CAPTIVE
PARADISE

CAPTIVE PARADISE

A History of Hawai'i

James L. Haley

St. Martin's Press ≈ New York

www.stmartins.com

Design by Meryl Sussman Levavi

Library of Congress Cataloging-in-Publication Data

Haley, James L.
    Captive paradise : the United States and Hawai'i / James L. Haley.—First edition.
        pages   cm
    Includes bibliographical references and index.
    ISBN 978-0-312-60065-5 (hardcover)
    ISBN 978-1-4668-5550-2 (e-book)
    1. Hawaii—History.   2. Hawaii—Annexation to the United States.   I. Title.
    DU625.H28 2014
    996.9—dc23

                                                            2014026108

St. Martin's Press books may be purchased for educational, business, or promotional use.
For information on bulk purchases, please contact Macmillan Corporate and Premium Sales
Department at 1-800-221-7945, extension 5442, or write specialmarkets@macmillan.com.

First Edition: November 2014

10 9 8 7 6 5 4 3 2 1

To Jody and Lesli,
and Spencer and Kate

Contents

If a big wave comes in, large fishes will come from the dark Ocean which you never saw before, and when they see the small fishes they will eat them up. The ships of the white men have come, and smart people have arrived from the Great Countries which you have never seen before. They know our people are few in number and living in a small country; they will eat us up.

—Davida Malo, adviser to King Kamehameha III

The nation that draws most from the earth and fabricates most, and sells most to foreign nations must be and will be the greatest power on earth. . . . This is to be looked for in the Pacific.

—William H. Seward, U.S. Secretary of State

Preface

hroughout recent years, activists agitating for the independence of Hawai'i occupy the grounds of the 'Iolani Palace in Honolulu, the only former royal palace on American soil.[1] They do this periodically. They want to draw attention to what, in their view, was the unconscionable way their country was annexed by the United States in 1898, in the name of cheap sugar and the needs of American imperialism (although, as we shall see, it was much more for the latter reason than the former). The full story of how the United States got its hands on the Kingdom of Hawai'i is virtually unknown among the mainland general public, and I began this volume as a history of Hawaiian annexation.

I quickly discovered, however, that such a narrow focus could not begin to embrace the kingdom's tumultuous journey, which ended with its absorption into the United States. Discovered by the British in 1778 as the most isolated and strategically important islands on earth, the country endured the clash of empires as the British, French, Russians, Japanese, and Americans all contended for influence with the native monarchy. From the mayhem of civil war every time a king died, a preeminent conqueror arose: Kame-hameha, who waged war and suppressed rebellion for thirty years before he could call himself master of all the islands in 1810. From a precontact culture of idol worship and human sacrifice, refugees from the Kamehameha conquest reached the United States, gained an education, insistently challenged American Christians to send missionaries to end the pagan terror, and in fact led the first mission-aries back to their homeland. And then the struggle was on for the next seven monarchs: to balance bringing their people into the In-dustrial Age while preserving for them some sense of cultural iden-tity; to maintain the sovereignty of their country while dealing with the greediest and most powerful empires in the world; to provide a modern economy and wealth for their people while becoming snared ever tighter in the grip of the American economic colossus. For all this to have taken place in the span of one human lifetime is a pageant of imperial triumph and human tragedy rare, if not un-known, elsewhere in history.

Dating back from annexation in 1898, the United States could never have captured Hawai'i politically had it not first come to dominate the islands' economy, and that moves the story back to the 1860s. Equally, it could not have dominated the economy without first capturing the people spiritually and culturally, and that moves the story back to 1820. But the American hand was felt even before that, in a bullying sea captain who inadvertently provided Kame-hameha the technology needed to conquer the country, and in the mostly American traders who introduced the chiefs to luxury con-sumer goods—and how to go into debt to acquire them. Annexa-tion, then, can only be understood in this broader context of the Americanization of Hawai'i.

Oddly, there has never been a narrative history of Hawai'i. There was a great deal of academic appraisal of the subject in the decades leading up to statehood in 1959, much of which has been reprinted for current reading. And James Michener's famous novel *Hawaii*, which rocketed him to literary stardom, came out in the very year of statehood. Modern academic studies have been rooted in the reigning "politically correct" paradigm of race, gender, and exploitation—which as it turns out are highly appropriate lenses through which to view the islands' history. But the Hawai'i I found is far more complex. Early in the process I had coffee with a distinguished history professor friend of mine, to discuss my possible return to graduate study, looking toward completing a long-abandoned Ph.D. He asked how my Hawai'i work was coming, and I said that while I was finding little to change my opinion that the 1893 overthrow was indefensible, I was also increasingly surprised and troubled by the pervasive oppression of the common people by their own chiefs and kings before Americans ever showed up. I cited several examples; the professor nodded and allowed that this was indeed the case, but he warned me that if I wrote the book that way and did not "position" the Hawaiians as victims of *American* racism and exploitation, as he said, it "won't help you get accepted back into grad school."

I marinated in this irony for a few moments and said, "This must be what they mean by academic freedom." Noting my shock, the professor went on to say that race, gender, and exploitation have ruled the scholarly paradigm for thirty years, and are entrenched for probably thirty more. He has made his peace with it, and he has disciplined himself to teach and write in that vocabulary. But it also seemed clear that when the actual facts of the history conflict with the reigning theoretical model, it may fall to nonacademic writers to disseminate a more nuanced narrative. The danger with this, of course, is that many "trade" writers who frolic in the vineyard of history are not trained historians, and are liable to seize upon the ill-conceived or the sensational—a trap that has admittedly also snared a history professor or two.

All this is meant only to express my sense of responsibility in handling a subject as multifaceted as Hawai'i. I knew going in that discussion and reexamination of how to interpret the islands' history is in active ferment, but what I found was an intellectual community in near riot over control of the narrative. "Revisionism," very often appropriate but sometimes excessive, provocative, and overreaching, is a given feature now of American history as presented in the academy. Hawai'i, however, has placed the phenomenon in a pressure cooker, by its isolation from other fields of history, by the long suppression of the native culture and the suddenness of a rich profusion of studies that incorporate it. Consequently, it is not unusual to find summaries of the American missionaries in Hawai'i that treat their presence as a foreign invasion, but it is incomplete and misleading to exclude mention of Opukaha'ia, or Hopu, or other refugees from the Kamehameha conquest, with their insistent challenges to the American Christian community to evangelize the islands and end the horrors of endless warfare and *kapu*—the ancient regimen of taboos. One history of the Chiefs' Children's School, apart from acknowledging that the enterprise was undertaken at the request of the *ali'i*—the noble class—treats it as a purely American ethnocentric gutting of the native culture, and omits any mention of the scholarly John Papa 'I'i, *kahu* of the king's niece and nephews, who functioned as a vice principal of the school, who appreciated the good that both cultures had to offer, and who was an important bridge from the old culture to the modern world.[2]

This debate over historical candor is hardly new. No sooner had Hawai'i's first printed chronicler, Samuel Manaiakalani Kamakau, begun relating "Ka Mo'olelo Hawai'i" (The History of Hawai'i) in the Hawaiian-language journal *Ka Nupepa Kuokoa* in June 1865 than he suffered robust criticism from readers who were offended that the knowledge was being imparted to those who had no permission to hear it. "This subject is not acquired by the common people," huffed Unauna in an opinion editorial, "nor by the country people; only through the chiefs was it gained. . . . In ancient times this was a very sacred subject, never to be given to another."[3]

Three years of research have chastened me with the sense that virtually nothing in Hawaiian history has a single cause, and virtually no one acted out of a single motivation. It is not a simple history, and it cannot be explained simply, certainly not with recourse to the easy remedies of a previous academic era—native savagery and simplicity—or of the current one—the Anglo sense of hegemony and entitlement. It is undeniable, for instance, that the arrival of Western venereal diseases decreased the natural fecundity of the islanders, but that does not, contrary to the impression one gets from museum displays, explain the expiration of the Kamehameha dynasty. Like Egyptian pharaohs, the *ali'i* had been preserving their *mana*—their spiritual force—by inbreeding for centuries. That probably was partly responsible for the fact that no Kamehameha after the Conqueror sired any (legitimate) children who lived to adulthood. Similarly, that Queen Ka'ahumanu witnessed the failure of *kapu* to prevent the decline of her people does explain in part her motivation to overthrow this ancient system of social control; it is also true that she adored power and had no intention of taking a backseat after the death of her husband, the Conqueror. It is true, for another example, that the prudishness and Anglocentrism of the missionaries wrecked a complex and in many ways lovely indigenous culture; it is also true that some facets of that culture were savage. As constrained as one is today to treat the values of differing cultures with respect, some of the traditional Hawaiian practices, such as human sacrifice and infanticide, were savage: No other word serves. It is true that the missionaries did not have the foresight to let the benefits of education and incipient democracy leaven the native culture in their own way. It is also true that neither did any other colonizing culture of that or any preceding era, and even if they had, it is doubtful that an enlightened native culture would have survived late-nineteenth-century imperialism, whether American, British, Japanese, or anyone else's. But as one native minister was heard to complain, "America gave us the light, but now that we have the light, we should be left to use it for ourselves."[4] If only *that* idea had caught on, the history and the lessons to draw from it might be radically different. But as it is, one Web site promoting

Hawaiian tourism writes on its history page that "it is difficult to find an objective Hawaiian history that is accurate and unemotional."[5] My goal with this book is to make that a little less difficult.

I should close with a word about native language sources. Hawaiian is a highly complex tongue that is not merely capable of great subtlety; it is a language in which subtlety is its daily stock-in-trade, with nuances of expression that escaped the American voyagers and still lead Anglo scholars astray. Most words have multiple meanings: first the literal meaning of the thing or action spoken, and then the *kaona*, the hidden meanings, either a spiritual overtone and/or, often, a highly irreverent sexual raspberry or double entendre. Among the historical sources one can consult, for instance, the reminiscences of John Papa 'I'i, who was raised in the Conqueror's court as a companion to his son and successor, Liholiho. Papa 'I'i provided a highly illuminating look at royal circles until his death midway through the reign of Kamehameha V. However, one recent skillful study[6] details the pitfalls of using the English translation of Papa 'I'i's memoirs, which first became available in 1959. My general examination of the Americanization of Hawai'i for a mainland audience that, mostly, does not know the story at all, may not be crucially dependent upon such sources, but I am wistful about how much better it would be had I a lifetime's facility in this language, whose gradations of meaning were honed by centuries of chant and high oratory.

Written Hawaiian utilizes twelve letters plus the 'okina, the reversed apostrophe that indicates a glottal stop to break two syllables, or to begin a syllable with a closed throat (with a tiny cough, if you will). At the risk of provoking the impatience of a mainland audience, in this text I have opted to use the 'okina, not to be pedantic but because it simplifies pronunciation for the mainland eye. The name, for instance, of the sister of King Kamehameha III, whom he desperately desired to marry, Nahienaena, is a confusing mouthful unless broken down as Nahi'ena'ena. Similarly, without the 'okina, virtually all mainlanders would misread the name of the crater

Halemaumau; it is pronounced Halemaʻumaʻu. Absent the ʻokina, however, paired vowels are indeed pronounced as a diphthong, but with more attention to the vowels' individual sounds than in English, as in Honaunau. The Western eye is also accustomed to reading double vowels in a standard way that would be incorrect in Hawaiian, hence the utility of the ʻokina in references to the Koʻolau mountain range, or the island of Kahoʻolawe, or names such as Princess Ruth Keʻelikolani.[7]

Finally, standard current usage has developed no fixed rules on which form of a word or name to use when it changed with the adoption of an alphabet. Before the language was standardized, the unifying conqueror-king of the islands, Kamehameha, was almost always referred to, and his documents were subscribed, Tamehameha. This form was used by his son Liholiho (or Rihoriho in the old style) as Tamehameha II, and then by Liholiho's younger brother as Tamehameha III.[8] The *K* that replaced *T* with the adoption of the alphabet is now universally backdated to the beginning, and one reads of Kamehameha from the arrival of Captain Cook. The same is true of Kamehameha's rival Kaumualiʻi, the king of Kauaʻi. Before the subsition of *K* and *L*, he is referred to most often as Tamoree. And there was a small fishing village on the south shore of Oʻahu that was called Honoruru until *L* took the place of *R*, but is now referred to as Honolulu from the beginning.

Contrary to this, *taro*, the starchy food staple brought from lower Polynesia by the first settlers, became *kalo* after the language was standardized, but modern usage has continued to use the archaic form. Similarly, Princess Ruth Keʻelikolani saw her name modify from Ruth to Luka after the alphabet was adopted, and she is so referred to in correspondence among the royal family, but the newer iteration is never seen in modern print—a fate opposite to that of Kamehameha the Conqueror, her great-grandfather.

My goal has been to confuse people as little as possible, and I have followed these established practices. In cases where a person's name changed significantly—Lydia Kamakaʻeha Paki did not become Princess Liliʻuokalani until her brother became king (although Elizabeth Kinaʻu gave her elements of the name at her birth)—a brief phrase in the text suffices to tip off the reader that this person has a significant future role to play.

The Kings and Queens of Hawai'i

KAMEHAMEHA DYNASTY

Kamehameha I, r. 1810–19; Queen Keopuolani (d. 1823),
Queen Ka'ahumanu (d. 1832).

Paramount chief of Hawai'i Island from 1782; king of Hawai'i, Maui, Lana'i, and
Moloka'i from 1794, O'ahu from 1795, Kaua'i and Ni'ihau from 1810.

Liholiho (Kamehameha II), r. 1819–24;
Queen Kamamalu (d. 1824).

Son of Kamehameha I; under premiership of Ka'ahumanu.

Kauikeaouli (Kamehameha III), r. 1824–54;
Queen Kalama (d. 1870).

Younger son of Kamehameha I; under regency of Ka'ahumanu to 1832; under
premiership of Kina'u to 1839.

Alexander Liholiho (Kamehameha IV), r. 1854–63;
Queen Emma (d. 1884).

Grandson of Kamehameha I; nephew of Kamehameha III.

Lot Kapuaiwa (Kamehameha V), r. 1863–72; unmarried.
Brother of Kamehameha IV.

William Lunalilo, r. 1873–74; unmarried.
First cousin of Kamehameha IV and V.

KALAKAUA DYNASTY

David Kalakaua, r. 1874–91; Queen Kapi'olani (d. 1899).
Great-grandson of Kamehameha I's first cousin Kepo'okalani.

Lili'uokalani (r. 1891–93; d. 1917);
consort HRH John Owen Dominis (d. 1891).
Sister of Kalakaua.

HRH Victoria Ka'iulani (heiress presumptive 1893–99, d. 1899).
Niece of Kalakaua and Lili'uokalani.

American Board of Commissioners for Foreign Missions
Missionaries to the Sandwich Islands (Owhyhee)

First Mission to Hawai'i, March 30, 1820

Rev. Hiram and Sybil (Moseley) Bingham
Daniel and Jerusha Chamberlain, five children
Rev. Asa and Lucy (Goodale) Thurston
Rev. Samuel and Nancy (Wells) Ruggles
Dr. Thomas and Lucia (Ruggles) Holman
Elisha and Maria (Sartwell) Loomis
Samuel and Mercy (Partridge) Whitney
Rev. William Ellis (from April 15, 1822)
Hawaiians Thomas Hopu, John Honolii, William Kanui,
    Prince George Kaumuali'i

Second Mission to Hawai'i, April 23, 1823

Rev. Charles S. Stewart
Rev. William and Clarissa (Lyman) Richards
Rev. Artemas and Elizabeth (Edwards) Bishop
Rev. Joseph and Martha (Barnes) Goodrich
James Ely
Louisa Everst
Betsey Stockton
Hawaiians William Kamoolua, Richard Kalaioulu, Kupelii

Third Mission to Hawai'i, March 30, 1828

Rev. Lorrin Andrews
Dr. Gerrit P. Judd
Rev. Jonathan Smith Green and Theodosia Arnold
Rev. Peter and Fanny (Thomas) Gulick
Mary Ward
Hawaiians George Tyler Kielaa, Samuel J. Mills Paloo,
    John E. Phelps Kalaaauluna

Fourth Mission to Hawai'i, June 7, 1831

Rev. Dwight Baldwin
Rev. Sheldon Dibble

Fifth Mission to Hawai'i, May 17, 1832

Rev. William P. and Mary Ann (McKinney) Alexander
Rev. Richard and Clarissa (Chapman) Armstrong
Dr. Alonzo and Mary Ann (Tenney) Chapin
Rev. John S. and Ursula (Newell) Emerson
Rev. Cochran and Rebecca (Smith) Forbes
Rev. Harvey and Rebecca (Howard) Hitchcock
Rev. David and Sarah (Joiner) Lyman
Rev. Lorenzo and Betsy (Curtis) Lyons
Edmund Horton Rogers
Rev. Ephraim and Julia (Brooks) Spaulding

Sixth Mission to Hawai'i, May 1, 1833

Rev. John and Caroline (Platt) Diell
Lemuel Fuller
Rev. Benjamin Wyman and Mary Elizabeth (Barker) Parker
Rev. Lowell and Abba (Tenney) Smith

Seventh Mission to Hawai'i, June 6, 1835

Miss Lydia Brown
Rev. Titus and Fidelia (Church) Coan
Henry and Ann Maria (Anner) Dimond
Edwin Oscar and Sarah (Williams) Hall
Miss Elizabeth Hitchcock (later married
    Edmund Rogers)

Eighth Mission to Hawai'i, April 9, 1837

Dr. Seth and Parnelly (Pierce) Andrews
Edward and Caroline (Hubbard) Bailey
Rev. Isaac and Emily (Curtis) Bliss
Samuel Northrup and Angeline (Tenney) Castle
Rev. Daniel Toll and Andelucia (Lee) Conde
Amos Starr and Juliette (Montague) Cooke
Rev. Mark and Mary Ann (Brainerd) Ives
Edward and Lois (Hoyt) Johnson
Horton Owen and Charlotte (Close) Knapp
Rev. Thomas and Sophia (Parker) Lafon
Edwin and Martha (Rowell) Locke
Charles and Harriet (Halstead) MacDonald
Bethuel and Louisa (Clark) Munn
Miss Marcia M. Smith
Miss Lucia Garratt Smith
William Sanford and Oral (Hobart) Van Duzee
Abner and Lucy (Hart) Wilcox

Ninth Mission to Hawai'i, May 21, 1841

Rev. Elias and Ellen (Howell) Bond
Rev. Daniel and Emily (Ballard) Dole
Rev. John and Mary (Grant) Paris
William Harrison and Mary Sophia (Hyde) Rice
Joseph—Hawaiian translator
Levi—Hawaiian translator

Tenth Mission to Hawaiʻi, September 24, 1842, and after

Rev. George and Malvina (Chapin) Rowell
Dr. James William and Millicent (Knapp) Smith
Rev. Samuel and Julia (Mills) Damon
Rev. Asa and Sarah (White) Smith

Eleventh Mission to Hawaiʻi, July 15, 1844

Rev. Claudius Buchanan Andrews
Rev. Timothy Dwight and Mary (Hedges) Hunt
Rev. John Fawcett Pogue
Rev. Eliphalet and Elizabeth (Baldwin) Whittlesey

Twelfth Mission to Hawaiʻi, February 26, 1848

Rev. Samuel Gelston Dwight
Rev. Henry and Maria Louisa (Walsworth) Kinney

Antecedent: Captain Cook

On January 18, 1778, Capt. James Cook, RN, strode the quarterdeck of his vessel of exploration, the converted collier HMS *Resolution*. She was stocky and slow, 460 tons. With a thirty-foot beam across a ninety-three-foot keel, she was a third wide as she was long, like sailing a great rectangular box. But she was overengineered, built to weather an epic voyage and withstand almost any challenge to her construction. Cook had pronounced her the fittest ship for service that he had seen, and if there was one kind of vessel on earth that James Cook knew how to handle, it was a collier—a coal carrier. The legendary Captain Cook had just turned fifty, with penetrating blue eyes set in a taut, angular face. On his last visit home he found himself such a celebrity that his likeness was painted by the great Nathaniel Dance. Unlike most of the serene portraiture of this era, dominated by the paintings of Thomas Gainsborough and Joshua Reynolds, with their subjects often recumbent in gardens of classical statuary, Cook was shown seated at a table, leaning forward, pointing to a speck on a map, his head cocked to one side and with the glint in his eye of a man possessed.

Indeed, his life's story had been one of dissatisfaction and hurry.[9] Unhappy on his parents' farm and unhappy as a grocery clerk when he was apprenticed out at sixteen, he was apprenticed again to coal merchants in Whitby and first went to sea on one of their colliers. While still a teenager, he devoured in his off-duty hours the study of astronomy, navigation, and mathematics, and by twenty-four he attained the rating of mate. He gained his own merchant command at twenty-seven, of another collier working the Baltic Sea, but joined the Royal Navy in June of 1755 once it was apparent that England and France were headed for a fight. As a junior officer in the Seven Years' War (known in America as the French and Indian War) he took part in numerous sea battles, sat successfully for his master's examination in 1757, and then in 1759 proved instrumental in winning Canada for Britain: Showing early his skill at cartography, as master of HMS *Pembroke* he charted the shore of the St. Lawrence River, piloting Gen. James Wolfe and his army to a landing from which they scaled the heights and surprised the French on the Plains of Abraham, leading to the capture of Quebec. This, and then his three years mapping the entire coast of Newfoundland with punctilious accuracy, marked him as an officer of singular determination and ability.

After the war the Royal Society—in full, the Royal Society of London for Improving Natural Knowledge, with its century of exploration and scientific quest already accomplished—desired to mount an expedition to Tahiti to observe the expected transit of Venus across the sun. After a canvass of the Royal Navy for its best navigator and mapmaker, it was Cook who was promoted to lieutenant and seconded to the Royal Society. In a momentous three-year voyage he delivered his onboard astronomer to Tahiti to have his gaze at Venus, and then sailed west, circumnavigated and mapped the coast of New Zealand and explored the eastern coast of Australia. He returned home in July 1771 with thousands of botanical specimens, journals that were published to wide fascination, and claim to a vast South Seas addition to the British Empire.

Although the Royal Society did not know much more about Venus than it had before, Cook was lionized for his exploration, promoted to commander, and offered another mighty journey. The ignorance of the West concerning the undiscovered regions was as massive as it was opaque. The most knowledgeable geographers for years had postulated the existence of a great southern continent, a *Terra Australis*, a mighty landmass that must fill the far-southern Pacific to counterbalance the weight of Asia—otherwise the planet must wobble out of its orbit. In his second voyage Cook's commission was to discover *Terra Australis*, and claim it for the empire. From 1772 to 1775 Cook pursued the goal, running a vast search pattern in the open waters of the southern ocean, becoming the first mariner to cross the Antarctic Circle. But in the six thousand miles west-to-east of the southern Pacific, traversed not once but twice, he proved that there was no *Terra Australis*. When he was back home again, the geographers would not have it, but Cook left them to grapple with the earth's rotation as best they could: He had been there, and he knew better. Cook was brusquely thanked with the Copley Gold Medal and made a fellow of the Royal Society; then he was retired from active service and given a post at Greenwich Hospital.

It was a retirement that he did not want, and Cook found a way to fight it. Over the years he had acquired the friendship, and the patronage, of the formidable John Montagu, the fourth Earl of Sandwich, a man of sobering means and weighty influence, who since the end of Cook's first voyage had acted as First Lord of the Admiralty. Cook knew him also as a man of vision (his later reputation for incompetence was overwritten by historians), and Sandwich offered him a third commission that would dwarf the others in importance. Almost from the time that Columbus had proved that the world was round, the Holy Grail of navigation had been to discover the Northwest Passage, a sea route that must lie to the north of the

New World. It would link Europe and the Orient by a voyage a fraction of the distance required by rounding the tip of Africa and crossing the Indian Ocean. All who had attempted to descry it failed, crossing the Atlantic only to be frustrated by the maze of icy islands in the Canadian arctic. But, no one had tried to find it from the west. The Bering Strait was known, separating Siberia from Alaska, but what lay north and east of there? That breathtaking task was handed to Cook, but no one must know. None of the competitors in the scramble for imperial expansion—the Spanish, the French, the Dutch, and now above all the Russians, for the Bering Strait was their back door—must have any inkling of the reason for Cook's heading to sea once more.

It was put out for public consumption that the purpose of this third voyage was to return a native Tahitian named Omai to his home. This first South Sea islander to visit the West had accompanied Cook to England, had been the toast of London, and now gave convenient cover for the third voyage. Cook was promoted again, to captain, commanding the stout *Resolution* and accompanied by a second ex-collier, half the size of the *Resolution*, HMS *Discovery*, Capt. Charles Clerke commanding. Leaving Omai once more with his people on Tahiti, Cook turned north toward Alaska, the Bering Strait, and glory in finally finding the Northwest Passage. Some 2,700 miles later, in the very heart of the vast central Pacific in what was assumed to be open ocean, he raised an island. It was the morning of January 18, 1778. Its tall mountains were obvious, although rendered dark blue by the distance over the water. The winds had been weak, and occasionally Cook found himself becalmed altogether. Throughout the day the island slowly slipped by them to the east, then another island appeared before them. When a lazy wind finally filled their sails it was from the east, making it easier to steer for this second island ahead of them.

Becalmed again during the night of the nineteenth, the ships drifted a bit to the west, and on the morning of the twentieth they finally approached the south coast of the second island. Cook found no anchorage here, but he could see that it was well populated, the landscape heavily dotted with grass houses and agricultural plots. A few canoes knifed their way out to them, paddled by a handsome swarthy people who closely resembled the Polynesians that Cook had left far behind. They were friendly, but apprehensive. Cook and his officers recognized the language as a variant of what was spoken in Tahiti and the other Society Islands—a different dialect, but communication was possible.

The natives were too cautious to come aboard, but Cook lowered gifts to them, brass medals and bits of iron. Once the islanders understood the visitors' friendly intentions, they pitched overboard the stones they had brought to hurl at them had they proven otherwise. Cook had no idea of the impact that the gift of metal would have on these people. In trade, the islanders sent up quantities of fish and sweet potatoes, and then paddled heartily away to spread the news: This alien race of men brought *iron* to trade.

To find an anchorage Cook turned west, toward the lee side of the island, and soon a third mass of land appeared on the horizon to the west. As the discoverer, Cook named the archipelago the Sandwich Islands, in honor of his patron, the earl. As the two ships proceeded, more canoes approached them with produce to trade, all for iron. "Such is these People's avidity for iron," wrote Captain Clerke of the *Discovery*, "a moderate sized Nail will supply my Ship's Company very plentifully with excellent Pork for the Day, and as to the Potatoes and Tarrow, they are attained on still easier Terms." The natives appeared to have an advanced culture, but no source of metal.

On the west side of the island Cook put in at a shallow bay from which they could see a village on the shore, perhaps sixty grass houses, and farther inland, a number of curious, flimsy white towers. As more canoes paddled their way out, Cook learned that the island was called Kaua'i, with a glottal stop separating the final two vowels. The village was called Waimea.

Here at last the natives came aboard the *Resolution*, and were awestruck at the experience. Some prayed; some threw themselves prostrate on the deck before the officers. As remembered in Hawaiian traditional lore, two men at the fore, a priest and a chief, tied *malo* sashes in their left hands; "they went before *Kapena Kuke* [Captain Cook] bent over, squatted down, and offered prayers . . . then took the hand of Kapena Kuke and knelt down; then rose up free from any tabu." Cook presented the priest with a knife, who then named his daughter Kua-pahoa (After this Knife.)[10] Once convinced that they were welcome, the islanders inquired into matters of etiquette and proper behavior. In their society men did not swallow their saliva, but spit incessantly, and they asked where they might do so. But again they were almost frenzied at the presence of iron. One man seized a meat cleaver and leapt overboard with the prize, racing for shore with others in his canoe. Lt. John Williamson, who was just lowering the pinnace to find a landing spot, pursued him; his men were under orders not to fire, but when Williamson shot his pistol after him, his men leveled a musket volley. Terrified natives dived overboard and swam, but the cleaver was not recovered.

As soon as the first English boat slid onto the beach, a native spied the iron boat hook and determined to seize it, and Williamson shot him. The locals carried his body away with no great show of mourning; apparently life was cheap here, and to English eyes the incident was soon forgotten. It occasioned much discussion among the natives, however. The thief may have been a chief named Kapupu'u (Forbidden Hill). In this culture, chiefs were accustomed to taking what they pleased, and this one ignored the priests' warnings, took the iron, and was killed. There was sentiment to avenge him, but the fear that this was a visiting god convinced them that hospitality was the safer course.[11]

Aboard the *Resolution* the natives at first showed a disposition to help themselves to anything the visitors had, but once they understood that this was not acceptable, they settled down to trade, eagerly and amicably. "No people," wrote Cook after convincing them they could not just take what they wanted, "could trade with more honesty than these people." Within a short time the ships had taken on nine tons of fresh water and a host of provisions, all acquired in exchange for more bits of iron.

During their days at Waimea, Cook went ashore three times. As a distinguished visitor, he was conducted to the most important sites in the village. The first was one of the white towers that he had seen rising above the forest; Cook estimated its height at fifty feet, but noted others even taller farther away. At its foot was a grass house, with a small altar outside on which food offerings had been left. It was the grave of an *ali'i*, a member of the ruling noble class. The second was a burying ground nearby, marked off by skulls set on the ground; this was the cemetery of the *kanaka kapu*, commoners (*kanaka*, or more formally the *maka'ainana*, people of the land) who had been privileged to be sacrificed to the gods. *Kapu*, among these people, was the same as *tabu* among the Tahitians, meaning set apart, holy, forbidden.

The English assessed an essentially Polynesian culture, with a diet based on taro, bananas, fish, pork and dogs, with clothing of *tapa*, the inner bark of mulberry or selected other trees, thinned by pounding until it became a coarse but flexible cloth. Cook recognized the culture well. Their weapons, though inventive, were edged with stone or sharks' teeth. The English also noticed two distinct classes of people. With some exceptions the *ali'i*, the chiefs, loomed in size over the low-status *kanaka*, and exercised unquestioned power.[12] Commoners fell on their faces before them. Cook did not meet any of the high chiefs, who were withheld by their retainers until they could learn more about this white foreign race and their vast powers.

Anxious to continue with his exploration, Cook took the *Resolution* over to the island visible to the west, called Ni'ihau. Clerke and the *Discovery* lingered at Waimea, where at last he met the island's handsome young king and his wife. The monarch was escorted out to the ship with great ceremony, but his attendants would not allow him to go farther onto the vessel than the gang-plank. They "took as much care in getting him in and out of the Canoe," wrote the amazed Clerke, "as tho' a drop of Salt Water wou'd have destroyed him." Clerke patted him on the shoulder in greeting, and the retainers looked on agape: To touch the king meant death; only some higher being would dare such familiarity.

After briefly probing the coast of Ni'ihau, Cook desired to top off his stores before venturing into the northern reaches of the Pacific, but wind and sea made it impossible to return to Kaua'i. Cook therefore sent three boats of armed men—a provisioning party—to ascertain a landing spot on Ni'ihau. Once they were ashore the surf increased, and it was clear that they would have to spend at least one night there. This displeased him, for Cook knew what would happen. He himself never partook of native women. During his brief visits home he had fathered five sons and a daughter with his wife, Elizabeth, to whom he had been married for fifteen years. Tolerant of his men's needs, he was also conscious of his role in empire building, with a sincere exertion to limit the spread of sexual diseases from his crew to native populations. But the English quickly learned how aggressive the women of these islands could be. This culture had developed a keen sense of eugenics, and to mate with a superior person was greatly desired. On Kaua'i, according to Lieutenant Williamson, the women "used all their arts to entice [the sailors] into their Houses & even went so far as to endeavour to draw them in by force." Cook had only allowed men with no venereal symptoms ashore on Kaua'i, although he knew that was no guarantee, but now with twenty stranded on Ni'ihau, infection was sure to be introduced.

On Ni'ihau, Cook left behind a gift of diversified diet: seeds of pumpkins, onions, and melons, a ram goat and two ewes, and an English boar and sow. Then, in company with *Discovery*, he sailed north to unlock the mystery of the Northwest Passage. Over a pe-

riod of months, Cook explored and mapped the wester
North America from California to Alaska, filling in th
tween charts left by previous Spanish explorers to the
Russian explorers to the north. He discovered the Cook
realized it was a dead end. Rounding the southwest
Alaska, he perceived that the Bering Strait was the only
outlet of any Northwest Passage. Repeatedly he tried
through to the northern sea but was driven back. Frusti
angry, increasingly hobbled by pain in his stomach, Cool
frayed and he took it out on his crew. At one juncture I
them, when they complained of their rations, to eat wal
total number of disciplinary lashes meted out for all offens(
had totaled only 288 on the second voyage, now number(
Cruelty was not unknown in the British navy, as would on
made clear by Cook's own sailing master on the *Resolution*,
four-year-old William Bligh, but for Cook this was new bel

Conceding defeat for the winter, Cook sailed due sou
visit his Sandwich Islands, which lay just south of the T
Cancer. Two thousand miles or more from the nearest land
any direction, the most isolated archipelago yet discovered o
their strategic importance to future trade and imperial pow
become vast, and a thorough exploration and claim for
would be signal.

For the better part of two months the *Resolution* and t
covery coasted the islands: the two Cook had visited a year
the tall volcanic island that the natives called Kaua'i and the s
agricultural Ni'ihau, as well as the island he had first seen
southeast, which they called O'ahu. Having been at sea for
the sailors were almost crazy to get ashore, but Cook was int
his exploration and took no notice. In later years Cook's thir
age inspired memoirs from about two dozen of his officers
more reverent than the previous in his praise for the captain.
together they created an iconic, almost godlike Captain Cook
account, however, written by the only American on Cook's v

and later resolutely buried by British historiography, took a different view,[14] John Ledyard of Groton, Connecticut, was a corporal of marines aboard the *Resolution*. He was twenty-eight, from a wealthy family, and had been on a recreational excursion when he was shanghaied in England and press-ganged into the Royal Navy. Ledyard accepted his fate, which seems astonishing but for the fact that he had been intent on exploring the world anyway. He had signed aboard a merchant vessel as an able seaman once before, and once impressed into the Royal Navy he even volunteered for marine duty on the famous Cook's ship. But he had a darker memory of Cook's cooping the men on board for two months within sight of rest and women—and not just women but eager, lusty, aggressive women. "This conduct of the commander in chief was highly reprobated and at last remonstrated against by the people on board both ships," wrote Ledyard. Cook seemed to care only for his chart making, disregarding the needs of his crew, "the brave men who were weaving the laurel that was hereafter to adorn his brows."[15]

East and a little south of Oʻahu, Cook raised the lozenge-shaped island of Molokaʻi, whose sea cliffs plunged three thousand feet down to the water; then small, pear-shaped Lanaʻi; and tiny Kahoʻolawe, a desert that lay in the rain shadow on the leeward side of an island called Maui, which was dominated by a tall, dormant volcano. Beyond that cluster lay the largest by far of all the islands, which the natives called Hawaiʻi.

The island chain extended from northwest to southeast, directly across the prevailing trade winds. They were volcanic islands, with high mountains that squeezed the moisture from the passing winds, so that the eastern sides of the islands consisted of the rankest dense jungle with innumerable streams and waterfalls, leaving the western sides of the islands semidesert. Cook found no coral atolls. In later years it would be understood that these are new islands; not enough time had passed for their mountains to be pummeled back beneath the surface of the ocean, leaving their telltale coral rings. Likewise, the many beaches were beautiful but intimately small. It

takes eons of time for the waves to pound rock into sand, and these islands were still in their youth.

At Maui, Captain Cook found a sheltered anchorage and finally allowed the natives aboard. A quick examination of the eager women showed many of them to be infected with syphilitic chancres; Cook was heartsick that the venereal disease his men had left on Niʻihau only a year before had raced all the way through the chain—ample evidence of the sexual libertinism of this native culture. But there was no need to deny his men their pleasures, either, and the women were led belowdecks to vent their enthusiasm in mating with this alien species of white and obviously very powerful men.

That English sailors introduced syphilis to Hawaii has become an indispensable element of the historical recitation, but in justice to Cook, he only assumed that his men were the origin of the disease he found on Maui because he believed that he was the first outsider to discover the islands. There was in fact an extensive native tradition that there had been contacts previous to his.[16] Of the Spanish, Dutch, Chinese, and Japanese candidates who may have landed and brought the disease before Cook did, the latter are the likeliest possibility. Syphilis had been introduced into Japan more than 250 years before, perhaps as many as two-thirds of Japanese sailors were infected, and demographers estimate from three to twelve instances of storm-driven Japanese ships becoming marooned on Hawaiʻi before Cook. So venereal disease in Hawaiʻi may have predated Cook and come from a different vector entirely.[17] Cook, however, assumed that the responsibility was his, and once the women of Maui were sated, Cook provided them with what medicines the era afforded.

This largest island, Hawaiʻi, anchored the archipelago at the southeast, and Cook surveyed it leisurely. Over a period of weeks the *Resolution* and the *Discovery* sailed in a clockwise direction down the northeastern and southeastern sides, and then north up the western side. He had no idea what significance this action had for the natives. On this island it was the season of *makahiki*, the lengthy, intricate festival celebrating harvest and year's end, and the beneficence of Lono, the god of storms, harvest, and fertility. One of the four primal gods of Hawai'i who had existed before Creation, Lono had a particular history with this island. Long ago Lono had sent two of his brothers down to earth to find him a beautiful woman to marry. They found such a woman, named Kaikilani, and Lono descended to earth on a rainbow and lived with her, making their home at Kealakekua Bay (*ke ala ke kua*, meaning "the Road of the God") on the western shore. One day Lono overheard a local chief singing a love chant to her: "O Kaikilani, your lover salutes you! Pull his out, stick mine in: you will still be filled." Outraged at the suggestive lyric, Lono struck Kaikilani down, but before she died she proclaimed her innocence and her love for him. Frantic and remorseful, Lono raced about the island, challenging any to wrestle him—the origin of the seasonal games held in Kaikilani's honor. Finally in despair Lono sailed away in a magnificent vessel the like of which none had ever seen before, with tall masts that reached into the sky and great square sails of Ni'ihau matting.

Beginning in October and lasting nearly four months, *makahiki* was a time for games and sports. A *kapu* was laid against work and war, which for the other eight months of the year occupied much of the islanders' time. A stylized image of the god was processed around the perimeter of the island—clockwise—through each district, as inhabitants brought offerings out to the god's keepers. The procession always ended at Kealakekua Bay, where Lono had loved and lost. High overlooking the south shore they erected a mighty *heiau*, or temple, called Hikiau (Moving Currents). Throughout the islands, hundreds of *heiau* had been erected over the centuries, of various types. This was a *luakini heiau*, one in which sacrifices were offered to the god to whom it was dedicated. Hikiau *heiau* was a platform of stacked lava rocks, 100 feet wide, 250 feet long, and 16 feet high, surrounded by a walled court and presided over by numerous *ki'i*, carved wooden images of gods fashioned to be as terrifying as imagination could make them.[18]

Each year the *makahiki* procession ultimately converged here, and the people built a wicker raft, which was laden with offerings and sent to sea as the people remembered Lono's promise that he would return one day with gifts and bounty beyond their dreams. Then, toward the end of the festival, the semiannual *kapu* against eating *aku* (a tuna known to the West as bonito, or skipjack) was lifted by the *kahuna*, the priest, who ceremonially ate first the eye of an *aku* and then ate also a human eyeball, gouged from the face of a sacrifice.[19]

What made this *makahiki* different from all others was that now, as the festival season ended and the people converged on Kealakekua Bay, two ships sailed into it, of a type none of them had ever seen before, but that fit to an unnerving degree the kind of vessel in which Lono was said to have departed: tall wooden masts, taller than any of them had ever imagined, with enormous square sails. The natives greeted the arrival with awe: Could it be that Lono, their god, had returned to them at last?[20]

CAPTIVE
PARADISE

1. The Loneliness of a God

After rounding the southern tip of the island, Cook's ships headed north up the western side. About thirty miles on, a small bay opened up on their right, about a mile across that bit half a mile into the coast. On the south shore lay a beach;[1] the east side vaulted steeply up to a beetling precipice several hundred feet high that sheltered the bay from the trade winds. Its face was so inaccessible that its caves held the bones of generations of kings, and the natives called it *Pali Kapu o Keoua*, the Sacred Cliff of Keoua, after the dynastic founder. Then it descended on the north shore to a lava shelf just above the water, as low and flat as a wharf. *Resolution* and *Discovery* entered Kealakekua Bay and dropped anchor in seven fathoms of turquoise water.

Within moments a throng of thousands teemed on the shore, and the people raced out in their canoes to discover what manner of gods had come to visit them, and what gifts they had brought. "Cook," wrote Ledyard, "ordered two officers into each top to number them with as much exactness as they could."[2] Both counts exceeded three thousand canoes in the water, with as many as six natives in each, with more thousands of people on the shore, rejoicing. Overall, Cook made a rough guess that between 350,000 and 400,000 natives inhabited the entire archipelago—a number that, interestingly, has stood as a sensible midrange figure in a scholarly debate over the size of the precontact population, figures that have ranged from 200,000 to more than 1 million.[3]

But of the three thousand canoes knifing toward him, Cook was not alarmed, for he knew the Polynesians to be fulsome, festive people. Women swarmed on board to give themselves to these godlike creatures; they chanted their intentions, reinforced with stunningly suggestive hula, as recorded by twenty-eight-year-old ship's surgeon David Samwell, of the *Discovery*:

> *Where, oh where*
> *Is the hollow-stemmed stick, where is it,*
> *To make an arrow for the hawk?*
> *Come and shoot. . . .*
> *A penis, a penis to be enjoyed:*
> *Don't stand still, come gently,*
> *That way, all will be well here,*
> *Shoot off your arrow.*[4]

Leaving behind the mass mating on his ships, Cook was rowed ashore in his pinnace; chiefs who accompanied him motioned the crowding canoes aside with long white poles—necessary because three thousand canoes in less than one-half square mile of water, and then crowding about Cook, created an unmanageable confusion. Ashore, "as they passed through the throng, the chief cried out in their language that the great Orono [Lono] was coming, at which they all bowed and covered their faces with their hands until he was passed [*sic*]."[5] To Ledyard's consternation, Cook made a joke of the natives' groveling: Having prostrated themselves, they rose once he went by and stared after him; then Cook would spin around and face them again, forcing them to fall to the ground once more. Cook was feted with the best that the islanders had to offer, although as a god, he could not be troubled by having to chew his own food. He was attended by chiefs, who reverently chewed the food for him and placed the masticated wads in Cook's mouth, which he managed to swallow. Contrary to the Captain Cook cult fostered by his officers, Corporal Ledyard was mortified by what he saw, and in later years American missionaries who heard the story from old natives blamed Cook darkly for his hubris in accepting their homage as a deity, which, they declared, made him responsible for his own looming disaster.

After preliminary contact was made, and with suitable advance preparations, Cook returned the courtesy and welcomed aboard Kalaniopu'u, the king of Hawai'i Island, an old man, noticeably not as huge as other chiefs of his class, wizened and palsied from years of consuming 'awa, a native hallucinogen.[6] Among the king's gifts to the god was an 'ahu'ula, a feather cloak that featured vivid geometry in red, black, and yellow; such cloaks were the epitome of the islands' handicrafts. The king removed the cape from his own shoulders and placed it on Cook's, then removed also his matching feathered helmet, his *mahiole*, and gave it as well; perhaps a half dozen more cloaks were laid at Cook's feet, gifts of stunning value. The rarest feathers were the yellow; the bird from which they came, the 'o'o, was jet black, with a single yellow feather beneath each wing. Professional birdcatchers harvested the yellow feathers and released the birds to regrow them. It would have been difficult for Cook to realize the wealth that was offered at his feet.

Accompanying Kalaniopu'u onto the *Resolution* was his son and heir, Kiwala'o, and a representative sample of the young *ali'i*. The most striking of them, to British sensibilities, was the king's nephew. A massive young man, he was variously described as from six feet four inches to seven feet in height. Heavyset and to Western eyes ugly, he was intense, brooding, with the thick, downturning mouth of the Polynesian, a low, prominently ridged brow, and heavy-lidded eyes. He was aloof, observant, his every glance seeming to be an appraisal. His name was Kamehameha, which in its full iteration meant "the Loneliness of a God."

Because of a variety of factors—his destiny to forge the modern Hawaiian kingdom, the fact that his own early history took place before the advent of written records, and the modern scholarly contest over control of the narrative—Kamehameha's early years are impossible to piece together with certainty. Sources equally probative differ beyond reconciliation, but within wide latitude general features are known:

King's nephew he may have been, but it was a miracle that Kamehameha had lived to see this day. He was born on the Kohala Coast at the northern point of the island, and shortly thereafter the *kahunas* laid the noble infant on the Naha Stone, a three-and-a-half-ton block of lava, to divine his royal worth: If he cried, he would be tossed out to the common people to share their miseries; if he was silent, then truly he was an *ali'i*, born to rule. The baby did not cry, and he was given the name Pai'ea, meaning "hard-shelled crab"; an important *kahuna* prophesied that he would one day overturn the chiefs of Hawai'i and rule the entire island. This, the priests saw with consternation, the baby had the lineage to do, and in Hawaiian culture, bloodline was everything. His mother, Kekuiapoiwa II, was an important chiefess of the Kohala district, and he had two fathers—a condition known as *po'olua* (two heads). In this polyamorous culture, paternity could be shared among a woman's husband and lovers, and of these two Kahekili was king of Maui, and Keoua (who had placed his ancestors' bones in the caves above the bay) was the grandson of the last chief to nearly unite the island of Hawai'i.[7] Kamehameha himself preferred to claim Keoua as his father, and after his rise to power he made it treason—and death—to question it, perhaps reason enough to suspect Kahekili.[8] Keoua's father and uncle were defeated in battle by an insurgent chief named Alapaʻi, who took the surviving orphans into his own clan. Paiʻea, therefore, was born into the extended family of the king, but because of his lineage and the dangerous prophecy, Alapaʻi placed the baby under a death sentence.[9]

The danger was real, for infanticide was accepted, though not common among the chiefs.[10] Most often it was imposed on babies produced by a chiefess but gotten of a father too low in rank for the elders to accept as her mate. This was a different case, as it concerned not just social disapproval but a prophesied overthrow of the king. Kekuiapoiwa could not openly defy Alapaʻi, but the women of Hawaiʻi were renowned for their shrewdness. She determined to save her baby by resorting to the custom of *hanai* adoption. Hawaiian *aliʻi* almost never raised their own children; families of high rank strengthened their ties by each handing over newborns to be raised by relatives, and accepting others' babies in return. The practice may have been a holdover from still more warlike days, when hostages were traded to ensure a peace; certainly it provided security for the children of a war-riven country to have two sets of parents, and in this instance it saved the infant Paiʻea's life. His mother sent him out for *hanai* to another noble family beyond the reach of Alapaʻi's assassins. Five years later the king withdrew the condemnation and sent for the child to be raised in the royal court. Already a suspicious loner, the boy was renamed Kamehameha, and as such he spent his youth, training as a warrior in traditional weapons and tactics.

In the arts of war he had a tutor, Kekuhaupiʻo, under whom he mastered the traditional weapons of the islands: the bloodcurdling twelve-foot spears, and the ability to dodge one, snatch it from midair, and launch it back toward the enemy; the war clubs studded with sharks' teeth, and the *pahoa*, the double-bladed dagger that could stab both left and right. His agility he honed by rolling through the town balanced on a rounded lava boulder (still preserved in a local museum), an astonishing feat for a man of his height.

When old Alapaʻi died about 1754, the island of Hawaiʻi was thrown into civil war. In this culture all land belonged to the king. The high chiefs held their domains as his vassals, and under them the chiefs (and chiefesses, for in this society genealogy trumped gender and women could be very powerful) held their parcels of land, called an *ahupuaʻa*. This was usually a wedge of an island from highest peak to shore. Whether by accident or design, this form of landholding allowed most of the chiefs to be largely self-sufficient, for the average *ahupuaʻa* contained all the productive topographies of an island, from tidal fishponds and irrigated taro fields to upland crops and forest. Commoners were not tied to the land like European serfs, but that was virtually the only distinction between their status and that of the peasants of medieval Europe. Whichever chief's *ahupuaʻa* they lived on, they were allowed to keep only perhaps a third of all that they produced—fish, taro, fruit, *tapa* cloth.[11] The other two-thirds they handed up the hierarchy, to the chief, the high chief, the king, and the *kahunas* who placated the gods. In addition, *kanakas* had to hold themselves in readiness to serve as the chief's warriors when he called for them. It was all very feudal, a system that Norman barons would have recognized, except in one important respect: There was no expectation that a chief's land tenure would survive the king. Once a king died, his successor held the right to redistribute all the land as he pleased. When there were rivals for the throne, as there almost always were, chiefs and high chiefs curried favor and struck alliances with contenders who would bestow the most favorable lands on them. Thus, more often than not a king's death occasioned a bloodletting free-for-all.

Kalaniopuʻu whom Cook greeted was Alapaʻi's great-nephew, and had not been in the line of succession but became king by conquest. Kamehameha was too young to have taken part in this war, but as he matured into the fearsome warrior he was acknowledged to be by the time of Cook's arrival, he would have been indispensable in quelling later rebellions against Kalaniopuʻu's rule. Nor were the circumstances of Kamehameha's fortuitous birth forgotten, and he was installed third in importance after the king and his son Kiwalaʻo. But second in line was not as good as inheriting the kingdom. Kalaniopuʻu was old, Kamehameha was ambitious, and once the kingship was vacant he would have to fight his cousin to establish his own rule.

Now aboard Cook's ship, as the others traded and visited, Kamehameha could not conceal his wonder at the ship's weapons. Their superiority over native spears and war clubs was stupefying. Iron to the Hawaiians was almost a legendary substance. They knew that it existed, for they had acquired small pieces of it—strong, malleable, extremely useful—from the drift of shipwrecks and, it seems likely a few times over the centuries, storm-driven Japanese fishing vessels whose survivors became assimilated into the population. But before Cook's arrival they had no dependable source of it. And here on this white men's ship were huge weapons—cannons—made of iron, which seemingly weighed as much as the Naha Stone. The chief who could gain possession of such weapons, and master them, could conquer the entire island. The British did not need to know of Kamehameha's birth prophecy, because his covetous rapture over their big guns shouted his ambition all too loudly.

The islanders' avidity for iron, and their desire to know how to work it, was such that Cook had the *Resolution*'s forge brought on deck, and the blacksmith fashioned implements before the astonished natives' eyes. Cook also observed a telling aspect of the culture: The chiefs wanted the iron for themselves: "If a common man received anything, the chief would take it. If it was concealed and discovered the man was killed."[12] When Cook requested a place on land to establish a camp to note down astronomical data, the chiefs, believing him to be Lono, were quick to offer him the Hikiau *heiau* on the south shore, since the temple was dedicated to him anyway. Cook established the scientific station there with a guard of marines; the chiefs laid a *kapu* against women approaching the sacred ground, but the sailors and the marine guard had no disposition to turn away the women eager to offer pleasure to these exotic men. The chiefs withdrew the *kapu* to save face, but were displeased that Lono's retainers would defile their own temple. "It was the beginning," wrote Ledyard, "of our subsequent misfortunes, and acknowledged to be so afterwards when it was too late to revert the consequences."

Another disquieting incident occurred when William Watman, one of the *Resolution's* gunners, suffered a stroke, requested to be buried ashore, and died. The natives had not suspected that one of the god's attendants could die, albeit he was not the god himself. They accorded him a mighty funeral within the limits of the Hikiau *heiau*, heaping the grave with flowers and sacrificed pigs. But their awe of the English began to disintegrate. Soon after, William Bligh instructed about fifty Hawaiians to haul *Resolution's* rudder, which had been taken on land for repair, back to the shore. Their response to being ordered about was typically Hawaiian. As Ledyard noted, they took up the rope, "and pretended to pull and labor very hard, though at the same time they were in fact doing all they could to retard the business, to ridicule and make their pastime." Bligh, as he later became famous for doing, responded by beginning to beat them, but was stopped by a chief; Bligh demanded that the chief make his people help. The chief then joined his people, who "laughed at him, hooted him, and hove stones."[13] Ledyard sought permission to arm his detail and ran to assist Bligh, but it was the English sailors who eventually hauled the rudder back to the *Resolution*; the *kanakas* had had enough of them.

After a stay of eighteen days, Cook sailed the ships away to find a better anchorage on Maui; happy to be rid of him but still thinking that he might be a god, the Hawaiians sent him off with ceremonies fit for the divine. But then on February 4 gale-force winds cracked the *Resolution's* foremast. In deciding where to put in to repair, Cook made a fatal error. Had he visited the new island he could have enjoyed the ecstatic welcome all over; but despite his misgivings he chose to return to Kealakekua Bay, where he knew the terrain and believed he had a friendship with the people. He arrived there on February 10 after a hard sail in adverse conditions.

Makahiki had ended, however. The food stores were exhausted and working life had resumed. Not only was Cook's reappearance unexpected, in the native mind no god would return with a broken mast. The *kahunas* of Lono's Hikiau *heiau* continued to treat the British with deference, laying *kapu* against disturbing the white men who were repairing the mast. But the chiefs' and their people's respect crumbled with continued familiarity. Thefts of iron implements from the ships became more common; watering parties sent ashore began to be stoned and driven away.

Events climaxed on February 14 with the theft of *Discovery's* cutter. The incident may have begun with a chief named Polea, *ai-kane* (young male lover) of the king, whom English sailors had knocked to the ground when he tried to prevent their taking his canoe. "He was angry," according to native folklore, "and thought he would secretly take one of the ship's boats, break it all to pieces for the iron in it, and also because he wanted revenge for the blow which knocked him down."[14] Cook was more tolerant of native behavior than most British or indeed other European officers, but stealing one of his ship's tenders was an act that he must not allow. Going ashore with a lieutenant and nine marines, he intended to handle the situation the same way he had in Tahiti; he invited Kalaniopu'u out to the *Resolution*, intending to hold the king hostage until the cutter was returned and the thieves punished. At first Kalaniopu'u agreed and walked toward the shore, but Cook's purpose was guessed, and in a growing cacophony the crowd prevailed on the king to listen to his retainers and not get into the waiting boat. Threats were made, weapons appeared. Cook was compelled to fire one of his double musket barrels, but the gun partially misfired and the ball struck a warrior's body mat harmlessly. The crowd surged forward, but a musket volley from the marines drove them back, leaving several dead. As they were reloading and Cook's three small boats stood in to rescue them, Cook killed another native with his second barrel.

One of the warriors lunged at Cook with a large stone dagger, but he evaded the thrust. He had noticed this type of weapon before, as he wrote in his diary: "They have a sort of weapon we had never seen before, and not mentioned by any navigator, as used by natives of the South Sea. It was somewhat like a dagger; in general, about a foot and a half long, sharpened at . . . both ends, and secured to the hand by a string. It is used for stabbing in a close fight; and it seems well adapted to the purpose."

Cook was stabbed in the neck and was then overwhelmed, clubbed, and repeatedly stabbed facedown in the surf. Four of the marines also died before the rest of the party was plucked from the shore. The Hawaiians immediately thought better of the violent outburst, and they treated Captain Cook's corpse with the same reverence as they did that of the highest *ali'i*. They baked his body in an *imu*, or underground oven, but only to make the flesh easier to remove from the bones. They did not eat him, as some British sailors came erroneously to believe—although three children did come across Cook's heart, which had been placed in a tree fork to dry, and believing it to be a pig's heart helped themselves. Cook's bones were washed and wrapped, for to the Hawaiians, the bones of a powerful man held enormous *mana*.

Kalaniopu'u went into hiding in a cliff cave but sent out word that Cook's remains would be returned. His nephew, the suspicious Kamehameha, too wary to return to the ships, showed his peaceful intentions by sending out an enormous pig as a gift, and the British returned word that his gesture was accepted. These attempts to salvage the situation were not followed by the people, who gesticulated, mooned, and threw stones at the English at every opportunity. Captain Clerke, now in command, adopted a policy of restraint, but when he first asked for the return of Cook's body, he received a parcel that, when opened, contained to everyone's horror only "a piece of human flesh from the hind parts."

Seeing a man among the crowd on the shore waving Cook's hat, Clerke opened up with his four-pounders, scattering the people with some casualties including, it was learned, an injury to Kamehameha, who learned firsthand the power of the weapons he had been coveting. But only after a village was sacked and burned were more of Cook's remains handed over—skull, scalp, feet, long bones, and his hands (recognizable from the distinctive scars of old wounds)—which were given burial at sea. With *Resolution*'s foremast repaired, Clerke sailed out of Kealakekua Bay on the evening of February 22, 1779.[15]

Three years after the English departed, old Kalaniopu'u died, and the Big Island was thrown into chaos once more. He had sought to avoid the traditional war over the succession—and its spoils—by naming his son Kiwala'o as his heir. This he was bound to do, for Kiwala'o bore the *ni'aupi'o* rank, the highest possible *kapu*, which he inherited from his mother.[16] Kamehameha was the better fighter, and hoping to placate him the king entrusted him with custody of the war god, Kuka'ilimoku, a responsibility almost as great as being king. He also made him high chief of Waipi'o on the northeast coast, perhaps the most beautiful, historic, wealthy, and productive valley on the island. Far from placated, Kamehameha knew his time was approaching. He was the son of the king of Maui and grandson (through his other father) of the most powerful king of Hawai'i before Kalaniopu'u. With that lineage, and with his reputation as the island's mightiest warrior, he would have no difficulty enlisting allies to unseat Kiwala'o. Indeed, five powerful chiefs of the Kona district came to him first, including his father-in-law, three of his uncles, and Kekuhaupi'o his mentor in warfare, to announce that if Kiwala'o did not reapportion the lands to their advantage, they would align with Kamehameha in a war to overthrow him.[17]

The split began over a sacrifice before the old man was even dead. In the thousand years since this isolated archipelago was first settled by voyagers from the Marquesas Islands, and in the perhaps four hundred years since the Tahitian conquerors arrived and subjugated the original settlers, the religious system developed around two concepts: *kapu* and *mana*. The common people were kept under control by the regimen of *kapu*, a complex list of foods, lands, and practices that were forbidden to defined classes of people. *Mana* was the source of spiritual power for the chiefs, and *mana* was gained somewhat by descent but more by killing one's enemies in battle, sacrificing them to the gods, and/or having possession of their mortal remains—hence their reluctance to hand over more than a token of the bones of such a powerful man as Captain Cook.

Even though Kamehameha had become keeper of the war god, it was the king's prerogative to make sacrifices to him, so that the *mana* of the victims would flow to him. When Kamehameha himself sacrificed a rebellious *ali'i* to Kuka'ilimoku and took that *mana* for himself, it was a serious challenge to the power of Kiwala'o. Six months after the death of Kalaniopu'u a sharp, brief war erupted; the death of Kiwala'o at the Battle of Moku'ohai in July 1782 left Kamehameha supreme ruler of three of the Big Islands' six districts: Kona along the west coast, Kohala at the northern end, and Hamakua, southeast of there. Emboldened to seize his dream to conquer the entire island, Kamehameha opened a campaign against the Hilo district in the east, but suffered a blistering defeat and was forced to withdraw.

Then followed a series of conflicts with Keoua Kuahu'ula, the younger half brother of the deceased Kiwala'o, who had escaped that fatal battle to his own district of Kau on the southern point of the island. The two fought repeatedly, depleting land and people, with no decisive victory. In 1785 Kamehameha returned to his own stronghold at Kailua, midway up the Kona coast, regrouped, and married a new wife, Ka'ahumanu, the teenage daughter of a Maui ally. With her he shared both an intense devotion and bitter combat for the rest of his life. By now Kamehameha had also gained control of two districts on Maui, but those chiefs rebelled in 1786 and maintained their freedom against an army that he sent under one of his brothers. The destructive stalemates continued for some four years before fate—and America—handed him a breakthrough.

⚜

Even as it was an American—marine corporal John Ledyard—who viewed Captain Cook as having a different impact on Hawai'i than the one memorialized by his officers, so it was an American who, albeit unwittingly, gave Kamehameha the means to transform himself from only a partially successful war chief, who was defeated as often as he was victorious, into the Conqueror.

Capt. Simon Metcalfe was a Yorkshireman by birth but American by long residence and disposition—deputy surveyor of New York and a supporter of the colonial Americans' revolution. Imprisoned by the British for a time in Montreal, and his Vermont property lost during the war, he settled his wife and younger children in Albany, and went to sea as a trader. At fifty-two, in 1787, he acquired a brig called the *Eleanora* and entered the Pacific fur trade, installing his son Thomas Humphrey Metcalfe as captain of the small schooner *Fair American* to sail and trade in concert with him. Two years later the two ships were ensnared in the trading dispute between Britain and Spain known as the "Nootka Crisis," and became separated; the *Eleanora* managed to escape Spanish capture but the *Fair American* was taken briefly to Mexico.

Father and son had, it is believed, agreed in case they were separated to rendezvous on the west coast of Hawai'i. January of 1790 found Simon Metcalfe's *Eleonora* off the Kohala coast on the northwest of the Big Island, where Metcalfe received a local chief aboard his vessel. The nature of the incident is lost, but the chief did something to offend the captain. Brittle, severe, authoritarian, and ignorant of the station of the *ali'i*, Metcalfe had the chief flogged with a rope's end. It was Metcalfe's bad luck that the headman he abused was Kame'eiamoku, a high chief and cousin of Kamehameha's mother, and one of the first chiefs to rally to the Conqueror in his campaign to rule the entirety of the Big Island. He remained one of Kamehameha's most trusted advisers. Mortally insulted, he vowed to avenge himself on the next foreign vessel he encountered.

Oblivious, Metcalfe then sailed the *Eleanora* across the strait to Maui to trade. There one of his crewmen disappeared, along with a small boat, and he made sufficient inquiry to learn that it was not a desertion, that islanders had stolen the boat and killed the man. As an American on a far frontier, Metcalfe behaved just like later Americans on the Western frontier, arrogating to himself the roles of judge, jury, and executioner, and he determined upon massive retaliation to teach the natives a lesson. Learning that those who stole his boat were from Olowalu, about four miles south of Maui's main settlement of Lahaina, Metcalfe sailed there and indicated his eagerness to trade. No canoe, however, might approach his port side; all the transacting would be done to starboard. The *Eleanora* carried seven guns below the main deck, all of which were moved to the starboard side and loaded with small shrapnel. As the swarm of canoes gathered, the gunports were opened and a broadside fired into the canoes only a few feet away. At least one hundred Hawaiians were killed and countless more wounded.

The place where he massacred the natives, Olowalu, was a *pu'u honua,* a "city of refuge." In Hawaiian culture, common persons be they born ever so low, if they violated a *kapu* and if they reached a city of refuge before they could be apprehended and killed, could be ritually cleansed and returned to their lives without fear of further molestation. For Metcalfe to kill people there, aside from mass murder, was an unspeakable sacrilege.

Ignorant of the Olowalu massacre and unaware of the near presence of his father, whom he was searching for, Thomas Metcalfe in the *Fair American* called on the Kohala coast—the domain of Kame'eiamoku. That chief and several men came aboard under the guise of trading; one account had the high chief himself presenting Metcalfe with a feather helmet. Metcalfe was in the act of setting it upon his head when Kame'eiamoku seized him and pitched him overboard, his men doing the same with the remainder of the crew.

As they floundered in the water, more warriors in canoes beat them to death with paddles. The lone survivor, a Welshman named Isaac Davis, was taken half dead into a canoe, and Kameʻeiamoku might have completed his vengeance on him, but for the intercession of another chief who cited Davis's brave fighting and asked that he be spared. Davis, the *Fair American*, and its cannons were all presented to Kamehameha.

Sometime later Simon Metcalfe, unaware of the near presence of his schooner or death of his son, entered Kealakekua Bay to see what trading he might generate there. Aware that there were other foreigners residing in the west coast's principal settlement, Metcalfe sent ashore his English boatswain, forty-eight-year-old John Young, to make contact. Kamehameha, fearful lest the new ship learn the fate of the recently captured schooner but not knowing of the relationship of the captains, detained Young ashore, and laid a *kapu* against any canoes going out to the *Eleanora*. He also, according to a native historian, leapt at the chance to dragoon these immensely capable foreigners into his service.[18]

Metcalfe waited, and then wrote a threatening letter to the foreign community ashore: "Sirs, As my Boatswain landed by your invitation if he is not returned to the Vessel consequences of an unpleasant nature must follow. . . . If your Word be the Law of Owhyhe as you have repeatedly told me there can be no difficulty in doing me justice in this Business, otherwise I am possessed of sufficient powers to take ample revenge which it is your duty to make the head Chief acquainted with."[19]

The standoff continued for a few days before Metcalfe weighed anchor and sailed for China, leaving John Young behind. So far as is known, Metcalfe never learned of his son's death or its circumstances, and he never returned to New York. (He was killed, ironically, four years later when Haida Indians in the Pacific Northwest boarded the *Eleanora* ostensibly to trade, suddenly realized their superior numbers, and massacred all the crew save one.) But it was Metcalfe's visit to Hawaiʻi that altered the course of those islands forever; it was his self-righteous bloodlust that handed John Young and Isaac Davis over to Kamehameha. That chief now had not only the cannons and muskets from the captured *Fair American*, he had two white sailors to teach his warriors how to use them. To Young and Davis he gave a choice: Serve him and be richly rewarded, or be put to death. The two Britons became close friends; they attempted an escape, once, and were thwarted, before accepting their fate. Both served Kamehameha ably and faithfully for many years, and were showered with land, power, and highborn wives.

In the eight years since Kalaniopu'u died, word spread in the West of the existence of the islands, and other foreign ships began to arrive: the first traders in 1785, two British warships, *King George* and *Queen Charlotte* in 1786. In that same year the French explorer the Comte de Lapérouse, an admirer of Captain Cook, arrived with an expedition in the *Boussole* and the *Astrolabe*, before continuing on to disaster. The next year one of Kamehameha's high chiefs, Ka'iana, left for China aboard the *Nootka* and returned the next year from Oregon on the *Iphigenia*, the first Hawaiian to travel beyond his native shores.[20] The *Imperial Eagle* brought the first (willing) white resident, John Mackay, in 1787. The next year the trading ships *Prince of Wales* and *Princess Royal* tarried for three months. In 1789 the first American trader, Capt. Robert Gray in the *Columbia* (the first American vessel to circumnavigate the earth), arrived to do business, the same year that a visiting Spanish captain recommended the islands' seizure as a strategic outpost for that empire. Most of the American ships that called were in the fur trade, such as the brigantine *Hope* and the brig *Hancock*, which came in 1791. There were other fiercely independent chiefs in Hawai'i, but Kamehameha, because his domain was the largest, and because of his fame and history with Captain Cook, was the most sought after. Always and ever he required one currency for his trade: weapons—cannons, muskets, powder, even ships. This condition was quickly seized upon by other traders, such as the American captain John Kendrick in the *Lady Washington*, with a whole cargo of guns and ammunition.

Kamehameha was quick to grasp the concept of money, and soon his storehouse contained a chest of coins, which was equally effective in trading for more armaments. And now he had Davis and Young to train his army, and they also had cannons mounted and lashed to large double-hulled canoes. Gaining in ambition, Kamehameha diverted his attention from the Big Island to trade invasions with Kahekili of Maui, who had watched his possible son grow in power. While Kamehameha failed to establish a permanent conquest of Maui at this time, he came away with a valuable possession. Thinking their cause lost and with Kahekili on the Big Island, the surviving royal family fled in canoes to Moloka'i. There Kamehameha overtook them, strengthening his claims by marrying the highest-ranking girl in the islands, one whose *kapu* was almost equal to that of the gods themselves. Her name was Keopuolani, daughter of Kiwala'o whom Kamehameha had sacrificed. The girl's grandmother Kalola, exercising the Hawaiian woman's wonted shrewdness, realized that the Conqueror after winning his battles would want to cement his rule by having children with the highest-ranking females he could acquire. Keopuolani was born so far above him that even he had to strip to the waist in her presence. But no one now could doubt his right to rule, or that of his children by her, who would also outrank him. She was still a girl of perhaps only twelve, and Kamehameha did not have sex with her for some years more, but she was a signal possession that ended any dispute over his lordship.

The year that Kalaniopu'u died, Kahekili conquered O'ahu and added that to his domain, building the House of Bones with the skeletons of O'ahu *ali'i* who had opposed him. Looking to his own defense, he also took to actively trading for Western weapons. He and Kamehameha fought to a stalemate: In a sea battle fought in the Maui Channel both the rival kings had cannons, but Kamehameha had Davis and Young to aim and fire his, and Kahekili's fleet was decimated. But the king of Maui was more than a match on his own island, and the two withdrew to their own kingdoms to regroup and round up more warriors to pour into the fight.

If any natives doubted the new king's *mana*, they were convinced in 1790, when Kamehameha attacked the district of Puna in the east to add it to his domain. While his back was turned the troublesome Keoua Kuahuʻula invaded again. After conquering Puna, Kamehameha returned to suppress Keoua's uprising. Aided with cannons and muskets from the *Fair American* (Keoua had also once captured firearms but was virtually helpless in how to use them) Kamehameha slowly gained the upper hand, and when Keoua retreated past Kilauea, that volcano erupted and about a third of his army perished in a cloud of poisonous gas.

This unexpected "miracle" was a sobering portent to victors as much as victims, and Kamehameha consulted with priests how to safeguard his power. He had always been devout in his observance of *kapu*, and always quick to testify that his success in war was attained by the gods' favor. At the small *heiau* near his family compound in Halawa, "many people were burned on the adjoining hill for breaking the *kapus*."[21]

Now the *kahunas* directed that he build a grand *luakini heiau* for sacrifices to the war god and dedicate all his victories to him. This Kamehameha did, at Kawaihae, on the coast some thirty-five miles north of Kona, at a place called Puʻukohola, the Hill of the Whale. He delegated the work to his popular brother, Keliʻimaikaʻi, who organized a human chain of thousands to pass red lava rocks from the Pololu Valley, fourteen miles east of there. The gargantuan platform was completed in less than a year. Kawaihae had been old Alapaʻi's capital; Kalaniopuʻu had located himself further north in Kohala, and now Kamehameha determined to anchor his own kingdom here. In mid-1791 he sent emissaries down to the disaffected Keoua Kuahuʻula to come north, meet, and discuss their differences.

He was suspicious of Kamehameha's motives, but with his own army sapped by years of battle and then the eruption of Kilauea, he accepted. Keoua arrived at Kawaihae in state befitting a high chief, with retainers in a great double-hulled canoe. From the harbor he could not miss seeing the colossal new *heiau* surmounting the Hill of the Whale, which was perhaps his first inkling that his end was at hand. Keoua gashed himself, thinking to make himself unacceptable as a sacrifice, but it did him no good, for *mana* resided in the bones that survived decomposition. Nor was it necessary that the victim be taken alive to the temple; the offering of a dead body was equally efficacious. At the last he hesitated, but was coaxed ashore. "Rise and come here," Kamehameha greeted him, "that we may know each other."[22] Cut down as soon as he landed, Keoua was the first *ali'i* whose body was laid on the altar of Kuka'ilimoku, followed by those of his slaughtered retainers.

In good part American-armed, Kamehameha was now undisputed king of Hawai'i Island, and he could stand in his birthplace of Kohala and gaze with confidence across the thirty-mile-wide channel at Maui.

2. "Disobey, and Die"

Young and Davis adjusted to their captivity. They proved their loyalty, and with Kamehameha never certain when his own chiefs might turn on him, he entrusted the Englishmen with crucial administrative posts, which came with land and *kanaka* tenants. Young built a comfortable stone house, probably the first on the island, on the coast at Kawaihae, within sight of the sanguine temple on the Hill of the Whale. The Conqueror gave him his niece, Kaoanaʻeha, for his wife,[1] and created him governor of Hawaiʻi Island. Not entirely marooned, Young found many opportunities to visit with English sailors, as on the visits of Capt. George Vancouver, who had first come with Captain Cook, and returned on the first of March, 1792. Tellingly, everywhere he landed the Hawaiians wanted guns, but he refused to arm any faction and departed as quickly as he arrived. He came back the following spring, having looked after British interests on the western coast of America; he was pleased to think that Kamehameha had grown into his role as king, and that "his riper years had softened that stern ferocity which his younger days had exhibited, and had changed his general deportment to . . . an open, cheerful, and sensible mind, combined with great generosity and goodness of disposition." To reciprocate his hospitality Vancouver made a gift of cattle from America, which Kamehameha turned loose, protected by his *kapu* that they not be disturbed for ten years, to allow the herd to increase.

Modern scholars typically prefer to emphasize Kamehameha's generous treatment of Davis and Young after they proved their loyalty, rather than dwell on the unpleasant terms of their cooperation— service or death—which might be seen as somewhat coercive. In any event his actions prove the sophistication of Kamehameha's governing style, of pairing punishment with reward, of the ability to maintain his focus on a distant objective that he perceived to be important to his goals. Shrewd and patient, he grew his strength. Kahekili died midway through 1794, and similarly to Kalaniopu'u, he sought to keep the peace by dividing his kingdom: His son Kalanikupule was already lord of O'ahu; Maui he left to his brother, Ka'eo. Thinking to swiftly dispatch his nephew, Ka'eo invaded O'ahu and put him to flight; the outcome seemed all but decided when Kalanikupule managed to rearm from the trading ships *Prince Lee Boo* and *Jackal*, and then also *Lady Washington*, which came on the scene. The tables were suddenly turned, and Kalanikupule lured Ka'eo into battle along the eastern loch of the Pearl River estuary, where English sailors in boats could support him with impunity. Ka'eo was killed, and Kalanikupule found himself king of both O'ahu and Maui. On New Year's Day 1795, his own ambition now afire, Kalanikupule's warriors swarmed *Jackal* and *Prince Lee Boo*, killed their captains, and made forced labor of their crews (*Lady Washington* escaped to Canton after an errant cannon shot from *Jackal* killed her captain and several others).

As Kalanikupule indulged his dreams of glory, the first mates and crews of the captive vessels retook them and killed or ejected the natives. The king and a few chiefs, who had already boarded for the voyage of conquest, were put ashore and the ships made straight for Kawaihae. Leaving letters telling John Young all that had happened on O'ahu, and by one native account disgorging the last of their armaments for the benefit of Kamehameha, *Jackal* and *Prince Lee Boo* made sail for Canton and left the Hawaiians to work out their mayhem for themselves.

Kamehameha was ready. When Vancouver returned for a third visit, Kamehameha "ceded" Hawai'i to the British Crown, probably in his own mind for purposes of counting on their protection.[2] With Kahekili dead and Maui exhausted, he invaded in 1795, with ten thousand men in twelve hundred war canoes. The campaign was short but bloody, and Maui was soon his. Now lord of all the southern islands, Kamehameha turned his attention to O'ahu, which was still ruled by intelligent, ruthless (as the captains of the *Jackal* and *Prince Lee Boo* discovered) Kalanikupule. Well aware of the growing threat from the south, the king of O'ahu had laid in more firearms, including artillery, from traders. To help prepare his defenses he obtained the services of a turncoat chief from Kamehameha's army, Ka'iana, the same who had been to China and America. Although an important *ali'i* in his own right and with ambitions of his own, Ka'iana may also have been fleeing Kamehameha's wrath for sleeping with the king's wife—not the sacred Keopuolani, but his favorite recreational wife, Ka'ahumanu.[3] Her relationship with the Conqueror continued devoted but tempestuous, and she took lovers when it pleased her—although they came to her at their own risk.

Kamehameha's men stormed ashore at Honolulu, a fishing village with a natural harbor on the south shore, and at Waikiki several miles east of there, and Kalanikupule staged a fighting retreat to higher ground inland. Northeastward from Honolulu, the Nu'uanu Valley rose higher and higher until it crested in a precipitous overlook, the Nu'uanu Pali, more than a thousand feet high, commanding a view of the opposite side of the island. Here Kalanikupule had his men chip gunports into the high lava ridge, making a natural castle of the heights. Kamehameha pursued the retreating army of

O'ahu until the mountaintop cannons roared to life and stopped him in his tracks. Pinned down and taking losses, Kamehameha sent part of his army to the other side of the island, where they scaled the Pali—no mean feat in itself—and put the guns out of action. Resuming the attack, Kamehameha's army cornered Kalanikupule's at the precipice, and some four hundred of O'ahu's warriors were driven over the cliff, plunging to their deaths a thousand feet below. Later Kamehameha's men moved through the bodies at the foot of the Pali, slicing off their heads so that the *mana* would accrue to him. Two generations later, American hikers at the foot of the Pali found skeletons in abundance, but no skulls; their burial place was discovered generations later during highway excavation. Kalanikupule himself escaped and lived for months as a fugitive, but was eventually captured, taken to the Big Island to Kuka'ilimoku's *heiau* on the Hill of the Whale, and sacrificed.

Present on O'ahu during the Battle of Nu'uanu Pali was Kamehameha's captive child bride, Keopuolani, now old enough to fulfill her function, and the Conqueror consummated their relationship. Thereafter she lived out her life as the sacred royal wife, though little affection attended the title. The king was fastidious in respecting her prerogatives, but he chafed under her rank and they did not live together. He acquiesced that she could have her own lovers, and she accepted that his call, when he wanted her, took precedence over her other men. During her life Keopuolani bore fourteen children, four of them by Kamehameha, of whom three lived: two sons, Liholiho, born about 1797; Kauikeaouli, born probably in 1813; and a daughter, Nahi'ena'ena, born in 1815.[4]

From O'ahu it was some sixty miles across the Kaua'i Channel to the remaining prize. If Western muskets and cannons were superior to clubs and spears, Western ships must be superior to native canoes; basing himself in Honolulu, Kamehameha undertook construction of a forty-ton vessel. The ship and its vast flotilla of war canoes departed in about June of 1796, but soon returned in disarray. Kamehameha seems to have put it out for public consumption that his force was disabled by storms in the notoriously turbulent channel, but the story touted on Kaua'i was that the vaunted Conqueror did land, and his warriors were defeated on the beaches. Early informants remembered a dozen of Kamehameha's warriors, captured in the Battle of Koloa Beach (today's Mahaulepa Beach), being taken to Kaua'i's Polihale *heiau* and sacrificed to the war god.[5]

Kamehameha was then recalled to Hawai'i to suppress another rebellion, this one led by the incensed brother of the traitor Ka'iana, who had been killed at the Pali. Learning from the behavior of restive *ali'i*, the king left O'ahu under the governance of Isaac Davis, who depended solely on him for favor and advancement, and who knew what would happen if he betrayed him. Davis had grown as content as Young in his new life, but with a different style; he "went native," preferring grass house to stone and accepting the station of high chief. With residences at both Kailua Kona, on the west coast of the Big Island, and Waikiki, Kamehameha bided his time for seven years, strengthening his government and the economy, but never forgetting to continually build up his military might.

During this period Kamehameha concentrated on creating a centralized government for his kingdom, and as merciless as his conquest had been, the administration he installed was stable and farsighted. He tapped the services of an able and vigorous young chief, Kalanimoku, as second in command in all things; Westerners equated his office with that of a prime minister, and even named him "Billy Pitt" after his close interest in and regard for Britain's then–prime minister, William Pitt the Younger. He probably became attached to Kamehameha's court when the king married Ka'ahumanu, who was Kalanimoku's first cousin.[6] He was demonstrably as intelligent as she, quick and curious around the increasing number of foreigners, their languages, and their ways, and he became an invaluable conduit between them and the king, to whom he was intensely loyal.

Peace begat productivity among the people, and Kamehameha grew wealthy on the tribute handed up by the chiefs and high chiefs, rounded up from their *kanakas*, who now could at least tend their fish, pigs, dogs, and crops without fear of sudden terror and death. Although there was no written language or numerals, tax collectors had a witheringly accurate system of accounting: "a line of cordage from four to five hundred fathoms in length. Distinct portions of this are allotted to the various districts, which are known from one another by knots, loops, and tufts, of different shapes, sizes and colors. Each tax-payer in the district has his part on this string, and the number of dollars, hogs, dogs, pieces of sandalwood, quantity of taro, &c., at which he is rated, is well defined."[7] With the bodies of his rivals baked and boned after lying on the altars of the war god, the king also sequestered the foreign trade to himself. While he personally preferred life on the west coast of the Big Island, foreign vessels needed a more sheltered anchorage and sought out the harbor at Honolulu. To be near the scene of the commercial action Kamehameha installed himself there for several years, ever gaining in power.

By 1803 Kamehameha was ready to mount a new assault on Kaua'i. On that island King Kaumuali'i prepared to repel the second invasion, but he also built a large modern ship to carry him to the western Pacific in case of defeat. Fate intervened, however, as Kamehameha's swelling army, and the people of O'ahu as well, were decimated by the *oku'u*—an epidemic of what was probably Asiatic cholera brought by a foreign ship. Incapable of believing that the gods had deserted him, the king ordered the *kahunas* to open a search to discover who had broken a *kapu* and caused such a calamity. At length three men were found who had eaten forbidden foods; they were apprehended, their limbs snapped, their eyes gouged out, and then they were sacrificed at a Waikiki *heiau*.

It was an unusually gory offering, for human sacrifice in Hawai'i was not generally as sanguine as it was, for instance, in Mesoamerica. The usual mode of dispatch was strangulation, often after the victim was tied to a tree. Occasionally, however, and particularly in older times, sacrifice could be much more vivid, depending on the nature of the ceremony. At the Mo'okini *heiau* at Kamehameha's birthplace in Kohala, a defeated chief might be strung upside down, so that the *kahunas* could anoint themselves in his sweat before he was bludgeoned and gutted.[8] The gruesome fate of these three hapless *kanakas* must have been a measure of Kamehameha's wrath and determination to make an example.

Remaining on Oʻahu kept the king closer to the independent and occasionally impudent Kaumualiʻi, the one annoyance that continued to nettle him. While Kamehameha raked in trade, primarily from the English and the Americans, a different empire cultivated the friendship of Kaumualiʻi and began to make its presence felt. In June 1804 two Russian ships, the *Neva* under Yuri Lisianski, and the *Nadezhda* under Ivan Johann von Krusenstern, called at Kauaʻi, opening an imperial bid that would not play out for some years. Anxious to gain knowledge of these mighty foreign nations, Kaumualiʻi placed his young son and heir, who became known as Prince George Kaumualiʻi (the king maintained his friendship with the British by naming his children after members of the royal family), on an American ship, with the charge to return with a Western education.

Eventually Kaumualiʻi acknowledged the inevitable, that Kamehameha would only keep coming. And Kamehameha, who profited handsomely from increasing foreign trade, accepted that peace was more beneficial than war. The Conqueror sent word through his retainers that he would be content to leave Kaumualiʻi in power on Kauaʻi and Niʻihau, but as his vassal, acknowledging Kamehameha's sovereignty and paying tribute. Remembering the fate of Keoua, and of Kalanikupule after him, Kaumualiʻi hesitated to travel to Oʻahu and pay homage in person.

His fears were well founded, for a council of Kamehameha's chiefs was even then sifting through the most advantageous circumstance in which to assassinate him, and decided to invite the visiting king on an excursion to the diving pool at Waikahalulu, out of the Conqueror's sight.[9] Kamehameha would not approve, and after about two years of trading gifts and assurances with his rival, he utilized the good offices of Capt. Nathan Winship to bring him over to Oʻahu. Fearing to be massacred, some Kauaʻi chiefs still held back, but Winship, leaving his first mate behind as hostage, bore Kaumualiʻi and a retinue over in late March or early April 1810. In his own canoe Kamehameha was rowed out to meet him, with a suckling pig in his arms as a gift, and said, "Homai ko lima" (Give me your hand).[10]

After some days of feasting and trust building, the king of Kauaʻi and Niʻihau offered his islands to the ascendant king, and was allowed to continue ruling them as Kamehameha's vassal, and as a symbol of his new office he received a splendid *kaʻei*, a feather cordon some five yards long.[11] Few of these feather stoles existed, and they were objects of tremendous *mana*, centuries old, trimmed with the teeth of sacrifices whose spiritual power transferred to the new owner. Kamehameha would never have handed over such a powerful thing unless he meant to keep his bargain. Thus Kaumualiʻi escaped being sacrificed, but there was an important casualty. In traditional society, if an *aliʻi* overburdened his serfs with taxes and tribute, they were free to leave him and offer their services elsewhere. Indeed, the incentive for chiefs not to abuse their *kanakas* was enforced here and there throughout their history with the violent deaths of tyrannical chiefs, even kings.[12] The chiefs of Kauaʻi bitterly resented having another level of tribute—to Kamehameha— being placed over them, and either they or Kamehameha's own chiefs, led by Haiha Naihe, determined to poison Kaumualiʻi—a favored method of assassination in the islands.[13] Isaac Davis, whom Kamehameha had made governor of Oʻahu and who had been involved in the negotiations, learned of the plot in time to warn him, but was instead himself poisoned. (Ironically Davis's daughter Betty later married Kaumualiʻi's son, Prince George.)

Davis's death was a hard blow to Kamehameha, who valued loyalty and ability as ardently as he punished treachery. But by 1810 he was undisputed king of the Sandwich Islands, and the *ʻahuʻula*, the feather cape that he donned, where others in the islands were predominantly red and trimmed in the rare yellow, was solid yellow, comprising perhaps a quarter of a million feathers of the *mamo*, a native bird now extinct. Amassing his empire was accomplished by twenty-eight years of blood, terror, and at the end, negotiation. Honored today as the "unifier" of the Hawaiian Islands, that characterization has been softened by time, and serves a modern need. In his own day he was feared and despised as widely as he was revered.

Kaumuali'i himself chafed under the overlordship, and when the Russians came back he was willing to make some intrigue with them. The Russians had been surprisingly slow to attempt to consolidate their claim to North America's upper Pacific coast, with its rich fur trade, and buffer their claim to Alaska. In 1815 Aleksandr Baranov, governor of the Russian American Fur Company, sent a vessel under a German commander, Georg Anton Schäffer, to salvage a cargo wrecked on the shores of Kaua'i three years before. His visit had a subtext, however, which was to capture as much of the trade as he could for Russia, and then on his own responsibility Schäffer set about trying to transform the islands into a Russian colony.

John Young, in league with the growing number of Americans, saw through Schäffer even as he tried to pass himself off as a curious naturalist and salvage operator. Kamehameha dismissed their warnings, Ka'ahumanu gave Schäffer land from her own holdings, and the German adventurer proceeded to Kaua'i. He overreached himself when two more Russian ships arrived in 1816, and he started to build a fort at Honolulu—a project that the king dispatched John Young to break up, although he very sensibly finished and occupied the fort. Kaumuali'i had followed these developments, and offered the Russians huge land and trade concessions if they would help him conquer the islands that were, he said, rightfully his—all of them, save Hawai'i.[14] Schäffer's delusions of grandeur only inflated; he gave Russian names to Kaua'i geography, sent out surveyors, and began erecting fortifications. Two things toppled his empire. The first was a port call by Otto von Kotzebue (son of the famous German

playwright) in a Russian ship, who expressed his shock to Kamehameha at Schäffer's audacity, and assured him that Russia had no
territorial ambitions in his islands. Second, the king, now six years
stronger than when he made his peace with Kaumali'i, sent his command to Kaumuali'i to evict Schäffer or face the consequences.
Finding safety the better part of ambition, and learning that Schäffer
had no standing, Kaumuali'i became again the obedient if reluctant
vassal, and threw the Russians off his island.

The Russian adventure was a gaudy distraction for a year, but it
ended with no harm even as it emphasized Hawai'i's importance to
Pacific geography. Once the existence of the Sandwich Islands became known, their strategic location made them the crossroads of
the Pacific, the stopping place for vessels of every seafaring nation.
And they brought to trade Western dress that became the craze
among the *ali'i*, furniture for their houses, tools and appliances, and
amenities they had never imagined. The Hawaiians proved happily amenable to all the enlargements the foreign visitors brought
to their way of life. The mainstays of their diet up to this point their
ancestors had brought from their home islands centuries before—
pigs, dogs, bananas, yams, breadfruit, sugarcane, and taro, whose
starchy corms they cooked into a pasty lavender gruel called poi.
Now, however, they assimilated a variety of new foods into their
diet. Captain Cook himself had given them seeds to grow onions,
melons, and pumpkins on his first landing at Ni'ihau. Vancouver's
cattle were increasing happily in lush upland meadows on the leeward sides of Hawai'i. The greatest benefactor of their diet proved
to be the Spanish mariner Don Francisco de Paula Marín, who introduced exotic fruits from the colony in the Philippine Islands:
lemons and limes, guava, papaya and later mangoes, and one plant
that gained great local favor and became an island staple: pineapple.
Kamehameha himself took note of the boon that Don Francisco was
providing to diet and trade, and brought him into his circle. He gave

the Spaniard an estate on the south shore of Oʻahu, where Marín settled and later planted Hawaiʻi's first vineyard, and then coffee. A natural linguist, hospitable, funny, and somewhat raffish (important virtues in the native culture), with an undetermined number of children by three wives, Marín often acted as the king's host and interpreter, and did very well in trade with visiting mariners.

Marín was the first in the islands to turn from subsistence agriculture to cash crops, and by 1810, just as Kamehameha completed his conquest, the kingdom made its debut on the stage of world commerce. When Simon Metcalfe had cruised the Hawaiian waters twenty years before, he was on the lookout for sandalwood, which was extremely valuable in the China trade, to augment his usual cargoes of fur from the American Northwest. The wood was known well enough among the islanders, who called it *iliahi*, and ground up the heartwood to rub into *tapa* to perfume the cloth. Westerners discovered it only the year before, and quite by accident, when some was burned for firewood.

Early attempts to sell *iliahi* wood in China failed, because islands in the southwest Pacific had species of sandalwood superior to the Hawaiian, and there were no buyers. Chinese demand, however, eventually exhausted the Fiji and Solomon Islands sandalwood, setting up Hawaiʻi for its first big venture in resource extraction. The American captain Nathan Winship's aid in cementing peace with Kaumualiʻi placed Kamehameha in Winship's debt, thus when Winship approached the Conqueror with a business proposition in 1810, he got an attentive hearing. If Kamehameha would set his tenants to felling sandalwood trees, and give Winship, his brother Jonathan, and their partner, Capt. William Heath Davis, a monopoly on the trade, they would transport the product to China, sell it, and pay the king one-fourth of the proceeds, either in specie or such fine Chinese goods as Kamehameha might desire. He agreed, and laid a *kapu* against any people but his own felling sandalwood trees, and the

Winships took their first shipload to China—where they learned
that the United States and Great Britain had entered upon the War
of 1812.

While the United States' few tough, brilliantly engineered frig-
ates gave a good account of themselves in the Atlantic, American
activities in the Pacific were almost entirely at the mercy of the vast
Royal Navy, and three of the Winships' vessels were blockaded in
Honolulu for three years. Kamehameha owed Winship consideration for his peacemaking services, but the king's eye for business
placed a limit on his obligation. Kamehameha had some eighty
thousand dollars with Canton factors, half in coin and half in merchandise, which the Winships dared not risk on the high seas. As
the delayed payment became increasingly difficult to explain to the
king, his English captive-turned-adviser John Young used the opportunity to play a small role in the war, and convinced Kamehameha that the Winships had played him false and absconded with
the sandalwood with no intention of paying him. Even if he still believed the Winships faithful, the king learned an object lesson on
the respective power of the British and American navies when a
British privateer entered Honolulu Harbor on May 23, 1814, as an
American prize taken by Lt. John Gamble, U.S. Marine Corps. He
sailed on June 11, but the ship was back in Honolulu two days later,
the prize of HMS *Cherub*, with Gamble a prisoner of war.

At length a neutral (Portuguese) vessel was engaged to ship Kamehameha's merchandise and cash to Hawaii, and even then was
delayed by monsoons. The Winships, annoyed that Kamehameha
had suspended their contract, instructed the captain to unload the
merchandise when he arrived in Honolulu, but to keep the money
on board until they were certain of the king's intentions. If a British
man-of-war entered the harbor, however, the specie was to be safely
given to the king at once. There was a story that—if it cannot be
confirmed nevertheless displays exactly the kind of shrewdness that
Kamehameha habitually displayed—the Winships' plan was betrayed to him. All ships arriving in Honolulu were heralded before

they ever crossed the reef by lookouts on Diamond Head, one signal for a small vessel and a larger commotion for a major ship. All Kamehameha had to do was arrange for the lookouts to alert the port of the arrival of a nonexistent British warship, and the forty thousand dollars was in his custody before the ruse was discovered.[15] He also was astute enough, after learning that one of Ka'ahumanu's ships was charged piloting and docking fees in Macao, to begin collecting money for the same thing at Honolulu—eighty dollars for anchorage, and twelve dollars for piloting payable to his English pilot, Capt. John Harbottle. The fees were not unjust because Honolulu had a tricky reef to navigate and a waterfront to develop, but the levy undoubtedly surprised ship captains who had not thought the king would so quickly adopt Western streams of income.[16]

Academic discussion of the sandalwood trade usually treats it as an exponent of American exploitative imperialism,[17] but once the scent of profit was in the air, there is no question that Kamehameha knew how to cash in with little prompting from American traders. Thus the king went into the sandalwood business, for cash and luxury goods, but he never lost his eye for weapons. As late as 1818, the Boston mercantile firm Bryant & Sturgis advised the captain of one of their ships, the brig *Ann*, "You have probably double the number of muskets and more Powder than is wanted . . . and it would be well to dispose of some at the Islands. . . . If you can sell the King any articles of your cargo on advantageous terms, to receive your pay in Sandal Wood . . . we think you had best do it."[18] Kamehameha could even pay cash for ships, such as the 175-ton *Lelia Byrd*, which became his flagship.

For Americans the sums of money to be made were addictive; where they might have to pay Kamehameha ten to fifteen thousand dollars to fill a hold with sandalwood, that cargo in Canton could fetch four times that amount. The Conqueror himself fell to the addiction, commanding the tenants who worked his vast lands to leave their fishponds and taro fields to go into the forests to cut *iliahi*, and squeezing still more in tribute from his chiefs, who wrung it from their own tenants. In remarkably little time there was no food, and *kanakas* were reduced "to eat[ing] herbs and fern trunks." The aging Kamehameha repented his excesses and ordered his tenants back to the production of food. And more than that, he was quick to notice when sandalwood began to be difficult to find, and he laid a *kapu* against the taking of saplings, so that there should be a future supply.

By 1818 there were perhaps as many as two hundred foreigners resident in the Sandwich Islands,[19] English and predominantly American, including Anthony Allen, a free Negro who was the first of several African-Americans to discover the fresh air of living in a country unmarred by any feeling of racial inferiority. This blending of English and American influence was perfectly symbolized in the new nation's flag: with red, white, and blue American-like stripes, but the superimposed crosses of Saint George and Saint Andrew in the upper left corner where American stars would have been.

Leaving administration to able minions, Kamehameha retired to his favorite residence, Kailua Kona, living out his days on the quiet beaches at the foot of Hualalai volcano. His decline was gradual enough that there was time to send for *kahunas* to chant over him; they prescribed human sacrifices until he should recover, but the dying king, almost as though he anticipated his country's massive pending change, forbade it. Even Don Francisco de Marín was sent for to try to doctor him, but all to no avail. He died on May 8, 1819, having ruled for thirty-seven years, only nine of which were over the unified kingdom he created. But the twenty-eight years of war, terror, and human sacrifice that it took to create his nation bore consequences that echoed even to the other side of the globe, consequences that were about to return to Hawai'i and change it forever.

3. The Suicide of *Kapu*

It was probably in 1783, during Kamehameha's conquest of the Big Island, that he at one stage had repaired to Laupahoehoe, north of Hilo, to regroup. With no major battles imminent, he took one canoe and its crew on a pillaging sortie down the coast. Like those of Vikings in a longboat, such lightning raids could gain supplies and spread terror very effectively among the defenseless coastal *kanaka* population. Spying two or three fishermen on the shore, Kamehameha had the canoe beached, and they pursued the frightened locals on foot. During this hot chase the king's foot became wedged fast in a lava crevice. One terrified fisherman, named Kaleleiki, turned and hit the Conqueror over the head with his paddle as hard as he could, shattering it. Kamehameha was knocked unconscious, but rather than finish him off, Kaleleiki fled. Once he came to, Kamehameha found his way back to his warriors; reflecting upon his fortunate escape, he proclaimed thenceforth a *kapu* against attacking noncombatants. "See to it," he intoned, "that our aged, our women, and our children, lie down to sleep by the roadside without fear of harm." In the formality of *kapu*, he added, "Hewa no, make"

(Disobey, and die). It became known as *Kanawai Mamalahoe*, the Law of the Splintered Paddle, which later became enshrined in the Hawaiian constitution. Kaleleiki, later cast before Kamehameha to face his justice, was pardoned.[1] It was the first crack in a social system that, for the *kanakas* since time immemorial, had been rooted in terror.

Word of the protective *kapu* spread, but also the knowledge that it was virtually unenforceable. It was ancient to Hawaiian culture that in their ubiquitous warfare, if an enemy force was defeated, they would fall upon their families, hacking and pillaging to the point of gory surfeit, even as warriors in all times and in all cultures, when their blood is up and the killing has started, press an attack without discrimination. Such was the case when Kamehameha's warriors overran a settlement in the Kau District. A young boy of about twelve named Opukaha'ia escaped with his parents and baby brother, and the family hid in a cave until thirst drove them to water at a nearby spring. "Here," Opukaha'ia recalled, "they were surprised by a party of the enemy while in the act of quenching their thirst." The man fled, but "the enemy, seeing the affection of the father for his family, put them to the torture in order to decoy him from his retreat. . . . Unable to bear the piercing cries of his family, he fell into their hands, and with his wife was cut in pieces."[2]

Attempting his own escape, the boy swung his three-month-old brother onto his back and fled. The spear flung after them skewered the infant to Opukaha'ia's body, killing the baby but only wounding the youth. He was too old to require care and too young to cause trouble, so his life was spared, and he was taken in by the warrior who killed his family. Later it was discovered that Opukaha'ia was the nephew of a *kahuna* of Lono. The boy had worked his way into the affections of his new family, and his "keeper," as he called him, vowed that if he could not keep the boy he would kill him, but he was powerless to defy a priest of Lono. Now perhaps fourteen, he was sent to the god's Hikiau *heiau* at Kealakekua Bay to study to become a *kahuna* as well, learning the precision of the chants and the protocol of sacrifices. In 1809, while visiting his one surviving aunt, he hid in terror as men invaded the dwelling and dragged her away. She was accused of violating a *kapu* and thrown from a cliff to her death.

"While I was with my uncle," Opukaha'ia later wrote, "I began to think about leaving that country. . . . I did not care where I shall go to. I thought to myself that if I should get away . . . I may find some comfort." From Lono's *heiau* the youth of now about sixteen swam out to a newly arrived American trading ship, the *Triumph*, Capt. Caleb Brintnall commanding, out of New Haven, Connecticut. One man aboard spoke enough Hawaiian to relay the boy's intentions. Unwilling to cause an incident, Brintnall fed him supper and invited him to stay the night, but required the priest's permission before taking him away. Opukaha'ia rowed ashore in the morning; his uncle was furious at the development and locked the boy in his room, although since it was a traditional grass house, he was able to work his way through the wall and escape back to the ship. The *kahuna* was eventually placated at the price of a pig, and the *Triumph* weighed anchor with Opukaha'ia on board.[3]

Also sailing away with Captain Brintnall was another refugee, a few years younger than Opukaha'ia, named Hopu, called Thomas by the crew, whom he served as cabin boy. Born on Hawai'i, he narrowly escaped death on the day of his birth. His mother, dispirited by the incessant raiding and terror, opined that it would be better for him had he not been born, and expressed the intent to kill him. Her sister overheard her and stole away with the baby to raise him in her husband's household. They returned him to his parents when he was four, but when he was eight raiders looted the family of all they possessed; the father relocated to Kealakekua Bay to start over, the mother died the next year, and Hopu availed himself of the *Triumph*'s presence to search for a better life.[4]

Hopu and Opukaha'ia were not unusual in fleeing their homeland; word spread quickly in maritime circles that the Sandwich Islands were a good place to bring depleted crews back up to strength. Once at sea, though, the boys learned that life to these new people was more precious than they were accustomed to. The *Triumph*, which touched at America for furs and then returned to Hawai'i before continuing to China, one day was making about nine knots before a stiff wind in a rolling sea. Hopu tending his duties as cabin boy, "stood by the main chains, outside of the ship, drawing up a bucket of water to wash my dishes, I fell overboard." There was just time to cry for help before the ship was beyond earshot, and then beyond sight. Hopu was a good swimmer and stripped off his clothes so they would not drag him under as he vacillated between despair and determination. Brintnall had been asleep in his cabin but was quickly alerted. "The Captain calls all hands upon the deck, and ordered to have all the sails pulled down in order to let about. . . . We turned our ship and went back after him, we found him almost dead. He was in the water during the space of two and a half hours."

Aboard the *Triumph* Opukaha'ia was befriended by Russell Hubbard of New Haven, who had been to Yale. "He was very kind to me on our passage, and taught me the letters in English spelling-book."[5] After a lengthy voyage, Brintnall docked in New York, a city that was a shock to the Hawaiian youths, although of all the strange new sights and sounds, nothing caused more consternation than seeing men and women eating together, which was a capital offense in their homeland, a keystone of the entire *kapu* system. They continued to New Haven, where Opukaha'ia lived with the Brintnall family, and Hopu with a doctor named Hotchkiss for a time before becoming a sailor. He disappeared for years, more than once shipwrecked, and captured and imprisoned during the War of 1812, before making his way back.

Opukaha'ia made a start at an education but became frustrated with others' lack of interest in him. One day "Obookiah," which was as close as the Americans could come to pronouncing his real name, was found sitting on the steps of one of Yale University's buildings, weeping. A solicitous student stopped to inquire what was wrong, and

Obookiah said, "No one will give me learning." The young man to whom Obookiah complained happened to be Edwin Dwight, nephew of Timothy Dwight, president of the college. "His appearance was unpromising," Dwight wrote of the meeting. "He was clothed in a rough sailor's suit, was of a clumsy form, and his countenance dull and heavy." Dwight almost passed him by without speaking, "as one whom it would be in vain to notice and attempt to instruct. But when the question was put him, 'Do you wish to learn?' his countenance began to brighten and . . . he served it with great eagerness."[6]

After but little religious instruction, Opukaha'ia's universe inverted. "Owhyhee gods," he exclaimed, "they wood! *Burn*! Me go home, put 'em in a fire, burn 'em up. They no *see*, no *hear*, no *any thing*. We *make* 'em. *Our God*"—he looked up in awe—"*He* make *us*."[7] Nothing was the same for Opukaha'ia, or Hawai'i, ever again.

It would be difficult to imagine drier tinder to receive such a spark.

The voyages of Captain Cook had a devoted follower in the person of William Carey, a prominent English Baptist preacher who puzzled over why, amidst the discovery of heathen nations utterly new to Western conscience, no effort was being made to obey the Great Commandment and preach salvation among them. Carey wrote a famous book, formed the Baptist Missionary Society, and then himself sailed to India to spread the gospel for four decades. The movement took root, and soon British missionaries fanned out across the Pacific, except for the one glaring exception of the Sandwich Islands. Carey's zeal spread to the United States, where one Samuel Mills, Jr., was inspired in 1806 to hold the famous Haystack Prayer Meeting, in Williamstown, Massachusetts, which led the American Congregationalist Church to form the American Board of Commissioners for Foreign Missions (universally referred to by its acronym, ABCFM). After taking an affectionate leave of Captain Brintnall, with whom he had lived for some months, Opukaha'ia lived with the family of Samuel Mills, Sr., while studying religion.[8]

As a student he won universal affection, as much for his ability to convulse other students with his dead-on mimicry of them and their teachers as for his scholarship. While residing with the Mills family in Torrington, Connecticut, he often paid visits to a friend (discreetly not named in Dwight's memoir) at Litchfield. That person was then studying for a doctorate in divinity and enjoying his immersion in the abstractions of theology, but Obookiah broached to him a soul sickness and desire that discomfited him greatly. "It was his object to converse with him upon the subject of accompanying him to Owhyhee. He plead [*sic*] with great earnestness that he would go and preach the Gospel to his poor countrymen. Not receiving so much encouragement as he desired, [Obookiah] suspected that his friend might be influenced by the fear of the consequences of introducing a new religion among the heathens." Upon which, though Opukaha'ia was still very new to the language of the scriptures, he demanded, "You 'fraid? You know our Savior say, He that will save his life shall lose it; and he that will lose his life for my sake, same shall find it?"[9]

Thenceforward it was a subject that would give Opukaha'ia no rest. His demonstrated zeal for spreading the faith came just at the time that the Second Great Awakening was kindling missionary fever throughout New England. As word spread of his determination to introduce the gospel to his native land, one elderly minister drew him aside to press on him the danger of martyrdom if he did so. "Suppose," he asked, "your countrymen should tell you that preaching Jesus Christ was blaspheming their gods, and put you to death?" Opukaha'ia was adamant: "If that be the will of God, *I am ready. I am ready.*" After being accepted into the church in Torrington, he agitated the question until he was finally taken in by the ABCFM for the purpose—to his unbounded joy—of returning to his home as a missionary.[10] In his study of Christianity, Opukaha'ia discovered to his surprise that one of the easiest subjects for him to learn was Hebrew, because to his mind it bore surprising structural similarities to his own language. He began a massive undertaking: to translate the Bible into Hawaiian, and he began with Genesis, bypassing English to transcribe from Hebrew straight into his native language. "I want to see you about our Grammar," he wrote a teacher friend. "I want to get through with it. I have been translating a few chapters of the Bible into the Owhyhee language. I found I could do it very correctly."[11]

In 1815 Thomas Hopu returned to New Haven, to learn when Brintnall might again sail for the South Seas—he was homesick and wished to return. "My friend Thomas come to me with a sad countenance," Opukaha'ia wrote in his diary on March 23, 1816. Hopu was already drawn into the new religion, but he was confused. He "wished that we might pray together in our own language. . . . We offered up two prayers in our tongue—the first time that we ever prayed in this manner."[12] Hopu threw in with the missionary effort, and then they discovered that there were still more of them in this strange and invigorating world. One was not just a countryman, but an *ali'i* of high *kapu*. Going by the name George Tamoree, he was in fact the son and heir of Kaumuali'i, the vassal king of Kaua'i. Entrusted to Americans to get an education, he had instead been used as a common laborer, served on an American frigate, and been wounded in the War of 1812. He was living in company with yet another Hawaiian, John Honoli'i, one of many *kanakas* who had shipped out on foreign vessels. And then there was William Kanui, who like Hopu and Opukaha'ia had had a narrow escape from death; his father was one of the few O'ahu chiefs to survive the massacre at Nu'uanu Pali during Kamehameha's conquest of the island in 1795. He fled to Kaua'i with his family in tow, where he became a vassal of Kaumuali'i. With war threatening again, the chief's two sons signed aboard the brig *Elizabeth* and joined the Hawaiian diaspora; the brother died in New York before Kanui was taken into the missionary circle.[13]

The ABCFM could hardly have asked for a more auspicious beginning for the evangelizing of Hawai'i. All five students had their portraits painted by Samuel F. B. Morse, and electroplate engravings of them were sold to raise money; in 1816 the society published *A Nar-*

rative of Five Youths from the Sandwich Islands to generate more support. The Hawaiians were enrolled in a religious school at Litchfield until the spring of 1817, when they began studying at the ABCFM's own new missionary school in Cornwall. And then disaster struck, as Opukaha'ia took a fever at the start of 1818. Diagnosed with typhus, he lingered for six weeks. "Oh! How I want to see Hawaii," he said. "But I fear I never shall—God will do right—He knows what is best." As he neared the end, his much-loved native confederates—Thomas Hopu, John Honoli'i, Prince George Kaumuali'i, and William Kanui—all pledged to him that they would continue in the new religion, return to Hawai'i, and end the horrors of *kapu*.[14]

"Go see my uncle," said Opukaha'ia. "Tell him I love him. I thank him for his care so long ago. And if my grandmother still lives, tell her I will return to her in my spirit."[15] He died on February 17, 1818. The passing of their star proselyte dismayed but did not dissuade American Congregationalists, for by his serene death in the faith Opukaha'ia finally galvanized what he had not been able to forge in life: the resolution to actually send missionaries to Owhyhee. His funeral was preached by Lyman Beecher himself, the forty-two-year-old lion of the Second Great Awakening. "We thought," he lamented, "we saw so plainly the hand of God in bringing him hither; in his instruction, his conversion, talents, and missionary zeal." His passing, however, must turn Christian eyes toward the Foreign Mission School. "His death . . . will awaken a tender sympathy for Owhyhee, and give it an interest in the prayers and charities of thousands. . . . Instead of fainting under the stroke, we are animated by it, to double confidence in God, and double diligence in this work."[16]

The churches of New England made good on Beecher's exhortation; they did not insist on a Congregationalist affiliation for candidates: Presbyterians or any other good Calvinist Protestant would serve as well. The understanding was that once they reached the Sandwich Islands, doctrinal quibbling was to be put aside in the greater effort to convert the heathen. Leadership of the forming expedition was awarded to Rev. Hiram Bingham. He was a Vermonter, a graduate of Middlebury College and Andover Theological Seminary, and newly wedded to Sybil Moseley. Unmarried persons were discouraged from emigrating as missionaries, so like Bingham, the other single men in the company made it their business to find eligible, zealous young women, marry them, and combine missionary effort with honeymoon—to say nothing of getting acquainted. With Bingham would go Rev. Asa Thurston and his wife, Lucy, who was destined to be the last survivor of the company; Samuel Whitney and his wife, Mercy, and Rev. Samuel Ruggles with his wife, Nancy, schoolteachers. Elisha Loomis, a young printer who had to ask for release from his apprenticeship in order to volunteer, was in danger of being left behind until he found Maria Sartwell during his trip home to say farewell to his family; there was also a doctor named Thomas Holman, and the farmer Daniel Chamberlain, taking passage with his five children. Like many of the more than one hundred missionaries who followed them, they had little expectation of seeing their homes again. Accompanying them, not least, were the four young Hawaiian men: John Honoli'i, Thomas Hopu, William Kanui, and George Kaumuali'i, the prince of Kaua'i.

The brig *Thaddeus* was chartered and loaded, sailing on October 19, 1819, one week before Bingham's thirtieth birthday.

Back in Hawai'i, changes were afoot. The first and smaller change was that the natives were becoming more vocal in their displeasure at their country being known to the outside world as the Sandwich Islands, which was a foreign designation wholly unknown to them. When the Russian captain Wassily Golovnin had an audience with the aging Kamehameha in 1818, the Conqueror went "so far as to object to the name 'Sandwich Islands,' . . . insisting that each one should be called by its own name, and the group, that of the king of Hawaii." The islanders themselves referred to the entire archipelago as *Hawai'i nei pae aina*, "these Hawaiian islands," and gradually, informally, the outside world began to use the names interchangeably. On official documents, however, the "Sandwich Islands" survived for another twenty years.[17]

The larger change was, to the native culture, cataclysmic. Among Polynesian women, fat was beautiful, and Kamehameha's favorite wife, Ka'ahumanu, was very beautiful. This imposing woman, estimated to have weighed five hundred pounds,[18] was also gracious, hospitable, and funny—important qualities in the wife to whom the king turned first for pleasure. However, she was also forceful and shrewd enough for Kamehameha as he grew old to name her as *kuhina nui*, or principal adviser and in effect coruler, to steady the coming reign of his son. He knew that the dissolute Liholiho would not be nearly the presence as king that he had been. The sacred royal wife, Keopuolani, had never regarded Ka'ahumanu's favored position as any degree of threat. As the mother of the new king, and herself possessing the highest possible rank, her social position was secure. Ka'ahumanu's position in retirement was less certain, however, and the favorite consort of the Conqueror had no intention of retiring from public life.

After his death, the two queens took charge of Kamehameha's body, assigning its preparation to male relatives. The corpse was baked in an *imu* and the flesh stripped from the bones that contained his immense *mana*. The bones of Hawai'i's previous kings were bundled and deposited in the cliff cave overlooking Kealakekua Bay, inaccessible but known. Kamehameha had proved himself greater than any of his predecessors, and it was imperative that the *mana* of such a protean figure should be sacrosanct. To those who believed in the gods, if his bones fell into the hands of enemies, they could cause incalculable harm. Even in benign hands, such as those of a fisherman, they could be crafted into hooks that, while they would be believed to possess near-magical powers, would be an end of incomprehensible humiliation for such a king.

As Kamehameha's body was prepared for burial, it fell to Liholiho to decree how many sacrifices were required to usher the king's spirit into the next life. As word spread that the time was drawing near, the commoners who had assembled to mourn began to vanish back to their homes. They may have venerated the Conqueror, but not enough to be strangled on the altar for him. Hawaiian mythology warned people against clever *kahunas* who would trick people into violating a *kapu* in order to nab a sacrifice;[19] far better for them simply to disappear. However, taking the example that the Conqueror allowed no sacrifice to win his recovery, Liholiho ordered no sacrifices to mark his passing—a startling change in custom.

Kamehameha's body was buried secretly, reputedly deposited in a cave whose only entrance was offshore, and the resting place of his bones has never been discovered. Liholiho at length returned to Kailua for his investiture, a ceremony now colored with Western touches. He emerged from a *heiau* "robed in scarlet and a feathered mantle, with several chiefs on either side bearing *kahili* [tall, feather-festooned standards that proclaimed royal rank] and spittoon, having on his head a princely hat from Britain." His retainers were armed not with spears but with muskets. It was his stepmother, as *kuhina nui* and guardian of the kingdom, who presided, addressing him as the Heavenly One. "O Kalani, I report to you what belonged to your father—Here are the chiefs, and the men of your father—there are your guns, and this is your land." Then came what was, for her, the moment of truth: "But you and I will share the land together."[20] The new king agreed, opening his reign as Kamehameha II, but sharing actual power with Ka'ahumanu as queen regent.

She realized there was only one way for her to maintain her power, and that was to destroy the *kapu* system. Not to break this *kapu* and that one—she had already done that with impunity—but to gut the whole system and destroy it, to pull down the altars, burn the idols. Nor was it entirely about maintenance of personal power. For years, as the king's hostess, she had observed foreigners break *kapus* repeatedly, and no volcanoes erupted, no wooden, shark-toothed *ki'i* roused themselves to life and smote them. The gods had not forestalled the advent of the foreigners' diseases, seen most terribly in the cholera that destroyed the army that was to invade Kaua'i. The officers and traders who called at the islands had no *kapus*, and they lived healthier and more abundantly than her people, even the *ali'i*, had ever imagined. It seemed perfectly plausible that in overthrowing the system, she had a rich new life to gain, and—apart from her life—only some old wooden statues and rock-piles to lose.

In this purpose she was joined by Keopuolani, and the way they chose to open their campaign was stunning. During the feast that followed Liholiho's installation, Ka'ahumanu in feather regalia, leaning on the Conqueror's tall spear, told him,

> If you wish to observe *kapu*, it is well and we will not molest you. But as for me and my people we intend to be free from *kapu*. We intend that the husband's food and the wife's food shall be cooked in the same oven, and that they shall be permitted to eat from the same calabash. We intend to eat pork and bananas and coconuts. If you think differently you are at liberty to do so; but for me and my people we are resolved to be free. Let us henceforth disregard *kapu*.[21]

Liholiho stared at her, perhaps drunk, perhaps in shock, perhaps incredulous that she might just have pronounced her own death sentence. But he said nothing. At that moment Keopuolani put her hand to her mouth, signaling her assent that he end *kapu* and eat with the women. So entrenched was the *kapu* against mixed eating that the men dared reproach even the sacred royal wife for suggesting this. It was true that in the paroxysms of grief that followed the death of a king, acts were permitted that would be forbidden at any other time, but for men to eat with women was an outrage. Liholiho was demoralized by the prospect, and his response was to absent himself. Thwarted only briefly, the queen mother then importuned her younger son, Kauikeaouli, who was only six, into taking food with the women, all but daring the men to do something about it. And they backed down, unwilling to challenge her *ni'aupi'o* rank.

Another step in the self-immolation of *kapu* occurred soon after. The new king journeyed to Honokohau nearby to dedicate a new temple, indicating that perhaps he was not of the same mind as his mothers. However, such a consecration required reciting a lengthy, complicated prayer, uninterrupted and unbroken, without mistake. Rum, which of all the imported liquors had become the most popular, flowed so freely that this could not be done, so the new *heiau* stood useless. Liholiho was only the most visible example of a surrender to alcohol that afflicted many of the *ali'i*, who discovered that its "euphoria which was so new and exhilerating [*sic*] . . . was so pleasantly different from the semi-paralysis brought on with the drinking of *awa*." And already sensuous by cultural heritage, the Hawaiians enthusiastically adopted a beverage that lowered their inhibitions even more.[22]

The party was broken up when a messenger from the queen regent arrived to announce that this god would not be respected at Kailua—her way of proclaiming the new order, and her control. Liholiho's response was to load his rum and retainers onto his ship and sail aimlessly off the Kona coast for a two days' bender. Ka'ahumanu used the time profitably, lobbying key chiefs to end the *kapu* system and winning over the islands' most powerful priest, Hewahewa. Finally she dispatched double-hulled canoes to fetch the king back to Kailua; the messengers reached him, found his ship becalmed, and towed him in. Again he was offered food with the women, and this time he relented. The shattering event was called *'ai noa*, "the free eating." The gods were dead, the only known time in the history of the world when a people threw over a long-established religious system with nothing to replace it.[23]

Ka'ahumanu had good reason to destroy the *kapu* system. But apart from maybe saving Ka'ahumanu's life, why the sacred widow, the new king's birth mother, went along with it is a harder question. She had always done well by *kapu*. She was an *ali'i* of the *naha* class.

She was the offspring of a half-sister marriage, and the granddaughter of a full-sister marriage. She was one of the few women in the islands who possessed the *kapu moe*: Commoners had to prostrate themselves before her, and even her husband the Conqueror had to partially strip in humility at her presence. Herself so highborn, her children also outranked their father. If foreigners beheld Kamehameha's children playing on his lap, they would have been wrong to believe that he was merely being paternal and affectionate. Lesser children, not sparing his own offspring by lesser wives, would have been executed for such an affront. For him to allow Keopuolani's children on his lap, or for him to lie on his back and let them play on his chest, was in fact his own submission to rank. Throughout her tenure as his consort, she gained fame for her kindness and amiability. (The same could not be said for her mother, who once hounded one of Kamehameha's lesser wives to suicide for miscarrying the Conqueror's baby.) How a child played was significant; Keopuolani's mother also once sent her grandson Liholiho, when he was very small, to climb on that wife's back to demonstrate that they were of higher rank than she.[24] There were times during Keopuolani's reign when commoners' shadows crossed hers, and she forgave them when she could have had them killed; in fact there is no story that she ever had any of her subjects executed for breaking *kapu*.[25]

And therein may lie the clue—that she was never awed by the sanctity of the forbidden. Indeed she demonstrated as much when she defied *kapu* by refusing to give her youngest daughter, Nahi'ena'ena, in *hanai* to anyone, and raised her herself, although she was restricted by the *kapu 'uha* (sacred lap) which decreed death to any child she tried to rear.[26] And, while famed for her gracious bearing, perhaps she never forgave her fate at being bartered off at the age of eleven to marry her father's killer. (That Kamehameha cared for her was certain; her health had always been fragile, and in 1806 when she grew dangerously ill, the Conqueror sacrificed people until she recovered,[27] but the feeling was proprietary. It could not be said that there was love between them.) She was also ten years younger than Ka'ahumanu, and while being mentored by her, may have been somewhat dominated as well. But whatever the reason, when Ka'ahumanu put her life on the line by advocating the destruction of *kapu*, Keopuolani threw in with her.

In far-off Kaua'i the vassal king Kaumuali'i happily agreed to abandon the idols and their *kapus*, and remarkably the reigning high priest, Hewahewa, also acquiesced in the new order, but the destruction of *kapu* did not take place without dissent. Many still believed in the power of the old gods and were prepared to fight for them. Even as in his youth Kamehameha had been named guardian of the war god, the Conqueror had entrusted the same office to the high chief Kekuaokalani, son of his younger brother, the "good chief" of Kohala. Now the nephew became a magnet that attracted dissenters. When Liloliho, coaxed in from his two-day bender, had endorsed and participated in the *'ai noa* with the women, those who did not approve picked up and followed Kekuaokalani south to Kealakekua Bay, where armed men collected about him. No doubt, the chiefs who followed him were also looking for better selections of land than they would get from the drunk and the women. It was the worst of the old days, all over again.

When negotiation failed, and Keopuolani herself made a personal appeal for peace, the two queens deputed the Conqueror's prime minister, Kalanimoku, to lead an army down to fight him. It was a wrenching task for him, for his sister Manono was the rebellious chief's wife, and she had resolved to fight at his side. The battle was brief; the dissenters fought gamely, but the royal forces had muskets and the rout was complete. The rebel army was driven down to the shore, where they were fired on by men in double-hulled canoes, one of which mounted a small cannon, commanded by Ka'ahumanu.[28] Kekuaokalani was killed and Manono after him, shot down while calling for mercy. Armed opposition to the new regime ceased there, and the common people continued to revere their household gods, but from this day the old religion was ended. *Heiaus* were dismantled; those *ki'i* that were not burned were either neglected or given away as souvenirs to foreigners.

The uproar over ending *kapu* was enough of a social upheaval to attend the new reign, without engaging in the usual fratricidal war over redistribution of land. Instead Kamehameha II and the queen regent decided to win the loyalty of the chiefs by ending the royal monopoly on sandalwood, giving them the freedom to earn the best they could at it. And the *ali'i*, after years of seeing the Conqueror's storehouses swell with luxury goods, fell upon their forests with a vengeance. Chiefs and chiefesses competed with one another for the latest fashions; household items such as mirrors that they had lived without for generations were suddenly seen as indispensable necessities, and merchants overcharged them mercilessly.

It was true that Americans had introduced Hawaiian sandalwood to an international market, and that they introduced the islanders to the concept of resource extraction to fund a consumer economy, but the nobility grasped the essentials of capitalism in a heartbeat. And when sandalwood trees became scarce, they were equally quick to comprehend the nature of a futures contract, paying for this year's purchases with the next year's product—which they then browbeat their tenants to scour the forests in search of. The difference between them and the Conqueror was that when Kamehameha saw the resource declining, he used his superior intellect to protect it, placing young trees under *kapu*. Some chiefs, on the contrary, when sandalwood was hard to find, actually ordered their jungle burned, with woodcutters commanded to follow their noses to the burning sandalwood trees and extinguish the fire before the valuable inner wood could be damaged—a ravenous act that hastened the disappearance of sandalwood by incinerating the saplings and seedlings.

The standard unit of measure for sandalwood was the *picul*, the equivalent of 133⅓ pounds, worth an average of ten dollars but varying from three to fifteen dollars depending on its quality. Within three years of the Conqueror's death, just one trading company had chiefs in their debt up to 23,000 *piculs* of product—a debt that they could not just repudiate because they knew exactly how powerful these new people were, and if they exacted their revenge, or even if they just stopped coming, all that remained was the old life, and now they had seen better: Possessions came with worry.

Before he died the Conqueror expressed his desire that the line of future kings stem from one of his sons by his sacred wife, united with one of his daughters by his sixth wife, who was Kaʻahumanu's sister.[29] The plan was given effect when Liholiho married his half sister Kamamalu, and then for good measure also married her sister Kinaʻu, both young women who rivaled their aunt in size, with Kamamalu by one account towering some six feet seven inches tall.[30] The new king hosted a lavish three-week luau to celebrate his accession and recognize Kamehameha Day. A large number of foreigners attended, and it was his half sister, Queen Kamamalu, who presided, dressed in Western satin and lace, personifying both the generosity of the culture and the relaxed etiquette of the luau: "She personally saw that none of the company was in any degree neglected; and extended her kindness even to those who had no claim to special civility. For instance, seeing a crowd of American seamen . . . she immediately gave orders to have refreshments served to them."[31] The coup that toppled *kapu* was now all but complete, and this was the face of the culture that American sailors saw when their ships anchored: festive hospitality, the bounty of nature readily shared, the chiefs supported by the labor of an enormous, imposed-upon but apathetic class of serfs. Only at the core of it now lay a spiritual vacuum.

⚜

During all these events the brig *Thaddeus* heaved southward on the rolling seas of the Atlantic. Conditions on board the little vessel were claustrophobic: "Chests, trunks, bundles, bags, &c., were piled into our little room six feet square," wrote Lucy Thurston, "until no place was left on the floor for the sole of one's feet.... With such narrow limits, and such confined air, it might well be compared to a dungeon." And in this tiny cabin she was confined for her first two days and nights with seasickness.[32] January 26, three months and a week into the voyage, found the *Thaddeus* attempting to enter the Straits of Magellan, and the missionaries discovered the legendary terrors of rounding Cape Horn. Lucia Ruggles (sister of Samuel, who would marry Dr. Thomas Holman) committed to her journal, "The wind having turned against us, we were driven off and on for 12 hours, in no small danger of being dashed against the rocks."

"Suffer much from the cold," she added six days into the ordeal, "there being no fire in the cabin, nor are we allowed a foot stove in the cabin as the Magazine is under us.... It is more than 3 months since I have seen a fire."

They exited the Straits a week later: "Last night, the winds began to blow and the seas to roll, as we had never before witnessed; so that the two conflicting powers seemed to agitate the ocean to its very foundations. Our vessel labored excessively, the seas constantly breaking over, threatened every moment to overpower her. I think I never so much realized the weakness of man, and the *power* of the Almighty."

Once safely through to the Pacific, the terrors abated and they rolled before favorable trade winds for a month, and then discovered the reason for the ocean's name. "A calm of 6 or 7 days has detained us here in the most sultry region of the globe," she bemoaned on March 11. "The hot and scorching rays of the sun are almost insupportable. We hoped to be at or near Owhyhee before this time, but the Lord would have it otherwise, and for wise reasons, no doubt." Six of the men ventured to go swimming that day, were in the water for some twenty minutes, and had just returned aboard when a ten-foot blue shark was hauled out of the water, which was found, when gutted, to have been following the vessel devouring table scraps.

Thankful for their escape, they continued until finally, on March 30, 1820, "the long wished for Owhyhee is in full view on our left." They could make out streams coursing down the flank of Mauna Loa. "The country before us is beautiful," wrote Lucia Ruggles, "wearing the appearance of a cultivated place—with houses and huts, and plantations of sugar cane and Tarrow." After 160 days at sea, the missionaries were awash with gratitude, their native Hawaiian converts overjoyed. At nine in the morning a boat was sent ashore to discover whether they would be received.

At four in the afternoon the boat returned, "with news of King Kamehameha's death; that the worship of Idolatry and other heathenish customs are entirely abolished. Such glad news we were not prepared to receive. Truly the Lord hath gone before us in mercy."[33]

4. Abhorring a Vacuum

The *Thaddeus* skirted the Big Island before dropping anchor at Kailua, and a deputation rowed ashore to announce their business. As usual, Kamehameha II was loath to commit himself to anything more than a spree. He declined to give the newcomers an audience for days, and when he did the meetings were inconclusive. Eventually he gave his consent that the missionaries could stay there in Kailua, provisionally, for a year. With a little more persuasion he consented to their starting a mission in Honolulu, and to run an errand north to Kaua'i to take Prince George home to his father. (Lucy Thurston believed they would not have been permitted to stay, except that the presence of the women proved the men's benign intent.[1]) Between the king's stipulations and the casting of ballots, the Kailua mission would consist of the Thurstons, Dr. Holman, and Hopu and Kanui. With the Binghams disembarked at Honolulu on April 14, the Ruggleses and the Whitneys sailed on to Kaua'i, where an ecstatic Kaumuali'i greeted his son and insisted that they stay and open a mission at Waimea. Kalanimoku, who had stayed on at the change of reigns as prime minister, and who now was even more important for having married the widowed Keopuolani, claimed Elisha and Maria Loomis for himself, to reside at Kawaihae. Although he was a printer by trade, Loomis had studied at the preparatory mission school enough to impart Calvinism's central elements to the prime minister.

The missionary effort was safest with Kalanimoku. He was more curious, sympathetic, and helpful than any others, and became the missionaries' most valued friend. Ka'ahumanu's bearing was ambiguous. She was the one who caused the destruction of *kapu*, so naturally she was interested in whether the Americans brought a religion that could do better by her people. But she had also seen enough of Americans, with their sharp dealing and overbearing ways, to be cautious with any endorsement. Thus Bingham and the others courted her, and she was kind but noncommittal. What eventually turned her was Sybil Bingham's nursing her through a dangerous illness, from which the queen regent emerged, to their perception, as the "new Ka'ahumanu."

The distracted king went on his rum-soaked way, dividing his time. To the traditional capitals of Kailua and Honolulu he now added Lahaina, on the leeward side of Maui, which was a favorite residence of his birth mother. As his reign lengthened and he shifted the royal household, with enormous disruption, among his islands, it became increasingly apparent that he was no Conqueror. Throughout his reign Kamehameha had built a fleet, by bargaining, by extortion, by cash purchase, and by compulsion of native labor. Liholiho, by contrast, became enamored of a fancy vessel built in Salem, *Cleopatra's Barge*, and bought her on credit, which probably meant sandalwood futures. Meanwhile he lost his grip on the Conqueror's sandalwood monopoly, which put him in financial straits. Hiram Bingham got a closer look at him when, on the spur of the moment, Liholiho boarded *Cleopatra's Barge* and materialized, suddenly and unannounced, in Honolulu. Cannons thundered in salute as he passed Waikiki, and by the time he entered the harbor his criers were working the town, "demanding hogs, dogs, poi, etc., to be gathered for the reception of his majesty (who was in his cups)."

To the Americans the worst part of the cacophony was the yelping dogs, tied to poles for slaughter. The missionaries, while dependent at first upon the kindness of the *ali'i* for their provisions, uniformly declined the offer of dogs, explaining that they were not part of their accustomed diet, but taking some chiding in return for their squeamishness.[2]

"Calling on the king at evening," wrote Bingham, "Mr. Thurston and myself" found Kamehameha II too drunk to talk. "We were struck, however, with the ingenuity of Kamamalu . . . who, in the dilemma, unexpectedly lifted the nerveless hand of her lord" to acknowledge their visit.[3] But with Kalanimoku's help, the mission prospered. They passed a milestone on January 7, 1822, when their printing press went into operation. And the following April 15 they received a boost with the arrival of William Ellis, twenty-seven, a veteran of several years' missionary effort in Tahiti and the Society Islands. Like the Americans, he was a Congregationalist, but he was British, part of that evangelizing effort that came out of England and preached seemingly everywhere in the Pacific except Hawai'i. Ellis's fluency in Tahitian made it easy for him to add the Hawaiian dialect to his portfolio of vocabularies in just a few weeks. He had intended only a short visit, but the Americans prevailed upon him to stay much longer.

Hawaiians who were not impressed with the missionaries took to referring to them lightly as *haole* (without breath—that is, unable to speak the language[4]), a term that evolved into a more dismissive epithet for any white foreigner, but particularly Americans. But most natives would listen to what they had to say. Early in their mission the Binghams and the Thurstons set out on foot to preach the first words of the gospel ever heard on the north shore of O'ahu. Accompanied by chiefs and interpreters, they ascended the Nu'uanu Valley, fascinated that the higher they went, the air cooled and the vegetation became more dense. The trail ascended gently from the leeward side, but on the windward side the precipitous wall of the mountain range deflects the trade winds upward, squeezing the moisture from the air and watering an almost impenetrable jungle.

As they reached the Pali, where the remnant of Kalanikupule's army had been driven over the cliff in 1795, the unobstructed trade winds nearly ripped the hats off their heads; Bingham was so undone by the vista of the rugged north flank of the Ko'olau Range and the jungle that extended from its foot to the ocean that he devoted two pages of his memoirs to its majesty—"the sudden bursting on the vision as by magic . . . its vast amphitheatre of mountains, and beyond it, the heaving, white fringed ocean"—before getting back to the matter at hand: threading their way down the path to the later site of Kaneohe to preach.

At their first comprehension of Bingham's purpose—the natives heard these alien people talking sternly in the presence of their native retainers about God and what he required—the crowd became restive in the fear that some of them were about to be sacrificed.[5] Of course, threatening people with hellfire in the hereafter was in reality less urgent than the possibility of being tied to a pole in a *heiau* and strangled, so the missionaries were already an improvement from the *kanakas'* standpoint.

A reinforcing company of about a dozen missionaries arrived on April 23, 1823, including some such as the Reverends Charles S. Stewart and William Richards, who would have an enormous impact on the country. Their goal in January 1824 was to establish the first mission at Hilo, on the verdant east coast of Hawai'i. Departing from Honolulu, it took them nine hard days at sea to reach their destination. Hilo was to be a major mission station; Ruggles and his wife were relocating from Kaua'i; William Ellis would join them, as would Joseph Goodrich and James Ely of the reinforcing company, and Chamberlain the farmer, most with their wives. Sailing in a little thirty-ton schooner, the *Waterwitch*, they put in at Lahaina to visit the Stewarts, and watched the sunrise gild the glaciers on Mauna Kea, 120 miles distant, which they took as their beacon pulling them on to the Big Island. Hilo, however, was still seven tough, seasick days away.

At Hilo the chiefs made available to them a thirty-by-seventy-foot canoe shed, with a thatched roof and no interior walls, in which to cook and sleep. Until they could arrange for houses for themselves they would live communally. The Hilo missionary effort commenced to consternation of a different nature than personal privacy, however. The queen regent had made a thatch building available to them in which to hold services, but the inaugural effort was scattered when "a large hog, black and fat . . . marched in swinging her head armed with huge tusks." The congregation surged away before her, carrying Reverend Ellis and company with them. Order was restored when the pig's handler, "more bold or skillful than the rest, approached the animal, and by repeated gentle *passes* of the fingers on her bristly back, composed her to a sort of *mesmeric* sleep." As the pig dozed, the congregation returned and Ellis finished his sermon. It seemed that the pig was a pet belonging to Ka'ahumanu herself, was named for her, and was *kapu* to her. It gave Ellis and Ruggles some pause to reflect that in this society the queen regent's pig—*kapu*, despite her having ended *kapu*—had more place in church than the people did.[6] But people came, and they listened.

The effort to Christianize the islands was furthered by the deathbed conversion of the queen mother. Keopuolani was about forty-five, and had lived the best and worst that *kapu* offered. After the missionaries arrived her interest in Christianity had been genuine, and she took a Tahitian convert as her personal teacher. In obedience to the new monogamy, she separated from the powerful Kalanimoku and kept the high chief Hoapili as her only husband. They took up residence at Lahaina, Maui, where she took evident pleasure in gaining an education. In August 1823 her health entered such a decline that relatives and nobles from around the islands were summoned to come pay their respects. By mid-September it was apparent that she was failing. To Kalanimoku, with whom she had remained friends, and separately to Hoapili she imparted similar messages: "The gods of Hawaii are false. My attachment to them is ended; but I have love to Christ. I have given myself to him. I do not wish the customs of Hawaii to be observed when I die. Put me in a coffin, and bury me in the earth in a Christian manner, and let the missionaries address the people. . . . Great is my desire that my children may be instructed in the religion of Christ, and know and serve God, and that you watch over them and counsel them to avoid evil associates, and walk in the right way. . . . Do no evil. Love Jesus Christ, that you and I may meet in heaven."

To her son Liholiho she spoke more in her royal voice: "This is my charge to you: Befriend your father's friends and mine. Take care of these lands and the people. Kindly protect the missionaries. Walk the straight path. Observe the Sabbath. Serve God. . . . If the people go wrong, follow them not, but lead them yourself in the right way, when your mother is gone."

Ellis and Ruggles arrived, and after hurried consultations about whether it was appropriate to do so, administered the sacrament of baptism. When Keopuolani expired on September 16 the outburst of native wailing was too heartfelt to stem, but otherwise perfect dignity prevailed. At the end of the funeral, Keopuolani would have been pleased that the gathered *ali'i* partially disassembled a nearby *heaiu* and used the rocks to build a wall around her grave. They hauled the heavy stones on their own shoulders, albeit attended by lackeys who bore the feather *kahilis* of their rank to attest that this tribute was performed by no ordinary hands.

British sailors, even more than visiting British dignitaries, found the American missionaries frosty and tightly laced, and the English with their easier manner stayed in the good graces of the noble class, so much so that Liholiho took it in mind to visit his brother king, George IV, in England. He chartered the British whaling vessel *L'Aigle*, only 114 feet long and 475 tons, and departed ten weeks after his mother's death. Kamamalu went with him, and at the head of their retinue was Boki, the governor of O'ahu, and his wife, Liliha. Boki was possibly the most influential voice against the missionaries and most of the Westernizing change in the islands, except on the points of alcohol, which made him a favorite companion of the king, and sandalwood, which gave him a lavish lifestyle and put him heavily in debt. It took from November to May 1824 for the suite to reach England. The outsized royal pair created a sensation, but the fashionable George IV almost wrecked the careful empire building of Cook and Vancouver when he delayed having to grant an audience to the "damn'd cannibals." It came to make no difference. Kamamalu was stricken with measles, a disease not native to the islands and to which she had no resistance, and died on July 8; the shattered king followed six days later of the same disease. It took until March 1825 for the news to reach home.

The absence of the ambivalent king and the hostile Boki accelerated the missionary effort in Honolulu. Less than a month after their departure, keeping the Sabbath holy became the law; there was to be no travel or work or—the hardest blow—gambling on Sundays, and the queen regent and prime minister loaded it onto the chiefs to see that the people obeyed. That was the stick, as it were. There was also a carrot. To some extent, people still credited the existence of *mana*, at least of some kind, and demonstrations of spiritual power could yet go a long way toward winning their hearts.

Near the end of the train of mourners at Keopuolani's funeral was Kapi'olani, niece of Kalaniopu'u through her father, and her mother had previously been a wife of the Conqueror. She was a high chiefess of the Hilo district, in her early forties, and like the widowed queens she was ready for the old ways to end. When she was about two, her father was killed in the service of Kamehameha during his lengthy contest for control of the Big Island. Kapi'olani was cast into brush as her father's soldiers escaped, but she was found and sent to live with an aunt near Kealakekua Bay. Learning the strictures of *kapu*, she became curious what there was about bananas that they should be forbidden to women, and had a servant procure some for her. When her crime was discovered, Kapiʻolani's life was spared on account of her tender years and high station, but the *kahunas* decreed that unless a suitable sacrifice were offered, she would lose her rank, live in poverty, and die unmarried. The guardian aunt offered the hapless servant in Kapiʻolani's place. He was described as her favorite page, a youth named Mau. The priests accepted him as an offering, took him into the nearby *heiau* at Puʻuhonua o Honaunau, and put him to death.[7] (Ironically for Mau, this temple was among those few designated as a City of Refuge; had he escaped and made it there on his own, he could have claimed sanctuary, been purified, and departed in safety.)

Thus chastened in the ways of *kapu*, Kapiʻolani grew into her station as a high chiefess. She was large (more than 250 pounds) and fierce, and the native historian Samuel Kamakau wrote that the *kanakas* learned to fear her. "She was not friendly with common or country women. No one durst stare at her." Her liaisons were many and lusty, and she took for her principal husband the powerful chief Haiha Naihe. They were often attached to the royal court, and they accompanied Kamehameha when he removed to Oʻahu and marshaled his forces to attack Kauaʻi. She nearly died in the *okuʻu* epidemic of cholera that broke up his intended second invasion.

After the Conqueror's death Kapiʻolani fell in league with the queen mother and queen regent to end *kapu*, but the American missionaries' first sights of her did not inspire hope: The Calvinists first beheld her, sunbathing on a beach, "like a seal or sea elephant," rubbing herself with coconut oil. The first time a missionary called on her, she was found lying on a mat with her two husbands, all of them drunk and nearly naked. Her reform, however, was equally dramatic. She was an intimate of Liholiho's half sister–queen, Kamamalu, and studied reading and writing with her. Before long Kapiʻolani was a committed believer.

After Kamehameha II and Kamamalu departed for England, Kapiʻolani determined upon a dramatic demonstration of her new faith. Despite the decreed destruction of the idols across the islands, there remained pockets of resistance where the old religion was quietly kept, but nowhere more so than at Kilauea, near the south shore of the Big Island. There in the floor of a vast, barren caldera of solidified lava lay an inner crater, Halema'uma'u, a deep gouge into the earth's crust at the bottom of which was a lake of boiling lava—rising, falling, emitting murderous vents of sulfurous gas, terrifying—and in traditional Hawaiian religion the home of Pele, the fire goddess.

In earlier times Pele had been considered a minor deity in the Hawaiian pantheon, but her frightful abode, more permanent than a stone-and-thatch *heiau*, kept her cult alive long after the arrival of the missionaries. William Ellis had seen the place in summer of 1823, during his tour to select sites for future missions. He had arrived famished after a long trek without food, and on the slopes around the caldera he gorged on the locally abundant *'ohelo* berries, looking like cranberries in thickets of bushes up to five feet high. The fruit of the *'ohelo* was considered sacred to Pele, and no local would have dared eat them without first sacrificing some to her. After Ellis's visit the *kahunas* pointed to subsequent violence from the crater as evidence of Pele's anger.

In February 1824 Kapi'olani became the first high chiefess to sponsor a church—other chiefs had permitted and tolerated them, but Kapi'olani had a thirty-by-sixty-foot house built for services, which James Ely began conducting in April. The following November Kapi'olani determined to visit Kilauea and challenge Pele with the power of the church. Although her rank allowed her to arrive in state by double-hulled canoe at the nearby shore, the high chiefess made a sixty-mile pilgrimage, on foot, without shoes, gathering a retinue as she traveled. By the time she reached Kilauea she had an enormous throng in tow, who heard the Pele *kahunas* predict her destruction. Loudly proclaiming her trust in God and Jesus Christ, the high chiefess picked her way five hundred feet down the precipice of Halema'uma'u to meet her fate at the lake of fire.

As the news spread, Kapi'olani's demonstration created a

sensation around the world. Some embellishments had her casting stones tauntingly into the lava lake, or herself eating 'ohelo berries without making a sacrifice, daring Pele to do her worst. Alfred, Lord Tennyson, composed a poem about her. To the *kahunas'* mortification, she emerged from the pit triumphant, unscathed but for bruises on her feet from the sharp rocks. It was a heavy blow to the traditional religion and to *kapu*. (Pele was decidedly less tolerant of missionary Gerrit Judd of the Third Company, which arrived in 1828. In the interest of science he descended into the pit of Halema'uma'u to collect a sample of fresh molten rock in a frying pan. Just as he reached the lake of fire there was a sudden upwelling of lava that pursued him to a vertical wall that he could not climb for its overhang. His Hawaiian companion pulled him up to safety with both hands as the lava closed beneath his feet, the heat blistering their exposed skin and burning their shirtsleeves. Another few seconds and Hawaiian history would have taken a significantly different tack.[8])

Back in England the British accorded Hawai'i's royal couple, sealed in multiple caskets of lead, mahogany, and oak, greater dignity than George IV had shown them in life. Interred temporarily in the church of Saint Martin in the Fields, and guarded against a rumored theft for display in a circus, they were returned home aboard a frigate mounting forty-six guns, HMS *Blonde*. She dropped anchor in May 1825 at a Honolulu in profound mourning already, for an American whaler had brought the sad news. It also occasioned the elevation of Liholiho's barely adolescent brother, Kauikeaouli, as King Kamehameha III, and not unimportantly consolidated power in the hands of Ka'ahumanu as *kuhina nui* and regent.

In October 1825, three months after this somber reminder of mortality, Kapi'olani was baptized. Within the church her fierce nature began to soften as she demonstrated charity to the fate-stricken and the needy. But she was still a high chiefess and guardian of her

culture, as she proved in 1829. Just south of the City of Refuge at
Honaunau was perhaps the holiest site on the Big Island, a log-
walled mausoleum containing the bones of Hawaii's ancestral kings
extending back to the 1600s. It was called the *Hale o Keawe*, the
House of Keawe, named for the Conqueror's great-grandfather who
had had it constructed. It measured about sixteen feet by twenty-
four, set in a palisade studded with the most ferocious idols that the
culture could conceive, with eyes of mother-of-pearl and grimaces
of sharks' teeth. In the earliest days of conversion, Reverend Ellis
was allowed to visit the place and peek inside, but not enter. The
hair stood up on his neck, not just from the perceived savagery of
the place, or the overpowering sense of history to see the bones of
dead kings neatly tied up and visible to the viewer. More than that,
at its construction and with each interment, *Hale o Keawe* was
drenched in human sacrifice. "At the setting of every post and the
placing of every rafter, and at the thatching of every 'wa' (or inter-
vening space), a human sacrifice had been offered." Until Liholiho
had abandoned the practice in services for the dead Conqueror,
every stage of preparing a royal corpse, "at the removal of the flesh,
at the putting up of the bones, at the putting on of the tapa, at the
winding on of the sennit," was accompanied by more ritual death.[9]

At a place of such crushing awe in that culture, it had been a
signal concession to the new religion in 1825 when Ka'ahumanu
had allowed officers of the *Blonde* to remove many of the *ki'i*, the
ferocious idols, and take them to England for display. But with the
removal of the guardians the place fell into disrepair. In 1829 news
of its condition occasioned a visit by Naihe and Kapi'olani; when
she, accompanied by Mrs. Judd, entered the *hale* they were the first
women who had ever been allowed to do so. The sight of the few rot-
ting offerings left to the piles of neglected bones overcame Kapi'olani,
who wept in grief. Later, after consulting with Ka'ahumanu, she rescued the bones of the Hawaiian kings and high chiefs. Eleven sets
of remains were placed in one large coffin, and twelve in another,
and they were carefully hidden in a cave, in the old way, and the

entrance rocked over. Then, with the precious relics removed, the mausoleum and its court were pulled down so that not a trace remained.

Kapiʻolani lived a dozen more years as a devout Christian; in fact her first American biographer considered that her life's significance was that it was, "in its essence, the tale of every life of spiritual aspiration" among the islanders.[10] Kapiʻolani was surely an example to her people, but one other incident associated with her, not related by later writers, must have had its influence in the spread of Christianity in Hawaiʻi. Some years after her conversion, she was visiting with Laura Judd, who asked her how, specifically, her servant Mau, who had procured bananas for her during her childhood, met his end. Kapiʻolani did not know, but sent for the *kahuna*, who was still alive, to further explain the incident. When he arrived he answered that the boy was taken into the *heiau* at Honaunau and strangled at the altar. That was the traditional mode of dispatch for sacrificial victims. "Those were dark days," he further admitted to Mrs. Judd and the high chiefess, "though we priests knew better all the time. It was power we sought over the minds of the people to influence and control them."[11] Puʻuonua o Honaunau, temple and City of Refuge, was one of the most important *heiaus* of the Big Island. For one of its *kahunas* to admit that the whole regimen of *kapu* was nothing more than a con to manipulate the people was a shattering admission, and a powerful weapon to hand the missionaries.

With the hostile Boki back in the country, the Calvinists—who had now grown accustomed to having their sermons backed by hand-billed notices giving legal effect to some of God's laws—began to encounter more vocal opposition. It was a tension that the officers of HMS *Blonde* were quick to notice, and in currying their own relationship with the Hawaiians, they tried to give them a more congenial alternative to New England Congregationalism. Lord Byron, captain of the *Blonde* (and recent inheritor of the title from his cousin the poet), was particularly irked by Hiram Bingham. "This man is, we have no doubt, truly zealous in the cause of religion; but . . . he has in a manner thrust himself into all the political affairs of the island, and acts as secretary of state, as governor of the young princes, director of consciences, comptroller of amusements, &c an interference that some may regard as political, and tending to establish an American interest in the islands."[12]

Lord Byron prevented Bingham from attending the royal funeral, which Bingham resented,[13] but after the greatest mourning had passed and the officers of the *Blonde* staged a Saturday-evening lantern-slide presentation for the entertainment of the natives, Bingham used his influence to discourage attendance. Saturday, it seemed, was the day before the Sabbath, when their attention should be more profitably given to preparing for the next day's worship. Among the gifts that the British Crown sent to their Hawaiian counterparts was an elegant silver teapot for Ka'ahumanu. Lord Byron noted that the Hawaiian ladies "have adopted tea, and almost rival the Chinese in their love of it." However, he griped, "the Americans, who chiefly supply them, have taken care that they shall have no experience of the best kinds." That, apparently, would be too pleasurable.[14]

Nevertheless the missionaries gained ground. By November 1825, the station at Hilo had made astonishing progress since the time Ka'ahumanu's namesake pig had scattered one of the early meetings. "The house of public worship will not contain half that assemble to hear the Word of Life," Joseph Goodrich of the Second Company wrote to the ABCFM in appealing for increased aid. "The chiefs have lately begun to build a new meeting-house of much larger dimensions. I am unable to supply one-twentieth part of the calls for books. . . . Nearly thirty thousand souls have open ears to hear the Gospel. Must they be left to perish because American Christians have exhausted their charities?"[15] Their school, Goodrich added, had been in operation only ten months, and already some natives had assimilated such urgency with their learning that they left to preach in more remote areas.

From the half year and more that it took such reports to reach New England, it was impossible for the Board of Foreign Missions to know whether the effort to Christianize—and perforce Americanize—the natives was indeed such a blazing success, or whether the missionaries' laudable zeal might be leading them to overestimate their influence. But it was clear that something remarkable was happening, and they marshaled increasing resources for the effort in Hawai'i. It had now been two and a half years since Goodrich and the reinforcement missionaries had arrived on the *Thames*, and while his appeal did not fall on deaf ears, it took another two and a half years before a third influx arrived. On March 30, 1828, the *Parthian* dropped anchor, carrying Mary Ward, twenty-nine, a spinster teacher; Rev. Peter Gulick and his wife, Fanny; Rev. Jonathan Smith Green and his partner in good works, Theodosia Arnold; and two men who would profoundly shape Hawai'i's future: Rev. Lorrin Andrews was thirty-three; he accelerated native conversion by establishing the Lahainaluna Seminary, and he bequeathed to the country his grandson, Lorrin Andrews Thurston— a name to remember for future years. And then there was Dr. Gerrit P. Judd. He was a month short of twenty-five, a graduate of Fairfield Medical College, married only six months to Laura Fish of his own Oneida County, New York. He established a medical practice treating natives—a ministry critically needed in a country as disease ridden as Hawai'i. His earnestness and skill helped him to navigate his wife through nine pregnancies, and eventually his dedication earned him the intimacy of the royal family and a second career, unsought, as their adviser, diplomat, and as one observer wrote with some exasperation, "Minister of Everything."

Eventually there were no fewer than eleven infusions of reinforcements for the original pioneers of the *Thaddeus*, totaling more than 120 men and women, spaced over the next twenty years, the last arriving at the end of February 1848. The two most important were the fifth, when the *Averick* disembarked a dozen preachers, teachers, doctors, and a printer in 1832; and the eighth, when the

Mary Frasier disgorged nearly double that number in 1837, including Amos Starr Cooke and his wife, Juliette, later noted as founders and headmasters of the Royal School, and Samuel Northrup Castle, remembered mostly because his children combined with those of the Cookes to begin the march toward a sugar monopoly.[16]

That last evil effect lay in the future, however, and for now the missionaries taught and doctored and ministered as best they knew how, sincerely, doggedly. Behind all their efforts loomed the enormous figure of the queen regent, Ka'ahumanu, shrewd, calculating, watchful for cause and effect, and the missionaries never lost sight of the fact that they depended upon her favor. She never let them forget it, either. Once when she dispatched servants laden with food to help the Americans host a dinner, and they thanked her and acknowledged they were indebted to her for the meal, she raised an eyebrow and teased, "Just this one?" To a certain extent she adopted Christianity similarly to Constantine in the fifth century: She was willing for her people to put their eternal faith in God, but she also expected it to cement their earthly loyalty to herself. Her interest in learning and the religion was genuine, but she never forgot her position for a moment. She attended church, but arrived in a great carriage pulled, in default of horses, by a dozen puffing lackeys. (Other royals attended, arriving in a gaudy parade of improvised litters and sedan chairs.)

When for reasons of state she acted outside Christian expectations, the missionaries learned to stay out of her way. Bingham, after long association with her, recognized her complexity. "This woman," he wrote, "with all her haughtiness and selfishness, possessed, perhaps, as true a regard for the safety of the state, as her late husband or his high chiefs."[17] They witnessed a case in point when, after several rumblings of renewed defiance by old Kaumuali'i of Kaua'i, she had Liholiho sail to Kaua'i, ostensibly on a journey of friendship to renew the existing agreement. Bingham went with him, and had an opportunity to see the new king in a more official and favorable light than he was accustomed to, and he also took in an object lesson on Hawaiian oratory and native politics—that what one heard was not necessarily what was meant. The errand nearly came to grief; the trade wind through the notorious Kaua'i Channel was roaring, but the king refused all entreaties to delay the trip, and the ship reached the point of foundering numerous times during the sixty-mile crossing.

Kaumuali'i renewed his allegiance, and after a lengthy sojourn, Liholiho invited his host to return to O'ahu with him. To outside ears it might have sounded like an invitation that could be declined, but it could not. Kaumual'i was now a prisoner of state, and once ensnared on O'ahu he was kept under close watch and then compelled to marry Ka'ahumanu to renew his fealty.[18] Then to seal the arrangement, and probably at least get some pleasure out of the situation, the queen regent also compelled his son to marry her, not Prince George Kaumuali'i who the missionaries had returned to his father, but a younger and more handsome one—Prince Keali'iahonui, twenty-one, six feet six, athletic, and "one of the handsomest chiefs in the islands." As it turned out, her distrust of the family was shrewd, as George had entered into a life of dissolution, and after his father's death he made a clumsy attempt to reestablish the independence of Kaua'i. He and some allied chiefs stole guns and powder from a fortification on August 8, 1824, but failed to capture the fort. Ten days later Kalanimoku had an army on Kaua'i, ran him to ground, and hauled him to O'ahu, where he lived under a kind of house arrest until he died of influenza the next year.[19]

Human sacrifice was now banned, but the difference in their fate would hardly have been noticeable to the disloyal. From that rebellion on Kaua'i, Reverend Stewart noticed that "one of the rebel chiefs, a fine looking young man, was made captive. . . . He requested to be shot, but was bound hand and foot, according to the custom of the country, and carried on board the pilot-boat. Mr. Bingham saw him in the evening, after they had put to sea, seated against the timbers of the vessel in her main hold. In the morning, the prisoner was gone; and on inquiry, the captain without speaking, but by very significant pantomime, made known his fate; he had been thrown overboard in the dead of night, with his cords upon him."[20] Simple execution, it seemed, was an adequate substitute for sacrifice.

To the missionary wives Ka'ahumanu learned to relate in a different and entirely womanly way than she did to the male preachers. "Ka'ahumanu treated us like pet children," wrote Laura Judd, who met the queen regent the very day they disembarked from the *Thames*. She "criticised our dress, remarking the difference between our fashions and those of the pioneer ladies, who still wear short waists and tight sleeves, instead of the present long waists, full skirts, and leg-of-mutton sleeves. She says that one of our number must belong exclusively to her, live with her, teach her, make dresses for her. . . . As the choice is likely to fall on me, I am well pleased, for I have taken a great fancy to the old lady." Like those before them, the women of the reinforcement were as overawed by her huge size as they were touched by her maternal affection. Ka'ahumanu, wrote Laura Judd, "could dandle any of us in her lap, as she would a little child, which she often takes the liberty of doing."[21]

The remarkable thing about Laura Judd's writing was not just that she was game for the adventure. She was a missionary's wife and believed that the way of life they offered the Hawaiians was superior to what they already had. But what buffed her memoir was her genuine respect and affection for the native people. The same could not be said for all of them. Lucia Ruggles, one of the original *Thaddeus* contingent, was frequently aghast at the people before them. "Finally I do not know how to describe their manners," she wrote, "for should I make use of language as indelicate and uncouth as they really appear, which I must do to give you any correct idea of their manners, you must be disgusted." Of their servants: "We have as many men and women servants as we please, and it will cost us nothing but the vexation of having them about, which is more than I can bear."[22] Nor was she fond of being pulled into the queen regent's lap.

⚜

Like Cook and others before them, the missionaries were struck by the difference in size between the *aliʻi* lords and the multitude of common *kanakas* who outnumbered them by several hundred to one. The chiefs "seem indeed in size and stature to be almost a distinct race," wrote Charles Stewart of the first company of reinforcements who arrived three years after the *Thaddeus* pioneers. "They are all large in their frame, and often excessively corpulent; while the common people are scarce of the ordinary height of Europeans, and of a thin rather than full habit." As exceptions he could point out only the sacred queen mother and the king of Kauaʻi, but otherwise he could well have believed that nobles and commoners descended from conquering and conquered ethnic stock.[23]

As they had with the arrival of iron with Captain Cook, and with the monopoly of sandalwood, the *aliʻi* were keen to make certain that any good things that foreigners brought with them were reserved for their own use, alone, not for the *kanakas*. The missionaries acquiesced in this to a degree, as when they devoted extra time and attention to instructing the chiefs and royal family, but they made it plain that God's message of salvation was for everyone. The missionaries' concern for the commoners as much as the *aliʻi* manifested itself in a particular crusade that receives scant attention now, against the native practice of infanticide. Culturally sensitive modern scholars give the subject a wide berth, either omitting it altogether, mentioning it only in passing,[24] or dispensing with it quickly and matter-of-factly without lingering on its moral valence.[25] But to the newly arrived Americans, the realization that overworked or sometimes merely disinterested native mothers thought little of throttling unwanted newborns, or more commonly burying them alive barely outside their houses, was unspeakable. The Englishman William Ellis would have been less shocked, for he would have been aware of the practice on Tahiti. "We have been told by some of the chiefs, on whose word we can depend, that they have known parents to murder three or four infants where they have spared one." Ellis was even more disturbed by the reason: "The principal motive with the greater part of those who practice it, is *idleness*; and the reason most frequently assigned, even by the parents themselves, for the murder of their children, is *the trouble of bringing them up* [emphasis in original]." He related the story of one mother who grew weary of her baby's crying, who "stopped its cries by thrusting a piece of tapa in its mouth, and digging a hole in the floor of the house, perhaps within a few yards of her bed, . . . buried, in the untimely grave, her helpless babe."[26]

William Ellis may have seen it all before but Charles Stewart, writing two years later, was aghast, asserting that "we have the clearest proof, that in those parts of the islands where the influence of the Mission has not yet extended, *two-thirds of the infants born, perish by the hands of their own parents before obtaining their first or second year of age!* [emphasis in original] . . . my soul often melts within me: and I cannot but think, how little . . . the inhabitants of Christian countries are aware."[27] Ultimately Kalanimoku endorsed the missionaries' remonstrations against killing babies, and Ka'ahumanu proscribed infanticide in 1824, reinforced by statute in 1835.

Capt. Lord Byron of HMS *Blonde*, while critical of the missionaries' assumption of temporal influence, allowed the sincerity of their spiritual mission, but the end of the decade found even some Americans put off by the missionaries' cold and pompous lifestyle. In 1831 the sick whaler Abram Fayerweather was put ashore in Honolulu for treatment; he wrote a scathing assessment to his father in Connecticut—home state of the ABCFM, to which the father was a contributor. Bingham, he wrote, lived in "a new house . . . which in America would cost six thousand dollars," while the *kanakas* subsisted in "the lowest state of degradation." The Americans had entered into commerce, and "spend their time mostly in trading and oppressing the natives, [who] say nothing for fear of them."[28] In justice to the Congregationalists, one man's effort at elevation and conversion another man might well see as oppression, but by the opening of the 1830s the missionary effort had taken on a different and somewhat more entitled complexion.

Fayerweather's charge might have borne some credence in the commercial environs of Honolulu, but probably more representative was the experience of John and Ursula Emerson, two of the Fifth Company of reinforcement missionaries assigned to Waialua on the north coast of O'ahu in 1832. It was an area spiritually devastated by the destruction of *kapu*, for just to the east lay what had been perhaps the holiest valley in the kingdom. In an age when ownership of each *ahupua'a* could be contested when the king died, only Waimea remained the permanent sanctuary of the *kahunas*. Two temples loomed over the entrance to the valley, their gods propitiated with human sacrifices, including in 1792 a lieutenant and three sailors from Vancouver's HMS *Daedalus* who had dared to draw water from Waimea stream. Thus the spiritual vacuum created when the temples were wrecked on the order of Liholiho and Ka'ahumanu was particularly acute. And then the *ali'i* lording over Waialua proved to be so avaricious in pursuit of the sandalwood that grew bountifully in the jungle that he set his people to extracting every tree they could find, even at the cost of neglecting their taro patches and fishponds. When the Emersons arrived to preach salvation, they found the local *kanakas* "dispirited" and more than ready to listen.[29] The Emersons tended their Waialua mission for the next thirty-two years.

In the traditional culture there was a limit, however undefined, on the chiefs' ability to abuse their commoners. Queen Lili'uokalani later insisted that "the chief whose retainers were in any poverty or want would have felt, not only their sufferings, but, further, his own disgrace."[30] Yet the missionaries often saw the other side of it, as Reverend Stewart once recorded, "A poor man of this description by some means obtained . . . a pig, when too small to make a meal for his family. He secreted it at a distance from his house and fed it until it had grown. . . . It was then killed, and put into an oven, with

the same precaution of secrecy, but when almost prepared . . . a ca-
terer of the royal household unhappily came near . . . deliberately
took a seat till the animal was cooked, and then bore off the promised banquet without hesitation or apology!"[31]

In such an environment any kindness shown by the foreigners
was bound to be received with little short of wonder.

5. The New Morality

In April 1821, almost exactly one year after the missionaries' arrival, the United States government established an official presence, under the title Agent for Commerce and Seamen at the Sandwich Islands. John Coffin Jones, Jr., obtained the post; he was only twenty-four, the son of the speaker of the Massachusetts State House, but he was already an accomplished seaman, had previously visited the islands, and indeed had presented an oil portrait of the Conqueror to the Boston Athenaeum in 1818, the year that Opukaha'ia died in neighboring Connecticut and kindled the whole missionary effort.[1] A more symbolic choice could hardly have been imagined. In this era when American diplomats commonly combined business with official duty, most of Jones's attention was devoted to being the agent of the Boston mercantile firm of Marshall and Wildes. Basing himself in Honolulu (a shrewd choice at a time when the royal court was still shifting among there, Lahaina, and Kona), he constructed a two-story warehouse convenient to the waterfront that did double duty as, and that the missionaries grandly referred to as, the American consulate.

He also lost little time, to the mortification of the missionaries, in going native. In 1825 he initiated a relationship with Hannah Holmes, the *hapa haole* (half-white) daughter of another Yankee sailor, and then almost as quickly became the lover of Lahilahi Marín, whose Spanish father had been so well rewarded by the Conqueror for his services. Jones prospered in his sinful ways, dwelt in a comfortable house on Fort Street, and within several years also had a retreat in the cool of the Manoa hills above Waikiki. How were the missionaries to persuade the natives to forsake their traditional sensuality when the American representative presented them such an example?[2] Even worse, in the growing business district near the waterfront, Jones showed the effrontery to conduct Unitarian services for seamen and ruffians who did not keep to the Calvinists' moral standards.

Peace, of a sort, with the waterfront was engineered with the arrival of Capt. John Diell, representing the American Seamen's Friend Society, who constructed a bethel at the corner of King and Bethel Streets. He was not one of them, but he had similar morals, and remembering the ABCFM's directive to keep doctrinal squabbling to a minimum, they accepted him into their circles. Plus, he had cultural possibilities; in the coral basement beneath where he held services, he began amassing a library and museum, and founded and hosted the Sandwich Islands Institute, a learned society of forty-two charter members at three dollars per year dues, each bound to deliver one scholarly paper per year or face a one-dollar fine. Diell gained credence with the missionaries for facing down the threat of a whipping from local grogshop proprietors for his habit of rounding up their patrons to attend prayer meetings; such a man deserved encouragement. Dr. Gerrit Judd of the Honolulu mission delivered one of the first treatises, which inevitably dispensed their own point of view: "Remarks on the Climate of the Sandwich Islands, and Its Probable Effects on Men of Bilious Habits."[3] The institute was a success among those with cultural aspirations, and Diell was presented with a three-hundred-pound bell to preside over their meetings, the cost subscribed by ship captains, the chiefs, and the king. In danger of being isolated from the influential element, Jones struck back, helping to organize the Oahu Amateur Theatre, whose first play, *Raising the Wind*, was presented on March 5, 1834. The venue was the large wood-frame 'Iolani Palace; the stage manager was the king.

Nothing could have shown more clearly the conflicts raging within the troubled youth Kauikeaouli, who became King Kamehameha III when he was only twelve years old, and whose early reign was dominated by the queen regent. The missionaries' persistence netted its greatest prize on December 5, 1825, when Ka'ahumanu submitted to baptism. As evidence that she was serious, she divested herself of her handsome recreational husband, Prince Keali'iahonui of Kaua'i,[4] and she lived out her life in hospitable piety, sympathetic neither to others' opposition to the Christian regimen nor to the young king being torn between the old life of unquestioned privilege and the new one of self-denial.

Kamehameha III was more than a handful. His name, Kauikeaouli, meant "Placed in Dark Clouds," and nothing could have been more prophetic. The Conqueror had promised him in *hanai* to Kuakini, Ka'ahumanu's youngest brother, but when it first appeared that the infant was stillborn, that chief would not accept him. The high chief Kaikio'ewa, a secondary husband of the Conqueror's formidable mother, sent for a *kahuna*, who declared that the baby would live. Prayed over and sprinkled with water, he drew breath, and Kaikio'ewa received him in *hanai*.[5] After serving as his mothers' instrument in destroying *kapu*, he fell under the sway of the recalcitrant Boki, governor of O'ahu, who encouraged him to insist on his ancient privileges and pursue the pleasures that were his birthright. Acquiring a favorite companion in the person of Kaomi, a Tahitian-Hawaiian hanger-on and sort of native Piers Gaveston, Kauikeaouli instituted a secret society called *Hulumanu* (Bird Feather) that was dedicated to pleasure and to bedeviling the missionaries. Some of the old life's luster dulled with the disappearance of Boki early in the reign; his improvident use of sandalwood futures had spent him into stunning debt, prompting him to fit out two ships and set sail for the New Hebrides, which he heard contained thick forests of *iliahi*. He never returned; the belief was that he was lost at sea, but evidence later suggested that he established a new life on Samoa.[6]

Bingham's policy of noninterference with Ka'ahumanu's state conduct, in the belief that a certain amount of backsliding could be tolerated when a greater good might result, proved wise. She came to faith largely through her own conviction, and inevitably her faith must become law. Such a bonus was reaped with a decree on September 21, 1829, "On Mischievous Sleeping," which outlawed cohabitation without benefit of marriage. It was a mild law, legitimizing existing relationships as now being man and wife, while forbidding unmarried cohabitation in the future, but it was a step in the missionaries' direction.[7] She took an even bigger step the following year, when she banned performances of the hula. In fact it was a huge step, for hula was not just a dance, it was a physical expression of the national poetry, much of which was written to be danced while being sung or chanted. Polynesian history was oral history, and hula was also the repository for the ancient legends and *mo'olelo*, their story. Like the chants dedicating a *heiau*, they were intricate and complicated, and to make a mistake was no small matter; there were teachers and schools dedicated to learning hula. To be sure it was idolatrous, dedicated to the goddess Laka, and being so embedded in the culture, hula could also be unashamedly sexual, as indeed the culture was. The highly charged dance that David Samwell witnessed in 1778 was probably the *hula ma'i*, the dance in praise of genitals, which may have developed as the dancers' way of ingratiating themselves with the chief. The dances in that time were fraught with meaning that escaped Westerners who merely sat mesmerized by swaying hips and swinging breasts. Not all hula was sweaty and naked and overtly sexual, but that and the idolatry doomed the art in the missionaries' eyes. Thus when Ka'ahumanu banned hula in 1830, she did not just outlaw the swaying pantomime familiar to generations of tourists; in what she thought was the service of her faith she struck at the heart of Hawaiian culture.

The decree "On Mischievous Sleeping" was issued over the young king's signature, but it is doubtful whether his heart was in it. Kamehameha III had just turned sixteen, he was chafing under his stepmother's domination, and the heart of the conflict was infinitely more vital than anything over grogshops and theaters. He had taken to dividing his time between Honolulu and Lahaina; his mother was buried there, but the magnet that pulled the young king irresistibly home was his sister, the Princess Nahiʻenaʻena. Only daughter of the Conqueror and Keopuolani, she was so beloved of her mother that the queen defied the custom of *hanai* and nursed her herself. He was deeply in love with her, and she with him. To the native culture and the now-silenced *kahunas* it was a match of dizzying brilliance, and children born to them would have been next to the gods in elevation.[8] The missionaries, however, the king's tutors and spiritual guides, were aghast: To them nothing could so have crystallized the pollution of the native heathen.

The matter lay unresolved at the death of Kaʻahumanu on June 5, 1832, which meant that the important office of *kuhina nui*, embracing not just prime minister but virtual coruler, had to be filled. The decision was an important one, because Kamehameha III, soon to turn nineteen, was being torn apart by conflict between the ancestral privileges and the new morality. The king turned to his older half sister and the queen regent's niece, Elizabeth Kinaʻu, daughter of Kaʻahumanu's sister by the Conqueror. At twenty-seven Kinaʻu was in some respects as strong-willed as her aunt, and had endured some battles in establishing her own identity. The deaths of her half-brother husband, Kamehameha II, and her sister Kamamalu in London had left her in the unusual position of being a dowager queen at the age of nineteen. Her second husband died in the 1826 epidemic of whooping cough. With Kinaʻu available once more, Kaʻahumanu had embraced a plan for her to marry the then-thirteen-year-old king, thus rekindling the Conqueror's desire that his heirs combine the line of his sacred wife with that of Ka'ahumanu's sister. Kina'u defied her and instead married the much-lower-ranked Mataio (a native rendition of "Matthew") Kekuanaoa, who was *po'olua*, a child of shared paternity one of whose fathers was the grandson of old Alapa'i who had placed a death sentence on the infant Kamehameha. The queen regent was furious with her, but Kina'u and Kekuanaoa made a good marriage and had five children together, including two future kings and a *kuhina nui*.

On state business Kina'u made a creditable prime minister, but she found the young king more interested in demonstrating his defiance of the missionaries than in tending to his duties. On March 15, 1833, Kauikeaouli decreed that he was ending the regency and was assuming absolute power; he brought back hula, he allowed Kaomi to seize land and to tax Christians to keep his debts paid, and generally mortified the chiefs. But he also took a step toward stability by confirming Kina'u as *kuhina nui*. When she then found more of the work falling upon her, she once confided to Laura Judd, "I am in straits and heavy-hearted, and I have come to tell you my thought. I am quite discouraged and cannot bear this burden any longer. I wish to throw away my rank, and title, and responsibility together, bring my family here, and live with you; or, we will take our families and go to America. I have money." Seizing the opportunity, Mrs. Judd praised Kina'u for her sensibilities, asserted (oddly, for an American) that Divine Providence had raised her to her rank, and, citing the example of Esther from the Bible, encouraged her to remain strong for the sake of her people.[9]

One large reason that Kina'u was overburdened was the king's long absences, agonizing at his sister's side over their inability to marry. The matter came to a crisis in June 1834, when Honolulu's two best doctors, Gerrit Judd and the Englishman Thomas C. B. Rooke, were summoned urgently to Pearl River, where rumor had it the king had tried to kill himself. The fact when discovered proved to be that Nahi'ena'ena, who was traveling in his suite, discouraged him from returning to Maui with her, because of the hostility of the missionaries and Christian governor, Hoapili. The dismayed Kauikeaouli then made an attempt to cut his throat. To get past this agonizing stalemate, the king's sister was betrothed to the son of Kalanimoku, whom she sullenly married on November 25, 1835, with a triumphant Rev. William Richards presiding. But when she became pregnant two months later, the king declared the exalted baby to be his, and proclaimed it heir to the throne. The child was born on September 17, 1836, but expired within hours, and Nahi'ena'ena sank into a dangerous condition. Rooke could not help her, and though he called in consultants, she died on December 30. Kamehameha III's grief at losing his sister and their baby was terrifying. He sat stone-faced by her coffin for week after week, and it took three and a half months, almost twice the usual period of a royal wake, before he released her body, on April 12, 1837, to return to Maui for burial with her mother. Impelled as much by duty as by attraction, he turned for comfort to a minor chiefess of Maui named Kalama, daughter of the commander of his Honolulu ships, and married her on February 14, 1837, while Nahi'ena'ena's body lay yet unburied. Kina'u vigorously opposed the match for Kalama's lack of royal rank, although the *kuhina nui* herself had done the same thing when she married Kekuanaoa. Now she was a fervent Christian, and probably her main objection was that Kalama had been an active part of Kauikeaouli's mockery of the missionaries—but the Americans counted their blessings that the young king had found a wife who was not his sister, and blessed the union. The marriage lasted, but even while married to Kalama, Kamehameha III still clung to the memory of Nahi'ena'ena and fathered a son, Albert, by his sister's close childhood companion, Jane Lahilahi Young.[10]

The conflicts between Kamehameha III and the missionaries over his choice of bride took place a world removed from the common *kanakas*, whose lives continued hard and poor. As the new companies of missionary reinforcements arrived every few years, they spread out to new districts yet unpreached to, and they discovered anew a squalor that reduced them to prayer, as much for their own strength and fortitude as for the natives' souls. The most visible maladies were skin sores and ulcers, which were rampant; scabies was so ubiquitous that Charles Stewart had been on land only two days before being asked if he had anything to cure "the itch."[11] Even more demoralizing to the Americans were the lice, which became a constant battle. Infestation was known among the royalty and became more prevalent lower down the social ladder, until "as to the common people, after a call of a few minutes, we think ourselves fortunate indeed if we do not find living testimonies of their visit, on our mats and floors, and even on our clothes and persons!" But what brought them near to fainting was the sight, among the *kanakas*, that "not only do they suffer their heads and tapas to harbour these vermin; but they openly, and unblushingly, *eat them!*"[12]

Paradise was also full of fleas. Forest or meadow, beach or cave, there was no respite from them. Native families thought nothing of sharing their bedding with pet pigs, dogs were everywhere, and the infestation was so relentless that many visitors called attention to it in letters and memoirs. The flea was not indigenous to the islands; probably at least one species arrived with the Polynesian voyagers' stock, but after several decades of foreign ship arrivals, there was a variety of species to torment people. A sailor on Maui who stayed at an inn with native proprietors had one vivid memory, "At 11 we droped [*sic*] on the mats . . . & the way the Flees & other vermin lit on us was a caution to all travilers [*sic*]. It had much more affect to keep us awake than a strong cup of tea would."[13]

Surrounded by lice and licentiousness, the compound that the Honolulu missionaries lived in became a partial refuge where they could commune with a more familiar life. The large house of which the young whaler Fayerweather had complained had been built in New England, disassembled and stored in the hold of the *Thaddeus*, and then reconstructed near the harbor in Honolulu, immediately behind the large traditional grass house that first served as the

Kawaiahaʻo Church. Fayerweather's criticism was less than just, as the wood-frame structure was actually a communal residence for the whole contingent, and it was not even all that comfortable. Honolulu was on the leeward side of Oʻahu, where it was often hot and dusty, and the families papered the dining room ceiling with *tapa* to keep the upstairs grit from sifting through the floor and down into the food. The house was designed to stay snug through frigid New England winters, and the Americans sweltered in it. Ten years later the compound added the Chamberlain "House," actually a two-story depository built of coral blocks in which they stored the supplies to be distributed to stations throughout the islands, and several years after that a separate building for the printing press to turn out Bibles, tracts, and lesson books. Even more than Gutenberg's press revolutionized learning in the West, this simple machine changed Hawaiʻi forever, as the missionaries provided the people with their first written language, which the *makaʻainana* learned with stunning alacrity.

After Bingham, the most famous resident in the *Hale Laʻau*, the "wood house," as the islanders called it, came to be Dr. Gerrit Judd, a New York physician who came with the Third Company of missionaries on the *Parthian*, arriving in April 1828. Judd opened a medical practice, treating commoners as well as nobles in an upstairs eave room. In this large house they also hosted company—the queen regent often spent the night in the guest room—and tried to come to grips with the proposition that American Calvinist Christianity was going to be a hard sell in Polynesia. It cannot be denied that the missionaries equated, and many would say confused,[14] their strict secular morality with Christian faith: In this era virtually everybody did. But this left them at a distinct disadvantage in Hawaiʻi. It was an outpost of Polynesia, whose attitude toward sex was generally frank, happy, and unashamed—qualities that made this portion of the globe legendary among lonely mariners. But the missionaries found it shocking. "For a man or woman to refuse a solicitation for illicit intercourse was considered an act of meanness," wrote Sheldon Dibble of the Fourth Company, which arrived in 1831. Any stroll by a native household would discover "emptied bottles strewn about in confusion amongst the disgusting bodies of men, women and children lying promiscuously in the deep sleep of drunkenness."[15] Reverend Whitney once asked a chief on Kaua'i whether having seven wives did not cause him anxiety, and the chief assured him that it did: "I cannot sleep for fear some other man will get them."[16]

It was also awkward to criticize sex to the natives when the missionary wives were dropping babies left, right, and center. Laura Judd had nine, and came to a stark realization of how the chiefesses felt about this when so many of them were infertile. When the Judds' second child was born, Kina'u begged and remonstrated to be given the baby in *hanai*, a custom that the Americans found mortifying. There were some tense moments about giving offense to such a powerful figure, before the Judds were able to convince Kina'u that naming the child after her was considered a great honor. Indeed the baby was named Elizabeth Kina'u Judd, and the *kuhina nui* kept an active interest in her upbringing—along with the five of her own whom she eventually bore.

In this society there was little notion of being too young or too old for sex. Children were expected to experiment as soon as they were curious. And there was no notion of what the newcomers could barely utter as the "Unmentionable Vice of the Greeks." Indeed, among the *ali'i*, on whose favor the missionaries depended, one particularly difficult custom to stamp out was the *aikane* relationship between a chief and his youthful male lovers. Much has been debated over the years about the actual nature of *aikane*— some denying that it had a sexual component at all, in order to make the old ways seem less scandalous to modern Western eyes, and others particularly in more recent years affirming it, to proclaim that there is nothing in the native culture to be ashamed of.[17] As with other aspects of native culture, control of the narrative today goes a long way toward controlling who learns what.[18] But it was no mystery to the first American in the islands. John Ledyard, the marine corporal aboard the *Resolution*, found it more an object of morbid fascination than censure, since "we had no right to attack or even disapprove of customs that differed from our own." At first Captain Cook's sailors could not believe their eyes. "As this was the first instance of it we had seen in our travels, we were cautious how we credited the first indications of it, and waited untill [*sic*] opportunity gave full proof." Yet the most cursory observation made it apparent that "sodomy . . . is very prevalent if not universal among the chiefs. . . . The cohabitation is between the chiefs and the most beautiful males they can procure about 17 years old. . . . These youths follow them wherever they go, and are as narrowly looked after as the women in those countries, where jealousy is so predominant a passion." Others of Captain Cook's chroniclers were more judgmental in their assessment of *aikane*, especially of old King Kalaniopu'u's delight in having his young lovers ejaculate on his royal person.[19] Indeed they were not mistaken in what they beheld. The native scholar Davida Malo was surprisingly frank in his assessment that "of the people about court there were few who lived in marriage. The number of those who had no legitimate relations with women were greatly in the majority. Sodomy and other unnatural vices in which men were the correspondents . . . were practiced about court."[20]

Ledyard was especially shocked that whether a chief's wives stayed or left seemed to be a matter of indifference to them; they were more possessive of their youths, whom they showered with gifts and open affection. (On this point Ledyard overspoke, for there was one famous instance in 1805 where the great high chief Kalanimoku, overcome with shame and rage when his wife, Kuwahine, deserted him in favor of a new lover, told Kamehameha, "I want to burn up the world." "Burn," shrugged the Conqueror, at which Kalanimoku set fire to most of Honolulu to drive her from hiding.[21]) And *aikane* was not without benefit to those younger partners, for in addition to the gifts received during the passion of courtship, young men could gain political and diplomatic status, and it also made them eligible later in life to marry a chiefess, and their children were recognized as *ali'i*—an otherwise unattainable social advancement.[22]

The missionaries, therefore, found themselves in a society where a sexual relationship between two males had no moral valence, and they wished to tread lightly in a new land but still preach their truth. Their somewhat prevaricating response was to translate *aikane*, in their budding Hawaiian-English lexicon, as "best intimate friend," with no mention of its original context. This came back to haunt them in a demoralizing way when the subsequent eleven shiploads of new missionaries fanned out into new villages to spread the gospel, relying on the Hawaiian-English dictionaries provided them. Learning the language as best they could, and relying on this translation, new preachers would sometimes announce to a local chief in their best new Hawaiian the desire to become his "best intimate friend," which was greeted with considerable surprise, not to say enthusiasm.[23]

Quiet native noncompliance with the missionaries' preachings about sex was reinforced by their witnessing increasing conflict among the *haoles* over morality—not just sex but drink and seemingly less portentous amusements, from theaters to card games. And the emergence of Lahaina as a town of royal residence and the establishment of a mission station there made it ripe for conflict when it became the leading Pacific anchorage for the world's—which meant mostly American—whaling fleets. Only two whalers visited in 1819, but then rich hunting grounds were discovered in the seas near Japan in 1820. With that country's perfervid isolationism keeping its ports closed to foreigners. Hawai'i was the perfect base of supply and recreation.

About sixty whaling vessels visited in 1822, a hundred or so in 1824, increasing to about 170 in 1829, and given the world demand for whale oil, ballooning thereafter. The islands' economy had stagnated since the exhaustion of sandalwood, but now wealthy shipowners, through their captains, could pay more for everything from supplies to transshipping to recreation. Some native women, once quite happy to dispense their favors for pleasure, found it an easy transition to take money for what still seemed to them harmless fun.

That, however, was a trade at which the missionaries drew the line; they sermonized incessantly, and recruited Kalanimoku's help to lay, as it were, a *kapu* against women visiting foreign ships. Interestingly, it was not a whaler but an American warship, the USS *Dolphin*, that generated the first crisis. The ship's commander, Lt. John Percival, known in the navy as "Mad Jack," had been sent to the islands at the request of American merchants, who hoped that the presence of a warship would inspire the chiefs to pay something toward their debts racked up with sandalwood futures. In Honolulu the sailors were shocked to discover that the celebrated women were now off limits; they grumbled for more than a month before taking action. February 26, 1826, a Sunday, Hiram Bingham was preparing to hold services at Kalanimoku's house when a mob of sailors arrived with clubs. Amid shattering windows Bingham escaped back to the mission house, but the riot overtook him there; the high chiefess Namahana interposed herself and was struck by a blow meant for Bingham. *Kapu* might have been dead, but chiefs were still venerated, and the natives present exploded. The melee subsided only with the arrival of Lieutenant Percival, who roughly corraled his own men even as Bingham saved one of their lives. It was Boki, the governor of O'ahu who himself had little love for the missionaries, who restored order when he had a deputation of willing women rowed out to the ship.[24]

There were easier pickings at Lahaina, and that town overtook Honolulu as the favored port of call for the whalers. Their presence was crowded into two seasons, fall and spring, and farmers there were alert to the seamen's preference for white potatoes, so they turned it into a staple Maui crop to keep them coming back. Port calls increased until they reached a high-water mark in 1846, when Honolulu recorded the visit of 146 whaling vessels, and Maui no fewer than 429, jostling each other up to a hundred at a time at Lahaina Roads.[25] Rev. Lorrin Andrews calculated that "on average they have $300 each. Ships 300 × dollars 300 = $90,000. . . . Whatever the people have been, I cannot now call the people poor on Maui."[26]

Seamen there no less than at Honolulu grew incensed at the *wa-hines'* newfound modesty, but Maui's royal governor Hoapili, the widower of Keopuolani, heeded her dying admonitions of Christian devotion and did his best to stem the vice. When the British whaling vessel *John Palmer* called at Lahaina, several women ignored the governor's orders and offered themselves on board. Hoapili detained the captain, Elisha Clarke, ashore; sailors turned their six cannons on the town, and more particularly on the house of the man they held particularly responsible: Rev. William Richards. In one of his reports back to the ABCFM, Richards made mention of another British captain buying a native woman for a sum of money, which found its way into newspapers. It became an international incident when news of it echoed to England and back. The British consul angrily vindicated the captain and demanded that the missionary be shipped to London to face a libel action, but a trial by the chiefs found for Richards.[27]

After Hoapili's death in 1840, Lahaina gained the reputation of a town where sailors could have a good time, but even when the whalers were behaving innocently, the missionaries made no friends for themselves with their stiff-necked self-righteousness. Capt. Gilbert Pendleton of the whaling ship *Charles Phelps* was laid up in Lahaina with "lung fever" that forced him to send his ship out without him. His doctor ordered him to take exercise, and when he passed their establishment, the missionaries refused him water because it was the Sabbath. It was true that whalers could be a rough lot, but many of the captains were New Englanders, too, and they could cite Bible stories with equal facility. "Christ himself went through the Cornfield on the Saboth [*sic*] & plucked the Ears of Corn because he hungered," he slashed in his diary. "I would thank any man whether missionary or what not to tell me why a weary hungry traviler [*sic*] should not be fed on the Saboth in this day & age of the world—Christ declared if any one give but a cup of cold water in his name he should not lose his reward."[28]

From such events Kamehameha III remained aloof as he

metamorphosed from the rebellious youth who at one time rescinded all laws except those against theft and murder (and briefly turned Honolulu into a haven of vice) into a grave young monarch who was determined to do his duty. He had suffered a crushing blow with his sister's death, and it is difficult to overestimate the effect this had on the Americanization of Hawai'i. Had Nahi'ena'ena and the baby lived, Kauikeaouli was a defiant enough young *ali'i* that he could have turned the clock back by years, and Hawaiian history might have taken a different direction entirely. After centuries of inbreeding for the refinement of *mana*, however, the clock finally ran out on the Conqueror's dynasty, and the twenty-three-year-old monarch emerged from the experience not just a shattered man, but a shattered king with a country to govern, and a genuine sense of obligation as his countrymen's *ali'i nui*, their highest lord. And, the most capable people around to help him were the *haole* missionaries. As the 1830s closed the Congregationalists' campaign for morality began, by sheer weight of determination and the shiploads of reinforcements, to take effect. Only three days before Nahi'ena'ena's burial on Maui, the *Mary Frasier* out of Boston disgorged thirty-two more of them, the Eighth Company and by far the largest contingent of New England Calvinists to spread the gospel, joining the sixty or so previously landed.

And their printing press was ever busy, so much so that it threatened to inundate the kingdom with tracts. Having given the Hawaiians a written language, they printed nine editions of First, Second, and Third Elementary Books, a text on arithmetic, and (judiciously) "The Thoughts of the Chiefs." Then followed a Decalogue and Catechism, the Sermon on the Mount, a hymnal, a history of scripture, and other works that took advantage of their near-monopoly on disseminating the written word. By the time the ABCFM published its 1833 report for its backers, the missionaries could enumerate having printed well over twenty *million* pages of texts and tracts. The value of paper on hand was nearly two thousand dollars, in readiness to print the remainder of the New Testament, selections from Numbers and Deuteronomy, and a geography book. They were expecting the arrival of a second press from home, with which they could expand their operations to Sunday school tracts, doctrinal sermons and their understanding of marriage, and further academic publications.[29]

Against this tidal wave of Christianity the king's further rebellion was hopeless. In his heart Kauikeaouli was sad and he drank too much, but he surrendered, and as Kamehameha III he became a good king.

In 1838 the colorful agent for American affairs journeyed to California and returned with a "Spanish lady," whom he introduced as his wife. Although John Coffin Jones's womanizing and informal cohabitations had been tolerated by the government up to then, Hannah Holmes, who had been with him the longest and claimed the station of his wife, sued for divorce on the grounds of bigamy. She won, and Kamehameha III, now grafted to American morality, not only sustained her but declared Jones persona non grata. "I refuse any longer," the king informed him on January 8, 1839, "to know you as consul of the United States of America." But even here was an echo of the old days: Jones had also been heard to utter a disparaging remark about the late Princess Nahiʻenaʻena, which would have earned him the king's cold shoulder faster than his own hedonism.[30]

Accustomed to centuries of privilege, Hawaiʻi's chiefly families responded to the new morality with varying degrees of individual compliance, according to the state of their own conversion to the new religion. But then their transition was hurried along with a sobering demonstration in the example made of Kamanawa II, a high chief of Hilo. He was an unreconstructed chief in the old mold, taking whom and what he pleased; his wife, Kamokuiki, became a Christian and disapproved of his continuing polyamorous wanderings. She sought a divorce, which was decreed on August 16, 1840, on terms that were biblical: Because she was the innocent party, she could remarry as soon as she wished; the chief, however, could not remarry while she lived.

Six weeks later Kamokuiki collapsed and died, and an autopsy found an inflamed stomach. At trial the chief testified that he administered "medicine" to his wife that was prepared by Lonoapuakau, a sailor and his friend. That friend testified that he had prepared poison, a cup of 'awa laced with 'akia, the "false 'ohelo," which in the old days was one mode of execution, and 'auhuhu, the "fish poison plant." But he argued he could not be found guilty because he did not administer it. The jury of twelve chiefs convicted both of murder, and death warrants signed by the king and kuhina nui ensued. No pardon came, and the two were hanged in Honolulu on October 20, 1840, before a throng of ten thousand, most of whom were probably astonished at the sight of a high chief, whose word had once meant life or death, himself swinging dead at the end of a noose.[31]

It was not only the unreconstructed old chiefs who resented this relentlessly growing influence of the haoles. Some of the newer generation, who had been educated enough to take a longer view, also had misgivings. Davida Malo, who had been raised in the Conqueror's court as a playmate for the young Liholiho, and who after the missionaries came was ordered to go to school for him and relay what he had learned, became one of the islands' first bona fide intellectuals and a trusted adviser to Kamehameha III. Halfway through his reign Malo wrote a letter to Kina'u, to pass along to the king, and in it he tried to explain the risk: "If a big wave comes in large fishes will come from the dark ocean which you never saw before, and when they see the small fishes they will eat them up. . . . The ships of the white men have come, and smart people have arrived from the Great Countries which you have never seen before, they know our people are few in number and living in a small country; they will eat us up, such has always been the case with large countries, the small ones have been gobbled up."[32]

6. Becoming Little Americans

After her conversion, the late queen regent had made a progress around Oʻahu in the company of Levi Chamberlain, the mission's commercial agent in Honolulu, "to encourage the people to learn to read and write, to instruct the land agents to take care of the teachers, and use the resources of the chiefs' lands to maintain the teachers, and not overburden them."[1]

The missionaries knew very well that all their best preaching would prove ephemeral unless they reinforced it with a strong system of education. And they knew from their experience with Opukahaʻia how readily these people could learn. He had died before finishing his grammar of the "Owhyhee" language, but others had completed it, and in January 1822, the printing press brought in the *Thaddeus* cranked out five hundred copies of an eight-leaf presentation of the alphabet, numbers, and simple readings. This *pi-a-pa* for years was the natives' first step to literacy.

By phonetically redacting the Hawaiian language to just twelve letters (whose inconsistencies and regionalisms were ironed out and standardized by 1826), and by concentrating on the preparation of native instructors, the missionaries succeeded far beyond their dreams in giving Hawai'i a written language and a literate population. They established common schools for elementary education; they were intended for children, but eager adults could not be kept away. By 1824 there were some two thousand pupils; by 1826, four hundred native teachers were giving lessons to twenty-five thousand; by 1831, there were eleven hundred schools teaching 40 percent of the population. The teaching effort made an important advance with the arrival of the Eighth Company of missionaries on board the *Mary Frazier* on April 9, 1837. Of the fifteen married couples and two single women, eight of the men and the two single women were teachers. Learning came with religious instruction, of course, so commingled that the Hawaiians could hardly discern the difference between the *palapala* (literacy) and the *pule* (religion). In fact the people came so to associate learning with the written word that they called it *palapala*, their word for the impressions stamped onto *tapa* cloth, which reminded them of the printing press.[2] By 1840 the government stepped in with a law that every community maintain a school, and royal adviser Davida Malo was given the superintendency.

If utilizing native teachers could spread education like a grass fire, how much better could the gospel be spread by Hawaiian evangelists? Those who returned from New England proved, mostly, to be disappointments. John Honoli'i was faithful, but like so many of his kindred, died young. Prince George Kaumuali'i, who himself had never professed faith but had been very useful in promoting good relations, died a frustrated prisoner on O'ahu. William Kanui had turned to drink and been thrown out of the Kailua church within three months of its starting, although he would be rehabilitated in his later years. Kamehameha III in his wild period was a bad influence on Thomas Hopu, where the missionaries had entertained the opposite hope. He grew disaffected and later left for California. What was needed was a seminary to train native preachers, there in the islands.

Repairing to Lahaina, Maui, where William Richards had

served as missionary since 1823, Lorrin Andrews of the Third Company began organizing the intended school, and the first classes at the Lahainaluna Seminary began for twenty-five chosen students on September 5, 1831, in a cluster of traditional grass houses. The first class included some of Hawai'i's brightest hopes: Davida Malo, the royal adviser who would warn the king about the danger of predatory fishes, and who later wrote a valuable history; Timothy Ha'alilio, the son of the governor of Moloka'i, who became Hawai'i's first international diplomat; and Boaz Mahune, secretary to Kamehameha III and later a contributor to if not the principal author of the Hawaiian Declaration of Rights and then the constitution.[3] Following soon after was the cultural historian Samuel Kamakau, whose "Ka Mo'olelo Hawai'i" caused a furor by publishing the islands' history for anyone to read in *Ka Nupepa Kuokoa*, thus destroying the old *kahunas'* monopoly on a subject they had previously declared sacred as part of their means of social control.

More substantial than the grass houses was the coral-and-timber *Hale Pa'i*, the "house of printing," in which was installed that expected second printing press in 1834, which began turning out a school newspaper and later Hawai'i's first paper money. (A reprint of the currency had to follow, with secret marks, after a student was expelled for counterfeiting.[4]) The ABCFM underwrote an expansion in 1836, including a new building and additional faculty. In 1842, of its 158 graduates, 140 were either teachers or in government service.[5] After launching the seminary at Lahainaluna, the missionaries busied themselves with new institutions of learning— the Oahu Charity School for foreigners' *hapa haole* children by Hawaiian wives in 1833; boarding schools for boys and girls at Hilo in 1836 and 1838, respectively, which emphasized homemaking for the girls and agriculture for the boys, which they took a step further with a school at Waialua that they meant to become self-supporting; a female seminary on Maui in 1837—all this in addition to the hundreds of common schools, which had never ceased functioning.

⚜

The new Calvinist morality—so utterly foreign to the Hawaiian heritage of easy sex and breezy relationships—came into the most anguished conflict over the matter of the young king getting an heir. He was twenty-six years old by 1839, and it was time to secure the succession.

By mid-nineteenth century the foreign diseases to which the natives had no immunity had reduced the native population by more than half, to about 150,000. Chiefs fell as well as commoners, but these *ali'i* faced an even greater obstacle: After centuries of incest they had inbred themselves into enervation and infertility.[6] Kamehameha had been a protean figure, but the first of his dynasty was also the last to produce any (legitimate) children who lived to adulthood. Keopuolani had been a granddaughter of Kalaniopu'u, so she was the Conqueror's cousin once removed on her father's side, and also his niece on her mother's—a distant-enough relation that three of their four children survived. But Liholiho and Kamamalu had died childless. The exalted baby of Kamehameha III and Nahi'ena'ena lived only a few hours. He and Kalama were not related, but both of their children died in infancy, thus there were no direct heirs. So, after consultation with court genealogists, the king drew up a detailed prospectus for the succession, beginning with remaining grandchildren and great-grandchildren of the Conqueror:

Heading the list were the children of Kina'u, herself the Conqueror's daughter by Ka'ahumanu's sister. She had successfully defied the queen regent by marrying not her half brother the boy king but Mataio Kekuanaoa; her children numbered the eldest, Prince Moses Kekuaiwa; then Prince Lot Kapuaiwa (later Kamehameha V); his younger brother, Prince Alexander Liholiho (later Kamehameha IV); and their younger sister, Princess Victoria Kamamalu, a future *kuhina nui*. Because of them the descent would remain direct through at least one preferred line. After them the succession should have fallen to Princess Ruth Ke'elikolani, and her case gave the king some pause. She was the Conqueror's great-granddaughter through a minor wife, but Ruth was also *po'olua*; her mother had left her husband and gone with a lover just about the time she would have conceived, which called Ruth's legitimacy into question. In traditional Hawaiian mores this would have caused no more doubt of her rights than it did with that most celebrated of all *po'olua*, the Conqueror himself. The missionaries had changed all that—a turning point in the Americanization of Hawai'i. But with Ruth there was still another consideration: As a baby she had been given in *hanai* to Ka'ahumanu, herself childless. At her death the queen regent bequeathed her vast landholdings, which amounted to about 10 percent of the entire kingdom, to her *hanai* daughter, making Ruth far and away the richest young woman in the country. Ruth also defied the times and refused to become a Christian, as Kamehameha III himself no doubt often wished he could have done. Whatever his own feelings were, he made Christian profession a requirement of eligibility, and he scratched Ruth out of the line of succession. The missionaries' notion of Christian morals, marriage, and legitimacy had robbed Kamehameha III of happiness with his beloved sister, and now the removal of Ruth Ke'elikolani from the succession shoved to the background a force of nature who, whatever commanding kind of queen she might have been, still managed in her time to dramatically alter Hawai'i's history.

After Ruth the succession fell to her cousin, Princess Bernice Pauahi, the last child in direct descent from the Conqueror.[7] Seven years old when the list was made, as she grew she enjoyed dressing in fashion, but she was also an avid outdoorswoman who became an expert rider. Every inch an *ali'i* who knew and followed her own mind, she also developed the tact to do so diplomatically. With no more hopeful record than the clan had amassed in having children, Kamehameha III extended eligibility beyond direct descent. The Conqueror's younger brother, Keli'imaika'i, the "good chief," had two great-great-grandchildren who were cousins, Princess Emma Na'ea, later queen consort of Kamehameha IV, and her cousin Prince

Peter Young Kaʻeo, later notable as the only royal to contract leprosy and be exiled to Molokaʻi. And there was a last-minute addition, Emma's half sister, Princess Mary "Polly" Paʻaʻaina. Accepting
that the Conqueror's father was indeed Keoua, the king also included Princess Elizabeth Laʻanui, descended from Keoua's elder
brother, and descended from Keoua's younger brother, Prince
(and later King) William Charles Lunalilo. Casting his net still wider
brought in descendants of two of Keoua's cousins—Kameʻeiamoku's
great-great-grandchildren, the siblings James Kaliokalani, David Kalakaua, and later Lydia (Liliʻuokalani) Kamakaʻeha, the latter two
being the last two sovereigns of the nation; and finally Kahekili's
descendants, the half sisters Abigail Maheha and Jane Loeau,
daughters of Liliha. By the end of the century Kamehameha III's
entire list of possibilities would be exhausted.

Having delineated a line of succession, the king determined to
give them a Western education, and so brought about the Chiefs'
Children's School. The chiefs passed a request to the Sandwich
Islands Mission in June 1839, which engendered uncomfortable
discussion. It accentuated the missionaries' position, which they had
always found delicate: needing to continue good relations with the
nobility but disliking to enable their chiefly prerogatives by providing
special education for their children alone. As with creature comforts
in the precontact days, as with sandalwood, as with the new religion,
the first instinct of the *aliʻi* was to hoard for themselves. "The miserable policy of the chiefs," wrote Gerrit Judd four years earlier, "is to
monopolize all the talent . . . for the purpose of maintaining their
own power. . . . Almost all the teachers of worth, on whom the labors
of this station have been expended, are kept by Kinaʻu constantly
about her person." But, they needed her, and they knew it.[8]

The prospect of educating the children of the *aliʻi nui* raised a
whole different spectrum of issues, largely centering on discipline.
Noble children were not born to inherit their station, they were recognized in their station, and its prerogatives, from the moment they
drew breath: They were, in a phrase, spoiled rotten. Rev. Charles

Stewart was stunned to see such pampered and uncontrolled tod-
dlers: "I have seen a young chief, apparently not three years old,
walking the streets . . . as naked as when born, (with the exception
of a pair of green morocco shoes on his feet), followed by ten or
twelve stout men, and as many boys, carrying umbrellas, and kahiles,
and spit boxes, and fans, and the various trappings of chieftainship.
The young noble was evidently under no control but his own will,
and enjoyed already the privileges of his birth . . . doing whatever he
pleased."[9]

Despite the missionaries' misgivings, the cornerstone for the
Chiefs' Children's School was laid on June 28, 1839, at the site of the
present 'Iolani Palace barracks. Chosen to preside over the new
school were Amos Starr Cooke and his wife, the former Juliette Montague, of the Eighth Company, which had arrived in 1837. He was
from Connecticut, she from Massachusetts, and like many of the missionaries, they had married only a month before they set sail for
Hawai'i. He was not a teacher by profession, but after two years
among them he was the one whom the chiefs requested be placed
over their children. Cooke accepted, on the two conditions that a
school be built and, aware of the children's awful reputation, that the
chiefs give him complete authority over them, which they agreed to.

For the task of *kahu*, a sort of governor and minder of the noble
children, the Cookes decided upon forty-year-old John Papa 'I'i,
trained from childhood as the companion of the king's late brother
Kamehameha II. He was a perfect choice, descended from a long
line of minor chiefs whose roles had been *kahu* to the *ali'i*. Still attached to the royal household, 'I'i had long since distinguished himself for thoughtful and loyal service. At that moment he was at
Lahaina in the royal suite, and William Richards was dispatched
with a letter asking him to take the appointment. Richards approached 'I'i in company with a new *kuhina nui*. After Kina'u's death
the office passed to her half sister Kekauluohi, forty-six, who was
deeply nested in the Kamehameha clan—cousin and stepdaughter
of the Conqueror, and widow of both him and Liholiho. 'I'i agreed

to be the children's governor on condition that the king and chiefs allow him to enroll his ward, the king's niece Victoria Kamamalu, who was barely two.

The missionaries had, discreetly, already cleared his appointment with the king, who engaged ʻIʻi in casual conversation at a luau before raising the real business. ʻIʻi repeated his wish to the king; the little girl had been extraordinarily dear to her mother, Kinaʻu, who had disregarded the *hanai* custom and nursed her herself. Kinaʻu had desired a Christian education for her daughter. "You go there with your child," replied the king, "and take my *keiki* [nephews] with you. If you do not go there, neither will my *keiki*."[10] Such an expression of the king's confidence led Papa ʻIʻi not only to take the job but to act boldly in overruling certain chiefs who hesitated before committing their own children to something as foreign to their way of life as a boarding school. Charge of the young *aliʻi*, day and night, was almost like a second *hanai*, and they were not convinced that it was good for them. Among them was Kekuanaoa, the birth father of the heirs to the throne. He was content to obey the king on their account, but with tears in his eyes asked ʻIʻi to hold back his youngest, Victoria Kamamalu. ʻIʻi cited both the wishes of her mother, and Kamamalu's destiny as a future *kuhina nui* to refuse.

A much more dramatic confrontation arose with the grandmother of the Conqueror's collateral heirs David Kalakaua and Lydia Kamakaʻeha. After once allowing their elder brother, James Kaliokalani, to attend the school, she withdrew him for the reason that he had been required to water plants in the yard, which was a servant's job. In the ensuing argument, ʻIʻi maintained that all the boys, and he himself, and the teachers took turns watering plants, for the exercise, which benefited them. "You have no right in the matter," he scolded her, and placed his left foot on her thigh as he forcibly removed James from her lap—a stunning affront to a high chiefess. She complained to Kekuanaoa, who she knew was close to the king. "I have tried," he told her, "without success. He has the power from the chiefs, so here we are."[11] (James Kaliokalani continued at the school, and was sixteen or seventeen when he died in an epidemic of measles, leaving the succession to his brother and sister.)

Papa 'I'i became, effectively, vice principal of the school. It was the first of many important advancements for him; over the next thirty years he became an extraordinarily influential voice in Hawaiian affairs, and an important bridge between the two cultures, both of which he respected. The first important decision taken in regard to the children, although it seems very harsh to modern sensibilities, was to separate them almost completely from their previous lives. What made this necessary was that when school started, the children came each attended by as many as two dozen lackeys, shading them with umbrellas, holding out boxes into which to spit, obeying their every whim. No progress was possible with such children, absent the shock of isolation. Eventually their attendants had to be banned because they loitered about, carping over how their precious were being treated. School convened in early May 1840, with eleven noble children ranging in age from three to eleven; the other chosen ones entered as they became old enough. Among them were four future kings, a queen regnant, a queen consort, and a *kuhina nui*. It was a scarifying time for the children, several of whom cried themselves to sleep. "Now all are asleep but one," wrote an exhausted Juliette Cooke on May 5, 1840, "and he is calling for the steward to come and sleep with him. It is a very trying time for them and for us, too."[12]

The school building was erected on the site of the first 'Iolani Palace barracks, just northeast of the royal residence and in the approximate location of the present Hawai'i Capitol. It was in the shape of a hollow square surrounding a courtyard with a well. The entrance was in the center of the south side, with the boys' and girls' classrooms to the left and the kitchen and dining room to the right. The Cookes' apartment was on the east side, one room for them and one for their children. Three boys' dormitory rooms were on the west side, and two girls' rooms on the north opposite the entrance. Papa 'I'i's apartment was at the northwest corner, strategically placed between the girls and boys, but a location from where, ultimately, he was not successful in keeping the precocious young people apart.

About six months after the school opened, the Cookes were informed that a condemned man, a murderer imprisoned in the fort and soon to be hanged, had asked to see David Kalakaua, who was only six. Thinking that such an interview would be a good object lesson on the biblical principle of an eye for an eye, they permitted it. They learned only later that the doomed man was High Chief Kamanawa II, sentenced to death for having his former wife poisoned so he would be free to remarry. Kalakaua was his grandson; the future king witnessed the execution of his grandfather—a traumatic event for the little boy that cannot help but have shaped his internal conflict between the old life and the new that played out so painfully during his later seventeen years as monarch. For common Hawaiians the double execution—Kamanawa was hanged with his accomplice—was no less shocking. For generations the high chiefs had held life-or-death power over *kanakas*, and here was one of them, the grandson of no less than Kameʻeiamoku the Conqueror's right hand, dangling lifeless at the end of a rope by the will of the white missionaries. What a precipitous change in power that was, with the gallows the new *heiau*, and those who violated the new *kapu* were the new sacrifices, even high chiefs. Thus to the persuasion of the pulpit was added the compulsion of the noose.

Days at the boarding school were rigorous: up at five, exercise with a ride or walk, prayers at six-thirty, an English-only breakfast at seven. Three hours of school were followed by a meal and three more hours of school, supper at five-thirty, and then evening prayers. One Bible verse was learned every day, in Hawaiian at the start of the day and in English at the close. All were in bed by eight, the younger ones at seven. Recognizing the children's boisterous natures, the Cookes were shrewd enough to include a healthy schedule of physical activity. They rolled hoops, flew kites, swung, learned to ride. The Cookes encouraged evident talent, which for several of the children was in music, and several of them became accomplished pianists and composers. Discipline was strict; lateness to a meal was a meal missed; willful misbehavior brought corporal punishment, once unthinkable for children of such station, but preceded by a talk to explain why it was being administered.

In time the square school building was replaced with a more substantial structure, one special feature of which was the "Boston Parlor," an upstairs drawing room to which the missionaries committed their finest heirloom furnishings. It was a daily exercise in this chamber for the royal children to practice their English and their social graces. One view of the students' progress was offered by the American consul George Brown, who was invited to a tea party at the school in November 1843, also attended by the other missionaries in the area. "Mrs. Cooke," he wrote home to his family, "has a large family to take care of, over twenty children of the chiefs male & female, among which is the heir apparent. They have made good progress in their studies & some of them speak English remarkably well. Some of the girls sing & play on the Piano very well for beginners, and most of them have a taste for music."[13]

The children were not allowed trips home, but their parents were permitted to visit the school. None was more vested in the school than the king, with his four adopted children all enrolled. He actually moved in next door to the school, into a large frame house built by his brother-in-law Kekuanaoa, of timbers that Ka'ahumanu salvaged from the *Hale Keawe* when it was pulled down. The king bought it from him when Kekuanaoa entered financial straits, and it became known as the first 'Iolani ("royal hawk") Palace.[14] Kamehameha III, like many visitors, remarked on the students' gift for music; he once heard his niece Victoria Kamamalu, still only a toddler, as she arced high in the swing during recess, belting out American songs at the top of her lungs. It was probably more than a glancing reference to her mother, Kina'u the *kuhina nui*, who had disagreed with him so vociferously over foreign and religious policy, when he said to her *kahu* John Papa 'I'i, "What a loud-voiced girl. She may have as great a voice as her mother's."[15] Kekauluohi, the present *kuhina nui*, had a grass house erected on the grounds so that she could sojourn in proximity with her son William Lunalilo.

The royal students' proficiency in English reached such a degree that one of the exercises in their notebooks was an extended fantasy on words ending in "tion:"

MARY MODERATION'S ANS. TO TIMOTHY OBSERVATION

Sir:

I perused your oration with much deliberation, & with no little consternation at the great infactuation [*sic*] of your weak imagination to show such veneration on so slight foundation. But after examination, & serious contemplation, I suppose your admiration was the fruit of recreation. . . .

It went on for several more lines before being subscribed, "I am without hesitation, yours, Mary Moderation."[16]

Nor were all their English lessons apparently in standard English. For reasons no longer obvious, the notebook of Prince Lunalilo, son of the new *kuhina nui*, shows him copying out the poem "The Louisiana Belle" in dialect:

> *In Louisiana, dat's de state,*
> *Whar ole massa eber dwell,*
> *He had a lubly colored gal*
> *Called de Louisiana Belle.*

The young *ali'i* of Hawaii, their dark skin notwithstanding, were not taught English in slave dialect, indeed the New England missionaries had a pointed antipathy toward slavery. The point of teaching this poem (and "Black Jupiter," among others) remains a mystery.[17]

In 1846 the name was changed to the Royal School. "Friday evening as we about retiring, his majesty and suite called on us, accompanied by martial music. The parlor and court were filled."

They desired to hear the piano, so the children did a command performance of several songs." "We passed cake, pie, grapes, figs, etc,. such as we happened to have on hand. . . . The queen is a very pleasant woman, and were it not that she is about as large as a barrel, she would be quite pretty. The children said she completely filled two chairs!!"[18] The presence of the royal family next door had one unintended consequence when Queen Kalama took a fancy to her husband's eldest nephew, Prince Moses Kekuaiwa. To the native culture, having a boy toy in the family was all in good fun, but the Cookes, when they learned of it, were horrified that the heir apparent was setting such a bad example—followed closely by his two brothers Lot and Alexander. They often slipped out at night to drink and carouse, enduring Amos Cooke's lectures and whippings only to slip out again.

Cooke's stern discipline of the boys gave no hint of his own misgivings about whether that was the best way to handle them. Gerrit Judd called one morning and imparted to Juliette Cooke "that he thought we were governing too much now-a-days by force . . . ," Amos Cooke wrote in his diary. "I have felt very bad about it ever since. . . . I stayed at home. I could not eat any dinner. Have read 150 pages in 'How Shall I Govern My School.' . . . This evening I feel like giving up the ship. The children are disaffected, and I have reason to fear the parents are also, and why should I sacrifice my life, and my wife's . . . for those who have no heart to improve by it."[19] The Conqueror's grandchildren were only the most prominent offenders. Princess Jane Loeau, who was the oldest of the students, was also the most precocious,[20] but all seemed to require vigilance, and the royal students' sexual capers drove the Cookes to distraction. The Royal Council eventually ordered Moses's expulsion from the school; his death shortly after from measles left his brother Prince Lot Kapuaiwa next in line to the throne.

The Cookes' contest of wills with Moses was little compared to the battles they had with Lot. At twelve, he fell heavily in love with Princess Abigail Maheha, fourteen. Being willful *ali'i* children, every remonstrance, coercion, and punishment the Cookes could devise failed to keep the pair apart, and Abigail became pregnant. For her shame, she was forced to marry not just a commoner but her mother's gardener, on February 3, 1847, and the pair was exiled to Kaua'i, where they were warned to remain in penitent quiet.[21] Lot was beside himself, and swore an oath never to marry—although he had been betrothed almost since birth to Princess Bernice Pauahi. They were first cousins once removed, but from different wives of Kamehameha I. If ever the inbred dying dynasty of the Conqueror had a chance at survival, that union would have been the likeliest possibility, but owing to Lot's fit of rage—and later during his years as King Kamehameha V he kept his vow—he likely doomed his line to extinction. It was not the only time that the history of Hawai'i turned on a royal tantrum—although Bernice had her own mind on the subject, announcing that she would marry Lot if commanded, but she did not like him and would as soon be buried in a coffin. (The child of Lot and Abigail did survive, and that line continues, so there remain on Kaua'i living direct descendents of Kamehameha I. Owing, however, to the introduced concept of legitimacy, they were excluded from further consideration.)

Such struggles at the school wore heavily on Juliette Cooke, who was also engaged in bearing and rearing her own seven children. Consul Brown found that, "Mrs. Cooke is a very interesting woman, but is not well. She has too much care . . . for one lady, without help. The Board ought to send out a woman to answer as housekeeper, so that she may have more time to apply to the essentials of her pupils. And it is highly important that these children, of all others, should be properly brought up, as they will have the Government of the Islands in their hands bye & bye. If Mrs. Cooke is not relieved, she will fail, & will be a loss not easily repaired."[22]

Despite these battles royal, both the Cookes and the students could put on quite a convincing show when company came calling. "I have seldom seen better behaved children," wrote Capt. Charles Wilkes of the U.S. Navy's Exploring Expedition, "than those of this school. They were hardly to be distinguished from well bred children of our own country, and nearly as light in color." No matter how fractious when among themselves, all presented a united front to the outside world. "Our teachers seek our good, sir," one of the princesses explained to another officer, in faultless English. "They have experience and know what is best for us. We have confidence in their judgment and have no inclination to do what they disapprove."[23] Frequent resort to the rod for discipline, especially among the boys, was for internal knowledge only; the chiefs could not be expected to keep the *kanakas'* respect if word got out that they allowed *haoles* to beat their children.

For the decade of the Royal School's operation, the Cookes could comfort themselves that they produced bilingual heirs and heiresses who were educated in geography, history, and the social graces, five of whom acquitted themselves as equals in the royal courts of Europe. But at what the Cookes considered to be their greater task, of producing genuinely converted, Christian youth, they admitted defeat. The children were all baptized, and marched into church every Sunday two by two for ten years, but of deeper conviction of the heart the Cookes saw no evidence. "The continual fact that there are no conversions," Amos Cooke reported home to the ABCFM, "is exceedingly humiliating & make [*sic*] it apparent to all, that we *fail* in many things, in *all* come short."[24]

After ten years of schooling, the operation came to a close with what the Cookes considered a success, the marriage of their last student (and one of their more peaceable ones) Princess Bernice Pauahi to Charles Reed Bishop of New York on May 4, 1850. Modern scholarly commentary criticizes the Royal School for being inherently Anglocentric, which it was, and for its unique equating of Christian civilization with Boston, which it did. It also finds the school, and the missionaries, disrespectful of, if not oblivious to, any virtues of the native culture they encountered.[25] Without the training received at the Royal School, however, its graduates would never have made the impression on, and gained the respect of, the world's royal courts, or conducted the affairs of their nation as ably as they did. That Hawai'i became a coveted prize of global imperialism would have occurred in any event; what consideration the royal administration did receive, from Britain, from France, from the United States, was the Royal School's success. The school most certainly did fail in its mission to turn its pupils into little Americans, but the education they received empowered those students in their later noble or royal lives to preserve their culture, and that was the nation's success.

Lahainaluna was judged a success, and the Chiefs' Children's School was up and going, but it left the missionaries, many of them now with growing families, in a dilemma over educating their own children. It was expensive, not to say emotionally wrenching, to send them home to boarding schools, but the Hawaiian children in the common schools were being taught in their own language, which the Americans did not think proper for their own. And there was the question of how to preserve their own children's morals in such a vividly sexualized society. They knew how raw it was, but seldom wrote about such indelicate things. One exception was when William Ellis warned them of the danger of allowing their children to fraternize too freely with natives; down in the Society Islands, racial mixing had not gone well. Samuel Whitney sailed to Tahiti to see for himself, and when he came back his wife, Mercy, wrote a breathless report of it. Several of the missionary children there

> have been ruined. . . . One was confined with a bastard child by a native man, not 3 months since. Three daughters of one of the Missionaries were not long since guilty of admitting 3 native men by means of a servant to their bed chamber, & secreting them under the beds till night, when the mother hearing a noise, lit a candle & went into the room, but on seeing the men,

fainted & fell & they made their escape. . . . Two lads, sons of
Missionaries, were lately expelled [from the South Seas Acad-
emy], for illicit connections with native girls.

Her catalog went on. Clearly, educating their growing broods in
company with native children was a dangerous idea.[26] The ABCFM
itself was little help, discouraging an exodus of children back home
with such platitudes as they would be spoiled by their grandparents, or God would use them as examples of decorum for the native
children. The missionary families reached their own conclusions,
some sending children home, some retaining them in the islands.
Interestingly, some of the missionary wives, as their families increased, voiced their frustration at being pinned down to domestic
drudgery when they had come to Hawai'i to convert the heathen.
They had hoped for a missionary appointment before they met their
husbands, and married them largely for the shared ambition to venture into the world to do good. They were not too bashful to point
out that they had ways to establish bonds with the native people
(witness Ka'ahumanu's fascination with their clothes) that their
preachy husbands did not, and they were not being well utilized.
Mercy Whitney found her "usefulness among the heathen . . .
greatly impeded, by having to devote so much of our time to the
education & care of our children." Others, such as Maria Chamberlain (wife of Levi, the missionaries' commercial agent), were content
to model Christian womanhood by their example, but she particularly was not enthusiastic at the prospect of providing lessons to her
seven children at home.[27] (Ironically, when the American ladies
were able to interact with the native women and provide an example
of being a good wife, it robbed the latter of "the very aspects of Hawaiian culture which afforded Hawaiian women some measure of
autonomy within their own social system."[28])

In 1841 the missionaries began to organize a school for their
own at Punahou, in the cool of the Manoa Valley above Waikiki. It
was on land that had been given, interestingly enough, to Hiram

Bingham by Boki and Liliha, who were not otherwise great supporters of social transformation.[29] The first class was held in a thatched-roof adobe building on July 11, 1842, making it the first English-language school west of the Rocky Mountains; fifteen students attended the first day, but there were more than thirty by the end of the year. The first teachers were Daniel and Emily (Ballard) Dole of Maine; he was a graduate of Bowdoin College and Bangor Theological Seminary, and they had arrived with the Ninth Company of missionaries the year before. Emily Dole died on April 27, 1844, four days after giving birth to their third son, Sanford Ballard Dole, who became an important figure in his own generation.

The year that Mrs. Dole died, Marcia Smith of the Eighth Company was imported to help with the teaching, and William and Mary Rice of the Ninth Company transferred from Maui to supervise the boarding students. William Richards undertook to turn the school into a college where graduates of the Royal School could complete their education.[30] In one guise or another, after receiving a royal charter in 1849, Punahou grew into a distinguished institution.

7. A Sweet Taste

Before discovery, the Hawaiian Islands contained about 2,700 species of plants, most of them "endemic," or not found anywhere else in the world. (Introduced foreign species now outnumber them by almost two to one, resulting in many crises of botanical survival.) As islands go these were a relatively new emergence from the sea, less than ten million years old, too isolated from other landmasses to share many species with them naturally. When the first aboriginal explorers arrived from southern Polynesia, they brought with them plants associated with some of their gods: gourds and sweet potatoes for Lono, breadfruit and coconuts as emblems of Ku', the bananas of Kanaloa, and the taro, bamboo, and sugarcane of the most powerful god, Kane.[1]

Europeans had regularly supplemented the local diet. After Cook had brought onions, pumpkins, melons, and mutton, Vancouver had brought in addition to cattle a variety of garden seeds. Observers in the early 1820s recorded chilis, asparagus, turnips, cabbages, and horseradish, in addition to garden flowers that would have been familiar in Europe and America. When HMS *Blonde* arrived in

1825, it carried not just the caskets of Kamehameha II and Kama-malu but a virtual orchard of sample fruit and nut trees to begin cultivating on the islands: fig, plum, apple, cherry, peach, and wal-nut, and grapevines. Stopping in Rio de Janeiro, she picked up or-ange trees and more grapevines, and also thirty coffee plants that were offloaded and consigned to the care of Don Francisco de Paula Marín. If anyone could keep them alive, that famous farmer could.

Sugarcane was not native to Hawai'i. It originated in the islands of what became Indonesia, and spread with human migration through Australasia and the South Pacific. There were many differ-ent varieties of it, which cross-pollinated readily into new hybrids. The Pacific islanders did not process crystalline sugar; the canes, whose inner fibers comprised about 12 percent sugar, were cultivated to be cut and chewed for the sweet raw juice.

The first people in Hawai'i to conceive of the commercial pro-duction of sugar were from China, where the art of making sugar had been known for generations. Their first recorded pass through the islands was in 1788, ten years after Cook, by which time traders had begun to arrive. In that year Kamehameha saw about four dozen Chinese carpenters, who had built the forty-ton schooner *North West America* for Capt. John Meares. Thinking ahead to his own fleet, the Conqueror asked Meares, without success, to leave him a couple to build him a ship. One of Vancouver's officers found a Chinese in the king's suite in 1794, and Chinese probably jumped ship regularly during the sandalwood years; John Papa 'I'i remem-bered three of them being well established in Honolulu around 1810. "Because the faces of these people were unusual and their speech . . . was strange, a great number of persons went to look at them."[2] In 1802 a mysterious Chinese, his name not recorded, was seen to be making sugar on the island of Lana'i. It was presumed that he came on a vessel seeking sandalwood and left by the same conveyance.

O'ahu witnessed a false start to a sugar industry in 1826, and it raised quite a ruckus among *ali'i* of competing sentiments. The ar-rival of HMS *Blonde* brought a reunion of sorts between Governor

Boki and one John Wilkinson, who had apparently agreed with Boki in London[3] to come to the islands and begin a commercial sugar operation. He arrived on the ship brittle in health and temperament; Boki turned over seven acres of his lands in the Manoa Valley, which Wilkinson put under cultivation, but he apparently had little more luck in coaxing labor from mocking islanders than Lieutenant Bligh had had in 1779. Money ran short, a flood destroyed the beginnings of a dam—sugar production requires copious quantities of water—and Wilkinson died in September 1826. Boki, perhaps seeing a way out of his sandalwood debt, increased the acreage, paid his workers generously, and built a road to the plantation. Levi Chamberlain was impressed. "If the natives persevere in cultivating the cane," he wrote on November 1, "and manufacturing it into sugar, the nation may be supplied with that article," and then added prophetically, "and a surplusage remain for exportation." By February 18 a British sea captain reported that he had seen the sugar, which "looks very good indeed," and that California might look for a shipload of it before long.

At that point Boki's elder brother, Kalanimoku, the prime minister, seems to have pulled rank, stripped the mill from Manoa, and rebuilt it near Honolulu to expand the industry to that area. Then Kalanimoku died, Boki reasserted control, and formed a new partnership with four *haoles* for the production—being Boki—of rum. His investors expended several thousand dollars in converting the mill into a distillery, but by then Ka'ahumanu had converted to Christianity; she decreed rum production illegal—the new word for *kapu*—and she supported the missionaries when they refused to allow their carts, which were the only ones on the island, to haul cane if the end product was to be alcohol.[4] The authority was the queen regent's, but goodwill for the missionaries on the harddrinking waterfront was scarce after this.

It was also the beginning of the end for Boki. With his rum operation shut down, he opened a hotel and mercantile in downtown Honolulu, exported merchandise to Tahiti and Alaska, but likely still had difficulty breaking even in those ventures. In the fall of 1829 there arrived in Honolulu the new eighteen-gun sloop-of-war USS *Vincennes*. Though the stop was intended only to be an amicable port call, the American merchants in Honolulu prevailed on the captain to speak to the government about the enormous amount of debt they were carrying on their books, which the chiefs owed them in *iliahi* futures. They reached a settlement of $48,000 for 6,865 *piculs* of sandalwood, or something over 450 tons of the trees now virtually extinct in Hawai'i, a debt of which Boki was apportioned one-quarter. This is what prompted Boki to follow news of large sandalwood stands in the New Hebrides, taking four hundred men in two ships, of whom only twenty ever returned to Hawai'i after dolorous misadventures. Boki was either lost at sea, or marooned, or more likely just sailed away from his problems and started over near Samoa. Thus Boki, ironically the chief who more than any other clung to the traditional ways and its privileges, became probably the first refugee from American-style debt.

The deal for the first large American-owned sugar plantation was made in 1835, when the royal governor of Kaua'i leased 980 acres for fifty years at three hundred dollars per year to Ladd & Company of Honolulu. The founders of that concern were not missionaries, but they were wholly contained in the Calvinist New England culture that subscribed to the missionary effort. William Ladd was twenty-eight, a native of Hallowell, Maine; Peter Brinsmade was three years older, from Hartford, Connecticut, a graduate of Bowdoin College who had attended both Andover and Yale Theological Seminaries. The two were brothers-in-law, married to relatives of Lucy Goodale Thurston, who was a keystone of the First Company of missionaries. William Northey Hooper was the youngest at twenty-six, from Manchester, Massachusetts, also married. The trio had arrived in Honolulu on July 27, 1833, on the sailing ship *Hellespont*, and immediately opened a mercantile on the waterfront. Lacking funds to improve a wharf, they sank an old hulk to serve the purpose, while the families shared the space on the second floor of their warehouse. They were something of an anomaly in the business district. Their connection to the Thurstons, and Brinsmade's background in theology, gave them good relations with the missionaries—perhaps one reason why they received little business from their neighbors, who called them the "Pious Traders," and they struggled for a year and a half.

The Ladd family Web site acknowledges that the missionaries interceded for them in acquiring the lease on Kaua'i.[5] It was an act that seemed harmless at the time, but it was a step onto the slippery slope of interfering with the government, something their missionary mandate prohibited, but that, as they grew more accustomed to their interpretation of God's law being equated with the law of the islands, became ever easier to resort to.

William Hooper, who knew nothing of sugar or milling, was dispatched to manage the venture. The land was at Koloa, near the southernmost point of the island, which had the requisites for growing cane: rich soil and abundant water. Kaua'i, its royal family's marital amalgamation into the rest of the kingdom notwithstanding, remained some degrees apart both really and psychologically. Changes to the traditional system wrought in the other islands could be slow to reach there. Establishing their plantation at Koloa not only met the climatic needs of the crop, it also allowed the "Pious Traders" to mount a frontal assault on the *ali'i*'s lingering overlordship of the serfs.[6] Workers were paid twelve and a half cents per day, which, allowing for the *kanakas*' famous ambivalence toward labor, still provided sufficient incentive for enough of them that the chiefs began growling that their traditional labors—and that translated to tribute—were not being maintained. Unlike previous attempts to lure the commoners to labor, here it was a success; people liked the idea of being able to buy things that they could not grow or make for themselves. The chiefs began posting thugs to intimidate workers away from taking jobs, but they backed down when faced with the combination of king and governor.

After constructing housing for laborers, Hooper planted the first twelve acres of cane, which he soon doubled, along with large tracts of coffee and banana trees (five thousand plants each), and forty-five fields of taro. In addition to their wage, Hooper provided the workers a meal each day of fish and poi. With no place nearby to spend their money, workers were paid in company scrip, redeemable for merchandise at Hooper's store, a system that became the standard in the sugar industry. Over time across the country as the sugar industry grew, payment in scrip limited to company stores became abusive, when real currency could have been spent elsewhere, but in this first plantation circumstance of weaning the *maka'ainana* away from subsistence farming to working for wages, it made little difference what medium was used in the only store around.

In 1836 Ladd & Co. shipped its first four tons of sugar and molasses to the United States. Once the feasibility was proved, other missionaries on Kaua'i established mills, "grinding cane on shares for native growers." Two years after Ladd's first export, there were twenty-two mills grinding sugar in the kingdom, two powered by water and twenty by animals.[7] From all sources sugar export rose to 44 tons in 1838, 50 tons in 1839, and 180 in 1840. It was, of course, the first sprinkle of what would eventually become a crystalline white avalanche of Hawaiian sugar, but its eventual dominance in the kingdom did not happen for lack of effort to create a more diversified economy. In fact the missionaries perceived precisely this need, and in 1837 presented a memorial to the ABCFM, requesting a shipload of vocational teachers who could encourage "the cultivations of sugar-cane, cotton, silk, indigo, and various useful productions adapted to the soil and the climate; and the manufacture of cotton, silk, clothing, hats, shoes, instruments of husbandry, etc." The profit from the venture would be turned to support of schools and other benevolent purposes.[8]

The Sandwich Islands Mission buttressed the memorial with a testimonial from a council of chiefs:

Love to you, our obliging friends in America. This is our sentiment: . . . Do give us additional teachers . . . whom we would specify, a carpenter, tailor, mason, shoe-maker, wheel-wright, paper-maker, type founder, agriculturalists . . . and makers of machinery to work on a large scale, and a teacher of the chiefs in what pertains to the land, according to the practice of enlightened countries. . . . Should you assent to our request, and send hither these specified teachers, we will protect them, and grant facilities for their occupations, and we will back up these works, that they may succeed well.[9]

The document was signed by all those with the greatest power and influence: Kamehameha III; Nahiʻenaʻena; Kinaʻu, the *kuhina nui*, and her husband, Kekuanaoa; Kekauluohi, who would succeed Kinaʻu as prime minister; and ten of the most powerful chiefs. Clearly, they were serious in their proposal; William Richards himself carried it to New England to present it to the ABCFM. The sentiment was progressive and noble, but the timing was awful. The United States had entered the throes of the Panic of 1837, which was the worst business recession in its history to that time—although because of that, willing emigrants should have been plenty. The larger obstacle was the ABCFM itself, which did not have the vision to perceive that, now with a largely literate population, something more than preaching was needed to assure Hawaiʻi's progress as a Christian nation. With *kapu* dead by the islanders' own hand, the missionaries had stepped into that vacuum and provided a conservative Christian alternative and conquered the spirits of at least the ruling elite, if not the majority of the *makaʻainana*. For them now to step away from the opportunity to guide the country's economic development along some kind of benevolent path left the next step in the conquest of paradise—the economy—to the tender mercies of the business community.

⁂

As it was, desultory efforts to diversify the economy were made. An experiment with silk production began on Kaua'i in 1836, with imported silkworms and mulberry trees. It looked promising at first, and some silk was even exported, but within a decade insects and drought wrecked the venture. An equally optimistic start was made at a cotton industry. Any good New England woman knew her craft at a spinning wheel, and upon her arrival Rebecca Hitchcock of the Fifth Company found four spare wheels in the storehouse at Lahaina, and had them converted to spinning wheels. Hawaiian women, no doubt enthralled at discovering a way to make cloth that did not involve pounding *tapa*, took it up with such enthusiasm that before long they had in their hands what Mrs. Hitchcock believed was the first cotton cloth woven in the islands. Sensing the commercial possibilities, several of the missionaries wrote letters home to the ABCFM to send machinery.

The Board found that expense prohibitive, and instead dispatched Miss Lydia Brown with the Seventh Company, one of the few single women to win appointment as a missionary. She was fifty-five, a spinster, an expert at spinning, weaving, and knitting who was keen to pass on those skills to the Hawaiian women. While seed was later sent for planting, natives knew where cotton already grew abundantly, having spread to the wild from fields planted years before by Don Francisco Marín. Miss Brown set up a weaving school for women at Wailuku, Maui. Before long they could boast that they were wearing clothes entirely of their own making; with two more years, they turned out some six hundred yards of cotton cloth. When Miss Brown added dyeing to the class regimen, her pupils were so thrilled with the result that she wrote with some pride, "I have not seen so much heathenish gesticulation since I have been on the Islds. as when they came to see it."[10] Brown's success drew the attention of the governor of Hawai'i and later O'ahu, John Adams Kuakini, brother of Ka'ahumanu. He built a thirty-by-seventy-foot cloth mill that rolled out another four hundred yards at Kailua, had a small gin brought in from China, and commissioned a carpenter to turn out a number of spinning wheels. But this industry, too, played out—mostly after Kuakini discovered that, as proud as he was of introducing a new industry to his country, cotton cloth and clothing could still be imported cheaper than they could be produced at home.

Western food crops left an equally spotty history. The Maui white potatoes that American whalers so looked forward to passed from economic importance to the islands, first with the decline of the whaling fleets and then further with increased potato farming in the American West. Early on, the widespread opinion in the United States was that cereal grains would not prosper in Hawai'i. This was found not to be the case, but the climate and insects presented obstacles; one early grower noted that his acreage had fattened the largest crop of weevils he had ever seen.[11] Americans in Hawai'i promoted corn as a healthful supplement to taro, which would improve both the native diet and fatten their pigs. Once introduced, there was always some acreage of corn but it was not a major crop. Wheat likewise elicited a lukewarm reaction; as many as three mills ground out a small export of flour, but it also never caught on.

Coffee had more staying power. Plantations of various sizes were begun on Kaua'i, O'ahu, Maui, and at Hilo on the Big Island. But it was the slips that missionaries planted *mauka* (up the mountain) from Kailua Kona sometime before 1830, on the slopes of Hualalai, that became the heart of the coffee industry. Coffee, however, proved itself highly susceptible to both meteorology and labor disputes, with exports rocketing or plummeting in response. Another industry that did make its impact was cattle. The Conqueror's wisdom in laying a *kapu* against disturbing the cattle that Vancouver introduced, along with later arrivals, eventually produced thriving wild herds in the uplands of the Big Island. They were hunted like wild game, professionally by some who lived rustically on the upper slopes of Mauna Kea. (David Douglas, a young botanist for whom the Douglas fir was named, was killed by a wild bull on that mountain in 1834).[12] This established a creditable hide and tallow industry, exporting between two and five thousand hides per year and some salt beef. Ranching the cattle also began in this era, including the development of a community of Mexican *vaqueros* who dazzled islanders with their colorful ways and feats of horsemanship. The *vaqueros* departed after several years, but were replaced by natives who mastered riding and roping.

Thus, while other enterprises made some showing they did not, except for cattle and coffee, take root. Nor was the economics of sugar entirely promising at first. In fact, Ladd's Kaua'i plantation itself ran into trouble. The capital expenditure to construct the mill, boiling house, sugarhouse, dam, carpenter and blacksmith shops, and provide housing and food for the laborers, who were paid twelve and a half cents a day plus food—for a product that sold for four cents a pound—was a difficult set of numbers. To be commercially profitable, sugar had to be produced on a massive scale.

By the spring of 1839 the Hawaiian government, with the missionaries behind the king, won the recall of the riotously living American commercial and seamen's agent, John Coffin Jones, and the new appointment, with appropriate lobbying, went to Peter Brinsmade, one of the "Pious Traders." And Kamehameha III, still only twenty-six but with fourteen years on the throne, importuned William Richards to resign from the mission to become his adviser. To rescue Ladd & Co. from its financial distress with a bold stroke, Brinsmade gained an interview with Richards in November 1841 to propose issuing common stock to form a company whose purpose would be nothing less than bringing into cultivation all the idle lands in the country. The contract would be good for a hundred years, the land would be selected in a year, settlement and development would begin within five, and the sovereign could buy in for whatever amount he pleased. Large-scale dispensation of land to colonial impresarios had worked effectively in other countries to speed up bringing empty land into productivity. And the idea was not too different in complexion from what the mission had requested of the ABCFM a few years earlier, only instead of sowing the land with teachers, tradesmen, and husbandmen, the same result was to come through private enterprise. Richards was not opposed but inserted a stipulation that the agreement would be observed provided the islands remained an independent country. Hawai'i's relations with the West had turned suddenly problematic, thanks to a blustering British consul who had been stationed in Honolulu and a French frigate captain who looted the city of twenty thousand dollars to satisfy French "honor." Honolulu was increasingly hosting a parade of foreign warships, most on friendly visits, but the presence of so much visiting firepower could not fail to intimidate. Richards thought it would be well for foreign investors in the country to have an incentive to press their home governments to respect Hawaiian integrity.

Brinsmade agreed to the terms. Wearing his business hat he sailed to the United States to show off the agreement and the prospects for Koloa sugar, but found a stunning silence of interest. Wearing his diplomatic hat he won a meeting with Daniel Webster, the U.S. secretary of state, to ask him to consider formal recognition of the Hawaiian government. He then traveled a circuit through Britain to France, where he again met Richards, who was in company with the native scholar and budding diplomat, Timothy Ha'alilio, to press for French recognition. Brinsmade and suite then traveled to Belgium, which was just emerging from its eight-year war of independence from the Netherlands, and whose king, Leopold I, was known as a sharp investor with an eye for the main chance. On May 16, 1843, the two parties signed a contract; Belgian colonists would embark for the islands under the auspices of a newly chartered Royal Community of the Sandwich Islands, the Belgian company would get Ladd & Co.'s interest in the project, and the cash-starved business would receive two hundred thousand dollars.

Brinsmade hardly had time to sigh in relief before shattering news arrived: Kamehameha III had ceded the government of the

Hawaiian Islands to Great Britain. Circumstances of the cession were unknown— the development stunned no one more than the British—but the deal that Brinsmade had been offering to everyone was predicated upon Hawai'i's continued independence. Leopold froze the deal, and Brinsmade hustled in high anxiety to London in an attempt to discover what on earth had happened.

8. Captains and Cannons

During Kamehameha II's doomed visit to Britain, his suite included a French purser named Jean Rives. After the deaths of the queen and king, Rives absconded to France, and it was soon discovered that a large amount of the king's traveling cash was missing as well. In Paris Rives promoted himself as a great man in Hawai'i, persuading the Foreign Ministry to back a French colonizing venture that he would lead. Part and parcel of the settlement was to be a contingent of Catholic missionaries.

Rives returned as far as California, where he learned that his doings had been uncovered, and he again disappeared. But by then Pope Leo XII had created the office of Prefect Apostolic for the Sandwich Islands, under the governance of the Picpus Fathers (Congregation of the Sacred Hearts of Jesus and Mary). Three priests—the Frenchmen Alexis Bachelot, prefect, and Abraham Armand, and the Englishman Patrick Short—and six lay brothers sailed on *La Comète* from Bordeaux on November 21, 1826, arriving in Honolulu the following July 7.

Catholicism was far from unknown on the islands. The Abbé de

Quélen, the ship's chaplain, had baptized Kalanimoku aboard *L'Uranie* in 1819, in the presence of the new king and queen regent, just after she ended *kapu* but before the American Protestant arrival. Boki and Liliha, no friends of the Calvinists, accepted Catholic baptism on board HMS *Blonde* as they brought back the bodies of Liholiho and Kamamalu. There were also a number of Catholic communicants in the foreign community, most prominently the famous braggart, bigamist, brewer, and vintner, Francisco de Paula Marín. To outside eyes it would have appeared only that the American Calvinists were about to get some competition in the contest for souls, but to the Sandwich Islands Mission it was an issue spiked with profound moral implications. In their minds, having papists loose in the country was only a half step above a return to wooden, shark-toothed *ki'i* leering in the *heiaus*. Ka'ahumanu was now an ardent Protestant, and on being warned of the danger, she summoned Boki to send Bachelot and company away. He was Catholic; they would take the news better from him. Boki could not be found, and the priests disembarked after two days' limbo. *La Comète*, rather like Rives, then disappeared before consequences could materialize.

It was a highly pregnant, if not actually dangerous, time in the kingdom. The great Kalanimoku had died five months before, and Boki, the perennial malcontent, was determined finally to emerge from his older brother's shadow. Ka'ahumanu dominated Kamehameha III and spread the new religion, but the boy king sought Boki's companionship with the familiarities of the old life, its privileges, and its hedonism. Under the old system Ka'ahumanu had far higher *kapus* than Boki, and under the new system as *kuhina nui* and regent she had far more power. But one thing Boki could still do was curry the favor of the Catholic missionaries for whatever use it could be against the queen regent. While to outward appearances Boki was attending Mass and performing his office as governor of O'ahu, the tension between him and Ka'ahumanu escalated for the better part of two years. What the Calvinists found even more troubling was the Picpus Fathers' success at winning converts.

All this occurred even as Honolulu was in the throes of its moral transformation, to the fury and threats of visiting sailors. Before leaving on a visit to Hawai'i Island, Ka'ahumanu forced Boki to renounce opposition to her rule in a council of chiefs, but while she was gone he began assembling an armed force to greet her return. Kekuanaoa tried his best to talk him out of it—without success, for Boki meant to revisit the old days and have a war. It was Hiram Bingham who defused the situation. He invited the feuding principals to tea, after which the fifteen-year-old king expressed his wish to sing, so Boki and the queen regent had to swallow their hatred of each other in a fest of psalm singing. Bingham considered the outcome to be a triumph of the gospel. He also took criticism for crossing the line into political affairs, largely without getting credit for preventing the country from slipping back into the butchery of the previous generations.

And then it was all to do over again. Boki left on his sandalwood expedition, never to return, leaving the governorship of O'ahu with Liliha. She was as much of an obstacle to the new order as he had been. With the king and high chiefs off visiting other islands, she heard that they had actually left to perfect plans to depose her, and she assembled a small army to receive them. This time the peacemaker was her father, Hoapili, the Christian governor of Maui, who talked her into coming home, where she lived until 1839. Those same chiefs took it in mind that the root of the trouble was the Catholic presence in the islands, and they struck on Christmas Eve, 1831. Father Armand had departed previously, but Bachelot and Short were seized, hustled through the streets, and put aboard the schooner *Waverly*. With a derisive cannon salute from the fort they were sent off to California, a land already planted thick with missions. The chiefs did this on their own authority, but Bingham was present when they made the decision.

This left the Hawaiian Catholic community severed from the sacraments, but the chiefs met complaints with persecution; there were beatings and jailings, to the Calvinists' probable relief, but without their expressed sanction. Ka'ahumanu died on June 5, 1832, her last words reputedly those of the hymn "Lo, Here am I, O Jesus." Among the minority of chiefs with a traditional bent, there was a thought to make Liliha the new *kuhina nui*, but that went nowhere, and she remained on Maui, having attached herself to the king's hedonistic circle, occasionally comforting him over his unsuccessful battle to marry his sister. The office of coruler instead went to Ka'ahumanu's niece, Elizabeth Kina'u, a woman of similar proportions and imperious demeanor, the Conqueror's daughter and therefore a half sister of Kamehameha III. She also was a Calvinist, and one whose face was set against the Catholics even more sternly than her aunt's had been. Under her premiership, scrutiny of native Catholics was sharpened, and Catholicism itself was banned from the islands at the end of 1837. Many of them had sought refuge in Boki's stronghold of Waianae in western O'ahu, but they were raided and sixty-seven of them marched to Honolulu. The thirteen who did not recant were jailed and set to hard labor. More than once Hiram Bingham, in person or in writing, alone or in company with Judd, Chamberlain, Bishop or others[1] advised the king and chiefs that imprisonment—of anyone—for conscience was not a good idea, and that they should ease off, but they did not interfere. British and American naval officers also importuned the king on the issue, but heated exchanges between the king and *kuhina nui* left Kina'u victorious on the policy.

By 1835 Bachelot had made his way back as far as Valparaiso, from where the vicar sent to Hawai'i not him but an Irish brother named Columba Murphy to make a report on the current conditions. Murphy was allowed in first because he was merely a lay brother and could not administer sacraments, and second because he was in an investigative, not a pastoral, capacity. But when Father Arsenius Walsh followed him the next year, Kina'u's government denied him permission to land, a decision that was reversed with the timely arrival of the French scientific vessel[2] *La Bonite*, with additional intercession by the captain of HMS *Actaeon*. The authorities allowed Walsh ashore, but on the condition that he tend only to the foreign Catholic community, not preach to the natives.³ Bachelot and Short slipped quietly into Honolulu in April 1837, but the authorities put them back onto their ship, the *Clémentine*, owned by the informally acting French agent Jules Dudoit. Once again the chiefs backed down, under the guns of HMS *Sulphur* and the French *La Vénus*, whose captains pledged that the fathers would obey the laws.

It was a great deal of strife for a government whose king was intent on pleasuring himself on Maui. Kinaʻu was left with the work, and it was she who got the king's signature on the total ban on Catholicism in December 1837 (just as that community lost a sizable piece of its visibility with the death of Marín). Kinaʻu died of mumps on April 4, 1839, so she did not live to see the result of her anti-Catholic vitriol; her death was followed a week later by Chief Kaikioʻewa's (a cousin of the Conqueror, whom Kaʻahumanu had installed as royal governor of Kauaʻi after Prince George's abortive rebellion), who had been her principal support on the council for Catholic persecution. Barely two months after Kinaʻu's death, Kamehameha III, perhaps having been warned of an impending French reprisal, verbally instructed the chiefs to end the persecution. His order was not published, and it did not amount to an "Edict of Toleration," but it gave the king some semblance of cover for when the French showed up—which they did, as soon as July 10, when a heavy frigate flying the French flag eased into Honolulu Harbor. She was *L'Artémise*, mounting fifty-two guns, under command of Capt. Cyrille Pierre Théodore Laplace, forty-five, one of France's leading naval officers and famous for having circumnavigated the globe nearly a decade before in *La Favorite*. He carried orders that were stern and unambiguous: He was to "destroy the malevolent impression you find established to the detriment of the French name; to rectify the erroneous opinion which has been created as to the power of France; and . . . you will not quit those places until you have left in all minds a solid and lasting impression."

The terms that Laplace meant to impose on the islands included freedom to practice the Catholic religion, payment of twenty thousand dollars in indemnity for the honor of France, and a salute to the French flag with twenty-one guns. The first that the Americans learned of his mission was a notice "To the Citizens of the United States resident at the Sandwich Islands," from the American commercial agent, Peter Brinsmade, that unless his terms were met, Laplace would open fire three days hence. And "in case of war, I am desired, under his kind Favor, to proffer to all American citizens, excepting the Protestant Clergy, an asylum, and protection on board the Frigate." Noting that they had been especially excluded from protection, the Sandwich Islands Mission hurried a note back to Brinsmade, signed by Bingham, Judd, Richards, Castle, and half a dozen others, requesting protection of American lives and property, which Brinsmade extended to them within his walls.[4]

The chiefs sent urgently to Maui for the king, but saw only one way out of the difficulty and that was to accede to Laplace's demands in all particulars. The weight of his office heavily upon him, Kamehameha III arrived and negotiated an agreement with Laplace that further stipulated that Frenchmen accused of crimes could be tried only by juries approved by the French consul, and, most odiously to the missionaries, Hawai'i was opened to the import of French wines and brandies, taxed at not more than 5 percent. French marines escorted the priests ashore, where they held Mass; cannon salutes were exchanged, the money rounded up and paid as a "bond" to insure future good conduct.

The business district in Honolulu viewed the "Laplace Affair" with some satisfaction for its casting the missionaries in a bad light, notwithstanding that they had to front much of the twenty-thousand-dollar indemnity. The January 15, 1840, number of the *Sandwich Islands Mirror* contained "An Account of the Persecution of Catholics in the Sandwich Islands," with primitive woodcuts (by Dudoit), including an illustration of one Juliana Makuwahine lashed to a

tree, "for the unpardonable sin of believing in the Church of Rome."
Another depicted Kimeone (Hawaiian for "Simon") in chains, his
cross defiantly around his neck, "released from his chains by the
magnanimous conduct of Captain Laplace."[5] Once back in business, the priests did not lack for converts seeking some shelter from
the uncompromising frost of American religion. The natives' "habits are fixed," wrote Juliette Cooke at this time, "and are not improved by all their intercourse with civilization & religion." One
young chief "has declared his intention of being a Catholic because
he says they are not so *strict* as the Protestants. He can be religious &
go to heaven & retain his sins into the bargain. His wife is not much
better, a young person of 16—She is said to be a ringleader of wick-
edness."[6] The Honolulu business leaders, happy to see the Congregationalists spurned, were even more pleased to learn that Hiram
Bingham, keystone of the Sandwich Islands Mission since their arrival, had been recalled by the ABCFM. He and Sybil took ship on
August 3, 1840, ostensibly for a rest because of Sybil's failing health,
but in fact the ABCFM was unhappy with his continued involvement in the affairs of the kingdom. Sybil died at the end of February 1848, but despite Bingham's wish the ABCFM did not return
him to Hawai'i. He made himself useful instead ministering to an
African-American church; he remarried, and died in New Haven in
1869, aged eighty.[7]

French truculence and bombast in Hawai'i naturally led the British government to undertake a review of their own relations with
the islands, which had been discovered by an Englishman and with
which they had a cordial friendship. The incoming foreign minister was George Hamilton-Gordon, the fourth Earl of Aberdeen,
characterized as kind, scholarly, unflappable, and "a profoundly
good man." As the Foreign Office communicated to the Admiralty,
all British officers were "to treat [the islands'] rulers with great

forbearance and courtesy, and, at the same time . . . afford efficient
protection to aggrieved British subjects, not to interfere harshly or
unnecessarily with the laws and customs."[8]

Great therefore was the Hawaiian shock when, on February 10, 1843,
a British frigate entered the harbor at Honolulu. HMS *Carysfort*, 925
tons, twenty-six guns, was under the command of Lord George Paulet, thirty-nine, erect, self-assured, the third son of the Marquess of
Winchester. Atop everything else, the Hawaiian government had
been fighting a running battle with the British consul, Richard
Charlton, who had taken his station shortly after the errand of HMS
Blonde in 1825. A man with no diplomatic experience, he was a bully
by nature, sour of temperament, litigious, hypocritical, derisive of
Americans and islanders; he was chosen largely because the owner
of the trading ship that Charlton commanded advanced him.[9] He
drank, enjoyed native women, and hated the American missionaries
with a passion. He was quick to seek vindication for all things British. When William Richards accused an English whaling captain of
buying a local girl (which he did, for $160, although they were later
married), Charlton tried to have Richards extradited to Britain to
face a libel charge. He made himself particularly unpleasant over a
certain tract of land in Honolulu, which Kalanimoku had leased to
him apparently without it being his to lease, and Charlton kept his
lawsuit over it alive for years.

In 1842 he stomped out of the country to lay his many griev-
ances before the Foreign Office, his charges now expanded to include one that English subjects were being abused. Worse, Charlton's
personal creditors in Valparaiso sued him in Hawai'i and won a
ten-thousand-dollar judgment, to satisfy which the court attached
Charlton's property, which prompted his urgent note to the commander in chief of the Pacific squadron to send a warship to protect
British interests. As acting consul in Honolulu, Charlton left Alexander Simpson, a diplomatic journeyman and junior Machiavelli

who harbored dreams of adding Hawai'i to the empire. His sentiments were well and publicly known, for which reason the Hawaiian government declined to receive him as the British consul.

At anchor in Honolulu, Paulet inquired immediately who was in
local charge, and directed a letter to "M. Kekuanaoa, Governor of
Woahoo," requiring to know the whereabouts of the king, as he
would conduct his business only with him, and whether he had been
sent for, as otherwise Paulet intended to take his ship to find him.
"As we were not informed of the business," Kekuanaoa replied, "we
have not yet sent for the king. . . . He is at Wailuku, on the east side of
Maui. In case the wind is favorable, he may be expected in 6 days."[10]

Summoned again from Maui, Kamehameha III had every reason to be confused. He was now thirty, he had surrendered his attachment to the former life and was now a serious (although often
not sober) monarch. In the previous four years he had done everything that the Americans had asked of him. First Richards and then
Judd had resigned from the mission to become his advisers, and
under their guidance he had granted his people a declaration of
rights and a constitution. Richards he had sent abroad with the
scholarly Timothy Ha'alilio, and they were making progress in winning a joint recognition of Hawaiian sovereignty from Britain,
France, and the United States. But now another frigate was in Honolulu Harbor ready to roll out her guns.

The king informed Paulet that Dr. Judd would speak for him,
but Paulet refused to see him. Instead he responded with a list of
demands; if they were not met by four o'clock the next day, he
would open fire on Honolulu: The attachment on Richard Charlton's property was to be lifted at once, and conveyance made to him
of all land he claimed, with payment of damages; recognition of
Simpson as consul; no imprisonment in irons of any British subject,
unless the crime he was accused of would be a felony in England;
and retrial of land disputes before new juries, one-half of whom
were to be English subjects approved by the consul.

Residents took Paulet's threat of violence seriously. When an empty brig was towed out to shelter British residents, "the streets were crowded with carts containing money chests, Book Safes, Trunks, Personal Clothing, &c. all hastening toward the wharfs to be placed on board of the ships."[11] At the same time an eighteen-gun American sloop-of-war, the USS *Boston*, offered asylum to American residents, the commander having no instructions about what to do in such an event. The king pointed out that he had ministers in London to negotiate all such matters at that very time, a fact that carried equally little weight.

"Some of the demands which you have laid before us," the king wrote coldly, "are of a nature calculated seriously to embarrass our feeble government, by contravening the laws established for the benefit of all. . . . We shall comply with your demands, but we must do so under protest." Flushed with victory (notwithstanding the king's sending a personal note of protest to Queen Victoria), Acting Consul Simpson then added new demands: one hundred thousand dollars in indemnity, reversal of court verdicts by royal decree without retrial, the king's personal endorsement of Charlton's lease, and more.

While much commentary has assessed the French bullying and thuggery, Laura Judd was equally shocked by Lord Paulet's conduct:

> Daily interviews with the king were demanded, and granted, only to pour upon him insult upon insult. Decisions in the courts were required to be reversed; claims to large tracts of valuable land to be confirmed; and a great amount of hypothetical damages demanded. The king was neither judge nor constable, and was utterly ignorant of the facts in many of the cases brought before him. . . . The demands which the defenseless king was obliged to acknowledge, ran up in a few days to about eighty thousand dollars, quite enough to cripple the nation. The ship-of-war was brought around, so that the mouths of her guns yawned continually upon the town.[12]

Nearly two weeks after the *Carysfort's* arrival, it became obvious that what Simpson wanted, with Paulet's guns behind him, was for the king to cede the islands to Great Britain. The cabinet split over what to do. Some urged defiance: "Let them fire." Others wondered who would pay for the American property that was sure to be destroyed. They considered ceding the country to France, but that was an even uglier prospect; perhaps they could place the country in trust with France and the United States jointly, but either case would only provoke a forcible seizure by Britain. Or rather, a seizure by Simpson and Paulet, which surely the British government would not allow—and that was where it rested. They would have to depend on London to redress this hideous conduct. After much anguish Kamehameha III pronounced, "I will not die by piecemeal. . . . I will yield the breath of my kingdom, and trust . . . to the magnanimity of the British government to redress the wrong and restore my rights."[13] Even this step the king felt he had to clear with Paulet, and on the evening of February 24 Paulet agreed that if the islands were ceded provisionally, he would not consider an appeal to London to be a hostile act.[14]

A ceremony was agreed for the next day, at the fort. In making the news public it was ironic, almost comical, that Kauikeaouli used the high oratory of the ancient chiefs to express his own powerlessness. "Hear ye! I make known to you that I am in perplexity by reason of difficulties into which I have been brought without cause. Therefore, I have given away the life of the land . . . but my rule over you, my people, will continue, for I have hope that the life of the land will be restored when my conduct is justified." Simpson and Paulet were furious with him. The Hawaiian flag was lowered, and the *Carysfort's* band played "God Save the Queen" as the Union Jack was raised. Then, at the special request of a female British resident, they also played "Isle of Beauty, Fare Thee Well," which Laura Judd took as "a refined cruelty, which could only emanate from a woman."[15]

After the cession, Kamehameha III repaired to Maui in grief.

"Every avenue of communication with the king or foreign countries was most jealously watched and guarded by his lordship," and Paulet prevented any criticism of his coup reaching the outside world. He made himself head of a government commission, in conjunction with the king or his deputy, which proved to be Dr. Judd, and others named by Paulet. He, however, proved to be a less accomplished plotter than he imagined. He requisitioned three Hawaiian government schooners to undertake his business. One of them, the *Hooikaika*, renamed *Albert*, he sent to the fleet at San Blas, Panama, with Simpson on board to flesh out the written report to Adm. Richard Darton Thomas, the squadron chief. The *Hooikaika* belonged to Ladd & Co., which agreed to place the vessel at the disposal of Paulet's commission if he would allow them to carry out a previously chartered errand to return specie to them from San Blas, and allow their agent on board to accompany it.

Paulet readily agreed, never suspecting that Ladd & Co.'s agent, James F. B. Marshall, would really be in the service of the king. With Dr. Judd involved in the scheme, "dispatches, prepared in the silence of midnight in the royal tomb, with Ka'ahumanu's coffin for a table, were sent off in canoes from distant points of the island; and once, when the king's signature was required, he came down in a schooner and landed *incognito* at Waikiki." By such means information of the takeover was sent to Washington, London, and the British squadron chief, but throughout the spring and half the summer Judd and the cabinet had no word what effect their effort might have had.

Paulet's commission, meanwhile, assumed a ham-handed sort of government. More than 150 trials were reversed, with natives put off their land as it was awarded to English residents. Paulet recruited a new native constabulary, named it the Queen's Regiment, and ordered Judd to pay them out of local finances, which Judd declined to do, provoking a new crisis; Judd resigned, and the king declined to name a replacement, placing the entire responsibility in English hands. To all the Calvinists, the nadir of Paulet's visitation was his constructive decriminalizing of prostitution, which, according to the American seamen's chaplain, "resulted in a veritable flood of immorality" at the fort[16] (perhaps one reason that Paulet's sailors, according to an observer a few years before, were devoted to him). The humiliated king had no choice but to allow it.

Finally, on July 25, residents in Honolulu saw the native alert from Diamond Head of a sail sighted, and soon, "an immense man-of-war hove in sight, floating the flag of an English rear admiral."[17] She was HMS *Dublin*, a ship of the line mounting fifty guns, the flag was that of Adm. Richard Thomas, commander in chief of the British Pacific Fleet. Thomas was sixty-five, having served in the Royal Navy since 1790. After making suitable inquiries, and with Lord Aberdeen's more enlightened statement of policy in hand, Admiral Thomas wrote the king that

> the Commander-in-Chief of Her Britannic Majesty's ships and vessels in the Pacific . . . as the highest local representative . . . hereby declares and makes manifest that he does not accept of the Provisional Cession of the Hawaiian Islands, but that he considers His Majesty Kamehameha III the legitimate King of those islands: and he assures His Majesty that the sentiments of his Sovereign towards him are those of unvarying friendship and esteem, that Her Majesty sincerely desires King Kame-hameha to be treated as an independent sovereign, leaving the administration of justice in his own hands.[18]

At 9:30 in the morning of July 31, 1843, Thomas and his entourage met the king and his entourage at the fort, where the British flag was lowered and the Hawaiian flag once again raised to thundering cannons and pealing bells. Paulet, most pointedly not invited to the ceremony, had destroyed all the Hawaiian flags he could confiscate, so Thomas had a new one sewn together on board the *Dublin*.[19] The speeches were not recorded, but one of the king's sentiments was subsequently rendered, *Ua mau ka ea o ka aina i ka pono*, or, "The life of the land is preserved in righteousness," which many years later became the motto of the state of Hawaii. Given the vagaries of translating from Hawaiian, other shades of meaning may be equally valid, especially that of Hawaii's first chief justice, William Little Lee, who rendered a slightly different version: "The life of the land is preserved *by* righteousness." About ten thousand people witnessed the ceremony. "The soldiers had made sure to take care of their actions . . . twice they encircled the King, with beloved acknowledgment to him. They saluted him often with gunfire, marching here and there."[20]

Afternoon saw a service of thanksgiving at the missionaries' Kawaiaha'o Church, which had undergone a stunning transformation. It stood on the site of a former spring that belonged to a high chiefess named Ha'o—*Ka wai a Ha'o*, the "water of Ha'o." Built to the design of Hiram Bingham, beginning in 1836 and finishing in 1842 in place of the grass church rose a monumental edifice of fourteen thousand half-ton blocks of coral cut from the Honolulu reef. Reminiscent of medieval peasants laboring for years on the great cathedrals of Europe, *kanakas* had dived from ten to twenty feet deep with hand tools to chisel the blocks, and raise and transport them to the mission compound. It was a suitably magnificent structure in which to celebrate the redemption of the kingdom.

Ceremonies done, the court retired to the king's new summer house, Kaniakapupu, a substantial residence of lava-rock walls built high in the Nu'uanu Valley above Honolulu. There the event was celebrated with a gargantuan luau attended by at least two thousand people. In the forest the tables bearing the food were chronicled as thirty-two fathoms long and two fathoms wide, and they creaked beneath sixty pigs, three hundred chickens, forty turkeys, fifty-three ducks, and about seven hundred fish, in addition to poi, sweet potatoes, coconuts, and fruit—all supplied by the chiefs, both the king's vassals and those of Kekuanaoa. Gerrit Judd, now one of the landed class, contributed two pigs, eight fish, and seven measures of poi.[21] Part of the fun at the luau was a performance of a "Restoration Anthem," contributed by Rev. Edwin Oscar Hall of the Seventh Company of missionaries, sung to "God Save the King." It had three verses, one praising the king, one praising Admiral Thomas ("Quick o'er the wave"), and the third one praising God.[22] Before Thomas and the *Dublin* sailed away, he hosted the king at a review of the ships in the harbor, with thundering cannon salutes all around. In perhaps the most eloquent testimony to the importance of the occasion, the king was seen to be happy—and sober.

This hopeful chapter of Hawaiian history had yet one sour note that was largely missed in the general jubilation. There is evidence that Admiral Thomas, while accepting the homage of the islanders, had effected the restoration less out of outrage at what Paulet had done, or from a sense of justice. Likely he acted more out of pique that Paulet, an upstart young enough to be his son, had gained such an inflated view of his own importance that he undertook to correspond directly with London rather than through the fleet commander—himself. When William Richards returned to Hawai'i he imparted to Samuel Castle that he had been told—he did not remember if by Lord Aberdeen himself or by his undersecretary—"that if Admiral Thomas had not restored the flag, the British government would not have done so."[23]

Independence now seemed even more precious, and it became even clearer what kind of imperial bullet Hawai'i had dodged when word came of the fate of Tahiti—the French had seized it and declared a protectorate. "Poor Queen Pomare," committed Laura Judd to her journal, "is dispossessed of power and property. The people are strongly attached to the Protestant faith, and numbers refuse submission to Roman Catholic masters, and have fled to the mountains. They will doubtless be hunted down and compelled to surrender."[24] She proved to be correct but had no idea that it would take the French four years and heavy losses to secure their empire in the South Pacific.

The American commissioner, George Brown, newly on station, echoed her sentiments when the French frigate Boussole arrived from Tahiti . . . with the news of the taking possession of the Society Islands by the French, in complete sovereignty, & the dethronement of the Queen. Poor soul I pity her, but this never would have happened had the English government & Eng missionaries done what they were in duty bound to do. It seems that the French admiral arrived there with a squadron on the 2d Octr with the expressed intention of landing the French Commissioner, and informing the Queen that the French King had accepted the Protectorate of her islands. But the Queen refusing to haul down the flag which had been given her by the Capt of the Eng frigate Vindictive, the French admiral chose to consider it an insult, and she still refusing, after representations & threats were made to her, he landed his troops & took possession of *all the islands.*[25]

It seemed as though the Pacific had gone mad with imperial seizure.

9. A Nation Among Nations

The Honolulu of the mid-1840s, at the height of the American whaling boom, was a far cry from the dusty fishing village of a half century before. On January 9, 1847, the *Polynesian* published an assay of the city that was more detailed than a census would have been. They counted 1,347 residential dwellings, 875 of grass, 345 of adobe, and 127 of wood, stone (which meant cut coral), or a mixture of both. None of them were of brick; Hawaiian clay lacked the binder necessary for brickmaking so adobe was substituted, and those walls had to be maintained, because they melted beneath the rain, leaving piles of formless goo "ankle-deep" around their perimeters. Of the twelve finest stone houses, two belonged to the former missionaries who entered government service, Gerrit Judd and William Richards. Most of the rest were owned by chiefs.

The *Polynesian* estimated the population of the city at ten thousand, of whom 617 were "foreigners," mostly American, followed by British, about a dozen French, and a scattering of other nationalities, plus 472 foreign-born who had become naturalized subjects of the king. In addition there were about a hundred members of a new class of people loosely called "floaters," native Hawaiians who had abandoned their sharecropping for the chiefs to move into the city, work for wages, and discover a kind of independence they had never known before. For those who could afford it, foreign and native, there were four hotels located *mauka* of Hotel Street, where a comfortable room and board cost seven dollars a week, somewhat less than in a private boardinghouse.

Centered in the city's commercial district, the foreigners' various occupations made Honolulu, apart from being the only city in the central Pacific, a cosmopolitan crossroads worthy of its geographical importance. There were thirty-eight carpenters, twelve masons, and five painters, who stayed busy from the $170,000 of new construction that was under way. Professionally there were five doctors, five lawyers, two watchmakers, ten printers, and a bookbinder. Eight tailors, nine tinkers, and two barbers kept the public looking good; seven blacksmiths kept them mounted or rolling. Two pilots got the ships through the reef and into the harbor, to disgorge their cargoes at five commercial wharves and one government wharf, much of it destined for the eight commercial warehouses, most of which touted red fireproof slate roofs.

Also crowding the city were the "country people," the rural *kanakas* who came to vend their wares. The Honolulu police arrest record tells an interesting tale of the relationship between these natives and the law, actual crime as opposed to moral crime, and the *kanakas'* success in bridging that gulf: Between April 1846 and April 1847, the police arrested 2 natives for polluting a stream with human bones, 4 for attempting to pray others to death, 3 for blasphemy, 39 for breaking the Sabbath, 43 for drunkenness, 48 for fighting, 57 for gambling, 211 for theft, and 806 for fornication. But when the natives were not stealing or trying to have sex, their vending stalls were located *makai* (on the seaward side) of what became King Street, or they just importuned pedestrians. Their chickens averaged thirty cents each, ducks fifty cents, turkeys up to a dollar depending on their size. Local produce was cheap—Irish potatoes as little as two dollars a barrel, oranges two cents each—but dairy products were dear: milk twenty-five cents per half gallon, butter thirty cents a pound, eggs averaging fifty cents per dozen. Fresh beef, though, was just six cents per pound, about half the cost of mutton.

For construction, lumber came in all precut sizes from the Pacific Northwest, as did premilled doors, windows, and moldings, kegs of nails, and window weights—enough iron to make a precontact native faint. Mariners also found boathooks, whale line, blubber hooks, sail canvas and huge curving needles to mend them, even anchors. Seamen who came into port sick or hurt found treatment in the American Hospital, which treated 156 of them in the previous year, or the British Hospital, which doctored 63. French sailors doubtless preferred the French Hospital, which treated 9.

Of consumer goods, there were hats and caps as disparate as Glengarry and Guayaquil; dry goods from Chinese satin to Scottish cambric to English wool to American duck; and a world market of ladies' fashion, including unmentionables of the finest make. Gentlemen could purchase cigars from Manila or even Havana, and if they could withstand the missionary glare they could choose wine from Bordeaux, Madeira, Sicily, and more—or carbonated sodas for the temperate. The general stores were a riot of playing cards, bath salts, writing paper, steel pens, lead pencils, sealing wax, riding tack, including bridles and whips, soap, glue, spermaceti candles, and Jew's harps.[1]

To administer the cosmopolitan new capital the king provided a vastly modernized government, but that had been a hard study and he had not done it alone. In fact, it was Hawai'i's good fortune that during this time the chiefs still held real power. After his adolescent rebellion against the oversight of Kina'u, they eventually had enough of his self-indulgence. They jailed his Tahitian favorite, Kaomi, for a time, and in other ways impressed on the king that it was time to live up to his responsibilities. Once broken to harness, and even while he was suffering varying degrees of lovesickness for his sister, he undertook the transition from Kauikeaouli to King Kamehameha III.

Decades of foreign contact, years of close observation of the missionaries, and the rapid Westernization of their society convinced the chiefs that, until they codified their laws in a Western way, *haoles* would continue to act as they pleased and appeal to their own governments for protection from what, in their eyes, amounted to no more than tribal custom. On January 5, 1835, the king promulgated a penal code prescribing punishments for homicide, theft, adultery, fraud, and drunkenness. The chiefs also desired to have their rights and responsibilities to foreign nations spelled out, but no one in the islands was competent to advise them in matters of law. Through William Richards they requested the ABCFM in 1836 to send them someone to instruct and advise them in politics; that brought a quick refusal, as it clearly crossed the Board's line against political involvement. So at the king's request Richards himself resigned from the mission to become royal adviser, translator, and instructor in "political economy," starting in July 1838. The king and *kuhina nui*—Kina'u until her death and Kekauluohi thereafter—and the council of chiefs heard Richards's lessons with focus and attention.

Their decrees began to take Western form: "Be it enacted by the King and Chiefs of the Sandwich Islands, in council assembled. . . ." And then on June 7, 1839, Kamehameha III issued the Declaration of Rights, a first and a signal turning point for the kingdom. While the document was written under Richards's general direction, much of the work was carried out by Boaz Mahune, a graduate of the Lahainaluna Seminary. He had become recognized as one of Hawai'i's ablest scholars, he was appointed secretary to the king, and he refined the paper several times after consultations with king and council. Thus one important torch was passed in the Hawaiian Declaration of Rights: Hawai'i now had its own native acolytes ready to claim and own Western political philosophy and adapt it to the islands' culture and circumstances. The philosophy of the document was unmistakably Western, even American, even as its language was just as unmistakably Hawaiian: "God hath made of one blood all nations of men, to dwell on the face of the earth in unity and blessedness. God has also bestowed certain rights alike on all men, and all chiefs, and all people of all lands. These are some of the rights He has given alike to every man and every chief: life, limb, liberty, the labor of his hands, and productions of his mind."

Until this document the common *kanaka*, while not technically a serf because he was not bound to the land, yet had no redress against a chief, except to leave and seek the patronage of some other chief. The Hawaiian Declaration of Rights opened a chasm away from the old days that could never be bridged again; there was good reason that the paper became known as Hawai'i's Magna Carta.

Scarcely a month after its promulgation, Captain Laplace and the frigate *L'Artémise* sallied into Honolulu and distracted the country with his raid in promotion of Catholicism and French wine. Once that annoyance was past, it was time to fulfill the Declaration's promise with an actual constitution. This was brought forth on October 8, 1840, another preeminently Western document in which the king laid down his absolute power. He and the *kuhina nui* still shared executive authority—a uniquely Hawaiian safeguard against runaway tyranny—with lesser powers accorded four island governors: those of Hawai'i; Maui and the leeward islands; O'ahu; and Kaua'i and its dependencies. The instrument also provided for a representative house, elected by the people, giving the *kanakas* a voice in government for the first time, and for a supreme court, comprising the king, *kuhina nui*, and four judges to be appointed by the lower house. The existing council of chiefs was rolled over into a house of nobles, of whom fourteen would perform a function roughly similar to any upper house of a legislature. Significantly, it included women as well as men, a continuation of the traditionally meaningful role that women played in ruling circles. Among them, in addition to the *kuhina nui*, were Keohokalole, the mother of the Kalakaua dynasty, and Hoapiliwahine, recently the widow of the solid Hoapili.

The 1840 constitution also contained a subtle but important change of style. Without remark or explanation, the official appellation "Sandwich Islands" was quietly dropped in favor of "Hawaiian Islands," a permanent alteration that reflected both the native preference that had always been in use, and American satisfaction to dispense with this first tie to England. The week before the constitution's promulgation, the *Polynesian*'s American editor, J. J. Jarves, published his opinion that "nothing so denationalizes a people than to change their language. . . . the natives have ever used 'Hawaii nei' as applicable to these islands," and Jarves maintained that their sense of patriotism should be "studiously encouraged."[2]

The document had important practical consequences beyond structuring the government, and even beyond providing an avenue of redress for the *maka'ainana* for the first time. The new constitution gave foreigners, and more to the point foreign governments, confidence in the country's judicial system, and in fact "was a key element in keeping the sovereignty of the Hawaiian monarch intact."[3]

The growing influence of foreigners and particularly Americans in the bureaucracy during the rule of Kamehameha III demonstrated, on the one hand, the king's desire to staff his administration with the efficient and the able. On the other hand, it also made clear just how limited the reservoir of talent really was. In 1842 the king prevailed on the multiskilled Gerrit Judd to follow Richards in resigning from the mission to be his adviser, and through subsequent years others in the foreign community referred to Judd with some jaundice as "Minister of Everything," as he held the portfolios of foreign minister (November 1843 to March 1845), interior minister (March 1845 to February 1846), and finance minister (April 1846 to September 1853). Richard Armstrong followed still later to superintend the kingdom's school system.

Help was also welcome from abroad. One rootless American to show up in the islands in 1844 was a lawyer named John Ricord, a French-descended native of New York, who was made attorney general of Hawai'i less than two weeks after his arrival. He had in the Republic of Texas lately served as private secretary to President Sam Houston, for whom he had undertaken sensitive confidential missions and was later appointed a district attorney. He owed his appointment as attorney general, however, more to the fact that he was at that time the only lawyer in the islands. He renounced his American citizenship to become a Hawaiian subject, and gave the country his professional effort for the next two years. While Ricord hardly came to Hawaii with professional references in his pocket, Judd brought him into the administration anyway, partly for the reason that if the only lawyer in the kingdom did not work for the government, he might well be employed against it.[4] When another itinerant attorney drifted through, it was William Little Lee of New York, and he was made chief justice. Help was where the king could find it. James Jackson Jarves was only twenty-two when he materialized in the islands in 1840, on the run from marital and business failures, but he was a good writer and effective newspaper editor. His *Polynesian* "became the official organ of the government."[5]

Indispensable help in the realm of foreign affairs arrived in the person of Dr. R. C. (Robert Crichton) Wyllie, a rail-thin yet room-filling Scot who could maneuver in any intrigue. Indeed it was later written of him that "no drama in the Pacific was complete without the fastidious, meticulous and verbose Scots busybody."[6] In January 1844, HM sloop-of-war *Hazard*, eighteen guns, dropped anchor at Honolulu with a new British consul on board, William Miller. That gentleman continued on to present his credentials throughout the South Pacific, leaving behind in Hawaii his physician friend, the investor and adventurer Wyllie. He was forty-five, from Ayrshire, Scotland, and fresh from disappointment in the attempt to seize California as forfeited collateral from Mexico and make it a British colony. He acted as British consul until Miller returned fourteen months later, at which time Kamehameha III relieved Judd of his portfolio as foreign minister and handed it to Wyllie. He cast a long shadow over Hawai'i's international relations for the next twenty years that he ran the Foreign Ministry—and not in ways that the Americans often liked.

Captain Laplace's humiliating sortie convinced the government that they needed to take steps to place Hawai'i in a more dignified posture with the Western powers, and another visiting dignitary had just that idea. He was Sir George Simpson, the more circumspect and sensible cousin of Alexander Simpson the would-be empire builder, and governor of the Hudson's Bay Company. His suggestion, accepted with alacrity, was to send a deputation abroad to negotiate treaties of recognition with the powers, in furtherance of which Simpson would speak favorably for them in London. The two commissioners who sailed away on July 18, 1842, were William Richards and the king's private secretary, also a member of the king's Treasury Board and a recent founder of the Hawaiian Historical Society, Timothy Ha'alilio.

On board the steamboat *Globe*, bound for the United States, Richards got a cold reminder of political realities there. He had now been ministering and working in Hawai'i so long that it must have struck him as a dissonant echo from his premissionary days. Word of the incident filtered down to the Royal School, where the last of the Kamehamehas, thirteen-year-old Princess Bernice Pauahi, wrote incredulously that on board the ship, as she had heard:

Before they sat down to breakfast, Mr. Richards went to the office window to procure two tickets for breakfast. But the Captain's secretary gave him 1½. He returned the half ticket and requested two. The man told [him] to give the half to Haalilio (his servant). Mr. Richards said to him, "He is not my servant, I am his. He is an ambassador from the king of the S. I. to the President of the United States, and has been received as such."

"That does not make any difference," said the man. "We do not wish any colored man to sit down at the table."[7]

At their first stop, in Washington, they spent almost the entire month of December lobbying for recognition. President John Tyler and his secretary of state, Daniel Webster, were besieged by highly contentious territorial expansion questions in Texas and Oregon, in which the British were vitally interested, and they were not anxious to make a pronouncement about Hawai'i, with its strong British ties. Eventually Richards stated that if the United States would not guarantee Hawaiian independence, he would have no choice but to allow the country to become a British protectorate. (Interestingly enough, that was the same card that the Republic of Texas played to win annexation at almost the same time.) Two days after Christmas, Richards and Ha'alilio obtained an audience with Tyler and his cabinet, and three days after that they won not a treaty but an unequivocal statement that U.S. ties of culture and commerce to Hawai'i gave it a greater interest there than any other country's, and that "no power ought either to take possession of the islands as a conquest, or for the purpose of colonization, and that no power ought to seek for any undue control over the existing Government."[8] Tyler, in effect, extended the Monroe Doctrine over the islands.

With the first part of their mission accomplished, Richards and Ha'alilio journeyed on to London, where Sir George Simpson could smooth their way with Lord Aberdeen. Sadly for their cause, Richard Charlton was also on his way there, spreading poison about how the Hawaiian government had swindled him out of his leases. They reached London on February 18, 1843; Simpson's testimonial on behalf of the government, plus the favorable interest of such figures as Belgium's King Leopold, who was interested in investing in Ladd & Co.'s colonization scheme, persuaded Aberdeen that official recognition was in order. The French foreign minister, François Guizot, was prepared to follow suit, but then the shocking news arrived of Lord Paulet's seizure of the islands.

The famously unflappable Aberdeen would have realized that Admiral Thomas must not have received, and thus could not have shared with Paulet, his mild instructions to the Admiralty on how

to proceed with Hawai'i. It took until autumn to get everything in
order, but on November 28, 1843, France and Great Britain jointly
recognized the Hawaiian kingdom. The United States declined the
invitation to join the declaration, the new secretary of state, John C.
Calhoun, citing American policy against "entangling alliances."
The United States concurred; it just would rather not sign. Richards
and Ha'alilio waited for the Atlantic storm season to pass, then returned to America in the spring of 1844, and took ship for the
arduous voyage to Hawai'i in November. Ha'alilio was probably
suffering from consumption, and died off the coast of New York on
December 3. His body was carried on to Honolulu, where Richards
arrived in March, two years and nine months after they left.

During Richards's absence, Gerrit Judd had advanced as the man
on whom Kamehameha III most leaned for advice. As perennially
good-natured, hopeful, and earnest as Laura Judd's journal entries
were, her husband veered in a different direction. As a physician he
had done much good treating the natives in the attic of the big
house, but since he resigned from his missionary post and entered
the king's service, the "Minister of Everything" had, in the perception
of many, grown fond of power.[9] Crossing him could cost an appli-
cant any chance of success in his commercial aspirations. Under the
guise of being busy he quickly sorted through who was worth his
attention, and was dismissive of those who did not pass the bar.
The business community and the foreign representatives all took an
immense dislike to him, but he only became more powerful after
the death of Richards on November 7, 1847. Richards was fifty-five,
and he left his wife and children in such hard circumstances that
the government granted her a house site and an annuity of eight
hundred dollars per year.

   There was another loss that year. The American consul, George
Brown, had been persona non grata for some months when Anthony Ten Eyck arrived to replace him, and Brown finally left for

home. "He sailed," wrote Laura Judd later, "*via* China, and there is every reason to fear that the vessel went down in a typhoon, as nothing is yet heard of it."[10] Her fear was well founded: George Brown's numerous letters to "Dear Wife and Children" had made it safely home; he was lost at sea.

Richards's death was not the only shakeup in the cabinet. John Ricord, the attorney general from Texas, wished to return home but he found himself a man without a country when Ten Eyck told him that he could not simply renounce his renunciation of American citizenship and get it back, and therefore the consul could not protect Ricord from his creditors, who were after him for nearly two thousand dollars. The rest of the cabinet thought well enough of him to float him a loan, albeit on strict terms and with a resolution that it wasn't to become a habit. Ricord then did a very unlawyerly thing: He absconded to San Francisco. (In later years he tendered his services to the king of Siam, and while en route to Liberia in 1861 died in Paris in the home of his uncle, who was physician to Napoleon III.[11])

On February 1, 1848, a new French consul arrived in Honolulu, Guillaume Patrice Dillon. France had already healed some of the previous damage to relations between the two countries by repaying the twenty thousand dollars that Laplace had impounded, and now Dillon bore a gift, a gigantic portrait of his king, Louis-Philippe. Two weeks later a parade left the French consulate for the wooden pavilion of the 'Iolani Palace: brass band, color bearers, a dozen sailors bearing the huge painting, Monsignor Maigret and other clergy from the Catholic mission, and most of the French residents of Honolulu. In the palace Kamehameha III "took Mr. Dillon's hand with much emotion." Dillon's instructions from the Foreign Ministry at last began to resemble Lord Aberdeen's British policy of many years: "Avoid in your conduct any show of pugnaciousness. It is fitting that moderation . . . consolidate the fruits of firmness." None in the company knew that Louis-Philippe was at that moment in the middle of being deposed and exiled, but the transition to the Second Republic was not expected to cause any wrinkle in the new friendship.

Several months' experience of R. C. Wyllie at the Hawaiian Foreign Ministry and Judd at Finance changed Dillon's attitude. "Two thirds of the time," he wrote, "my inclination is only to laugh at the fuss that is made about this Lilliputian kingdom [with its] negro King whose life is mostly wasted in orgies with stable-grooms."[12] No fewer than seven times did Dillon ask for a French warship to call at Honolulu and vindicate him.

Finally, in August 1849, the frigate *Poursuivante*, fifty-two guns, under command of Rear Adm. Louis-François-Marie-Nicolas Legoarant de Tromelin, sixty-three years old with nearly fifty in the navy, commander in chief of the French forces in the Pacific, entered Hawaiian waters. Accompanying him was the corvette steamer *Gassendi*, mounting seven shell guns, which he had just fortuitously encountered. Having been apprised of Dillon's many complaints, Tromelin called at the Big Island, met the king and Dillon's special enemy, Gerrit Judd. "Nothing in their reception," the admiral wrote, "could lead me to suppose that anything more existed than a difference of opinion." He arrived at Honolulu on August 12, traded cannon salutes with the fort, and traded cordial visits with Governor Kekuanaoa and Foreign Minister Wyllie. But when Dillon came aboard and delivered a fusillade of particulars, he convinced Legoarant de Tromelin that the honor of France was at stake.

On August 19 the king returned from Waihea aboard his yacht *Kamehameha* and walked into a hornet's nest. Two days later the sixteen-guns sloop-of-war USS *Preble* entered the harbor, two and a half months out of Hong Kong and crippled by the loss of twenty-one crewmen from dysentery. Kekuanaoa quickly got the remaining sick on shore and into a makeshift hospital at the armory, next to the fort.

"The King and Government of the Hawaiian Islands," wrote Wyllie to Tromelin two days later in response to a list of French demands, "are not aware that there are matters pending between

them and the Republic of France. . . . If, however, Admiral Tromelin and M. Dillon are of the opinion that there are any matters . . . it
would please His Majesty if they would specify them." The French
declared this an insult. "The time for deliberation is past. . . . In
case justice is not done, [we] will employ the means at [our] disposal to obtain complete redress."

This time the French list of demands had ten items, from grand
concepts such as renewed guarantee of the freedom of religion, all
the way down to refunding twenty-five dollars to a French whaling
ship taxed for entering the harbor with alcoholic spirits, and punish-
ing certain schoolboys who had disrupted Mass. Some of the
demands seemed gratuitous—the removal of Kekuanaoa as governor of Oʻahu for allowing police to make an arrest in the priests'
residence—and even touched on the bizarre, requiring installation
of French as an official language of commerce in the country. Catherine Lee, wife of Chief Justice William Little Lee, wrote indig-
nantly: "There are not a dozen French on all Hawaii, and to grant
this claim would not only require a host of interpreters, but would
afford every other nation a right to make a similar demand."[13] Two
of those resident dozen Frenchmen were merchants, one of them a
tavernkeeper, but no French commercial vessel had dropped anchor in five years to supply them. The outrageous nature of this last
particular demand may have had a more personal impetus. Of all
the things in Hawaiʻi that offended Dillon, none was worse than
Foreign Minister Wyllie, whom the French consul characterized as
an adventurer and, "so long as he is in office, a permanent insult to
France." Wyllie was not fluent in French, and Dillon wrote his windy
invective only in French, which Wyllie had to labor after hours to
translate. Insisting on French as an official commercial language was
a sure way to get under his skin.[14]

The impasse grew angrier, and Kauikeaouli ordered that no resistance be offered if the French started shooting, that everyone be
cautioned to say nothing that could be taken as another insult. But
there was to be no cooperation, either, even to opening a door. His

officials should "allow the French, if they choose, to take the keys out of their pockets, but on no account to give them voluntarily."

On August 25, Dillon lowered the flag from his consulate, threatening retribution if any damage was done in his absence, and boarded the *Poursuivante* for safety during the coming action. On board USS *Preble*, Cmdr. James Glynn observed *Gassendi* train her guns on the fort, and realized an errant shot from the ship could land among his stricken sailors at the armory. Glynn quickly interposed his vessel between *Gassendi* and the fort, threatening to maul the corvette if she opened fire—it was a bold bluff, for Glynn did not have enough men left to operate the guns. But it worked. Instead, Tromelin landed boatloads of armed sailors and marines. They stormed the fort and had an easy victory, as it had been evacuated and was tended only by Kekuanaoa and the marshal of the kingdom, Warren Goodale. The marines made patriotic work of spiking the cannons, smashing firearms, and throwing a huge store of gunpowder into the harbor, which blackened the water. King and cabinet waited out the storm in the palace, uncertain whether they were to be raided as well. That did not happen, but the French marines utterly vandalized Kekuanaoa's house, which was located within the fort, despoiling it even of keepsakes of his late wife, Kina'u.

In the meantime, through the French fathers, Tromelin had handbills posted in Hawaiian, announcing that he had come in peace to discuss why the terms of the previous agreement were not being observed, but he had been obliged by intransigence and insults of the Hawaiian government to vindicate the honor of France. When Tromelin finally sailed away he took as prizes a number of ancient artifacts, and the king's yacht, *Kamehameha*. The entirety of the foreign community was appalled. "These gallant Franks," fumed Catherine Lee, "perpetrated their outrage without a finger being raised against them. . . . Every foreign Consul sent in a protest against their proceedings, and they left loaded with the execration of the entire community not excepting their own countrymen."[15] At least when Tromelin sailed, he took Dillon with him, so some good came from the visitation. A travel writer on the scene a few years later accurately assessed the incident when he wrote that the French "affected to spring out of a misunderstanding . . . but, in reality, [they were] to gratify the consummate vanity of France in the extension of her territory in the Pacific Ocean."[16]

The bill for the French vandalism surpassed a hundred thousand dollars. A surprised French government was at first disposed to consider it sympathetically, but then changed its mind and never compensated Hawai'i for the destruction. Dillon, at least, was cashiered for wrecking the rapprochement that the government had been trying to effect with the islands.

Upon reflection, it occurred to king and council that since Richards's and Ha'alilio's mission to Europe and the United States to win recognition had been so successful, perhaps a new effort could get to the bottom of the French trouble and collect the hundred thousand dollars in damage that Tromelin had wrought. Accordingly the government dispatched the valuable Gerrit Judd, taking with him the king's two eldest nephews, Lot Kapuaiwa, eighteen, and Alexander Liholiho, fourteen, the first two (their older brother having died) in line for the throne. They were veterans of the Royal School, and such a trip would broaden their education in ways that the Boston Parlor could not.

Months in Paris brought no result, and then the unthinkable happened. On December 13, 1850, with Judd and the princes still abroad, residents of Honolulu awoke to find another French warship, the corvette *La Sérieuse*, with a new French commissioner, Louis-Émile Perrin, on board, threatening to resort to the "extraordinary powers" of France if certain demands were not met. It was becoming surreal. This time negotiations dragged on for nearly three months, during which time a new U.S. consul arrived, Luther Severance, but he had no instructions on dealing with renewed French bullying. Neither did the British consul, William Miller.

An American warship in the harbor, the aging but creditable sloop-of-war USS *Vandalia*, eighteen guns, was asked to delay its sailing to protect American interests in case the French started shooting.

Miller's response, when he had one, grievously disappointed the king and council. Britain's 1843 treaty obligations with France, he said, made it unlikely that they could protect the kingdom from French enforcement of their demands. Miller had, however, conferred with Perrin (which the king likely did not regard as good news) and been assured that France had no intent to seize the islands. King and cabinet were not comforted. Of the three great powers netted in Hawaiian affairs, France seemed insane, Britain had acted honorably in restoring the kingdom after the Paulet outrage but was now proving unreliable. That left the United States, which had already recast much of society in its own image and had imparted a constitutional government, but had never made any move to seize the country. And Kamehameha had in his back pocket the statement of the American secretary of state, John M. Clayton, that the United States would protect the islands, even unto war. The very evening of their last frustrating interview with Miller, the king signed a new decree placing the country under the protection and flag of the United States—but only provisionally. The document was shown to Luther Severance before being sealed and given to him, to open officially in the event he observed the American flag flying over the fort.

Miller, upon learning of their intention, imparted that the entire direction of the events made him suspect an American plot to get their flag over the islands. He warned the king against even considering annexation to the United States. They are, he said darkly, "very hard upon the natives of the countries they obtain."[17] Miller did not succeed in getting the proclamation withdrawn, but he did succeed in angering the cabinet. Perrin, when he realized he had been outflanked and outgunned, signed an interim agreement with Wyllie and quit the country, returning to France for fresh instruction.

The fact that Kamehameha III first raised the possibility, indeed his willingness, to place the country under U.S. protection, even to be annexed to the United States if need be, ignited energetic discussion on the subject in the United States. Commissioner Severance loaded the American consul, Elisha Allen, with dispatches and sent him to Washington to get the best clarification he could on the U.S. posture toward Hawai'i. The prospect of extending Manifest Destiny halfway across the Pacific enthralled some newspapers, especially on the West Coast. The Millard Fillmore administration wanted no such thing, however. Daniel Webster was back at the State Department, having succeeded Clayton, and he issued a policy statement that the United States still honored its 1842 agreement with Hawai'i in recognizing its independence, and had no territorial ambition there. At the same time, he wrote, the United States "can never consent to see those islands taken possession of by either of the great commercial powers of Europe." And Webster bound the United States to maintain its Pacific Fleet at such strength and readiness as to vindicate Hawaiian integrity, if called upon.

In the conquest of paradise, much has been written of American avarice in annexing Hawai'i later in the century. Much less has been written of the fact that here, in the first instance, it was French thuggery and British vacillation that drove Hawai'i into American arms.

10. The Great *Mahele*

R. C. Wyllie took time from his duties as foreign minister to
contribute to other civic endeavors, one of which was assembling the nucleus of a national archive. One document
that fell into his possession was the diary of Francisco de Paula
Marín. Wyllie became so taken with Marín's botanical legacy that he
helped to establish the Royal Hawaiian Agricultural Society, contributed papers, and himself established a plantation at Hanalei Bay,
the most sheltered spot on the north shore of Kaua'i. It was a spectacular property, backed by 4,400-foot Namolokama and nineteen
waterfalls that cascaded from the surrounding mountains. There
Wyllie erected a comfortable estate, hired an Austrian manager, and
began planting coffee. The soil and climate, however, were against
him, and when the coffee venture failed he turned to sugarcane.

Even more than agriculture, Wyllie was devoted to history, and
his efforts to collate the papers of the nation were invaluable. For
years "every scrap of paper that came to him or emanated from
him . . . was preserved and backed and sorted into its proper repository, the whole, at his death, forming a voluminous portion of the

Government records."[1] And Wyllie had a full sense of his own importance, keeping a journal and letter books of such mass—at least fifty-eight numbered volumes by the end of his career—as only a Victorian could generate.[2] He fully expected a biography of himself to be written one day, and he committed pages and pages of notes to paper every day, although his handwriting was universally held to be execrable. Kamehameha III and the next two kings relied on him, but the American missionary faction came to revile him, and sensed in him a mortal danger to the Hawai'i they were trying to create.

And the Industrial Age with both its wonders and its pleasures was changing Hawai'i before their eyes. A lighthouse, small and primitive but the kingdom's first, went into operation at Lahaina in the fall of 1840. A sight equally bizarre shocked them late in that year when Hannah Holmes entertained a party of American officers with the ascent of a large hot-air balloon. Also in 1840 the king put his new public school system into operation. To protect public health, a new law went into effect requiring contagious diseases to be reported to the government within twenty-four hours; another one banned unauthorized burials in Honolulu. Some time after, the missionary doctor Dwight Baldwin treated a chief for a curious combination of symptoms; it was the kingdom's first case of leprosy, but he didn't know what it was. A start was made at a public waterworks in Honolulu when fresh water was piped from a source a short distance above the town to a tank near the harbor. Its water was ladled by buckets into the city's first pumping fire engine, and a volunteer fire department was formed.

1845 saw mail service undertaken from San Francisco to Honolulu, although it was spotty; occasioning greater comment was Theophilus Metcalf's opening a daguerreotype studio in the capital, providing patrons with precise photographic likenesses before such a service was available in most of western North America. An even greater commotion greeted the arrival of the first paddle-wheeled steamship, HMS *Cormorant*, in May 1847. The sight of a vessel entering Honolulu Harbor without benefit of sail, slow and stately, its towering wheels barely moving, put the natives "in a state of great excitement," according to one observer.[3]

1847, as a measure of the limits on the influence of the missionaries, also witnessed the inauguration of the 275-seat Thespian Theater, the kingdom's first professional company. As a double bill on September 11 they presented both the melodrama *The Adopted Child* and the farce *Fortune's Frolic*[4]—although a histrionic drama that turned on adoption must have been a curious subject for a population to whom adoption was part of normal daily life. The company folded in only four months, but was quickly replaced by the Royal Hawaiian Theater, which successfully occupied its premises for decades, surrounded by a fence plastered with playbills. For those not so bold as to be seen in a theater, the reading collection in the Seamen's Bethel had now become a functioning public library of more than three hundred books, with a quiet reading room. It was a welcome refuge because the harbors were busier than ever—whale hunting peaked in 1846, when some 746 vessels called at either Honolulu or Lahaina.

Visiting naval and marine officers whose character was elevated above the waterfront nevertheless enjoyed dancing, and a growing urban commercial class, unattached to the scowling missionaries, was happy to provide social occasions for them. And with the missionaries' own proliferating broods of children reaching ages to want to experience more of the world, those Calvinists of the first generation found themselves waging a fighting retreat on the matter of musical entertainment. Foreign Minister Wyllie made himself particularly troublesome to them, hosting the kingdom's first fancy-dress ball at his comfortable Nu'uanu estate, Rosebank. It was a brilliant evening: French chef, German musicians. Governor Kekuanaoa came, incongruously, in Highland attire, but the evening's most splendid costume was counted as that of the Catholic bishop of Honolulu—clothed in his own vestments.

Wyllie sparkled in conversation, he was classically read and witty, but his formidable preparedness for intellectual repartee, while not wasted in Hawai'i, was of limited utility in his international diplomacy because of the kingdom's sheer isolation. He had a chance to shine at the visit of the Danish corvette *Galathea*, which was circumnavigating the globe in furtherance of science and Denmark's commercial interests. Capt. Carl Steen-Andersen Bille was authorized to appoint Danish consuls, and his instructions took particular note of Hawai'i's trade potential. Taking a liberal view of his instructions and favorably impressed by king and court, Bille negotiated an amity and commerce treaty, subject to his government's approval. It contained none of the assumptions of superiority that the British and French kept loading into their documents, and it became a template for treaties that followed with the Hanseatic free cities of Bremen and Hamburg.[5]

Usually, however, Wyllie found it necessary to instruct emissaries and send them abroad with powers to negotiate. Undertaking careful diplomatic minuets from his corner of the globe and making sure that complete understandings had been reached would have been prohibitively time consuming. Mail service still moved at the caprice of wind and wave—and at the sufferance of distracted mariners. Chief Justice William Little Lee discovered that a newspaper sent him by a friend in Buffalo, New York, had undertaken a remarkable journey before reaching him: "From the U.S. it [rounded] Cape Horn and first landed at Valparaiso. From thence it took passage on a Chilean vessel for Tahiti. At Tahiti it exchanged the Chilean vessel for a French Man-of-War, the 'Sarcelle,' and went to Callao and the city of Lima in Peru, and then by the same vessel came with a large American mail to Honolulu. But the stupid Frenchman, forgetting that he had a mail on board, sailed without landing it, and carried the newspaper to Christmas Island, where after an absence of a month, it returned to Honolulu and made a safe landing, all 'tattered and torn.'" But Lee confessed that to his amazement, "I have never had any letters directed to me at the Sandwich Islands miscarry," which was a comfort because, "to lose letters at this distance from home is provoking beyond all measure."[6]

Interisland mail, at least, was soon put on a more regularized basis; in 1851 Hawai'i followed the United States by only four years in the issuance of prepaid postage stamps, an innovation first introduced by the British in 1840. The rate was thirteen cents to send a letter home: five cents for postal handling in Hawai'i, two cents for the ship's captain, and six cents for forwarding in the United States.[7] That paid for letters up to one-half ounce in weight—hence the habit of several missionaries to write two pages of text on one sheet, one written at a right angle to the other, to save paper and avoid additional postage, but they could be maddening to try to read.

When free domestic postage ended in that year, the missionaries saw to it that the legislation provided for natives to continue sending letters without charge, as an encouragement to practice their skills in reading and writing. The postal service was placed under the interior minister, who at that time was Prince Lot Kapuaiwa, who agreed that despite some financial burden to the government, he would endorse free postage for the islanders as "contributing in some degree to the advancement of the nation in civilization." The native Hawaiians, employing their often-demonstrated skill at descrying loopholes, began using the postal service to ship large parcels such as sacks of fruit, with the expectation that the attached letter qualified the whole lot to post for free. A new civil code was enacted in 1859 that imposed a two-cent postal rate for all domestic correspondence, and despite the missionaries' fears that native letter writing would be discouraged, postal use increased steadily.[8]

Hawai'i's increasing cultural amenities and maturing social life, nicely appointed as they were, were secondary in importance to the program of governmental reforms that Kamehameha III pursued doggedly under the tutelage of his American ex-missionary advisers. The changes that he undertook in the 1839 Declaration of Rights and the 1840 constitution articulated basic changes in the hierarchical structure of the society, but they had to be given effect with a whole program of enabling legislation that would earn the respect of the great powers. First came the creation of a treasury board in May 1842, composed of John Papa 'I'i, *kahu* of the Royal

School; the king's secretary, Timothy Haʻalilio; and the trusted Dr. Judd. It took them four years to do it, but organizing the country's finances cleared the national debt. The treasury board also had the job of taking the first steps toward a vast reordering of land tenure in the kingdom.

Of all the reforms espoused in the declaration and constitution, none was more fundamental than the idea that the king held the land not for himself but in trust for the whole people. That was a sea change from the days of the Conqueror and before, when each king distributed the land as he pleased. Looking toward a day not of revocable tenancy but of widespread ownership of land on the Western model, the treasury board began ferreting out which lands the king would retain as his personal property, and which would pass to the government.

Working on another front, Attorney General Ricord prepared a series of "Organic Acts" to regularize a permanent government structure. The first, which began operating in March 1846, established the executive branch of five portfolios, with a minister for each: Finance, Foreign Relations, Interior, Law, and Public Instruction. Those ministers, with the four governors, would comprise the king's privy council, assisted by others that he might appoint. The second Organic Act took another step toward land reform in establishing the Board of Commissioners to Quiet Land Titles—in short address, the Land Commission—to oversee the country's transition from mass tenancy to fee-simple ownership.

The great flaw in the Hawaiian land system that had remained uncorrected up to this date was the fundamental insecurity of land tenure: Every level of occupancy could still be overthrown at the whim of the next higher lord; the chief could evict the *kanaka* tenants; the high chief could evict the chiefs; the king could evict the high chiefs. In fact a prudent chief diversified his holdings under the favor of different high chiefs, so that if one turned on him and seized one *ahupuaʻa*, he could avoid penury by taking refuge on another parcel under the governance of a different high chief.[9] The whole was a powerful disincentive to development, but the chiefs clung to it in the belief that the power to evict their inferiors was critical to controlling them. As one chief told William Richards in 1841 regarding his tenants, "If we cannot take away their lands, what will they care for us? They will be as rich as we are."[10] There was a complicated but ill-defined etiquette when it came to a high chief dispossessing a lesser chief. As with the arrest of Kaumuali'i or other unpleasant matters, all was framed with courtesy, but resistance was futile. Generally "chiefs acted entirely at their own caprice, and it was always considered that a chief could revoke his grants."[11] Indeed, the chiefs' behavior in sometimes arbitrarily seizing the produce of tenants who did show initiative in working their land harder than their neighbors led *kanakas* to scoff at the idea of wearing themselves out to improve their circumstances. Thus many were reinforced in lives of cynical indolence.

Yet there was broad agreement that something had to be done for the common people. Under Kamehameha III they no longer faced the prospect of warfare and mayhem among feuding chiefs, but their labor was in many cases preempted by the command to search for sandalwood or perform some other service for the chiefs they supported, in addition to raising their own sustenance. In an economy that functioned for centuries without currency, they still paid their taxes in produce and a certain number of days' labor, and during the 1830s "the lot of the common people was harder. . . . than it had been during the time of Kamehameha I."[12] The Western concept of working for wages began to crack the system in the mid-1830s, as exemplified by the Ladd & Co. sugar plantation on Kaua'i, freeing the *kanakas* from the grip of the chiefs. As the practice spread, it led to the creation of a new class of native Hawaiians who handed up no tribute, the "floaters," which began to supply the towns with a labor force.

Under the authority of the Land Commission the entirety of the kingdom began to be apportioned and the results entered in a voluminous log called the *Mahele* (Division) Book. The Crown Lands, retained by the king as his personal possession, totaled nearly a million acres. The remainder of the land that he had formerly controlled as his personal property, rather more than half, he surrendered as public domain, which became known as Government Lands. The chiefs, now recognized as *konohiki*, or landlords, were required to register claims for the lands they wished to keep and pay a commutation fee to register their titles. Lacking cash, they often paid in land less dear to them, which was added to the pool of Government Lands. At the end, the 235 chiefs kept for themselves about 1.5 million acres, or about ten square miles each, on average—rather a generous settlement on a class of masters who, themselves, had done little more than order their *kanakas* about for as long as anyone could remember. In other revolutions in other times, such a class might simply have been eliminated, or told to pick up a hoe and dig some taro for themselves. But even then the chiefs retarded the process. Their ingrained sense of entitlement was difficult to shed; they were lackadaisical in registering their lands, as they had never been required to establish their ownership before and saw no emergency to do so now. Filing deadlines were repeatedly missed and had to be extended with new legislation, as late even as 1892.

And then there was the question of the surveys, which were disorganized, duplicative, and inconsistent. At various times some thirty-three surveyors worked for the Land Commission; some were thorough and exacting, some were careless to the point of dereliction; some had faulty compasses, some saw no fault in setting pins a distance beyond the end of the chain to give the grantee a little extra land.[13] The result was a chaos of gaps and overlaps.

Finally, last in line, not eligible for land until passage of the Kuleana Act of August 6, 1850, were the *maka'ainana*, the "people of the land" themselves. The foreign community in the islands warmly espoused the concept of giving people the fishponds and taro patches they had tended for decades, not just for the inherent justice of the act but as a means to arrest the alarming decline in native population. The prospect of becoming a freeholding yeomanry could not but have a salutary effect on the beaten-down and disease-ridden *kanakas*. British consul Miller had once gotten so carried away on the subject that he proposed a plan to the king to promote child-bearing: that commoners be freed from the labor tax on the birth of a first child, and that they be given land title on the birth of a second, the size of their plot to increase with the size of the family.

Especially during and after 1848, increasing the number of natives was a topic of acute concern, owing to the onset of crushing epidemics. "Much sickness prevails here at the present time," reported the *Polynesian* on October 14. "The whooping cough made its appearance a few weeks since, and during the last week several cases of the measles have occurred in town. By an arrival from Hilo, we learn that the measles prevail extensively among the native population of Hilo." In the first two months of the siege, nearly seven hundred people were reported dead in Honolulu alone, and that number was surely underreported. After a year the *Missionary Herald* reported "whole neighborhoods, even whole villages, prostrate at once . . . there not being enough persons in health to prepare food for the sick." Whooping cough wreaked such havoc in the countryside that in some areas, nine in ten newborns and infants were carried away. And then influenza came for the very old: "The aged have almost all disappeared from among us," the missionaries sadly reported.

The doctors among the missionaries worked themselves to exhaustion. In his nearly seventeen years in the islands since arriving with the Fourth Company, Dr. Dwight Baldwin of Maui had seen nothing like it. "Never was I driven so to distraction, week after week & month after month, with no respite—& probably never did I lie down at night" without being wracked with frustration that some suffering family had sent for him, "but whom I c'd not reach before night overtook me, or c'd not find, owing to a large part of Lahaina being without roads."[14] So many factors ran against them. The weather took an unseasonable and relentless bend toward cold and rain. Stocks of medicine ran out; Amos Cooke noted in his journal that he and John Papa 'I'i had helped Edmund Rogers of the Fifth Company make ipecac and calomel pills to treat diarrhea. Some began using native herbs. Even their closer communication with the outside world worked against them: In the old days it took half a year or more before a ship reached the islands, and infected people died at sea or recovered before ever touching shore. Now with California only some two weeks away, new disease was only a new arrival away—which was how measles first landed at Hilo in 1848.

Native schools were suspended, some church congregations decimated. Naturally the missionaries' first instinct was to turn to their faith. The king appointed December 6, 1848, "as a day of fasting, humiliation, and prayer to Almighty God," but it took another six months for the pestilence to lift. When it did, some ten thousand native Hawaiians had died, perhaps 10 percent of the remaining population. The native chronicler Samuel Kamakau believed the total to be much higher, up to 30 percent,[15] but no accurate count could be made. That the epidemics were underreported is certain, and given that in remote areas whole families might die unrecorded, he may have been closer to the truth. In any event it was the worst siege of disease since the 1804 *oku'u* thwarted the Conqueror's intended second invasion of Kaua'i. And the most terrifying pestilence—smallpox—was yet to come.

The plummeting population colored every other consideration in the islands. It was a large factor in turning to imported Asian labor for the sugar plantations. One reason Kamehameha III was willing to entertain ceding his country to the United States was that he believed his own race was headed toward extinction. Thus the humanitarian aspects of the Kuleana Act, to get Hawaiian natives in possession of their own land and give them a reason to hang on, were quite real.

Once they were eligible, some ten thousand *kanakas* applied for ownership of the plots they had long been cultivating, and at the end of the day, the total of all such land distributed to the *maka'ainana* was only about thirty thousand acres. This was less a miscarriage than it seems at first, for the few acres of one *kuleana* given to a *kanaka* was fertile, arable land, whereas vast tracts of the chiefly or royal lands were taken up with lava flows, escarpments, or other features that were not materially productive.

Thus the first assay of the Great *Mahele* was that in a real sense it *was* the "great division" of the lands, with the net result that some ten thousand commoners actually owned land, a prospect that would have been unthinkable a generation before. But if the road to hell was paved with good intentions, then the road to a completely Americanized Hawai'i was paved with the Great *Mahele*. At the outset virtually everyone agreed that its effect would be to transform the class of *kanaka* tenants into landowning stakeholders in their own country, but its actual effect, disastrously, was the opposite.

For the individual commoners the biggest factor involved in receiving desirable land was luck, and many of them wound up with less land than was actually needed to support their families. A busy government commissioner might assign one family a plot containing a taro patch of only two or three acres. But taro depletes the soil, and a patch must lie fallow for at least two years before being replanted; an agent who understood this awarded larger tracts. The luckiest commoners were those for whom the missionaries acted as commissioners, especially those missionaries who came to understand the tension between the tenants and the chiefs, whose disregard for the *kanakas* could be quite heartless. Such a missionary was willing to bite deeper into the chiefly lands and might award a *kuleana* of thirty acres or even more[16] to insure that the *maka'ainana* really did become self-sufficient. Chief Justice William Little Lee, during his stint as chairman of the Land Commission, received many letters from commoners so anxious for sustainable tracts of land that they even addressed him as their *Pu'uhonua*, their City of Refuge, to whom they looked for a new beginning in life.[17]

But the real poison pill that doomed the Great *Mahele* was not the small size of average plots awarded to *kanaka* families. It was the passage, a few weeks before the Kuleana Act, of the Alien Land Ownership Act. During the preceding decades, international interest in Hawai'i had surged; its potential for trade and imperial defense were widely noticed, but the remnant feudal system of land tenure had proved a potent discouragement to foreign investment in the islands' economy. American and European capitalists were deeply wary of sinking money into agricultural ventures (and large-scale development required vast sums of money) without some guarantee more binding than the chiefs' smiling assurance of goodwill that their investment was secure. The provision of a Western-style constitution and courts set a system in place by which redress could be sought, but it was still illegal for foreigners to own Hawaiian land in fee simple.

Widespread misunderstanding of the Hawaiian concept of a lease had in the past been at the root of many ugly conflicts with foreign residents, European consuls in particular, but not limited to them. To Western minds one leased the whole of a property—land and improvements together. The chiefs, however, considered that one leased the improvements on the land, and enjoyed the use of the land, but they never entertained a notion that they had alienated the land itself, even for a period of time. Passage of the Alien Land Ownership Act of July 10, 1850, opened the floodgate of foreign capital, which filled the land just as thousands of native commoners found themselves in possession of real estate, however modest their acreage, that they were free to sell. Freedom to sell they understood very well, and the most sinister factor in the failure of the Great *Mahele* was that the *kanakas*, similar to American Indians at the time of forced severalty (individual ownership), had little understanding of the nature or responsibilities of ownership. Whether because of that, or because they owned parcels too small to support their families anyway, or whether they needed quick cash to doctor or bury victims of the hideous epidemics, or whether, acting on caprice, they seized a chance to have a good time in town, or to get to town and investigate making an urban living—whatever the combination of factors, the Great *Mahele* had the net effect of evicting thousands of native Hawaiians from the countryside and leaving them worse off than they were before.

Even as the Great *Mahele* matured over time into a feast of unintended consequences, so too did a second momentous development of 1848: After twenty-eight years of support and oversight, the ABCFM cut the Hawaiian Mission loose. It was not unexpected, as for several years a philosophical rift had been quietly but earnestly widening between Boston and the islands. As far back as 1832 the "foreign minister" of the ABCFM had been Rufus Anderson, a Maine man now of fifty-two. Like many of the missionaries he was a product of Andover Theological Seminary; unlike them, he nursed a tightly held vision of missionary work that was purely evangelical in nature: Preach, move on, and preach again. Their business, as he was wont to say, was with the unbelievers, not the believers. Teaching, doctoring, and pastoring were not their concern—high irony as it was for the issue to reach a boil during the epidemics. Natives were to be trained as rapidly as possible to take charge of native congregations. Hiram Bingham led the others to Hawai'i twelve years before Anderson took charge, Anderson had been spurring them for a further sixteen years, and even then Hawai'i had only a couple of seminaries and a handful of native Christian graduates.[18]

It was all tidy theorizing from a man who had never served in a mission station (he had wanted to go to India but the church kept him in a secretarial capacity). Had his model been followed, the Congregationalist missions in Hawai'i would have been not just failures but abject failures. The more than one hundred missionaries and wives taught and doctored and pastored because that was what was required for Christianity to take root in the islands. William Kanui and Prince Kaumuali'i had been examples of giving responsibility to native converts too soon. Moreover the missionaries enmeshed themselves in the lives of the islanders because they

cared for them. In 1820 they encountered a native culture that practiced human sacrifice and infanticide, in which the multitude of
commoners were beholden to and terrorized by a tiny caste of chiefs.
Modern scholars criticize the missionaries for their equating Boston
morality with Christian virtues, and they have a point—apart from a
heavy dose of "presentism" (that is, the fallacy of judging nineteenth-
century people through twenty-first century sensibilities). But those
who rhapsodize over the natives' lost innocence and languorous sensuality also gloss over the horrors of precontact life. The change that
the missionaries wrought, turning it within a generation into a constitutional monarchy with one of the highest literacy rates in the
world, was stunning. The habits of centuries could not have been
broken with a couple of sermons and a lecture series.

But Rufus Anderson was certain that he knew best. Others in
the ABCFM knew that his patience was wearing thin. "Whatever
methods may be adopted," one of the Boston insiders warned them
in 1844, "you must pursue this object of raising up . . . successors in
the gospel ministry. . . . Think as favorably as you can of those
whom you have brought forward, confide in them as much as you
can . . . and in this manner aim to make them . . . respect themselves." The issue was considered in Honolulu; they had been licens-
ing native preachers since 1841, and they took steps to increase the
pace, but it did not happen fast enough, and Anderson lowered
the boom in April 1846. "The great point is," he wrote them, "*to get
a NATIVE MINISTRY.* In this I understand you to have failed."

To Anderson's credit, so far from desiring the Americanization
of the islands, he did regard the expeditious training of native
clergy as essential to the future independence of the kingdom. "I
believe that if the churches are officered by foreigners, the offices of
the government will continue to have foreign occupants. Nothing
will save the native government but a native ministry placed over the
native churches. . . . It is better to have a very imperfect native ministry," he insisted, "than to have none at all. . . . The most effectual
rebuke for ambitious foreigners in the civil government, will be . . .

creating native pastors for all the native churches. . . . When the natives see that you are putting them forward in the churches, they
will feel an impulse . . . to become qualified for the posts . . . and
an upward direction will be given to the native mind."[19]

That was one part of the story. The other was a sea change in the
ABCFM's policy toward the missionaries' involvement in Hawaiian
life. Until then they had been forbidden to engage in politics, and
were discouraged from becoming citizens or owning property. (Judd
and Richards had had to resign from the mission in order to accede
to the king's request to help him run the government.) When others
of the missionaries began returning home, ostensibly to oversee their
children's education but almost certainly never to return, Anderson
realized that he did not want what he called this "homeward current" either. Thus an accommodation was reached, by which the
ABCFM relaxed the restrictions, making it easier for them to live in
Hawai'i as Hawaiians, and to help make the mission self-supporting
as he weaned it off of home support.

In 1847 the ABCFM reduced the Hawaiian missionaries' sala-
ries to five hundred dollars per year—half the level of support given
those sent to China. And the timing was terrible; news of the discovery of gold in California reached Hawai'i before becoming
known in most of the United States, and starting in 1848, the diversion of goods and produce to sell in California caused prices to
skyrocket in the islands. "You will like to know how we live in these
times," Castle wrote a friend soon after. "Well, I will tell you something of how we live—or, rather, how we don't. We have not bought
a bunch of bananas in many months. . . . much of the time we have
neither Irish nor sweet potatoes. . . . Almost every species of fruit is
beyond our means."[20]

Some of the missionaries got jobs, some took in boarders, some
prepared to return home. With the closing of the Royal School,
Amos and Juliette Cooke were among those who found themselves
at loose ends. "Pray for me!" Cooke wrote to his New England relations. "I love to preach, but, you know, my talents are limited. I left

a mercantile life to prepare to preach. Shall I now leave the prospect of preaching to return to my former life?"[21] That question was
answered for him when Levi Chamberlain, who had long assisted
Castle in running the mission's supply distribution, died of consumption on July 29, 1849, and one of the workers at their depository left to edit the *Polynesian*. Badly in need of help, Castle and
Cooke, in a long night of discussion with their wives, decided to form
a partnership and capitalize the mission's supply base into a commercial mercantile. Their plan was still to sell supplies to the missionaries at cost, but then recover some profit by selling to the general
public as well.

It was not an easy plan to implement. Many of the missionaries,
particularly those on the outer islands, had each believed for years
that he was at the end of the line when it came to receiving badly
needed supplies, and now all feared that they would be gouged,
notwithstanding Castle and Cooke's determination to pass materi-
als along with no markup. Then the ABCFM itself weighed in, requiring the two to charge 5 percent over cost even to the several
missions to pay for the company's overhead—a condition they were
in some position to make, as they offered favorable terms to Castle
and Cooke to privatize the mission's inventory of supplies. As a single exchange of letters required the better part of a year, it seemed
doubtful that terms would ever be consummated. Both Castle and
Cooke became naturalized subjects of the king during 1850, the
new firm of Castle & Cooke obtained wholesale and retail merchants' licenses on June 3, 1851, and the two principals signed a
partnership agreement two days later. The ABCFM retained them
as agents for the mission at five hundred dollars per year, allowed
them to draw on the warehouse's funds for start-up expenses,
offloaded unneeded merchandise at cost, and gave them permission
to open a second location if business warranted.

As Castle & Cooke used its location in Honolulu, the center of
the kingdom's commerce, to open a multifaceted business concern,
the scores of missionaries scattered across the islands were hard put

to keep their operations together. At Kohala on the northern tip of the Big Island, Elias and Ellen Bond fretted for years how to keep their flock of believers faithful and out of trouble. The Bonds were from Maine, he had just turned twenty-seven when, following the pattern of so many of their predecessors, they married on September 29, 1840; he was ordained the next day, they sailed for Hawai'i six weeks later and set to work producing their eleven children. They came with the Ninth Company, arriving in Honolulu in May 1841 in time to see the splendid Kawaiaha'o Church being raised. Before he could entertain any visions of his own grandeur, Bond was dispatched to windy Kohala, where Isaac and Emily Bliss had been laboring in a modest thatch church for four years. By his own sweat Bond expanded the mission complex, adding a kitchen, washroom, carpenter shop, and other improvements, and he repaired the storm-battered 'Iole Mission Station while ministering to the flock at the Conqueror's own birthplace.

At the time the ABCFM divested itself of the Hawai'i Mission, Bond offered to continue with no salary if the governing body would turn over to his ownership the mission complex he had so labored on. The ABCFM, however, required five hundred dollars for it. Bond, in response, answered to his own sense of justice and was able to use the terms of the *Mahele* to simply acquire the property. The kingdomwide decline in population hit Kohala particularly hard, not just the mortality of disease but defections as Bond's bored and work-averse natives departed for more interesting—and sinful—lives in Hilo and Honolulu. At length, "It came to me clear as sunshine, that it must be sugar cane. . . . There was no work in the district by which our people could earn a dollar . . . yet my figuring led me to believe implicitly that, with proper management, a plantation could be made to pay expenses, whilst retaining our people."[22] Bond journeyed to Honolulu and met with Samuel Castle, whose firm became Bond's agent in a public offering of stock. Elias Bond did not set out to make a fortune; in fact Kohala Sugar Company once it became organized was popularly known as the Missionary

Plantation. For years thereafter he plowed earnings back into the operation, and contributed profits—large soul that he had—to the ABCFM.

Bond's paternal ministry to his flock found its way into the plantation rules:

1. Said company shall not distil nor manufacture any spiritous [*sic*] liquors from the products of the plantation.
2. The laborers and all belonging to the plantation are requested to attend church once at least every Sunday. . . .
3. There is to be no card playing.
4. No fighting is allowed under penalty of one dollar for each offense, the money to be laid out on books and papers.
5. No quarreling with or whipping wives is allowed under penalty of one dollar for each offense. . . .
6. No tittle tattling is allowed, or gossiping.

Much has been written of the missionary families' success in business, and that success was largely attained in later years through exploitation of native and imported labor and devious politics. It is worth remembering that those charges are better leveled at their children and grandchildren. The missionary generation itself entered business uncertainly and unwillingly; for many of them, such as Elias Bond, the requirement for self-sufficiency was molded around their desire to continue as missionaries, and in the case of Castle & Cooke, to aid them in that effort.

11. The Anglican Attraction

Kamehameha III passed away on December 15, 1854, having reigned through regency and majority for nearly thirty years; he was only forty-one when he died, but he was spent. His two children with Kalama had lived but a short time. His infant son, Albert Kunuiakea, by his departed sister's companion Jane Lahilahi, was vigorous—indeed he lived out the century—but the missionaries had introduced the concept of legitimacy, and he was never considered for a royal role. In the old days being gotten of the king's loins was its own legitimacy, and here was one way in which the missionaries bent the course of Hawaiian history away from where it might have gone. As with the banishment of Lot's "illegitimate" daughter and her mother, Princess Abigail Maheha, from the Royal School, and as with excluding Princess Ruth Keʻelikolani from the succession because she was *poʻolua*, the missionaries unwittingly sent Hawaiʻi forward with a weakened dynasty.

Next in line were his two nephews. The elder, Lot Kapuaiwa, had just turned twenty-four, but he was stubborn, hotheaded, somewhat antisocial, and the king did not think that he would make a success of ruling the country. By his will and the council's approval the throne passed instead to the younger nephew, Alexander Liholiho, who was just twenty. The foreign enclaves welcomed the choice, for he was widely esteemed for his intelligence and handsome looks; the missionary community accepted the succession but viewed it with consternation. At the Royal School, Lot and Alexander along with their older brother the heir apparent, Moses Kekuaiwa who died in the onslaught of measles in 1848, had made life miserable for Amos and Juliette Cooke. Although he was born fourteen years into the missionary era, there was an extent to which Liholiho suffered the same cultural trauma as his uncle, caught between the old ways and the new. As a tot he showed up at the Royal School with no fewer than thirty servants. He was the son of an ardently Christian *kuhina nui*, but he was also the grandson of the Conqueror, and like all children of the *ali'i* he was accustomed to having his way. Once his battalion of minders was sent away, Liholiho was alone in the care of Amos Cooke, who was not known for sparing the rod, and the beatings were the cost that Liholiho paid for an excellent education. Where most of his relatives tended to corpulence, he grew tall and athletic—he was gifted in music and cricket, but he also suffered from chronic asthma, whose alarming symptoms made problematic how long he might live.

His experience in the Royal School was probably the smaller source of his dislike of Americans, for he understood the value of the education he received there. The larger source he came by more directly, on the diplomatic mission that he and Lot undertook in 1849–50 with Gerrit Judd. In Paris, President Louis-Napoleon received them cordially and expressed the hope that the tiff between France and Hawai'i would be resolved. In London, Queen Victoria was confined with her seventh pregnancy, but Albert, the prince consort, received them. Liholiho took a liking to him, Lord Palmerston, and British society. In May 1850 they moved on to the United States, a reception by President Zachary Taylor, and exposure to real American society, which they had known only in small doses all their lives.

Ready to board their train from Washington to New York, Judd
asked Liholiho to get on first and secure their seats, as he and Lot
would see to their baggage. Alexander found their berth and seated
himself, and there occurred one of the pivotal moments of his life,
as he came face-to-face with the reality of how Americans regarded
darker-skinned people. He could still barely contain himself as he
entered the experience in his diary:

> While I was sitting looking out of the window, a man came to
> me & told me to get out of the carriage rather uncerimoniously
> [sic], saying that I was in the wrong carriage. I immediately
> asked him what he meant. He continued his request, finally he
> came around by the door and I went out to me[et] him. Just as
> he was coming in, somebody whispered a word into his ears—by
> this time I came up to him, and asked him his reasons for telling
> me to get out of that carriage. He then told me to keep my seat.
>
> I took hold of his arm, and asked him his reasons, and what
> right he had in turning me out and talking to me in the way
> that he did. He replied that he had some reasons, but requested
> me to keep my seat. And I followed him out, but he took care to
> be out of my way after that. I found he was the conductor, and
> probably [had] taken me for somebody's servant, just because
> I had a darker skin than he had. Confounded fool.
>
> The first time that I ever received such treatment, not in
> England or France, or anywhere else. But in this country I must
> be treated like a dog to go & come at an Americans bidding.[1]

After his return to Hawai'i, his uncle appointed him to the house of
nobles and the privy council, so he was already engaged with the
kingdom's affairs at the time of his accession. Throughout his reign
as Kamehameha IV, Liholiho's judgment of Americans remained
fixed: They were pompous, arrogant, overbearing, and often unjust
in their treatment of others different from themselves. The American missionaries were not optimistic that their Calvinism would

flourish in the new reign. At least the new king came by his disaffection honestly; even Judd had to admit that as a youth the prince had been compelled "to morning prayer meeting, Wednesday evening meeting, monthly concert, Sabbath school, long sermons, and daily exhortations," and these on top of academic instruction. Small wonder that his heart was "hardened to a degree unknown to the heathen."[2] Judd's judgment was too harsh, for to the Calvinists rejection of Boston morality was the equivalent of rejecting the gospel. In truth the new king did give way on some points, such as not making a holiday of Christmas, which the Congregationalists eschewed as a "pagan" observance. Instead Kamehameha IV proclaimed December 25 as a day of national thanksgiving,[3] thus allowing the missionaries their point without spoiling the season for the non-Calvinist *haoles*. (He did tire of this annoying tittle and proclaimed Christmas a holiday six years later.) His other reproofs against the missionaries were equally measured, as when the Ministry of Public Instruction was demoted from a cabinet post. Richard Armstrong was retained to run the school system, a task at which the missionaries excelled, but they no longer had a voice at the cabinet level. They were not happy with him when he relaxed restrictions against letting even the culpable party to a divorce remarry; they preferred Governor Kekuanaoa's understanding: Once a pillar of salt, always a pillar of salt. But the new king framed the issue in a conciliatory way as one of increasing the anemic population.[4]

The year following his accession the king determined to marry, and his eye fell on Emma Na'ea Rooke, his classmate in the Royal School, a high chiefess of the Kohala District on the Big Island, born in 1836[5] and raised partly in an idyllic, sheltered seaside compound at Pu'ukohola. Thus she grew up in the morning shadow cast by the Hill of the Whale and Kamehameha's imposing but long-silent *heiau* to Kuka'ilimoku that had vouchsafed his conquests. Emma was beautiful, not just in the Polynesian sense but to Western eyes as well. She loved the outdoors, she was an expert equestrienne, and she was thoroughly bicultural: a granddaughter of John Young, she had been given in *hanai* to the English Dr. Thomas C. B. Rooke, and raised in luxury with an English governess even before her manners were polished in the Cookes' Boston Parlor.[6] Great-great-granddaughter of the renowned Kekuiapoiwa II, she was immensely popular and possessed of a gracious sense of noblesse oblige, which it was said she inherited from her great-grandfather, Keliʻimaikaʻi, the Conqueror's favored younger brother, whose memory was still revered in Kohala as the "good chief."

The match was almost universally acclaimed; the couple was elegant and charming, court life promised to be brilliant, and the only muttering against her came from mentors of other young aspirants to the matrimonial throne. Indeed Emma left one of the round of engagement parties in tears when she overheard the whispered clucking that her rank was insufficient—and she being part *haole* to boot—to be accepted as queen.

Their marriage on June 19, 1856, was remarkable from numerous standpoints and showed a Hawaiʻi still in transition. The short procession of carriages from palace to Kawaiahaʻo Church, with cavalry outriders, might as easily have been proceeding down the Mall in London—except for *kahili* bearers, and the commoners along the street, who fell on their faces as in the old days—a sight rarely seen by that time. The ceremony took place in the center of Congregationalist faith, with Richard Armstrong officiating, but at the couple's request (and a mighty act of goodwill it was) he performed the Anglican service, to the scandalized murmuring of the Calvinists in attendance. The new queen had three bridesmaids whose presence together, unknown to any of them, packaged a whole drama of past history, future contest, and the downfall of the dynasty less than twenty years later.

First was the king's sister, Victoria Kamamalu, who was only sixteen but had already been serving as *kuhina nui* for over a year, and until there was an heir she remained second in line to the throne after Lot. As ardently as Liholiho was inclined to Anglicanism (although neither he nor Emma were yet baptized members), Kamamalu was just as fervently Congregationalist and pro-American. When she was a toddler, Kamehameha III had remarked on her fearless singing as she arced high in a swing at the Royal School, and now she led the choir at Kawaiahaʻo Church. Wyllie had tried to get her to give up this post as unsuitable for a princess–prime minister, but she wouldn't hear of it. Kamamalu was also, however, a Kamehameha and accustomed to taking her pleasures at will; the scandals of her private life were soon to rock the royal house. The other two bridesmaids were Mary Pitman, close friend and frequent companion of the new queen, the *hapa haole* daughter of wealthy Benjamin Pitman of Massachusetts and Chiefess Kinoʻole o Liliha, whose father had been one of the courtiers entrusted with hiding the bones of the Conqueror. And there was Lydia Kamakaʻeha, sister of David Kalakaua, whose father was said to be incensed that the king did not marry her instead. Lydia's close friendship with Emma now contrasted sharply with her later sniping at her when the dynasty changed eighteen years later.

Like many a nervous groom before him, Liholiho discovered at the critical moment of the ceremony that he had forgotten the ring, but the danger passed when Elisha Allen, now a privy councillor, slipped off his own ring and pressed it into the king's hand.

One of the first things that Kamehameha IV wished to do was reset the tangle of foreign relations from his uncle's rule. He retained R. C. Wyllie as his foreign minister, who was urbane, able, familiar with the existing messes, and not an American, which meant that the king felt he could trust him to advise for the country's best interest. Toward the end of Kamehameha III's reign, the kingdom had come perilously close to annexation to the United States, a step the new king was determined to avoid. Annexation originally had been held out as an alternative to Hawaiʻi's seizure by either France or Britain, but since then it had taken on a more economic tint. Hawaiʻi's growing sugar industry was largely in American hands, and Hawaiian sugar paid a stiff duty to enter the United States—an impediment to profit that annexation would answer. The king instead determined to seek a "reciprocity" treaty with the United States.

The most direct path to an equitable relationship with the United States was to make another run at persuading the Americans to guarantee, along with Britain and France, Hawaiian independence. That tack had failed some years earlier, not for want of American amity but because of their reluctance to enter treaties generally. Chief Justice Lee, whose health was failing although he was only thirty-four, agreed to work for the treaty in the United States, as he was already planning to visit California for medical advice. He reached Washington in July 1855, and met cordially with President Franklin Pierce and Secretary of State William Marcy. But as the tripartite proposal was picked over in detail it fell apart again, this time mostly over the American concern not to give Britain and France any leave to speak up over an ongoing situation in Cuba. What Lee did get in September was a reiteration of the U.S. commitment to Hawaiian independence, including an agreement "to station some portion of their naval force, at or in the vicinity of the Sandwich Islands," to deter any foreign ambitions. Significantly, the United States also undertook to protect the islands against filibusters from its own shores, as California adventurers who failed in the search for gold made noise from time to time about forming a private army and just taking over the country.

Lee returned to Hawai'i, where he died about a year and a half later, probably of tuberculosis. Elisha Allen took up the cause in the United States; he was a curious choice, and an interesting figure in Hawai'i's Americanization. He was a former congressman from Massachusetts who went to Hawai'i as the American consul in the Millard Fillmore administration. The diplomatic corps being patronage positions, he was ousted by a new consul appointed by the Pierce government. In response Allen became a Hawaiian citizen and served ably as finance minister and in the house of nobles—and flexibly; he had supported Gerrit Judd's advocacy of American an-

nexation, but when the king made his preference known for a reciprocity treaty, worked for that in good faith.[7]

The terms that Hawai'i suggested for such an agreement seemed
advantageous to both countries: Hawaiian sugar and molasses, coffee, arrowroot, and other specified products would be admitted
duty-free to the United States, and American grain, lumber, and
other products that were heavily consumed in the islands would
enter the kingdom equally free of tax. When he arrived in San
Francisco, Allen first heard that the treaty would be expeditiously
ratified, but when he reached Washington he got a pointed lesson
on how the American iteration of politics made strange bedfellows.
On other fronts Northern and Southern senators were at one another's throats over slavery, but a sudden alliance coalesced when
Louisiana senator John Slidell attacked the treaty as dangerous to
his state's sugar growers, and he struck an alliance with Jacob Col-
lamer of Vermont, who was eager to protect New England wool.
Favor waxed and waned for more than a year until Southern intransigence killed the measure in February 1857. By way of a small apology, a general Tariff Act revision just a couple of weeks later lowered
the duty on Hawaiian sugar from 30 to 24 percent.

The year 1857 also brought finally a respectable treaty with France,
but it wasn't easy. About a year and a half after Judd's and the
princes' mission to Paris, President Louis-Napoleon staged a coup
d'état and began ruling as Emperor Napoleon III. New negotiations
began on a more hopeful footing, as rather than Hawai'i having to
send a commissioner to Paris, the French commissioner to Hawai'i
was given power to deal. Sadly for progress, that was Louis-Émile
Perrin, the same man who had arrived on *La Sérieuse* threatening
to resort to France's "extraordinary power" if his demands were
not met, which ultimately resulted in the arrogant 1846 agreement.
Commissioner Perrin should not be confused with the more famous
Émile Perrin, who at this time was director of the Opéra-Comique

in Paris, but for purposes of getting a new treaty, the latter could have produced the negotiating sessions. Wyllie and Perrin detested each other, and there were times when Elisha Allen, the new finance minister and cocommissioner with Wyllie, almost had to physically separate them. Perrin's government allowed him to discuss anything while still insisting upon the main points of the 1846 document: French as an equal diplomatic language of the kingdom (notwith-standing the dearth of Frenchmen in the country); French citizens in Hawai'i to be tried only by juries nominated by the French con-sul; and only low duties on French wines.

The last issue placed the king squarely between the French gov-ernment and the missionaries, who wanted to ban all alcoholic im-ports. Employing the national skill with loopholes, the Hawaiians had observed the 5 percent limitation on duties for French wine but had been collecting a five-dollar-per-gallon duty on brandy, which pleased no one but netted some revenue for the government. After nearly four years of back-and-forth and failed ratifications, a treaty finally went into effect in March 1858. The French dropped their demand for French-approved jurors, the duty on French brandy was lowered to three dollars per gallon, and commercial and diplomatic papers would be made available in French, although the French conceded that they did not have to be prepared with the same speed as they were ren-dered in English.[8] France's coming to terms was no doubt helped by the American de facto extension of the Monroe Doctrine to Hawai'i, but just to show that there were no hard feelings, the French emperor presented the king with an elegant silver service.[9]

In January 1858, Kamehameha IV took a cruise through his is-lands, courtesy of HMS *Vixen*, a 1,400-ton paddle sloop, George Frederick Mecham commanding. With a new royal mausoleum hav-ing been completed in Honolulu, the king had the vessel call at Ka'awaloa, near the source of so much history at Kealakekua. His mission was to take charge of the bones of the twenty-three ances-tral kings that Kapi'olani had rescued from their decaying resting place in 1829. He ordered the stones removed from the entrance to their cave, and the two large coffins were carried by torchlight aboard the British warship. Back in Honolulu on February 12, he consigned the venerated remains to his father and *kuhina nui*, Kekua-naoa, for a more Western-style interment. The commoners' unease over disturbing their rest, however, was given credence when Commander Mecham sickened and died of bronchitis five days later. (His successor, Cmdr. Lionel Lambert, was later murdered.[10])

This reflection on death was balanced with a joyous expectation of life: Emma was pregnant. When she was delivered of a baby boy on May 20, 1858, the country was almost delirious. His Anglophile parents named him Albert Edward Kauikeaouli, after the Prince of Wales (later Edward VII), although they followed the Victorian fashion and referred to him simply as "Baby." Four days later, on the suggestion of the privy council, he was created Prince of Hawai'i. If Emma gave the prince in *hanai* to anyone, it was a limited *hanai*, for the parents were intimately involved in raising the child. She did select a principal governess and somewhat an adoptive mother, in Esther Kapi'olani, great-niece of the Christian chiefess of the Big Island who descended into Kilauea to defy Pele. She was married to Emma's uncle, who was thirty-five years older than she, and she served the queen as senior lady-in-waiting.

While Finance Minister Elisha Allen was in the United States, he married and brought his bride back to the islands. Their son, Frederick Hobbs Allen, was born ten days after the Prince of Hawai'i, and the king and queen virtually took the Allens into their own family; the boys became playmates from the start of their lives. Kamehameha IV harbored a distaste for Americans generally, but he made many exceptions in advancing those who were loyal and talented.

Another on whom he relied heavily was his secretary, Henry Neilson, bright and companionable scion of a well-connected American family ("related by marriage to Hamilton Fish, secretary of state under President Grant"),[11] and he fit in well with the vivacious court life. The first five years of Kamehameha IV's reign, while notable for its preference for the Anglican religion, gave little sign of the return to primitive passions that the missionaries had feared. That the old days lurked, however, just beneath the social patina came home in a terrible way on September 11, 1859. The king's frequent attacks of asthma caused him much pain and depression, and court gaiety was sometimes maintained with a kind of grim determination. Excursions away from Honolulu were frequent, and September found the court headed for Lahaina, the king with Bernice Pauahi and her *hanai* sister Lydia Kamaka'eha in one boat; the queen with Lunalilo in another; the little prince with his nurses and Emma's mother in another; Kalakaua and his retinue in still another.

Three-quarters of the island of Maui consists of the massive shield of Haleakala (House of the Sun) volcano, and the object of the visit was a camping trip, on horseback, up its heights. They warmed themselves by blazing fires against the cold at ten thousand feet, then retired to their tents. Henry Neilson wrote that he had never seen the king more lively or in better spirits, but the exertion brought on a terrible attack of asthma. Accompanied by Neilson and a few others the king rode down to Lahaina. His mood changed, and in company with one attendant and the captain of his yacht, he went back to sea and remained the whole of the next day, drinking. That night he returned to Lahaina, and walked quickly and with purpose to the house where Neilson was staying. His secretary was on the porch and rose to greet him, when the king suddenly leveled a dueling pistol and shot him through the right side of his chest.

The royal court has probably never convened in which there were not gossip, self-serving rumors, and intrigue. By some means the word had reached the king that in some way never detailed Neilson and the queen had "compromised" themselves. Daylight, sobriety, and the quickest of inquiries proved the rumor false beyond question. The court was in shock, Neilson was badly wounded although it seemed possible that he might recover, but the king was shattered by what he had done. He had suspected his wife wrongly; he had committed wanton bloody violence on a faithful and unsuspecting friend—but he had done worse than that: He had proved Judd's and the Cookes' worst fears correct. Scratch the surface and he was still a savage. Kamehameha IV took full responsibility for his act. He made certain that Neilson had the best medical attention, and paid for it, and he wrote to Neilson, when he was well enough to read and respond, a lengthy and eloquent exoneration of the secretary's conduct, and a full admission of his own culpability. Most tellingly, he determined to abdicate.

One important courtier who had not been touring with the royal suite was the foreign minister. R. C. Wyllie was approaching his sixty-first birthday, confined to Rosebank with an illness that grew so severe that the king at length insisted he move into town. Wyllie ensconced himself in Washington Place, a lavish house a few blocks from the palace. It was owned by Mary Dominis, widow of an American ship captain whose voyages had built the house, but whose disappearance at sea (in the same ship that went down with George Brown) left Mrs. Dominis in such straits that she rented out rooms to support herself. She nursed Wyllie, whose illness worsened until his right leg became partially paralyzed, and he began to arrange his affairs before recovery set in. News of the contemplated abdication set him in motion.

He wrote the king a brilliant letter—humble, affectionate, occasionally even funny: "So long as God spares me in life I shall stand by Your Majesty's Throne to the last—and if I cannot do so on two legs I shall do so on one." He allowed that the king's feelings were motivated by a desire to recover his honor, but, "permit me to say, with all loyal respect, that they originate in a judgment pronounced by you against yourself vastly beyond any just occasion."[12] The council at once backed Wyllie, registering the belief that in the international climate, an abdication would render the nation's continued independence doubtful. The broken Liholiho returned to Honolulu. The council voted a generous cash settlement on Neilson, and the government began again, but the king never forgave himself. Had Neilson died, there would have been a finality to it. But by surviving, as an invalid, every breath he drew was a reproach to the king, and he lived for two and a half years.

The public became aware that the king had wrongly committed an act of violence against an innocent man, owned up to it, and was doing all he could to make it right. To all appearances it did not damage his standing with the people, but it turned the king's mind to religion, and if there was forgiveness to be had, he did not want it from the Calvinist God. Liholiho had been moved by Anglican services in London, and three months after the shooting he asked Wyllie to arrange to establish that church in Hawai'i. Wyllie, whose own interest in religion had intensified after lying close to death, began employing his connections. He wrote the Hawaiian consul in London, Manley Hopkins (father of the poet) to begin rounding up support; the king had pledged land for the church and parsonage, and one thousand dollars per year for a clergyman. As if the king's estrangement from the missionaries of his youth needed any emphasis, Wyllie sent a second, private, note to Hopkins: "The King desires me to make known to you, confidentially, that He and the Queen would prefer that the Episcopal Clergyman . . . be eminently liberal in all his principles and ideas."[13] Freedom of religion in Hawai'i was going to take a step forward.

The thorough Wyllie initiated discussion of a Hawaiian Episcopal church, not just in Britain from the Archbishop of Canterbury on down, but in the American Episcopal Church as well, which might be better situated over time to help sustain the effort. Word of the effort got out in Honolulu, and supporters started a building subscription fund to raise the church. News also reached New England, where Rufus Anderson, the same "foreign minister" of the ABCFM who had discontinued funding the Hawaiian Mission in 1848, was nevertheless jealous enough to fire off a letter straight to the Archbishop of Canterbury, protesting their crossing the informal equatorial boundary that had separated Anglican missionary efforts from their own. He also questioned whether the French and other powers might not interpret the injection of the Church of En-

gland into Hawai'i as a precursor of some kind of territorial assertion. The archbishop responded that all missionaries in the Pacific
"have the same great end in view"—the conversion of souls—and
that he should be very sorry if the Anglican Church's acceptance of
the king's invitation created jealousies among other churches.

William Richards, who was no longer a missionary but was
heartily connected to its philosophy, wrote to his old friend William
Ellis, his fellow worker from a quarter century before, now back in
London. He sought to guide the development rather than block it,
asking Ellis to do what he could to see that a man of evangelical zeal
was appointed: "A High Churchman, or one of loose Christian habits, would not succeed," and the existing community of evangelical
ministers would oppose him. Wyllie derailed this effort, however,
sending his own letter to Ellis, suggesting that he visit Manley
Hopkins—who could probably be counted on to tell Ellis of the
royal wish that the post go to anyone *but* a zealous evangelical.

The terrible epidemics of 1848–49 had not even passed from memory when a new scourge, smallpox, swept the kingdom in 1853,
leaving at least 2,500 dead. For many years seamen's hospitals had
offered care to the foreign community, but for the *kanakas* in the
countryside, and the poor floaters who were trying to make their
way in the towns, there was nothing. The dwindling population
weighed on Kamehameha IV's mind as much as it had his uncle's,
to the point that he once suggested initiating an immigration program from elsewhere in Polynesia to invigorate the native stock. To
the legislature he proposed the establishment of hospitals for the
poor,[14] which the legislature approved if the money could be privately
raised. One Congregationalist expressing his view on the subject
was the Rev. Samuel Damon of the Tenth Company, who felt that if
the natives were not lazy, drunk, and licentious, they would not
need a hospital. (Not all the American medical missionaries were so
contemptuous, especially the doctors who practiced unstintingly

among the poor.) The legislature referred the question of fundrais-
ing to a committee consisting of the acting finance minister, D. L.
Gregg, and Wyllie. The latter, perhaps partly in jest, suggested that
if the matter were turned over to ladies, they could raise the money
straightaway. But Wyllie also had enormous confidence in the queen,
and she and the king did raise the money, resorting even to importuning people on the street.[15] The Queen's Hospital, when it was
built, was a huge step forward in the country's public health.

After getting that project launched, Emma intended to spend a
long vacation at R. C. Wyllie's plantation at Hanalei Bay. She took
the baby and his governess, Esther Kapiʻolani; her favorite cousin,
Peter Kaʻeo; D. L. Gregg's wife and three children; and several other
friends. On the north shore of Kauaʻi they hiked, raced canoes,
swam, and indulged in such naughtiness as eating chicken with their
fingers—for the propriety of which Emma cited the example of
Queen Victoria. The king joined them after a month; in and out of a
fog of depression, after his daily work he often cared for Henry Neilson himself, his penance for having shot him. A few weeks at Hanalei Bay almost restored him—fishing, playing with the children,
learning the Tyrolean waltz—all under Wyllie's beatific gaze.

One chief cause of the Americans' dislike of him was his influence with the royal family. He renamed his plantation Princeville in
honor of the toddler Albert Edward. He encouraged Emma to open
a correspondence with Queen Victoria, rather a bold suggestion
because Emma was not confident of her spelling and expression—
"As you know," she once wrote her father, "I am not very good at
it."[16] She ventured a letter, however, and in fact she and the British
queen became affectionate if long-distance friends. Wyllie set the
cabinet ministers to wearing dress uniforms, and he formalized
court etiquette, both of which could be defended on the ground of
establishing the nation's dignity in foreign relations, but the
American-associated newspapers ridiculed him for it.[17] When he
promoted the idea of a Hawaiian peerage, though, opposition was
so fierce that he did not pursue it.

༄

Back in England, the wheels turned slowly to establish a church in Hawai'i. After much discussion, the bishops thought it better, since Hawai'i was already a Christian nation, to send not a missionary but a bishop with clergy under him—a prefabricated hierarchy. Ellis reported darkly back to Honolulu that the whole effort included Anglicans who were among "the greatest . . . perverts to Popery."[18] The process took so long that the royal couple began planning an event to coincide with the bishop's arrival: the baptism of the crown prince. Queen Victoria consented to be his godmother, and arranged for a proxy to bring a massive silver christening vessel. In the meantime they performed in Verdi's *Il Trovatore* at the Amateur Musical Society, of which the king was a contributor and sometime stage manager. They sailed down to Kona, a place rich with their family history, and stayed at Princess Ruth's Hulihe'e Palace. They began arranging alternative family seats, acquiring a summer villa above Honolulu in the Nu'uanu Valley, and a country seat above Kona on the slopes of Hualalai volcano.

On February 11, 1862, Henry Neilson finally died, giving the king a chance to mourn him and move on. The Prince of Hawai'i turned four, made his first appearance in the legislature, and behaved flawlessly. Many people had remarked on his sweet nature, but despite his parents' determination not to spoil him, there were storms. One day in Kapi'olani's care, he threw a tantrum over a pair of shoes he did not like. Liholiho suddenly doused him with cold water to stop the display. On August 19 the boy took a fever and stomachache and deteriorated by degrees. Three days later Victoria's proxy, William W. F. Synge, arrived to find him dying and his parents inconsolable. With an Anglican bishop and clergy not yet arrived, Ephraim Clark of the Kawaiaha'o Church performed an Anglican baptism on the morning of August 23, and the little prince died four days later.[19]

The prostrated Emma gave herself a new surname, Kaleleokalani,

"Flight of the Heavenly Chief." The king blamed himself and all but withdrew from public view; he had tortured himself for more than two years over what he had done to Henry Neilson; now this. He could not recover. The hysterical queen blamed Kapiʻolani, in whose charge the incident happened, and for the rest of her life could not bring herself (with rare state exceptions many years later) to attend a function where they might meet. The prince's symptoms, however, were consistent with appendicitis,[20] and there was probably nothing that could have been done.

Just over three years after the movement was initiated, Bishop Thomas Nettleship Staley disembarked in Honolulu, with his wife and staff, on October 11, 1862. He was thirty-nine, a Yorkshireman, a product of Queen's College, Cambridge, and intellectually everything that the king had asked for. King and queen were baptized and confirmed, followed by Wyllie, the king's father Governor Kekuanaoa, David Kalakaua, and other important members of the ruling class. It was a time for the American Calvinists to lick their wounds, but in fact the death of the toddler Albert Edward was a nail in the coffin of the British future in Hawaii, and the American reclamation faced one less obstacle.

12. Useful Marriages

The death of the crown prince cast a final pall over the reign of Kamehameha IV. He all but withdrew from public life, although he did not neglect his state duties. He proclaimed and maintained Hawai'i's neutrality when the United States descended into the nightmare of the Civil War, and that developed into an interesting refinement of the Hawaiians' understanding of the Americans' view of them. Many of the U.S. businessmen who staked their fortunes in Hawai'i were New Englanders, and they shared that section's approval of the abolition of slavery. That did not extend, however, to any notion that different races were equal. Besides, the evil of slavery would have been a curious doctrine to advocate in a country whose population had once consisted of a couple of hundred chiefly families living on the tribute handed up by about four hundred thousand *kanakas* living in near-serfdom. Nevertheless the dominance of New England Congregationalism and, perhaps as important, the intermarriage of Yankee businessmen to native chiefesses already well schooled in noblesse oblige, created a certain sympathy for the Union cause. Despite the king's proclamation of neutrality, three or four dozen young men from the Punahou School volunteered for the Northern cause, but what many of them discovered was the same racial schizophrenia encountered by the king when, as Prince Alexander Liholiho, he was almost forcibly ejected from the train in New York. Probably not atypical was the experience of Henry Ho'olulu Pitman, son of Queen Emma's bridesmaid Mary Pitman. Henry's father was banker Benjamin Pitman of Boston, where Henry was educated. He was about eighteen when he enlisted, and notwithstanding his nationality and nobility he was assigned to a Negro regiment. The Confederacy treated black prisoners of war harshly, and Henry, captured early in the war, died on February 27, 1863, in the notorious Libby Prison at Richmond, Virginia.

The few Hawaiians who entered Confederate service did so by quite a different route. Over the preceding decades about two thousand young *kanakas* had escaped their drudgery by signing aboard American whaling vessels. During the Civil War the remains of the Yankee whaling fleet became the regular prey of the dreaded Southern raider CSS *Shenandoah*. Captured whaling crews were given a choice between being clapped in irons below deck and then put ashore in the middle of nowhere, or joining the rebel crew. Twelve Hawaiian sailors made the latter choice.[1]

Wyllie used Hawai'i's neutrality to expand trade with the United States. The absence of Confederate sugar in the North quintupled the price of that commodity there, a hardship that Wyllie was quick to take advantage of by encouraging increased Hawaiian production. The attempt at a reciprocity treaty in 1855 had been defeated by the influence of Southern sugar planters, and their voice was no longer heard in the Congress. While sugar consumption in the North was being throttled, California was a Union state, and the market was open for as much Hawaiian sugar as could be produced.

As William Richards had predicted to Ellis, the Congregational establishment in Hawai'i was hostile to the English Church preferred by the royal family and many of their retainers. That opposition did not lessen when Rufus Anderson of the ABCFM himself visited the islands in 1863 to formally turn the remaining mission establishment over to the Hawaiian Evangelical Association. The Anglican Church gained an even larger public profile when the king presented a copy of the Book of Common Prayer—his own translation into Hawaiian. But they were now not the only competition that the Calvinist missionaries had to work around.

In the year of Kamehameha IV's accession the Mormons established the City of Joseph on Lana'i. The Congregationalists found Mormon beliefs even more appalling than the rituals and costumes of the Anglicans. The Mormons, however, stole a march on them by giving the natives positions of real responsibility in the local churches, as opposed to the Calvinists' habit of keeping them in seemingly endless pupilage. This danger of losing influence among the native believers was not unforeseen, in fact it was an important factor in Dr. Rufus Anderson's washing his hands of them. The Mormons, however, arriving late on a scene where thousands of natives could already read and write and understood the rudiments of Christianity (thanks to the missionaries), were able to capitalize on one certainty in Anderson's philosophy: that the natives would seize upon a church that made them feel important.

The Mormons had been quietly laboring in Hawai'i since the end of 1850, when ten young adherents abandoned the search for gold in California and came to the islands to mine souls instead. They quickly shifted their focus from white converts to native. Their most effective advocate in the islands was George Q. Cannon, English by birth but an early convert whose family was close to the heart of the movement—in fact his uncle John Taylor was wounded in the hail of bullets that killed the religion's founder, Joseph Smith. A year after he arrived in Hawai'i, Cannon began translating the Book of Mormon into Hawaiian, assisted ably and eagerly by one of his first native converts, Ionatana (Jonathan) Napela. Scion of a cadet branch of the ancient kings of Maui, Napela was nearly forty and a graduate of the Lahainaluna School—a shocking betrayal in the Calvinists' eyes, and he was deprived of his Wailuku judgeship at the time of his defection.

In 1853, when Mormons on the mainland were thinking to cloister the members of the church in a "gathering" in Utah as a bulwark against worldliness, the same sentiment led the church in Hawaii to fort up in the City of Joseph on Lana'i. Native emigration from the kingdom was illegal, and the church persuaded Chief Levi Ha'alelea of Lana'i to allow them to "gather" instead on his *ahupua'a* in the Palawai Valley. Renaming the land the "Valley of Ephraim," the Mormon Church anchored itself there for more than a decade.[2]

Cannon returned home after four years, and while Ionatana Napela remained a pillar of the Mormon community and an interesting figure in the history of the islands, Brigham Young's recall of the white missionaries to help fight the "Mormon War" left the church rudderless (arguably undercutting Rufus Anderson's theories on the efficacy of native church leadership), and prey to the machinations of a shadowy American figure, Walter Murray Gibson. He was about forty, his past was a mystery; no one knew where he was from, although the most entertaining story was that he had been born at sea to English nobility, switched at birth to a poor American family, and one day would claim his title. That melodrama alone should have alerted people that something unsavory was afoot. His utterance of pro-Confederate sentiments—not the quickest way to win friends in Hawai'i—made people think he was from the South. He had run guns in the Caribbean, and the Dutch jailed him on Java for revolutionary activities but he escaped. He had the gift of plausibility, and upon joining the Mormon Church in Utah persuaded Brigham Young to send him to the Pacific with the splendiferous title (he claimed) of Chief President of the Islands of the Sea and of the Hawaiian Islands. He won the confidence of the Mormons on Lana'i, who worked mightily to earn for themselves the *ahupua'a* of Palawai—a tract over which Gibson could rhapsodize in cracked King James English: "I am King . . . of Palawai on this day of grace. . . . Smile sweet valley, thy baby smile, thou hast no evils of manhood. No type of man's sins are here. . . . Oh smiling Palawai, thou infant hope of my glorious kingdom."[3] Only later did the faithful learn that Gibson took title to the land in his own name, not theirs or the church's. Ionatana Napela journeyed to Utah to see if Gibson really was legitimate; the Mormon Church sent a deputation in 1864, who excommunicated him but could not get hold of his title to the 2,500 acres on Lana'i. Gibson made himself scarce for a time, to resurface in a later reign.

In contrast to Gibson, if there was a hero among the missionaries in Hawaii, he was not among the Americans at all, but Father Damien de Veuster, a Belgian of twenty-four who was ordained two months after he arrived in spring 1864 into the Picpus Fathers, the original Catholic order that first came to Hawai'i (Honolulu by then had a bishop and a cathedral). At first he was sent to Kohala, where Elias Bond (informally but now ironically known as "Father Bond") was trying to keep his people busy and in good morals on the sugar plantation. Father Damien's calling, though, would lie in a different sphere entirely.

Kamehameha IV died, only twenty-nine years old, as much from a broken heart as from asthma, on November 30, 1863. Emma, still stricken by the loss of her son but performing her public duties, was almost beyond reach. The king had been unwell for two days, but none of the doctors believed there was any mortal danger. She was alone with him when he suddenly began gasping for breath and expired in her arms. Emma aided in the decision to postpone a funeral until the new royal mausoleum was completed at Mauna 'Ala in the Nu'uanu Valley—which meant that he lay in state in the throne room for two months—about the usual period of mourning for royalty in the old days. French consul Charles de Varigny wrote of the thousands of commoners who swamped the palace grounds, wailing in the first convulsions of grief. "The Queen," wrote Bishop Staley, "sits almost incessantly by the coffin. She has prayers in the room night and morning, in the Hawaiian language, so that all present may understand."[4]

The day after the funeral on February 3, 1864, Emma also presided over the reburial of Albert Edward. While she stayed in a tent during the days, she slept in the burial vault every night for two weeks, until the combined urging of Lot, Kekuanaoa, Wyllie, and Staley coaxed her away. Emma now changed her name from Kaleleokalani to Kaleleonalani—the plural form, "Flight of the Heavenly Chiefs."

The afternoon of Liholiho's death the council and *kuhina nui* proclaimed Lot Kapuaiwa king as Kamehameha V. The independent tack that his rule would take became clear when he refused to take the oath of office under the existing constitution. Toward the end of his reign Kamehameha III had granted a more liberal fundamental law than the 1840 document, and Lot wanted those royal prerogatives back. The usual time to convene the legislature was in April, but the king issued a call instead for it to assemble in July to revise the constitution. This was not the mode of amendment provided for in the existing document, as the American press demanded to know what the use of a constitution was if the king could change it at will. In July the convention deadlocked over the most controversial articles, and Lot dismissed them, abrogated the existing constitution, and said, "I will give you a Constitution." That document, which he signed on August 20, 1864, rescinded the universal male suffrage his uncle had granted and replaced it with both literacy and property tests. He abolished the office of *kuhina nui*, without whose signature laws had not been valid, and he freed his ability to act from the privy council. With those steps taken, he signed the document and took the oath as king—a suddenly very powerful king—on the same day.

For a monarch who intended to rule as well as reign, Kamehameha V chose a highly international cabinet to assist him. The former French consul Charles de Varigny took the finance portfolio, and he retained the Scot Wyllie as foreign minister. The American

C. C. Harris became attorney general, Elisha Allen of long service was chief justice, and the secondary positions were just as eclectic. As with his grandfather, what was paramount was loyalty to the chief.

In the first year of his reign Kamehameha V was compelled to deal with a new disease threat, not as imminently deadly as smallpox and not as widespread as measles or whooping cough, but a disease that was incurable and whose horror was biblically reinforced. The natives called leprosy *ma'i pake*, the Chinese disease, for the prevalent belief was that they were the ones who first introduced it, but that could not be certain. Its spread, however, was alarming. "The increase of leprosy has caused me much anxiety," the king told the legislature, "and is such as to make decisive steps imperative." Twenty-five miles across the Kaiwi Channel from O'ahu lay the island of Moloka'i, on whose north shore sea cliffs, virtually unclimbable but for a single dizzying mule track, vaulted three thousand feet above the ocean. Jutting from this north shore, the small Kalaupapa Peninsula became a colony to house the diseased, who were rounded up from among the population and deported. In a few years there were just over eight hundred, a few of them Caucasian but predominantly native, including the only *ali'i* to be afflicted, Emma's cousin and correspondent Peter Ka'eo, who early in the reign was in the house of nobles and a privy councillor. For several years the kingdom ill supported the colony, and conditions there deteriorated in some cases to the unimaginable, although to his credit Ionatana Napela visited and tried to help. Knowing leprosy to be contagious, the Catholic Church was hesitant to assign priests, but in 1873 Father Damien went willingly, and then volunteered to stay when the church would have begun a rotation. He did not just preach and pastor; he comforted the sick, dressed their lesions, organized recreational opportunities, and finally, in a real as well as a Pauline way, became one of them in December 1884 and died just over four years later.[5]

⚜

Stubborn on the restoration of royal powers, Kamehameha V proved equally stubborn on the topic of his marriage. The Cookes' icy destruction of his relationship with Abigail Maheha at the Royal School had worked dark damage on him, and no doubt contributed to his sour personality. From early in life he had been betrothed to Bernice Pauahi, but as the time approached for such a marriage to progress to concrete plans, she proved herself no less a Kamehameha than the men in the family. Her parents tolerated her friendship with Charles Reed Bishop, but they opposed him virulently once they found out she loved him. Lot's father Kekuanaoa, with all the weight he brought to the discussion, sided with her parents, and demanded that Bernice recognize her royal obligations and marry the prince.

She refused. The Cookes were in her confidence, and she let them see the letters she wrote disengaging herself. As Amos Cooke recorded,

> This afternoon Bernice wrote a letter to Lot requesting that he come to see her. She told him of the wishes of her parents and said she would marry him, in accordance with their commands, but she knew it would make her unhappy, for he did not love her and she did not love him.
>
> After this she wrote the governor [Kekuanaoa] and said that, if they wished her buried in a coffin, she would submit to their authority. That she would as soon they buried her as promise to marry Lot. The governor replied to it, saying she was deceiving herself.

Lot, learning the depth of Bernice's determination, showed himself gentleman enough to release her from their engagement, admitting that he was not worthy of her and would not be the cause of her misery.[6]

Lot's refusal to consider marriage, heavy as that was in import to the kingdom, was only one manifestation of the state that matrimony in the kingdom had come to be. Many of the highborn were torn between Christian sacrament and their ancient chiefly rights, and this fell harder on the women, who were now expected to be virtuous Victorians like their European models. Emma embodied this, and she was fortunate in that she loved her husband, whom she addressed affectionately, even in public, as "Aleck," and he responded with "Emma." For others in the family it was more problematic.

Not long after Aleck and Emma's wedding, with most of the family ensconced in the palace complex, the couple invited to dinner the married Englishman Marcus Monsarrat, a businessman and auctioneer, who recently was among a consortium that gifted the queen with a new carriage. After the family thought that the evening was over, a servant reported that Monsarrat was in Victoria Kamamalu's room. Prince Lot burst in and found Monsarrat at the stage of "arranging his pantaloons." While Lot threw him out of the house, the king blamed his brother "for not shooting Monsarrat down like a dog."[7] (He had not yet wrecked his own life by shooting down Henry Neilson, so bold speech was easy.) There was no criminal charge to make, but Liholiho banished the offender from the kingdom; he returned some months later, was arrested and banished again.[8] In the precontact days, sexual adventure was the right of chiefesses as well as the men, but purity in Hawai'i was coming to be as one-sided as it was in the Western world.

This raised the issue of what to do with the libertine Kamamalu, and that was settled in ways that reflect little credit on the men of the family. The *kuhina nui* was eighteen at the time of the Monsarrat incident, well old enough to know what she was doing. There had been talk of marrying her to David Kalakaua, and now that was off the table—although in the old days her sexual experience would not have been an issue. More culpably, it was well known around the court that she had actually been in love with Prince William Lunalilo, and he with her, but her brothers had forbidden the match. Lunalilo was the last male Kamehameha—although a collateral one, descended from the Conqueror's father via a secondary wife. Other branches of his family tree were formidable on their own: One of his grandmothers was a sister of Ka'ahumanu. Court genealogists had to tell the king and his brother that if Lunalilo and Kamamalu married, any children of theirs would outrank children of any other royal offspring, including those of Liholiho and Lot. Victoria Kamamalu therefore was doomed to a kind of limbo until her brothers could find someone genealogically harmless to them for her to wed—small wonder she turned to a British auctioneer. Kamamalu and Lunalilo, like Emma and Liholiho, were only second cousins once removed, and like the royal couple, they loved each other; they might have had children. It was sad for the future of the kingdom that the last two Kamehameha kings' jealousy of rank kept a potentially fertile branch of the dynasty from having a chance. A similar argument could be made for Lot and Bernice. He was the Conqueror's grandson, she was his great-granddaughter, through different wives. They might have had children, and the dynasty would have survived, but for his self-indulgent petulance in making himself too unpleasant to marry: The impending doom of the Kamehameha line was self-inflicted.

Equally serious for the future of the kingdom was the prevalence of mixed-race marriages. At first contact Hawaiian women could not wait to give themselves to the exotic and, even to their perception, vastly advanced white men. As decades passed the practice took on a different complexion. In England and America women, by and large, could not own real property, where in Hawai'i chiefesses controlled enormous estates. In Hawai'i, before the *Mahele* and its related statutes, foreigners could not own land, and after passage of the Alien Land Ownership Act, it was still easier, and cheaper, to come into control of a large tract by marrying its *konohiki*. In these Victorian times, it went without saying that this practice did not work in the other direction. White men might take native wives at will, but in the Anglo mind, the thought of a white woman being possessed by a native man, be he ever so highborn, was demoralizing. It was an inequity that aroused bitter comment from Hawaiian men, from Opukaha'ia to Kamehameha III.

The wedding of Princess Bernice Pauahi in 1850 was one of the most prominent and successful, and to all appearances free of mercenary motive. Charles Reed Bishop of Glens Falls (on the Hudson), New York, large-eyed, long-nosed, and handsome, originally came to Hawai'i in company with his aunt-in-law's brother, William Little Lee. They were on their way to seek their fortune in the Oregon Territory when their ship diverted to the islands to resupply, and they stayed. They became naturalized citizens, and Lee did admirable legal and diplomatic service until his untimely death. Bishop went into finance, his Bishop & Co. bank being the first chartered in the kingdom, and it was an idea whose time had come, as he raked in nearly five thousand dollars in deposits on the first day. Ladd & Co. hired him to unsnarl their land fiasco; he invested in a Kaua'i sugar plantation, and likely would have ended rich even had he not married Bernice, who was yet to inherit the vast pool of land she was heir to. Theirs was an example of a good marriage; in fact even her parents eventually accepted him, and they took up residence on the family estate. After her death he honored her memory with the founding of schools and the museum that bears their name.

Likely on the other end of the happiness scale was the 1862 union of Lydia Kamaka'eha with John Owen Dominis, son of the ship captain's widow of Washington Place. Lydia's *hanai* father Abner Paki had been so incensed that Kamehameha IV didn't marry her that he groused he would marry her off to some good white man, but apparently he had little to do with the Dominis match. His family was of vaguely noble Croatian heritage, via Schenectady, New York.[9] His boarding school was next door to the Royal School, and he made friends with the *ali'i* children over the top of the fence. After marrying Lydia he dedicated himself to becoming the indispensable man. He served on the boards of education, immigration, and health, and more than twenty years as royal governor of O'ahu, part of that time as governor of Maui also. His marriage should have been so dedicated. Dominis married Lydia and dumped her at Washington Place in the contemptuous care of his mother, who was an arrant racist. Lili'uokalani wrote discreetly in her memoirs that her husband "preferred to socialize without me," but that did not stop him from fathering an illegitimate boy by his wife's servant Mary Purdy Lamiki 'Aimoku. (According to his physician, Dr. George Trousseau, Dominis was a serial philanderer and was probably lucky that there was only one baby out there.[10]) Finding refuge in the spirit of *aloha*, Lydia partly blamed herself, for her apparent inability to have children, and later adopted the bastard son and, in one account, briefly considered trying to pass the child off as their own, which would have been illegal. (In this adoption she followed the example of Queen Dowager Kalama, who adopted Kamehameha III's illegitimate son, Albert Kunuiakea.)[11]

Another important royal heiress to marry white was Elizabeth La'anui, the great-granddaughter of the Conqueror's older brother. She wed Franklin S. Pratt of Boston in 1864, who spent years on the periphery of power without taking any key role: staff colonel to Kamehameha V and privy councillor; in later years his longest tenure was as registrar of public accounts before serving briefly as Hawaiian consul in San Francisco.

Americans were not the only practitioners of the mercenary marriage. From whaling in the Antarctic to cattle ranching in Texas, Scots were seldom second in line to banking a profit. Lydia's biological younger sister, Miriam Likelike, wed Archibald Scott Cleghorn in September 1870. He was from Edinburgh, the son of immigrant parents, and had been responsible for running the family store in Honolulu since he was seventeen. He already had three *hapa haole* daughters from a previous relationship, but once he graduated to the royal circle he served for eighteen years on the privy council and succeeded Dominis as royal governor of O'ahu. His marriage to Likelike, however, dissolved into bitter vituperation, which made things awkward in raising their child, when they finally had one fifteen years into the marriage. That was Princess Victoria Ka'iulani, heiress presumptive during and after Lili'uokalani's reign.

And those were just the most important marriages. Throughout the kingdom white, usually American, businessmen won the hands of chiefesses and acquired instant stakes toward future wealth. Both sides, at least, could play at this game, as land-rich *ali'i* women secured fortunes for themselves in exchange for their lands, as when Abigail Kuaihelani married the Scot James Campbell the year he sold the Pioneer Mill for half a million dollars. Some mixed-race families were already rolling into a second generation, as with John Adams Kuakini Cummins, born as early as 1835 to an American father and a high-chiefess mother. He became known for his lavish entertainments, and for friendships and service to Kamehameha V, Princess Ruth, and Queen Emma, among others. Between the marriages and the *Mahele*, much of the wealth of the islands passed out of purely native control.

Exhausted by losing baby and husband within fifteen months of each other, Emma gathered a suite for a European progress: her escort John Synge of the British Foreign Office; William Hoapili Kaauwai (the first native Episcopal deacon) as her chaplain and his wife as lady-in-waiting; her Canadian footman, John Welsh; Sister Catherine Chambers for companionship, and two chiefs' daughters to deposit in England for schooling. They sailed on May 5, 1865; Emma meant to rest and recover herself, and almost from the start the voyage had its effect. She enjoyed Acapulco and Panama, crossed the Isthmus and boarded the RMS *Tasmanian*. They were feted by the governor of the Danish West Indies, arrived at Southampton in mid-July, and were conveyed by carriage to London. In between rounds of sightseeing and a surfeit of Anglican church services, Emma was diligent to promote the cause of the Episcopal Church in Hawai'i, but highest on her agenda was to meet Queen

Victoria, with whom she had been corresponding with all the fervent affection of the era.[12] They met on September 9 at Windsor Castle; Victoria had been a widow for almost four years, Emma almost two, and both wore mourning.

"She is dark," wrote Victoria in her journal, "but not more so than an Indian, with fine features & splendid soft eyes. She was dressed in just the same widow's weeds as I wear. I took her into the White Drawingroom [sic], where I asked her to sit down next to me on the sofa. She was much moved when I spoke of her great misfortune in losing her husband and only child."

"The Queen received me most affectionately," Emma wrote home to the king, "most sisterly."

When Victoria returned from her habitual summer sojourn at Balmoral she invited Emma to spend the night of November 18 at Windsor, a mark of singular favor, and the visit cemented their friendship. Emma "is not looking well," Victoria recorded, "and coughs poor thing, for which reason she is ordered to go to the south of France." At dinner Emma was seated between the queen and her visiting eldest daughter, Vicky, now the crown princess of Prussia. Emma "was amiable, clever, & nice in all she said, in speaking of her own country. . . . The people now were always dressed as Europeans, & were all nominally Christians, but not very fervently so."

"Directly after breakfast," Victoria wrote of the following morning, "we went to wish good Queen Emma goodbye & I gave her a bracelet with my miniature and hair. She thanked me much for my kindness, & for consenting to be godmother to her poor little child."[13]

The group had a long vacation on the Riviera, during which Hoapili succumbed to the atmosphere and took a French mistress, for which he and his wife (who had not been a diligent lady-in-waiting) were sent home early. A letter from Emma's brother-in-law the king reminded her of the importance of going to Paris and presenting herself to the emperor. She did so, relaying to Lot that Napoleon III had no memory of meeting him fifteen years before, but they had a hearty laugh when Empress Eugénie asked if the king of Hawai'i spoke French, to which Emma answered, of course, and he had learned it in Paris. Emma's greatest surprise was the sight of an exotic Pacific plant growing in a vase of Sèvres porcelain. Emma explained to them that it was a *ti* plant, considered a nuisance in the islands, fed to cattle and used to wrap fish.

The party returned home by way of the United States, and Kamehameha V drew on his American experience to advise her: "They are a very sensitive people, your visiting them will disarm all the lies and insinuations directed against our family."[14] The dowager queen received a thirteen-gun salute in New York Harbor, and President Andrew Johnson received her in the Red Room of the White House—the first queen to visit the executive mansion.

Emma returned home on October 22, 1866—having missed some important events. R. C. Wyllie had died almost exactly a year before; Emma had deeply mourned the news, and she came home to find him interred in the royal cemetery at Mauna 'Ala, a high honor for his more than twenty years of service. More troubling, Victoria Kamamalu, the heiress presumptive, had died the previous May, throwing the succession into confusion. As the highest-ranking chiefess in the country, she had undertaken charitable activities such as founding the Ka'ahumanu Society for the relief of elderly and sick natives, which was widely subscribed and generously supported.[15] She was only twenty-seven, and yet unmarried, an unhappy hostage to her brothers' determination to preserve their status as the highest in the land.

Her passing might have been only a minor story in the American press, but it became known to large numbers through the pen of a remarkable author. In March 1866 the American steamer *Ajax* dropped anchor in Honolulu, disgorging cargo and passengers, except for one California journalist who stayed swapping stories so late that he spent another night on board. In the morning Samuel Clemens, lately famous for a short story about a jumping frog under the pen name Mark Twain, sauntered ashore. To all appearances he had come to dispatch home amusing anecdotes of the islands and people, yet there was a more serious intent as well. Twain's employer, the Sacramento *Union*, was one of those newspapers that was alive to the possibilities of Pacific empire, or at the very least trade, and the stories that he filed, while inimitably Twain, also convey much accurate and relevant information on the government, economy, and commercial potential.[16] The very ship that Twain arrived on, the *Ajax*, was intended to inaugurate regular steamship service between the islands and California, and he was supposed to generate tourist traffic. (She was a year ahead of her time, however. Service on the *Ajax* was suspended after two unprofitable voyages, but a similar service the next year on the SS *Idaho* did make money, boosted with a $75,000 per year mail contract with the United States.)[17]

Mark Twain arrived in time to witness the entire month of Kamamalu's funeral observations. And his senses were filled, for the king accorded her the traditional rites of their people. "A multitude of common natives," wrote Twain, "howl and wail, and weep and chant the dreary funeral songs of ancient Hawaii, and dance the strange dance of the dead." Indeed the king closed the palace grounds to all but the *maka'ainana* so they could mourn in their own way, annoyed that the funeral obsequies for his brother had been "criticized and commented on too freely."[18]

This stern but benevolent demeanor, whether seen in his insistence on a crown-empowered constitution, or in his use of that power, as when he quashed legislation that would have permitted the sale of liquor to natives ("I will never sign the death warrant of my people"), or in his judicious embrace of the ancient culture, earned Kamehameha V wide respect. His motto was *Onipa'a*, "immovable," and the *kanakas* considered him "the last great chief of the olden type."[19] "He dressed plainly," Twain wrote of him, "poked about Honolulu, night or day, on his old horse, unattended. He was popular, greatly respected, even beloved."[20]

In trying to relate an engaging story, Twain may not have understood the significance of the funeral's reversion to native traditions, but his journalist's eye certainly noted the decline of the Hawaiian people, and held the business and missionary interests equally to blame in accomplishing it: "The traders brought labor and fancy diseases . . . in other words, long, deliberate, infallible destruction, and the missionaries brought the means of grace and got them ready. So the two forces are working harmoniously, and anybody who knows anything about figures can tell you exactly when the last Kanaka will be in Abraham's bosom and his islands in the hands of the whites."[21]

The native indulgence of Victoria Kamamalu's funeral was only a temporary revival of native custom, however. More representative was the king's laying the cornerstone of Saint Andrew's Episcopal Cathedral on March 5, 1867, an act that could not help but showcase the royals' continuing disdain for their Calvinist upbringing. The cathedral had been a favorite project of Kamehameha IV and Queen Emma, who selected the stonework when she was in England. It was designed by the London firm of Slater & Carpenter, which dispatched to Hawai'i the prefabricated stonework and their master builder Benjamin Ingelow.

During 1869 events occurred that seemed to reinforce British relations with Hawai'i and left the American community in further doubt of their future. During her sojourn in England, Emma had not met Queen Victoria's second son, Prince Alfred, the Duke of Edinburgh. He had undertaken a naval career, a duty at which he excelled, and rose to command the frigate HMS *Galatea*. He was twenty-five and third in line to the throne after the Prince of Wales and his son, the infant Duke of Clarence. He proved to be a popular representative of the royal family wherever he called—notwithstanding an assassination attempt in Australia the preceding year.

In a stark contrast to the scowling missionaries, Alfred in Hawai'i asked to see a representation of authentic native culture, and the king assigned the task to his fellow graduate of the Royal

School, Lydia Kamakaʻeha. At thirty-one she was only six years older than the prince, and she was known as an enthusiastic promoter of preserving the native arts. At her Waikiki estate, Lydia assembled a sumptuous luau for Prince Alfred that included a progression of Hawaiian dishes and exhibitions of native sports, chants, and dances, including the hula. It lasted for six hours, from eleven in the morning until the guests were driven to shelter by a violent thunderstorm at five.[22] One display of native Hawaiiana all her own was the presence of the monumental Princess Ruth Keʻelikolani, the king's half sister, all 440 pounds of her, with her voice that people said sounded like distant thunder. The Americans were not pleased. "We regret to have to chronicle," clucked the *Hawaiian Gazette*, "that the disgraceful Hula-dance was a part of the programme, and trust for the sake of common decency that it may be the last time that this relic of heathenism may be performed." This American mouthpiece also took a dim view of the fact a number of Hawaiian women had been invited to the feast, but not their *haole* husbands.

Prince Alfred took advantage of the opportunity to steal a march on the Americans, presenting precious tokens to all the royals—gold studs to the king, a bracelet to Emma, and pearl ring to Kalakaua. Recognizing Lydia's musical accomplishments, Alfred gifted her with copies of two of his own compositions, in addition to a gold chain with an anchor clasp. When *Galatea* sailed, the Hawaiians responded to Alfred's kindness and interest by loading his ship to the gunwales with native bounty, even as they would have done in the old days—souvenirs of tapa cloth, and generous provisions of taro, pineapples, and pork. It was the Americans, however, who were left stewing.

Before Alfred left, Kamehameha V hosted a grand ball at the palace for him, and it was Emma who partnered him for most of the evening. She seemed recovered from her multiple bereavements. She and the king were confederates in promoting the English church in Hawaiʻi. "You and I perfectly feel the same," he once wrote her, "why the Mission from England should have had the support of all people who really loved their Country."[23] In 1872 Kamehameha V laid the cornerstone for a new royal palace just south and east of the wood-frame complex, this one to be built of coral blocks and named to honor his brother—'Iolani." (This was the Ali'iolani Hale, which was later converted to house the legislature.) Emma received from her uncle's widow the beautiful 4,500-acre *ahupua'a* of Lawa'i on Kaua'i. She sailed up to put the estate in order, and in directing the digging of a water ditch from the spring to the cottage, she encouraged the workers to finish it promptly—by providing them with beer.[24] Such sensible good nature kept Emma as popular as ever. When the king heard that she intended to visit Ni'ihau to add to her famous collection of native handicrafts, he sent word solicitously that the season of storms was almost upon them and she should not risk it.

Perhaps it was inevitable that even Lot's bitter heart would finally think of her tenderly. Emma was a vivacious thirty-five; they might even have children and solve the succession issue. With the utmost discretion he put out a feeler as to whether she might be able to return his affections. She replied with the utmost respect and kindness, but she said no.[25]

13. Mountains of Sugar

Whaling, which once anchored the islands' commerce with the outside world, had peaked in the early 1850s. But the decline in the number of whales, then losses of Northern ships to Confederate raiders, and the discovery of petroleum all damaged the industry. In April 1871 many of the remaining vessels sortied from Honolulu for the Arctic. Hunting was poor; they stayed too long and were trapped by ice. The crews were rescued, but thirty-nine ships with their cargoes were crushed and lost. Late in Lot's reign, fewer than fifty whalers a year called at Honolulu and Lahaina for supplies and recreation. The only resource on the horizon that could fill this gap in the economy was sugar, and sugar, they discovered, made a vastly different footprint on the islands. In supplying whalers, Hawai'i was a beneficiary but a bystander of an operation that required nothing of the islands. The whalers extracted a resource from the open ocean; it required no commitment of vast tracts of land, no financial investment, other than buying goods to profitably resell to the sailors. It did not rearrange the Hawaiians' landscape, maim their environment, or dislocate their society.

None of that could be said of sugar, at least after it came to dominate the economy, but in the beginning just getting an industry started was a struggle. The techniques of growing and refining sugar were learned by trial and error; down in Kohala, Elias Bond did not bring in a viable crop until January of 1865, and by then he owed his banker/agents, Castle & Cooke, thirty-five thousand dollars. Torn between his benevolent instincts and the need to convince his people that they must work, he dismissed a foreman whom he caught beating a lazy *kanaka*, but his people, when they looked at the labor needed to produce sugar, simply shrugged and moved to Hilo or Honolulu.[1] The bad news for any country dependent upon an agricultural base was that there was no escaping work. Coffee plantations were undergoing a blight, and an experiment at exporting *pulu*, which were tree-fern fibers used for mattress stuffing, was as much work as sugar, and was not a major factor in the economy.

Since the end of the reign of Kamehameha III, the simple export tonnage of Hawaiian sugar told an accurate story of both the laws and the times. In 1851 the crop failed, and the country exported a mere ten tons of sugar. The following two years it rebounded to about 300 tons, which was roughly similar to exports before the collapse. Six years later, after passage of the Alien Land Ownership Act—allowing time to acquire land, put it into production, and bring in a crop—the importation of coolies had begun, and with incrementally increased mechanization in the processing, exports tripled to more than 900 tons. By 1862, when the Civil War opened California to as much sugar as they could send, it was 1,500 tons, and two years later, 5,200 tons, and one year later, 7,600 tons. In 1866 Hawai'i exported more than 8,800 tons of sugar, and the nation achieved its first positive balance of payments.

The economics of growing sugar required large-volume production from a large-scale operation, which meant instituting a plantation system in a country that traditionally only understood subsistence farming. In a nation with a plummeting population, the problem of finding enough natives to work the fields—let alone finding those willing to work—was insuperable. Even as the king was considering whether to raid Polynesia for immigrants of similar ethnicity to restock the native islanders, plantation owners began looking to Asia as a source of labor—cheap, obedient, hardworking, controllable labor.

Very experimentally, 180 Chinese workers had been imported as early as 1852, opening unfavorable discussion in Western countries of what they called the "coolie trade," the signing of exploitative labor contracts with thousands, and then tens of thousands, of impoverished Asiatics to swelter in the Hawaiian cane fields. At first it did not seem so abusive, because the wage—three dollars a month—was about double what they could expect at home. But the system grew to such proportions that it not only captured its contractors, it changed the ethnicity of the kingdom forever.

1867, when sugar production was exploding, brought hard times on other fronts, however. The close of the American Civil War seemed an auspicious time to make another run at a reciprocity treaty, which could only tie the islands more closely to the United States. Negotiations opened afresh, and it was difficult for other foreign representatives in Honolulu to warn of its dangers without sounding merely as if they were attempting to thwart closer ties to the United States. But Varigny, speaking not as a Frenchman but as the Hawaiian foreign minister, issued a prophetic warning:

Suppose the tariff were in effect for a period of seven years . . . and thus assured us a remarkable prosperity for this period of time. What if, at the expiration of this term, the United States government should exert the right to annul the treaty and impose on our sugar a tariff rate. . . . Would not such a shift in future policy result in a terrible commercial crisis? Threatened by imminent ruin, would not our planters all rally round the notion of annexation to the United States, if only that nation would assuage the planters' fears of the future by permanently abolishing the tariff on sugar? . . . How would Hawaii survive it?[2]

Some of Varigny's fears may have formed in his mind thanks to the inopportune presence in Honolulu Harbor of an American warship, the USS *Lackawanna*, a screw-propelled, 1,500-ton sloop–of-war mounting, most prominently, two monstrous eleven-inch Dahlgren smoothbores, two nine-inch smoothbores, and a battery of smaller but still modern and imposing howitzers and rifles. *Lackawanna*'s port call was not meant to convey any threat—in fact the last time Hawai'i reached any agreement with the United States the kingdom actually *requested* American warships to visit or even be stationed in Honolulu, but times had changed. France was no longer a threat, and English friendship had never been warmer. On the other hand *Lackawanna*'s captain, William Reynolds, was a former resident of the kingdom who had issued statements favoring American annexation of the islands that the king found seditious, and Reynolds was persona non grata. Hawai'i announced that it would not take up consideration of the treaty until the warship was recalled. U.S. minister Edward McCook found this rather odd, considering it was Hawai'i that was pressing for the treaty, and sent Varigny a sarcastic note asking whether the kingdom claimed the right to select the captains of U.S. warships.[3]

Nevertheless McCook reported to the secretary of state that the Hawaiians felt intimidated, and agreed that Reynolds was not the best man to have in the vicinity. Unrelated to this discussion but with good timing, *Lackawanna* received orders to survey Midway. The day she steamed away, July 30, 1867, the king called the legislature to a special session and the treaty was approved by a vote of 33 to 4. Again unrelated to events but now with bad timing, *Lackawanna* returned only days later and stayed for eight months, which was the first time that Hawaiians felt the presence of an American warship, as opposed to British or French, to be a threat, although that was not the intent.

Varigny's fears of the long-term repercussions of a reciprocity treaty proved to be premature. For all their work on the treaty, what Hawai'i got was another lesson on the realities of American government. Both in concept and infrastructure American democracy was majestic, but when one came down to the actual, individual men who worked behind those imposing marble facades, the people were as likely as not to elect seedy, shortsighted, self-serving jingoes who embarrassed their offices. An equitable reciprocity treaty, signed by the principals and ratified in Hawai'i, reached the U.S. Senate, which was dominated by radical Republicans intent on impeaching Andrew Johnson, rubbing the former Confederacy's nose in its defeat, and squeezing the maximum spoils from dominating a Congress in which their main opposition was disenfranchised. The embattled administration worked in good faith on behalf of the treaty, but the Senate could not be bothered and swatted it down.

And then things got stranger. The United States, having exorcised slavery from its own midst, began manifesting concern for labor conditions elsewhere in the world, and the U.S. took its turn in condemning the "coolie trade." Congress in 1862 passed a law barring American ships from transporting them, and a following resolution in 1867 required the State Department to register American displeasure with countries who imported contract labor into the Western Hemisphere "or adjacent islands." In 1868 the United States learned that fifty Japanese laborers had been transported to Hawai'i, and McCook duly registered American concern. The Hawaiian government dodged that they had just established a national immigration bureau to prevent labor abuse, an aim with which they were in perfect sympathy, but the fifty Japanese were not actually coolies because they did not sign contracts before they left Japan. The United States was prepared to accept this explanation, with perhaps the arch of an eyebrow, but then the Japanese government, which had no regular representation in Honolulu, asked the American and British ministries to watch over the welfare of Japanese in Hawai'i, citing signs that conditions there were less favorable than they had been led to believe.[4]

The sugar planters, many of whom still had strong ties to the missions, but an increasing number of whom were businessmen who were in it purely for the profit, naturally found this annoying. Castle & Cooke issued a reminder that before the revolution, more than half of the American colonials either had been, or were descended from, indentured servants. Castle & Cooke became the sugar factor for a number of plantations, not just Elias Bond at Kohala, and sent out a circular to all their clients recommending provision of hot water for the Japanese workers' daily baths.[5] Castle was now sixty-one, vigorous and engaged (he would live to eighty-six), but in the matter of contract labor generally he was still Calvinist enough to believe that the law was the law, which he extrapolated to a contract was a contract, and the law must and would enforce a contract, even a contract for labor and even one for harsh terms. "Our 'forced labor' system," he wrote to the *Hawaiian Gazette*, "consists in laws requiring people to fulfill their contracts, specifically. They are just to both parties. . . . he who tries to throw odium upon our system abroad as a semi-slave system . . . unless he brings something practically better, strikes a serious blow at *every interest* in the country, not the planting interest alone, but the coasting, the mercantile and every other one."[6] What Castle refused to see was that equitable contracts arise from comparable bargaining power, and that was never part of the coolie trade.

But some people did see it, and not all voices sang the praises of contract labor. One of the most astonishing stands against it came from a polite but presumptuous upstart, Sanford Ballard Dole, son of Daniel and Emily Dole of the Ninth Company of missionaries. He had been born in the kingdom, nourished by a native wet nurse, and grew up partly in Koloa, which was a prime sugar area. He attended the Punahou School for a time before his parents shipped him off to Williams College in Massachusetts; then he worked for a Boston law firm for a year. He was only twenty-five and had just returned from the United States. A large public meeting convened in Honolulu in October 1869, and a succession of planters and factors praised the Chinese workers who have, "as a rule, been faithful, industrious, and reliable," even declaring that labor contracts had been not just advantageous but "quite necessary" to the Asians' well-being. They moved resolutions that the program be expanded.

Then Dole—tall, pole-thin, large eyed, apple cheeked—spoke: "I oppose the system from principle, because I think it is wrong. . . . I cannot help feeling that the chief end of this meeting, its heart and soul, is plantation profits. . . . Is this not so? The burden of your cry is *labor; we must have labor*, and the plan which promises that . . . you favor without asking many questions. . . . Tried in the balance of the 'free and equal rights' principle, the contract system is found wanting."

One can imagine the pall in the hall, but Dole was seconded by another missionary scion, Albert Francis Judd, son of Gerrit. He was thirty-one, another product of the Punahou School sent to the homeland for higher education, and he came back with his Yale undergraduate degree and his Harvard law degree. But the planters were most provoked by Henry M. Whitney, son of Samuel and Mercy Whitney of the very first company of missionaries and one of the first white children born in the islands. He was now forty-five, had been schooled as a printer in the United States, and as Hawai'i's first postmaster was responsible for issuing the first postage stamps. Now he owned a bookstore and published the *Pacific Commercial Advertiser*. Galled by unfavorable comments in his newspaper, the business element began meeting on other islands than O'ahu to escape his notice. (They also withdrew their advertising, prompting Whitney to sell the paper, start the *Hawaiian Gazette*, and he later founded the Hawaiian-language *Ka Nupepa Kuokoa*.) A quarter of a century on, both Dole and Judd would play important roles in the overthrow of the Hawaiian monarchy. Many scholarly articles have been written trying to defeat the popularly held but erroneous notion that the revolution was done in service of the sugar industry. The revolution suffered from many moral failings, but the stands taken by the junior Dole and Judd, and a few others, are the first exhibit that benefiting sugar was not one.

✤

As Kamehameha V passed forty he took less and less care for himself, and his weight ballooned to nearly four hundred pounds before his body began to give out. Diagnosed in that nineteenth-century way with "dropsy of the heart," the dying mountain of a king sent for his lifelong friend, but never wife, Bernice Pauahi, on the morning of December 11, 1872—his forty-second birthday. She had now been married to Charles Bishop for twenty-two years in the most congenial of the mixed-race marriages, managing her estates and charities while her husband made ever more money. When she arrived she found an extraordinary scene in the death chamber. Six possible claimants to the throne were there. Lot had said that surely God would not take him on his birthday, but when his doctors assured him that his time had come, he said, "God's will be done."

His attorney general, Stephen Phillips, was at the bedside, urging the king to dictate a will and name a successor. The king said he needed time to make such an important decision, but time was now the one thing he did not have. He turned to a trusted friend, the longtime governor of Maui Paul Nahaolelua, and asked whom he favored. Nahaolelua was known to favor Dowager Queen Emma, but she had already recognized the superior claim of William Lunalilo, whom the king disliked but knew to be immensely popular. Whatever he said, Nahaolelua would make five enemies. He finally parried, "They are all *ali'i*."

The scene was selectively recorded by Lot's close friend, privy councillor, and the governor of O'ahu, the American-born John Owen Dominis, who was also the brother-in-law of Lot's ambitious chamberlain, High Chief David Kalakaua. When Bernice arrived, the king told her that he wanted her to succeed him. "No, no, not me," she declared. "Don't think of me, I do not need it." The king protested that he was thinking of the good of the country, not of their friendship. Bernice refused again. "There are others, there is your sister, it is hers by right."

She was correct; the king's half sister Princess Ruth Keʻelikolani (also present) was, aside from her close friend Bernice, the only surviving direct descendent of the Conqueror. Kamehameha III had removed her from the succession over the question of her legitimacy, but when Lot answered that she was not suitable, he was probably alluding to her truculent bearing, her defiant paganism, and her contempt for foreigners, which would have made her a problematical monarch. Bernice would not be moved, however; King Kamehameha V entered extremis and expired an hour later.

Elizabeth Laʻanui, also their classmate at the Royal School, later claimed that before seeing Bernice Kamehameha V offered the throne to her and she declined. Such an offer would have been quite proper, if it happened, for she was a strong candidate, great-granddaughter of the Conqueror's older brother. Like Emma she was one-quarter white (granddaughter of Kamehameha II's shady French secretary Jean Rives); unlike Emma she was married to a white, Franklin Pratt of Boston. Emma also tended Lot in his final hours, but Dominis, alert to promote the interests of the Kalakaua family to whom he had tied his own fortunes, wrote her out of the scene, although all the principal claimants were right there in the room.[7] On his deathbed Kamehameha V was heard finally to mumble his assent that Lunalilo, "unworthy" as he was, would have to do, but that fell well short of a decree. Lot's constitution provided for just such confusion, so when no successor was named, the legislature would choose the monarch.

Of the four principal contenders to the throne, Bernice Bishop had recused herself, and Ruth Keʻelikolani was discounted for her questioned legitimacy and reactionary ways. David Kalakaua wanted the job badly and began lobbying his fellow legislators, but one big obstacle stood in his way: William Charles Lunalilo. It may have taken court genealogists to advise the Kamehamehas of his high birth, but it was no mystery to his mother, the *kuhina nui* Kekauluohi. At the very time of his birth she had chanted, "I luna, i luna, i lunalilo" (up high, up high, disappears up high).

Kamehameha I

Born into the *ali'i* (the ruling elite) before Western contact, Kamehameha grew up steeped in a culture of warfare, human sacrifice, and *kapu* (the indigenous religion). Because of his high lineage, *kahunas* (priests) foretold at his birth that he would one day rule the entirety of the Big Island. For this the ruling usurper king condemned the infant to death, but Kamehameha's high chiefess mother spirited him away to be raised by relatives. The king later changed his mind and raised the boy in the royal court.

Pu'ukohola Heiau

After that king's death, Kamehameha's uncle fought his way to power, and after his death, Kamehameha in turn defeated his cousin for the right to rule the western sector of Hawai'i Island. To enlarge his domain, his *kahunas* advised him to build a *heiau* (temple) to the war god, Kuka'ilimoku. Kamehameha responded by constructing the gigantic *Pu'ukohola* (Hill of the Whale) *heiau*, 225 feet long, 100 feet wide, surrounded by walls up to 20 feet high. The red lava stones were passed by a human chain from the Pololu Valley, fourteen miles away. Pu'ukohola was a *luakini* heiau, one at which opposing chiefs and warriors were sacrificed.

Nuʻuanu Pali

While Kamehameha gained allies where he could, other island chiefs opposed him fiercely, including Kalanikupule, king of Maui and Oʻahu. Key to Kamehameha's conquest was the Battle of Nuʻuanu Pali, fought in the mountains above Honolulu in 1795. After the battle some four hundred Oʻahu warriors who survived the fighting were forced over the 1,100-foot precipice of the *pali* (cliff). Their heads were cut off and offered in sacrifice at a *heiau* where the Pacific War Memorial now stands. Kamehameha's conquest of the entire archipelago required thirty years, after which he ruled a united kingdom for nine more years.

Queen Kaʻahumanu

Herself high-born but not the sacred mother of the heir, Kaʻahumanu remained Kamehameha's favorite among his numerous wives despite their tempestuous relationship. She was witty, shrewd and capable, and Kamehameha before he died named her *kuhina nui* (co-ruler) to share power with his dissolute son. After Kamehameha's death she, the sacred wife, and other high chiefesses combined to overthrow the ancient *kapu* religion, whose key features were the subjugation of women and the *makaʻainana* (commoners, or *kanakas*). She was the effective ruler of Hawaiʻi until her death ten years later.

Opukaha'ia

Today Kamehameha I is credited with unifying the
Hawaiian Islands, but his wars of conquest killed
or displaced tens of thousands. One refugee was
Opukaha'ia, who saw his mother and father cut down,
tried to flee with his baby brother on his back, and was
wounded when the infant was speared. Later escaping
on an American ship, he attended Yale, became
a Christian, and repeatedly challenged American
churches to send missionaries to end the cycle of horror
in Hawai'i. The Congregationalists finally agreed, but
Opukaha'ia died while in training as a missionary, and
translating the Bible.

Liholiho (Kamehameha II)

Queen Kamamalu

Taking power as Kamehameha
II in 1819, Liholiho possessed
little of the Conqueror's
foresight and charisma. Late in
1824 Liholiho and his half-sister
and wife Queen Kamamalu
journeyed to England, and
although they fascinated
fashionable society, a mortified King George IV would not receive "the damn'd
cannibals." With no resistance to Western diseases, the king and queen died
within days of each other in London, of measles.

Hiram and Sybil Bingham

Opukaha'ia's serene death in the Christian faith spurred the Congregationalist Church to finally send seven missionary couples, led by Hiram Bingham and aided by more native converts. When they arrived in Hawai'i in spring of 1820, they had the extraordinary luck to arrive in a spiritual vacuum: Ka'ahumanu's movement to destroy the native religion had succeeded, dismantling *heiaus* and burning the fearsome *ki'i* (wooden idols). Contrary to popular belief, the American missionaries did not destroy the native religion; it self-destructed before their arrival. Bingham's vision of the missionary calling embraced their roles as teachers and doctors, a philosophical difference with the home church that eventually led to his recall.

Kawaiaha'o Church

Capitalizing upon the deep vein of native spirituality, aided by the powerful High Chief Kalanimoku and by Ka'ahumanu's conversion, the missionary effort succeeded beyond what the Americans had dreamed. They worshipped at first in traditional grass houses, until the mighty Kawaiaha'o Church was dedicated in 1842. It was built of fourteen thousand half-ton coral blocks, hand-cut and raised from the reef outside Honolulu by native divers—an act of faith similar to that of European peasants helping to raise the medieval cathedrals.

High Chief Kalanimoku

King Kamehameha III

Queen Kalama

With news of Liholiho's death, nominal power passed to his twelve-year-old brother, Kamehameha III. After the conversion of both his mother and stepmother, he was torn between his ancestral privileges and the new Christian morality. He attempted suicide when the missionaries prevented him from marrying his sister, Nahi'ena'ena, and he then married High Chiefess Kalama of Maui instead. Broken to Christian traces, he laid down absolute power, granted a constitution, took instruction in Western political economy, and oversaw the Great *Mahele*, a division of the lands that was intended to grant ownership to commoners for the first time.

Mataio Kekuanaoa and Daughter Victoria Kamamalu

Hawaiian Princes in America, with Gerrit Judd

When Kamehameha III commissioned the opening of a school for the *ali'i* children, his brother-in-law Mataio Kekuanaoa sought to hold back his daughter, Victoria Kamamalu, who was only two at the time. After several years' education, Kekuanaoa's two sons, Alexander Liholiho (*left*) and Lot Kapuaiwa (*right*) accompanied Gerrit Judd (*standing*) to Europe and America on a diplomatic mission. While honored as royal princes in Europe, they were so insulted by the racist treatment they received in the U.S. that it colored their reigns as Kamehameha IV and V.

King Kamehameha IV
Kamehameha III and Kalama produced no children who survived, and he adopted the children of his half-sister as his heirs. As a small boy, Alexander Liholiho entered the Royal School with some thirty servants, and never lost his resentment at being stripped of his privileges while a student. As Kamehameha IV (1854–1863) he promoted the Anglican Church over the American Congregationalists, and pursued a foreign policy favorable to Britain.

Queen Emma
Granddaughter of the Conqueror's captive English sailor John Young, Emma was a success as queen—popular, gracious and moved by noblesse oblige. Her Anglican religion and Anglophilia distanced her from the American community, however. Nearly shattered by the deaths of her son and husband in the space of a year, she adopted the name *Kaleleonalani*, the Flight of the Sacred Ones. After the monarchy became an elective office, her cool bearing toward Americans cost her the throne.

King Kamehameha V

Prince Lot was older than his brother, but was moved down the succession for his lack of royal temperament. After the Cookes foiled his childhood romance with Princess Abigail, he angrily swore never to marry. As king (1863–1872) he kept his vow, bringing down the Kamehameha dynasty. He also refused to swear the oath as king until he was granted greater power under a new constitution, but his generally wise and discreet rule led to his being known as the Last of the Great Chiefs.

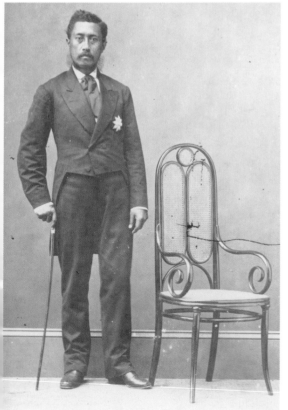

King Lunalilo

Higher-born than his Kamehameha cousins, they denied him marriage to their sister Victoria Kamamalu to prevent his having children who would outrank them. He was a shell of his former self at the time of his accession, far spent in alcohol and tuberculosis. He died after a reign of only one year.

King David Kalakaua

The election within the legislature to succeed Lunalilo was a fierce contest between Dowager Queen Emma and High Chief David Kalakaua, who was not in the royal line but who had served several terms in the legislature and mastered the art of American-style campaigning. When Emma received only six votes despite superior blood claim and her vastly greater popularity with the people, Honolulu erupted in rioting that required American and British marines to quell.

Queen Kapiʻolani

Esther Kapiʻolani was the niece and namesake of the high chiefess who, early in the missionary period, descended to the lava lake of Halemaʻumaʻu to defy Pele and proclaim her faith in Christ. Herself childless, Kapiʻolani founded a hospital for unwed mothers. She was a lady of good works, and she retained her popularity until her death in 1899.

'Iolani Palace

Performance of Hula

Kalakaua was the first monarch of any country to undertake a world tour, welcomed to the royal and imperial courts of Asia and Europe, and he was the guest of honor at the first state dinner ever hosted in the White House. Construction of the 'Iolani Palace allowed him to live in modest state, by Western standards. The palace featured electricity and a telephone before the White House did, but its ruinous cost placed him further in debt to the American business class who criticized his extravagance. They also opposed Kalakaua's determination to resuscitate native culture suppressed since the missionary period—the ancient chants and mythology, indigenous sports such as surfing, and the narrative dance form called hula—despite the fact that the modestly clad dancers here on the palace grounds were a far cry from the near-naked shimmying that enthralled early Western sailors.

Princess Ruth Keʻelikolani

Standing opposite the transition to Western ways was Princess Ruth Keʻelikolani. More than six feet tall, weighing 440 pounds, she refused to speak English, never became a Christian, and spoke for Hawaiians who clung to their traditions. Despite being the Conqueror's great-granddaughter she was removed from the succession ostensibly because of her possible illegitimacy—a term that had no meaning before the missionaries arrived.

Kapiʻolani & Liliʻuokalani in London 1887

The government preferred to project a different image to the West, dispatching Queen Kapiʻolani (seated) and Crown Princess Liliʻuokalani (standing) to London to attend Queen Victoria's Golden Jubilee in 1887. Victoria bestowed special favors on them, ordering their carriage to be escorted by her own household cavalry and having two of her own sons attend them at dinner, when German royalty refused to be seated with them.

COURTESY HAWAII STATE ARCHIVES

Queen Liliʻuokalani
Intelligent and capable, Liliʻuokalani nevertheless played into the hand of pro-American annexationists when she sought to replace the 1887 constitution with one of her own crafting, which would have restored the royal powers of previous generations.

Lorrin Andrews Thurston

Sanford Ballard Dole

While Lorrin Thurston was the firebrand who kindled the Hawaiian coup d'etat of January 1893, he knew that he was too closely associated with the overthrow to win respect abroad as head of the new government. Sanford Dole, who sat on the Hawai'i Supreme Court, had the reputation and gravitas to give the provisional government at least some color of legitimacy, and he became president of the Republic of Hawai'i.

USS Naniwa and HIJMS Boston Anchored Together
The *Boston* (right) supplied the sailors and marines who helped topple the monarchy. Here she rides at anchor next to the larger, faster and more powerful *Naniwa* (left), which the Japanese withdrew rather than have people think they were complicit in a suspected counterrevolution.

Landing Sailors and Marines in Honolulu
Curious townspeople gather to watch bluejackets and sailors from the *Boston* form up on the wharf. They landed ostensibly to protect U.S. interests, but later inquiry determined that they were better positioned in the town to support the coup d'etat, than to protect American property.

Liliʻuokalani Enters Prison
Although the deposed queen probably was complicit in the failed countercoup of 1895, her trial was conducted under rules that would never have been permitted in an American criminal court. Sentenced to five years at hard labor, she was instead confined for nine months in her bedroom in the ʻIolani Palace, whose throne room now served as the Republic's House of Representatives, before being paroled to her private residence, Washington Place.

Princess Ka'iulani

Before the former queen arrived in the United States to lobby against annexation, her niece and heiress apparent, Princess Ka'iulani, undertook an American lecture tour—to the consternation of her aunt's supporters, who suspected that she meant to become queen herself.

Ku'e Petition

George Frisbie Hoar

At seventy-two, Senator Hoar of Massachusetts had gained a reputation as a conscience of the Senate. He was a Republican but anti-imperialist, and despised efforts to establish an American empire. His support of the Ku'e petitions helped defeat the proposed annexation treaty, which needed to pass with a two-thirds majority.

COURTESY HAWAII STATE ARCHIVES

Lowering the Hawaiian Flag

When the Senate failed to annex Hawaii by treaty, President William McKinley accomplished it with a Joint Resolution of Congress, which required only a simple majority—a stratagem used to annex the Republic of Texas in 1845. Playing "Hawai'i Pono'i" as the Hawaiian flag was lowered overwhelmed several members of the former Royal Hawaiian Band, who abandoned their instruments and left the stage. They did not accompany the navy and marine musicians in playing "The Star-Spangled Banner" as the American flag was raised.

At one time he had the makings of a splendid king—handsome, popular, extremely intelligent and liberally disposed, he was a famously brilliant conversationalist and debater—and he aimed to accommodate the Americans where he could while stemming their march to take over the whole country. Once again, however, the Kamehameha family ruined their people's chances for happiness, this time by sabotaging Lunalilo's chances for happiness when they crushed his romance with their sister Victoria Kamamalu over fear of being outranked by his children.[8] (It was extraordinary how "genealogy" had simply become a new word for *mana*.) Distraught, Lunalilo then sought the hand of Kalakaua's sister, Lydia Kamakaʻeha, but she also declined him—at the urging of Kamehameha IV—and she entered that dismal marriage with Dominis.[9] The Kamehamehas' jealousy of Lunalilo's rank apparently extended also to refusing him a position at court, where he could have trained for the reign that most people assumed would one day be his.[10] William Lunalilo therefore gimped through adulthood as a lonely alcoholic bachelor, and was far gone in both drink and tuberculosis at the time the whole matter landed in the legislature.

Lunalilo announced that he would accept the throne only on condition that they hold a plebiscite for the people to vote their choice, and, wrote Castle, "I presume their expression will be in his favor as he is popular."[11] In that referendum the only candidate to stand against him was Kalakaua, and it was a fascinating campaign that showed Hawaiʻi in transition, with Lunalilo standing upon his royal rank but enlightened to seek the suffrage of his people, and Kalakaua running something like an American-style campaign, buttonholing key legislators for support, spreading stories about his opponent, and making promises he couldn't keep.

Lunalilo's only statement was that, notwithstanding his right to inherit the throne, "I desire to submit the decision of my claim to the voice of the people," with the single promise that if he were elected, he would restore the constitution of Kamehameha III, and "govern the nation according to the principles of . . . a liberal constitutional monarchy." His only misstep—whether it was published at his direction or only a widespread misconception—was a claim of direct descent from the Conqueror. A circular authored by a committee of "Skilled Genealogists" in Kalakaua's service quickly brought that up short, but it did nothing to dent Lunalilo's popular support.

Kalakaua did attain a measure of royal connection when he married Esther Kapiʻolani, the erstwhile governess of the unfortunate little Prince of Hawaiʻi, and whom Emma blamed for his death. (Kapiʻolani's Christian name is often rendered as Julia, but *Kulia*—Strive—was her motto, not her name.) Her elderly first husband, Emma's uncle, died, and she and Kalakaua wed not long after Kamehameha IV died. Kapiʻolani, unlike Kalakaua, was distantly related to the Kamehameha line, a tincture that would pass to their children, if they produced any.[12]

For his part, Kalakaua published a platform of windy but clever promises, first shrewdly tying himself to Kamehameha I by promising to enforce the Law of the Splintered Paddle—which he pointed out had been suggested to the Conqueror by Kalakaua's ancestor Keaweaheulu. Second, he promised to increase the population "and fill the land," although one can imagine any number of randy Hawaiians wondering with amusement how much personal attention he meant to devote to that pledge. He promised to repeal all personal taxes and pay off the national debt by putting native Hawaiians into government offices—which sounded mighty but made no sense whatever. The plebiscite would be a nonbinding referendum only, and at root, Kalakaua's chances came down to his ability to influence legislators who would actually decide which would become monarch. Britain and the United States both detected a possibility of trouble—if Lunalilo won the election, which he would, but Kalakaua turned the legislature, which he might, there could be violence. Both consuls requested warships to protect the property of their respective citizens, but only the 2,400-ton screw sloop USS *Benicia* arrived in time.

Lunalilo's triumph in the referendum was so overwhelming

that when the legislature convened to vote for monarch, his jubilant supporters thronged the grounds. Their numbers were sufficiently intimidating that one of their supporters in the legislature moved that the members sign their ballots when they voted—a sure antidote to any American-style skulduggery on Kalakaua's part. It worked, and the vote was unanimous, but for one—John Owen Dominis, Kalakaua's brother-in-law; he abstained.

Though a husk of his former self, Lunalilo took the oath as king on January 8, 1873. Mark Twain had met him in 1866 and liked him enormously, finding him "affable, gentlemanly, open, frank, manly; [he] is as independent as a lord and has a spirit and a will like the old Conqueror himself. He is intelligent, shrewd, sensible, is a man of first-rate abilities, in fact. . . . He has one unfortunate fault—he drinks constantly, and it is a great pity. . . . I like this man, and I like his bold independence, and his friendship for and appreciation of the American residents. . . . If I could print a sermon that would reform him, I would cheerfully do it."[13]

The solemnity of the investiture was largely destroyed when the new king, who was quite musical and had always wanted to lead the band, suddenly seized and donned the bass drum, and led the musicians in a march around the palace grounds, whomping it with abandon. As a youth Lunalilo had been diffident where girls were concerned, and in his student workbook he once composed a poem to inscribe in a girl's autograph book—if one should, he wrote, ever ask him to. Marching to church in the Royal School he was often paired with Emma Na'ea and the two had remained close friends. He had always been careful of his appearance, and recorded in his diary bathing in a stream with his father and using *palolo*, a traditional hair-straightening pomade.[14] Then came his wrenching romantic reversals with Victoria Kamamalu and Lydia Kamaka'eha, and Lunalilo, who might have ushered the Hawaiian kingdom into happier days than they had known under the Kamehamehas, instead came to the throne a broken man.

Indeed, much of the government's focus from the outset was on

keeping him alive, just at a time when national issues required vigorous attention. The 1872 sugar crop was not good, and in defiance
of the law of supply and demand, prices were depressed as well.
The subject of a reciprocity treaty with the United States was back
in circulation, but with their Reconstruction almost spent, the Southern states were about to regain a voice in Congress, so protection of
Southern sugar just promised further disappointment. Then Henry
Whitney of the *Pacific Commercial Advertiser* spoke up. Why not,
he suggested, offer the Americans a fifty-year lease on the Pearl River
basin west of Honolulu, in exchange for importing Hawaiian sugar
duty-free?

It did not seem suspicious. The presence in Hawai'i at that moment of a high-level American military delegation was easily explained away. During his decline, Kamehameha V planned to visit
the United States for medical treatment, and as a courtesy, the U.S.
Navy dispatched the USS *California*, a large, new, massively armed
wooden steam frigate, to transport him. She was under command of
Adm. A. M. Pennock, whose orders included turning the port call
into a goodwill visit, and to "use all your influence and all proper
means to direct and maintain feeling in favor of the United States."
Also present on board were Lt. Col. B. S. Alexander, of the Corps of
Engineers, and Maj. Gen. John M. Schofield, commander of the
Division of the Pacific. They, it was reported, were on a recreational
leave for Schofield's health—although Schofield was only forty-two.

What no one in the islands knew was that they were on a secret
mission, "for the purpose of ascertaining the defensive capabilities
of the different ports and their commercial facilities, and . . . to
collect all information that would be of service to the country in
the event of war with a powerful maritime nation." So far from
their interest in Pearl Harbor being coincidental, their orders also
warned, "It is believed the objects of this visit . . . will be best
accomplished if your visit is regarded as a pleasure excursion,
which may be joined in by your citizen friends."[15] What everyone
knew was that the Pearl River estuary was the most capacious and

most sheltered harbor in the Pacific, but blocked by a coral reef. Alexander being an engineer, short of taking soundings or otherwise arousing suspicion, he could estimate how much effort it would take to blast through it, how much dredging would be required to service a fleet, the best location for a coaling station, and other logistics.

Henry Whitney, who had sold the *Advertiser* and now published the *Hawaiian Gazette*, gave plausible reasons why and how a lease would benefit the kingdom. "It will defeat and indefinitely postpone all projects for the annexation of these Islands to any foreign power, at the same time that it will secure to us all the benefits claimed by the advocates of annexation, and will guarantee our national independence under our native rulers as long as the treaty may continue."[16] An important clause, that last one. If apples and oranges make a poor comparison, Whitney wrote an entire fruit basket on the question of how American warships in Pearl Harbor could satisfy the cases both for and against annexation.

The U.S. minister to Hawai'i, Henry Peirce, had apparently not been included in the plan to quietly assay Pearl Harbor's defensive potential, and when asked about the possible quid pro quo, repeated that the United States had no territorial ambition in the kingdom, but sent dispatches to Secretary of State Hamilton Fish detailing the activity and requesting instructions. The sick and unhappy king was persuaded to support the idea, but if the previous thirty years had taught the educated native class anything, it was that alienation of any part of *Hawai'i nei* was anathema. As the plan became more widely known—and helping to raise the alarm was Walter Murray Gibson, the excommunicated Mormon, now publishing a bilingual newspaper called the *Nuhou*—public gatherings against it were so large and angry that Lunalilo must have known that he had stepped amiss.

The king entered an acutely ill period; he probably knew his time was short, for at one of his last parties he commanded the band to play "God Save the King" seven times. He retreated to his cottage in Waikiki, but more trouble followed him there. Hawai'i had no real standing military force; most of the men in uniform were the band started by his predecessor. There was a small company of household troops sufficient to deal with any local disturbances, and in the quest for spit and polish, they were given over to a Hungarian martinet, Capt. Joseph Jajczay. His infliction of nineteenth-century military discipline was out of proportion to his command. On September 6, 1873, he discovered four treasury guards absent from their post, found them enjoying a Saturday night in town, and locked them up, shackled to balls and chains. The next morning, with the captain gone to church, those prisoners with four others in the cell knocked down the door with the balls they were chained to, and freed themselves but did not run away.

When Jajczay returned from church, other troops ignored orders to seize them; the captain hit one with the flat of his sword, and that soldier knocked him down. Governor Dominis and the Adjt. Gen. Charles Judd (another son of Gerrit) were called to the scene; when Judd tried to force the situation, he was knocked down. Then there was a full-on mutiny. Fourteen loyal troops sided with the government, forty barricaded themselves in the barracks with a six-pounder cannon seized from the palace yard. *Haole* families living in the area left their houses; the streets filled with celebrating *kanakas* who cheered the rebels and brought them food and water. And then, interjecting himself unbidden into the disturbance was David Kalakaua, presenting himself as mediator. Anything that embarrassed Lunalilo made him look good to the public, and he may well have made things worse. After a week three of the mutineers were given safe conduct to Waikiki, where the king promised them amnesty if they would return to duty, and that ended the affray.[17] The rebels were discharged and barred from further service, whites were put in charge of the armory, and many people, the *haoles* especially, tried to put it out of their minds. At some level beneath conscious acknowledgment it registered on them that it was significant how quickly the *kanakas* had stormed to support a mutiny, and thus how much resentment lay just beneath the surface.

Although Lunalilo was pressed to name a commissioner to negotiate yet a new attempt at a reciprocity treaty, this time on the
basis of a Pearl Harbor lease, he finally followed both his own instincts and the popular remonstrance, and withdrew his support.
He had tried to govern, through the ravages of whiskey and disease,
and in truth kept the one promise he made during the campaign:
He restored the universal male suffrage of the 1852 constitution.
The king was barely conscious when the election was held on February 2, 1873, and his death from pneumonia the next day saddled
the privy council with deciding which legislature must choose a
new monarch: the old one, which had not been prorogued, or the
new one scheduled to convene in April. They chose the latter.

One matter of which Lunalilo made certain before he expired
was to express his command not to be buried with the Kamehameha kings at Mauna ʻAla. His bitterness at their refusing him
their sister still burned. He was instead laid to rest in a small, stately
Victorian mausoleum in the Kawaiahaʻo churchyard, inscribed
simply LUNALILO KA MOʻI, "Lunalilo the King."

Through the king's persistent illness, Emma often nursed him,
but they seldom had any time alone. Thwarted in marriage by his
cousins, Lunalilo had taken for a mistress the green-eyed Eliza
Meek, *hapa haole* daughter of Honolulu's harbormaster. Hopelessly
overmatched in the company of the royal family, she became shrill
and shrewish, careful never to leave Emma and Lunalilo alone together, refusing to leave the room even when asked to be excused.
She insulted the king to such a degree that even in his exhaustion
he once found the strength to throw a chair at her. Emma took it in
stride,[18] knowing that there was a faction at court who believed she
was angling for his endorsement to succeed him. While the dowager queen basked in the love of the people, she was under no illu-
sions about her lack of popularity among the wealthy Americans.
But upon both major counts of her intransigent Anglophilia she was
unshakable: her Episcopal religion, and her preference for British
over American influence in Hawaiʻi. It looked increasingly as

though the new contest, sharpened as never before, would be a face-off between Emma and Kalakaua.

⚜

The grief over Lunalilo's death overshadowed any appreciation of a living reminder of their history glimpsed at the same time by the observant American writer Charles Nordhoff. Of that first generation of missionaries there was now a single survivor in the islands:

> Of the first band who came out from the United States, the only one living in 1873 is Mrs. Lucy G. Thurston, a bright, active, and lively old lady of seventy-five years, with a shrewd wit of her own. She drives herself to church on Sundays in a one-horse chaise, and has her own opinions of passing events. How she has lived in the tropics for fifty years without losing even an atom of the New England look puzzles you; but it shows you also the strength which these people brought with them, the tenacity with which they clung to their habits of dress and living and thought, the remorseless determination.[19]

In truth Mrs. Thurston had no difficulty maintaining the aura of old New England, for she had just finished her memoirs, using copies of her letters that her husband long before had encouraged her to make. "In the silence and solitude of night, with my study lamp," she wrote, "I was young again, and I saw my father's family surrounding me, so loving and so lovely. Many, many noble friends had assembled with them. . . . So real, so near they all seemed, that when about to open these lips to speak to them in an easy manner, a thrill went through me." Others may have seen an eccentric elderly lady clattering to church in her buggy on Sundays, but in her own mind she had been twenty-five again, and writing one of the most fascinating and readable memoirs of early American Hawai'i.[20]

Mrs. Thurston had six more years to live, but in the preface of her book she composed her own epitaph: *"She Hath Done What She*

Could." The sentiment could equally have memorialized the fellow travelers of her youth. It was true that they imposed a frowning and alien morality on the native culture, but they had also taught and doctored, pastored and befriended. In their own minds their most important contribution was to give the Hawaiians a faith to replace *kapu* and sacrifice, but they also gave them a written language and a literacy rate that was now the highest in the world. They gave them a head start on principles of constitutional government to which they must have come later than sooner anyway. And now some of their sons—Dole, Judd, Whitney—maintained a lookout for the integrity of the kingdom. But there was another element that would wreck it all. That was the sons and grandsons who increasingly dominated the islands' economy. They were possessed of an inflexible certainty that their moral right was only augmented by their financial might. They mistook, however, their own greed for the sense of purpose that fired the first missionaries.

Now there was David Kalakaua, who would make sweet deals with them if they would make him king. And he would find that in making his easily-given promises to the "Missionary Boys," he was making a deal with the devil.

14. Taffy Triumphant

On September 17, 1875, a distinguished visitor disembarked from the steamer *City of Melbourne*, two weeks out of Auckland, New Zealand. Anthony Trollope was sixty, and had assumed the mantle of the late Charles Dickens as England's most famous novelist. He spent less than two days in Honolulu before continuing his voyage, and was gone by the time the newspapers published his presence, but the brevity of his acquaintance did not prevent him from writing his impressions for the *Daily and Weekly Mercury* of Liverpool. Amenities at the Hawaiian Hotel, he noted, cost dearly, but the establishment produced its own gaslight, and local laundries could process any amount of work by a "steam apparatus" in as little as six hours. The parties glittered, Americans dominated the government, the mainstay of the economy was sugar, and the country was led by King Kalakaua, whose dynasty "rejoiced in the name of Ka-meha-meha."[1] Trollope was about to become even more famous with publication of the novel most often cited as his masterpiece, *The Way We Live Now*, whose central theme was the self-deception of greedy graspers who believe that dishonesty becomes acceptable if only it succeeds on a grand-enough scale. If Trollope had stayed longer in Hawai'i, he would have seen how closely life can imitate art, for the expensive, prosperous, American-accented Honolulu that he glimpsed was the fruit of a year of scheming, tumult, dissension, riot, and recrimination.

The death of a king once again without issue or declaration of a successor threw the matter into the legislature, and the two predicted figures came forward as claimants. The first was Dowager Queen Emma Kaleleonalani, who asserted that Lunalilo on his deathbed had declared his desire that she succeed him, but he expired before a decree could be prepared. To make this claim twice within a year would sound suspicious, but most observers both foreign and domestic were equally certain that he would have chosen her. And there, again, was David Kalakaua with his weighty but not royal family behind him, and his American-style political savvy that Emma felt was beneath her.

Emma's blood claim over Kalakaua's was commanding.[2] With the Conqueror's legitimate direct candidates now removed from contention, Emma's lineage was superior to that of any rivals, being the great-granddaughter on her father's side of Kamehameha I's only full brother, Keli'imaika'i. Kalakaua, as he had with Lunalilo, hired genealogists to dispute her claim; they maintained that her grandmother was *po'olua*, making Emma not certainly the Conqueror's great-grandniece. (That alternative great-grandfather, however, would have descended Emma from Kalaniopu'u, which would still best Kalakaua's claim.) In either event, Emma Kaleleonalani was a chiefess of high descent. On her mother's side, however, she was the granddaughter of Kamehameha's British captive servant John Young, leaving her vulnerable—as she had discovered at her engagement party—to a racist whisper that being one-quarter white disqualified her. More to policy, the legislature also had to consider that Queen Emma remained immensely popular with the native people, who had come to depend upon the hospital she had built and endowed for them, and to whom she remained philanthropically

devoted. Weighing against her in the largely Congregationalist legislature was her Anglicanism and her openly British sympathies in
the international arena. They would not forget that Emma's late
child had been named Albert Edward after the Prince of Wales,
and that Queen Victoria herself had been his godmother.

Only a day after the dowager queen made her candidacy known,
High Chief Kalakaua published his intention also to run for king.
Though not of the royal line, he was descended from Kamehameha
I's general and confidant Kameʻeiamoku (he who had captured the
Fair American and killed her crew, save Isaac Davis), and his mother
was a high chiefess of the Kona District—so his election would
mean a complete change of dynasty.[3] A sometime poet, he cleverly
framed his announcement, beginning in the style of the traditional
Hawaiian chant, which might draw some of the native support
away from Emma, and ending with a little American-style elec-
tioneering that would play well with the *haoles*: "Now, therefore, I,
David Kalakaua, cheerfully call upon you," it concluded, "and re-
spectfully ask you to grant me your support."

And the race was on. Kalakaua was a complicated man. His
name meant "Day of the Battle," and in that uncanny Hawaiian
way, foreshadowed his life of conflict. He was born in November
1836, making him only a few months, probably, younger than Emma.
She had been given in *hanai* to a wealthy English doctor, and grew
up in luxury and stability. He had been promised in *hanai* to Kuini
Liliha, but Kinaʻu intervened, perhaps disapproving of her and Boki's recalcitrant tendencies, and routed him instead to the High
Chiefess Haʻaheo, who died when he was seven. He lived with
his *hanai* father on Maui, then with his biological parents on
Oʻahu, when not boarding at the Royal School. He could be for-
given ambition born of not knowing exactly who he was. Emma
was beautiful, he tended to be fat; his nickname was "Taffy." At the
Royal School, because of their similar ages they were placed in a
group that took their lessons together, and he was always trying
to catch up to her. Owing to her home life, she spoke excellent

English; he struggled with the lessons. She grew up in a home with a sense of propriety, he lived closer to the life where the chief took what he wanted—until he saw his grandfather hanged for it.

And here they were at thirty-eight, with little changed in their respective relationship. Like Emma, Kalakaua despite his pandering to the Americans also desired to restore native rights and rehabilitate the culture, and bring the *haoles* to heel. In his younger years he had headed a group called the Young Hawaiians, whose motto had been "Hawaii for the Hawaiians." He was well known in the legislature, having served there for thirteen years after holding earlier positions in the administration of Kamehameha IV. The acting British commissioner quoted A. F. Judd, now attorney general, as saying that he would "almost prefer the chances of a revolution, to the nomination of Colonel Kalakaua."[4] Bishop saw things perhaps most clearly: that Kalakaua if he were elected would try to do a good job, despite his faults, but "there are strong fears, that Q. E. would be partial to a clique," by which he meant the English.[5]

His constant angling for the throne, though, and his possible manipulation of the palace troops' mutiny, only heightened Emma's disgust with his grasping. But she also realized that his ability to dedicate himself to a goal was a lesson by which she could profit. As she wrote her cousin Peter Ka'eo, "With Taffy's faults we must give him credit . . . he has exerted himself . . . he has not faltered, but keeps on trying for the end. This is a good point in him which we must copy." Copy, she wrote, using honorable means, not the crooked subterfuges that Kalakaua was all too ready to resort to.[6] In her memoirs, Kalakaua's sister Lydia Kamaka'eha relentlessly takes his part, depicting Emma as the one grasping for power, shamelessly importuning both the dying Kamehameha V and the dying Lunalilo to name her, even within Lydia's hearing. It is this last element, if nothing else, that falls too far outside the parameters of Emma's discretion to be credible.[7]

Perhaps as a measure of his desire to be king, Kalakaua paid up his back dues to the Masons, membership in which he had dropped in 1868, and began attending meetings again.[8] This time there would be no plebiscite, which Emma would have won going away; the entire contest would be waged within the legislature, behind the paired Ionic columns of the Ali'iolani Hale. As the campaign progressed, Emma left the city for her house in the Nu'uanu Valley. Stories began to circulate about her that had something of Kalakaua's sound about them: she had promised to abolish all taxes, she had promised to free convicts from the jail, she had promised to take no salary. Some of it may have been true; Emma's advisers were pressing on her that she could not win in the legislature, and she must compete with Kalakaua on his own ground. If she did make or consent to these pronouncements, it was out of her character and not well done. And it all happened with astonishing suddenness. Lunalilo had died on February 3, and the legislature met to make its choice on February 12.

American political interests could never have come to dominate Hawai'i without first capturing the culture, and Kalakaua's lobbying in the legislature gives some vivid examples of how complete the transformation had become. One of Kalakaua's backers there was the *hapa haole* John Adams Kuakini Cummins, the "Lord of Waimanalo," who previous to casting his vote against Emma offered that "I believe in beautiful women and fine horses, but no petticoat shall rule me."[9] Cummins was the offspring of another one of those useful marriages, this one between Massachusetts businessman Thomas Jefferson Cummins and a high chiefess of O'ahu five years his senior. Himself raised as a high chief,[10] there was a time when a man like Kuakini Cummins would have fallen on his belly at the approach of a figure like Keopuolani; for a decade and a half after the Conqueror's death, the important policy decisions of the kingdom were made by Ka'ahumanu and then by her niece Kina'u. For Kuakini to have entered the legislature as a knee-jerk mysogynist, and to refer to such a decidedly Western concept as "petticoat rule," demonstrates the sea change in the Americanization of cultural values—which certainly smoothed Kalakaua's path to the throne. To say that the seat on the privy council that Kalakaua then awarded to Cummins was a payoff for his vote might not be fair, for Cummins's wealth, social prominence, and favors rendered to previous monarchs recommended him for such a station, but over the next two decades Cummins proved himself an effective servant of the house of Kalakaua.

A large throng gathered before the Aliʻiolani Hale, most of them the queen's supporters—"Emmaites," their enemies called them. When the vote was taken there were 39 votes for Kalakaua, 6 for Emma, and it was apparent that Kalakaua had managed to do what observers feared he might do the year before—get himself elected monarch against the prevailing will of the people, by ingratiating himself with a majority of the legislators. Lunalilo had had the fact of a landslide referendum to prevent that; Emma had none. When the result was announced, a deputation of five legislators left the building for a waiting carriage to take the news to the new king.

But then "a hoarse, indignant roar, mingled with cheers from the crowd without was heard within the Assembly."[11] The crowd became a mob as shock gave way to utter outrage. They rocked and then tore apart the carriage as the deputation fled back inside. Wheel spokes became clubs; windows shattered as they surged inside. Most of the eighty policemen whom the marshal of the kingdom, William C. Parke, had assigned to crowd control, joined in. Inside, Parke stationed himself just outside his own office with a pistol, and the crowd avoided him, but the legislature was sacked. One legislator who was known to have supported Kalakaua was defenestrated and killed where he landed.

There was no help. Hawaiʻi's showy little army had never been reconstituted after the mutiny the previous year; the policemen were now part of the mob. Charles Reed Bishop, now foreign minister, Governor Dominis, and the king-elect called on the British and American consuls for marines from their warships—of which there were only three in the harbor—to restore order. About 75 marines landed from HM screw corvette *Tenedos*, and about 150 from the sloops-of-war USS *Portsmouth* and USS *Tuscarora*. The Americans cleared the courthouse and square; the British marched up the Nuʻuanu Valley to Emma's summer house, Hanaiakamalama, and dispersed her people gathered there.[12]

It was the most violent rioting that Honolulu had ever seen. At one point Kalakaua sent a message to the queen dowager, asking her to request her partisans to disband, but she refused. The tension was slow to dissipate; that night was punctuated by breaking glass and gunshots. That Kalakaua opened his reign by placing himself in further debt to the Americans played a suitable overture; that was a central theme of his seventeen-year tenure.

In arranging the royal household of his new dynasty, and himself being childless with Kapiʻolani, he declared his younger brother, William Pitt Leleiohoku II, twenty, his heir apparent, followed by his younger sister Lydia Kamakaʻeha, and next their youngest sister, Miriam Likelike. All were, by his prerogative, made royal highnesses, and he bestowed a new name on Lydia. When she was born in 1838 the *kuhina nui*, Elizabeth Kinaʻu, who had only seven months to live, was enduring a painful eye condition. She was close friends with the new mother, Keohokalole, with whom she shared a descent from Keoua, and she named the infant Kamakaʻeha, "Sore Eyes," preceded by Liliʻu Loloku Walania, "Painful Tearful Burning," with Lydia being her first name, and her oft-used surname, Paki, that of her *hanai* father. At his accession Kalakaua contracted her names to Liliʻuokalani, "Smarting of the Royal Ones," which her close friends shortened to the nickname "Liliʻu."

Soon after his election, Kalakaua undertook a royal progress to the different islands, which helped his popularity. And there were other ways in which he figured out how to help himself. One of his first accomplishments was composing the lyrics of a national anthem, "Hawaiʻi Ponoʻi" ("Righteous Hawaiʻi," more liberally translated as "Hawaiʻi's Own True Sons"), partnering with his bandmaster, Capt.

Henry Berger, who wrote the music. "Hawai'i's own true sons," it began. "Be loyal to your king, Your country's liege and lord, the chief." After each verse came the refrain, "Father above us all, Kamehameha, Who guarded in wars, With his spear." The song was a clever, clever fusion of patriotism, designed to promote an upwelling of national pride that the people would find in having a national anthem, and his own ingratiation with the people by tying himself to Kamehameha I, to whom he was not related, and whose descendents viewed him as something between a civil servant and ambitious grabber.

And the project also began to recast Kamehameha from Conqueror to Unifier. Many Hawaiians on Kaua'i still viewed him as the king who failed to subdue their island and had to negotiate for it; many on O'ahu reviled him for the massacre at Nu'uanu Pali, where hundreds of their own men had plunged to their deaths and had their severed heads offered in sacrifice. It would have been impossible for Kamehameha to have killed tens of thousands during the conquest and been kindly remembered everywhere. Kalakaua, in league with a controversial legislator—Walter Murray Gibson the ex-Mormon, who had wheeled and dealt and rehabilitated himself back into public employment—undertook a project to commission a heroic statue of Kamehameha to commemorate the centennial of Captain Cook's landing. A worldwide search for an artist led them to Thomas Ridgeway Gould, a Bostonian working in Florence, who had recently produced portrait busts of Junius Booth and Ralph Waldo Emerson. Gibson and the king raised ten thousand dollars, and commissioned Gould to execute a heroic standing figure of the Conqueror, to depict him at the age of about forty-five, which gave Gould some creative license since the only portraits of Kamehameha showed him in his old age.

The plaster model that Gould created was sent to Paris for casting in brass, the gilded finished statue was dispatched in August 1880, but the ship burned and sank near the Falkland Islands. The Hawaiian government used the insurance proceeds to pay for a second casting, unaware that Falklands fishermen had salvaged the original, although it was damaged. Painted in lifelike colors to conceal damage to the gilt brass, this original was later erected before the courthouse in Kapaʻau, near Kamehameha's birthplace in North Kohala. The second casting was placed before the legislative building, the Aliʻiolani Hale in Honolulu, and it too was eventually painted in natural colors. And Kalakaua was proved correct, as the statues were quickly accepted as iconic symbols of the Hawaiian nation; the more traditional natives accorded them the status of spiritual objects, and receptacles of *mana*, despite their being Western-created objects of heroic art. For those who could not see the statues in person, the image was widely disseminated on a twenty-five-cent postage stamp. Kalakaua was probably the first head of state to realize the propaganda value of the humble stamps. During his tenure as postmaster, issues of Hawaiian stamps—perforated, gummed, and beautifully engraved in Boston—became some of the most advanced in the world and were avidly sought by collectors.

Kalakaua was fascinated by science and inventions, and he keenly followed the doings of a British scientific expedition that arrived in June 1874, to record a transit of Venus across the sun—the first such event since the one that brought Captain Cook to the islands ninety-six years before. It also, happily for his purposes, put him in connection with the somewhat outcast Princess Ruth on a matter not related to the succession. The seven astronomers wished to be lodged as close as possible to where their instruments were set up. The site selected was in the Apua District on Honolulu, *mauka* of the business center. Ruth rented them a house that she owned, and the station was located next door on land that Kalakaua owned. The king proved to be rather an overgrown schoolboy, and wore his welcome thin, but he had facilitated their business by waiving customs inspections and in other ways, and the astronomers tolerated him with smiles—unlike the incessant heat, rain, mosquitoes, and a throng of curious locals.[13] The actual Venusian transit was not to occur until December 8; on November 15 Kalakaua imposed on them with several ladies of the court; it was as close to the transit as he would get, for he had to leave the country two days later.

He had gotten himself elected king on promises of relief for the sugar planters, and had to leave for America to make good on the pledge. Times for the industry had turned hard, but there was nothing in the American political landscape to indicate that landing a deal for sugar would be any easier than it ever had been. It was a risk, but Kalakaua concluded that he must go to the United States to dispense some royal charm—no reigning king from anywhere had ever visited America.

He sailed on the USS *Benicia* in company with his brother-in-law Governor Dominis—who left his wife and mother to coldly endure each other at Washington Place—and Henry Peirce the American minister, and aides. Kalakaua, who all his life had had to elbow his way to a place of prominence, actually proved himself good at being a king. While his negotiators thrashed out the details of a treaty that the United States did not particularly want, but which, recognizing its special relationship with Hawai'i, they were willing to entertain, the king addressed a joint session of Congress, visited P. T. Barnum's circus in New York (although it was uncertain at times whether he was a tourist or an attraction), and attended a glittering state dinner hosted by President U. S. Grant—a first for the nation.

By the opening of 1875, certain elements became clear. Pearl Harbor was off the table, but Hawai'i had to agree that no other reciprocity treaty would be sought with other countries. Hawaiian rice, which had been growing in importance, would also be admitted to the United States free of duty, but not wool. Unrefined sugar destined for the San Francisco refineries would be included. It had been surprisingly easy; Secretary of State Fish agreed to present the treaty to the cabinet. Kalakaua returned home on February 15 and the wait began, hopeful at first, but as the months dragged on, all were reminded of the many obstacles that could arise in the United States. But the Senate approved the treaty on March 18, and

Kalakaua ratified it a month later; but then the U.S. House of Representatives had to pass on it, and the next session would not be until December.

In the meantime the California refiners got cold feet. What if Hawaiian sugar flooded the market? Some of the Honolulu factors then moved intelligently, visiting San Francisco to say they would withhold their sugar from refiners who could not support them. Then there was the usual Louisiana objection. In fact the House did not vote until May 8, and it passed, but then the Senate had to approve that version. Acting in blind faith, the Hawaiian legislature passed the necessary enabling legislation to set the treaty in motion, and waited for news from the American Senate. And that did not come until August. But, he had done it. Kalakaua had made reciprocity happen, and Honolulu was delirious.[14]

Now it was time to really be a king. After four decades the royal residence that faced the legislative assembly building was nearing the end of its useful life. Called the 'Iolani Palace, it was a palace only in the meaning that it housed royalty; it was really a middling large pavilion, designed for ceremonial functions more than living in. It was built of wood and thus suffered the fate of all wooden structures in Hawai'i over time, riddled by insects to the point of collapse. The king commissioned the building of a new 'Iolani Palace that, while not on the scale of a Versailles or a Caserta, would at least allow the Hawaiian crown to conduct its business in a state somewhat similar to the rest of the world's monarchs.

And then, if he had accomplished so much on his trip to the United States, what might he do on a trip around the world? At a cabinet meeting on January 11, 1881, Kalakaua announced his intention to make a royal circumnavigation, something that no other monarch, from anywhere, had ever done. There was little time to discuss it. He would take Attorney General William Armstrong with him, and his chamberlain, Charles Judd; he appointed Lili'uokalani

as regent, and sailed on January 20. Usually dismissed as an opening extravagance of the king who gained fame as the "Merrie Monarch," Kalakaua on his world tour actually did what monarchs still
do: He promoted his country and its business interests, he built or
cemented relationships, and in fact he conducted a fair amount of
state business out of pocket.

The first call was at San Francisco to huddle with the sugar refiners about business there, and then he reversed course for Japan.
Twenty-four rough days out of San Francisco fighting high seas and
headwinds, Kalakaua's party docked in Yokohama on March 4, and
a week later were ensconced in suites at the Imperial Palace. Watchful for the dignity of his country, the king expressed his satisfaction
at being billeted in the same rooms that had hosted President Grant
and the Duke of Genoa. He was also able straightaway to conclude
his most important business, an agreement for an increase of
Japanese workers. "What you desired, mostly," he wrote to Chan-
cellor C. C. Harris, "skilled labor, can be had by proper applica-
tions through the Foreign Office at any time. . . . I would take no
heed of what the foreign news papers say. No foreign news paper is
allowed in Tokio. So their judgment cannot be taken as a fair representation of the inward working and policy of the country." A second letter, to Foreign Minister W. L. Green, alerted him that he had
concluded an agreement for a treaty allowing Japanese courts expanded jurisdiction "to the exclusion of the extraterritorial clause,"
which would soon be forwarded to Green by the Japanese Foreign
Office. He particularly asked Green to press the princess regent for
her approval. The king was anxious that Lili'uokalani gain a reputation as a successful administrator and believed that this would be
set down to her credit.[15]

During his sojourn Kalakaua was treated to visits to the naval
academy, an arsenal, a civil engineering school, a paper factory, and
a printing office, among others, and he was the honored center of a
military parade. All this left him with a feeling of the warmest fra-
ternity with Emperor Mutsuhito.[16] The Japanese politely raised a

barrier, however, when the Hawaiian king ventured one too-intimate proposal. Kalakaua sensed that at the end of all games, Hawaii was too small and weak to exist indefinitely as an independent country. He believed that it must, eventually, come under the dominion of either the Americans, whose cultural and commercial encroachment was already pervasive, or the Japanese—an outside chance, but one that he thought he could perhaps improve. The king's youngest sister, Princess Miriam Likelike, had married Scottish businessman Archibald Cleghorn, and their daughter, Princess Victoria Ka'iulani, was now five years old. Lili'u and Dominis had no children, which made Ka'iulani, after her mother, heiress apparent to the throne. Gently Kalakaua explored the possibility of Ka'iulani's betrothal to a Japanese imperial prince. That government, giving no hint of its mortification at the thought of racial intermarriage, declined with fulsome thanks on the ground that the prince was already betrothed to another.[17]

Hardly was the king out of Hawai'i when rumors and diplomatic intrigues began swirling about his actions and intentions. The king's increasing debt to the sugar industry was common knowledge, and the story gained currency that his true purpose in traveling abroad was to find a buyer for the country or some part of it, or to use it as collateral in securing a large foreign loan. Those stories reached the ear of James G. Blaine, the new U.S. secretary of state, who felt impelled to squash any European ambitions before they could take root. Buttonholing the French minister to Washington, Blaine characterized Kalakaua as "a false and intriguing man," and "thought it his duty to say plainly" that the United States would never allow a sale of Hawaiian territory to happen. He made similar remarks to the British minister, Sir Edward Thornton, who passed it up to the Foreign Ministry, with the observation that Blaine's comments left him certain that "the position of the Sandwich Islands is of such importance to the safety of the United States that they would never allow any other nation than themselves to have control over them." The British might have a free hand anywhere else in the Pacific, as far as Blaine was concerned, but Hawai'i was off limits. Thornton went on to suppose that, ultimately, this issue would drive the United States to take sole control of the islands.[18]

From the State Department the topic wafted up to the newly installed president James A. Garfield, who declared that such an action by Kalakaua would be a breach of the 1875 reciprocity treaty, which ruled out any alienation of Hawaiian territory during the life of the treaty. Blaine sent dispatches to U.S. ambassadors in European capitals to head off any attempts by Kalakaua to sell or mortgage his country by warning his hosts that the United States would not permit it.

Meanwhile, the British Foreign Ministry sent a copy of Thornton's report to its commissioner in Honolulu, James Wodehouse. Seeing a chance to advance Britain's case in Hawai'i (and blithely unaware that Britain was in a phase of rapprochement with the Americans over Hawai'i) Wodehouse used his cordial access to the queen dowager to show the letter to her, playing up the part about the American intent eventually to seize control of the country. Emma was shocked. This more than overrode her disdain for Taffy; she was a patriot and in her deep roots she was thoroughly antirepublican. Wodehouse also slipped the letter to Archibald Cleghorn, who then brought his wife, Likelike, to see it, and then to John Dominis, who asked for and received a copy to show to Lili'uokalani herself. All were stonefaced.

Two of the English-language newspapers in Honolulu had British editors, and Wodehouse lobbied them successfully to feature the subject in their journals, with accompanying editorials critical of the United States. Finally he felt emboldened to send to the British squadron at Esquimalt, British Columbia, to dispatch a warship to Honolulu to protect British interests. Satisfied that he had started driving a wedge between the United States and its client state, Wodehouse informed London of his little venture into geopolitics and spent $250 to host an elegant party on the occasion of Queen Victoria's birthday, which the princess regent attended and hoisted a glass to toast the British monarch's health.

When Wodehouse heard back from London, what he received was a frosty slap. Foreign Minister Earl Granville was horrified by Wodehouse's meddling; significant repairs must now be made with the United States, there was no need for a warship in Honolulu, and to top it off, Wodehouse had to pay for the queen's birthday party himself.

And all this took place in response to the mere *rumor* that Kalakaua was intending to sell the kingdom. Blaine's own horror at the scale of Chinese immigration contemplated by the sugar growers would have been assuaged had he only known the energy with which Kalakaua was working behind the sugar boys' backs. In China in early April, foul weather nearly frustrated Kalakaua's desire to visit Tientsin and Peking, but he persevered and was able to gain an important concession concerning Chinese labor: "First, of stopping if possible further immigration of Chinese to the Islands, without carrying with them their wives, and Secondly, to secure for our government the same privileges granted to the United States Government, the right to restrict, return or remove, the large influx of Chinese to our Islands. On these two subjects our mission has been successful."[19] The sugar boys back in Hawai'i would have gone into fits had they known what he was doing.

Kalakaua was in Hong Kong when he wrote on April 21 that he had learned of an outbreak of smallpox in Honolulu, and was right away concerned for the success of Lili'uokalani's administration. "I hope Her Royal Highness will continue admister [*sic*] her government for the good of the people, for I really empathize with her . . . that the small pox should make its appearance, imposing upon her anxiety and extra labor." He considered aborting his world tour and returning to Honolulu to deal with the epidemic, but a letter from Dominis that the king answered from Singapore let him know that the danger had been contained. The royal tour was costing money, and Kalakaua apologized for the single greatest expense: the manufacture of badges for the royal orders that he was handing out to the crowned heads and potentates. However, "badges have a powerful weight upon the minds of Asiatic Princes, especially those of Japan, Siam and Johore." He noted that European monarchs had already taken care to load them down with hardware, and if Hawai'i wished to be included in the family of significant nations, it could do no less.[20]

From Cairo on June 21 Kalakaua wrote his sister; he had learned that nearly three hundred Hawaiians had fallen to smallpox, and that she had led the nation in prayers to get through the epidemic. But then he loosed a broadside, showing that those years at the Royal School had not penetrated to the core of his *ali'i* identity, wanting results and not placated by incantations: "As you are a religious and praying woman, Oh! All the religious people praise you! But what is the use of prayer after 293 lives of our poor people have gone to their everlasting place. Is it to thank Him for killing or is it to thank him for sending them to him or to the other place which. I never believed in the efficacy of prayer and consequently I never allowed myself to be ruled by the Church. . . . The idea of offering a prayer when hundreds a [*sic*] dying around you. To save the life of the people is to work and not pray."[21] (His old schoolmarm, Juliette Cooke, would have predicted as much. "They do not speak much against religion," she had written of the royal children at the school, "yet their practices, conversations &c tell their true opinions."[22])

The king went on his way through Egypt as guest of the khedive, noting that he had intended to buy a set of pearls for Kapi'olani, but the five-hundred-dollar price was simply too much. In Italy he met King Umberto I and then Pope Leo XIII, then toured Europe, in all capitals being received, and acting like, a fellow monarch. He returned via the United States and arrived home on October 29, having been gone seven months—the average amount of time that it once took a shipload of missionaries to reach the islands from America.

The new 'Iolani Palace was nearing completion, less the subject of remark on its beauty, which was extraordinary, than on its cost, which was some three hundred thousand dollars—equivalent to an entire annual budget. It was imposing in its scale but had astonishingly few rooms. The forty-four tall windows spaced around this first floor looked out from only four principal chambers. Crossing the intricately tiled floor of the veranda, one entered the Grand Hall that extended straight through the building. At the far end a broad straight staircase of gleaming koa and other exotic woods rose to the second story. Eight bronze chandeliers hung from the elaborately plastered ceiling, their even, yellowish electric light not flickering like the previous gas lamps. Technology, as the British astronomers discovered, was Kalakaua's favorite hobby, and new inventions replenished his sense of wonder and amusement. The lights and their electric generator had doubled the cost of the building, but he had taken great pride that his 'Iolani Palace had electric lights, indoor plumbing, and a telephone even before the White House of the American presidents in Washington could boast of such amenities.

The second floor of the palace contained six rooms—the king's bedroom, study, and music room on the west side, and the queen's bedroom and two spare bedrooms on the east side. The latter were reserved mostly for use by Kapi'olani's sisters, Virginia and Victoria. The latter was the widowed mother of three sons who, after the immediate family, were the heirs of the kingdom. The great grief of Kapi'olani's life was that, as much as she adored children, she bore none. Thus, more than public spirit was involved in her establishing the Kapi'olani Maternity Home for native mothers and their babies, in a house that Victoria had bequeathed for the purpose when she died in January 1884.

A lavish banquet inaugurated the palace on December 27, 1882, followed by the coronation six weeks later, timed to the ninth anniversary of Kalakaua's accession. Crowns were the last remaining confirmation of the new dynasty, and they and the ceremony were paid for with appropriations from the previous two legislatures. The crowns were gold but not gaudy, the circlet of his crown thinly spaced with small diamonds, the circlet of her smaller crown equally thinly spaced with small opals. A modest pavilion was built on the grounds just southeast of the palace, and connected by a covered ramp. The ceremony was brief, an amalgam of European ritual—crown, scepter, sword, and ring—with Hawaiian custom—*kapu* stick to create a sacred space, *kahili* to proclaim his rank, and the great feather cloak of the Conqueror for continuity. Those Americans of the party critical of him, who might have been inclined to be moved by the coronation, or to accept it as a ceremony of some gravity, were disabused of the notion at the sight of Kalakaua crowning himself, picking up the crown by the golden bead that surmounted the arches and, according to one observer, plopping it on his own head with all the dignity of a golf cap. (Another ceremony during the festivities was the dedication, finally, of the heroic statue of the Conqueror by Thomas Ridgeway Gould.) With the coronation Kalakaua saw a chance to finally repair the rift between his family and the queen dowager. He issued new royal patents, designating Kapiʻolani as first lady of the realm, with Emma second in precedence, followed by his sisters Liliʻuokalani and Likelike. This was in the best European etiquette, but he could not, apparently, find the words to tell his sisters about it, leaving the crown princess to read about it in the newspapers. Emma saw it as a healing step, but also noted that he still excluded Bernice and Ruth, both of whom should have taken precedence over herself. She therefore followed their lead in not attending the coronation, but all three attended the dinner. Absent from the dinner were Liliʻu and Likelike, who stayed home and sulked—alone, as both their husbands did attend. The progress was that it was one of the few occasions when Emma and Kapiʻolani attended the same function, and no word of discord escaped the evening.

The coronation of Kalakaua and Kapiʻolani nine years into his reign provoked criticism, even disgust, from the sugar boys in a way that emphasized the differences between them and their missionary parents and grandparents. Their justification was an issue of public morals, but the real issue was financial waste. William N.

Castle, son of the missionary Samuel Castle and now one of Hawaii's leading sugar factors—banker, business agent, and marketer—filed criminal obscenity charges against one of Kalakaua's aides, William Auld, and Robert Grieve, the printer of the *Hawaiian Gazette*, who had printed the program that accompanied the hula performances. The judge had the court cleared as witnesses clarified the meanings of the verses in Hawaiian that were chanted in praise of certain body parts. Both defendants were convicted and fined, but Grieve's sentence was overturned on appeal, on the grounds that he had taken the program in good faith to be printed, and was unaware of the meanings of the native-language content.[23]

Restoration of hula was a hallmark of Kalakaua's reign, as part of a broader regime to restore the native culture. The many traditional forms of hula could be performed to act out the nation's oral history, or as part of the ceremonies in a *heiau*, where the worship could be spoiled by a single mistake among the company. Some hula indeed was danced just as a venting of celebration. Both men and women had their regimen of hula, but the missionaries fixated on the women's, and could not think past the naked limbs and swaying or even thrusting hips. Some Americans, while finding it tantalizing, could also appreciate it as an art form. "At night they feasted and the girls danced the lascivious hula-hula," wrote Mark Twain in 1866. "It was performed by a circle of girls with no raiment on them to speak of . . . placed in a straight line, hands, arms, bodies, limbs, and heads waved, swayed, gesticulated, bowed, stooped, whirled, squirmed, twisted and undulated as if they were part and parcel of a single individual." However, Twain added, the authorities had clamped down on it, requiring payment of a ten-dollar permit. "There are few girls nowadays able to dance this ancient national dance in the highest perfection of the art."[24]

There was a second point of contention between the king and his sugar creditors, and that was the rise to power early in the reign, of the unsavory Walter Murray Gibson. While the king was traveling the world, Gibson showed his care for the native people by publishing a health manual, *Sanitary Instructions for Hawaiians*.[25] He encouraged the king's steps in resurrecting native customs and sports, including the hula, which angered the American community. Kalakaua made him foreign minister, and Gibson sought the cooperation of various Pacific kingdoms in unifying under Kalakaua as emperor. The effort came to nothing, but Gibson managed to play to the king's vanity, validate the Americans' worst suspicions about him, and unify the Hawaiian business interests against him.

If the end point of this process was not obvious to those who participated in it, it was obvious to one outsider who surveyed it with a writer's eye. Hawai'i, wrote Anthony Trollope after only two days, must end as "the property of American or English sugar-growers, and the work on the plantations would be done by Chinese or coolie immigrants," the whole result being "very much opposed to the theory of those who have wished to build up an Hawaiian monarchy."[26]

15. A Voice Like Distant Thunder

David Kalakaua was keenly aware that when the legislature voted him the crown, he was not the candidate most qualified by blood. Kamehamehas III and V had excluded Ruth Keʻelikolani from consideration for different reasons, Bernice Pauahi was not interested, and Emma he had defeated, with some well-placed promises to legislators and a few companies of British and American marines to quash the outrage that his scheming produced.

Kalakaua completed the change of dynasty by stripping the honor of "royal highness" from the last two Kamehamehas, Bernice and Ruth. The latter felt the greater sting, for she was close friends with Kalakaua's mother and sisters, so much so that she was the *hanai* mother of the new crown prince, who was named for Ruth's first husband, William Pitt Leleiohoku I. Kalakaua also replaced her as royal governor of Hawaiʻi Island, a post she had held since 1855 and been reappointed to by Kamehameha V and Lunalilo. Whatever personal satisfaction Kalakaua might have gained by pushing the last of the Kamehamehas away from the throne, it was a move of colossal stupidity. In her will Ruth bequeathed her vast Kame-hameha lands to her *hanai* son, who died in 1877 aged just twenty-three. If Kalakaua had only shown her some respect, she might have been content for those lands to pass to the royal family, thus making them financially independent. After his repeated slights, however, she took him to court, recovered her lands, and left Ka-lakaua to beg, borrow, and plead throughout his reign for money from sugar barons, leading to the disaster of the Bayonet Constitu-tion in 1887.

Usually only glossed over in books of Hawai'i history, Princess Ruth actually provides an intriguing glimpse into the what-ifs, had the monarchy pursued a more native path to development. Kalakaua's effort to diminish Ruth's standing was a hot coal that really came back to rest on his own brow, for people continued to address her by titles not less equal for being unofficial: Ku'u Lani, "My Royal One"; Ke Ano Lani, "The Heavenly Reverence"; and most often Ku'u Haku, "My Leader."[1]

It was a devotion occasioned only in part by her high station; it was more the result of her lifetime of championing the native cul-ture in defiance of the country's inexorable transformation in to a Western exponent. In her obstinacy she was not alone, indeed the Calvinist Church begun with such energy in the early 1820s was, if anything, in decline. The American Board of Commissioners for Foreign Missions had long since cut the Hawaiian church loose, allowing it to sail its own way. By 1870, thirty-nine of its fifty-eight churches in the kingdom were served by native ministers, well or-dained, but commanding the allegiance of only one-quarter of the people. They now had not only Christian alternatives—Catholic, Anglican, and Mormon—but many cast an eye back to older ways. It was noticed in some quarters that where tavernkeepers could barely eke out a living after paying for their thousand-dollar-per-year liquor license, native purveyors of the traditional 'awa easily afforded their eight-hundred-dollar license fees and lived high. Even the most devout of the *ali'i*, such as the queen dowager, cherished

collections of cultural artifacts, and the less devout such as Kalakaua had long advocated the survival of the ancient ways.[2]

Especially in the towns, the rock-ribbed Congregationalists
were seen as increasingly out of touch and anachronistic. Mark
Twain, during his sojourn in 1866, took their measure with deadly
accuracy when he characterized them as "pious; hard-working;
hard-praying; self-sacrificing; hospitable; devoted to the well-being
of this people and the interests of Protestantism; bigoted; puritani-
cal; slow; ignorant of all white human nature and natural ways of
men . . . fifty years behind the age; uncharitable toward the weak-
nesses of the flesh . . . and having no mercy and no forgiveness for
such."[3] Among the natives who felt overwhelmed by the Calvinists'
purity, Ruth found a natural constituency.

Princess Ke'elikolani—the name meant "Leafbud of Heaven"—
was born on February 9, 1826, almost six years into the missionary
era. Her mother, High Chiefess Kalani Pauahi, was twenty-two, the
Conqueror's granddaughter, and died giving birth to her. The first
of her po'olua fathers was the Conqueror's nephew, who died before
she was a year old. The second, with whom Pauahi was living at the
time of the birth, Mataio Kekuanaoa, raised her fully as his own.
She was given in hanai to the powerful queen regent, Ka'ahumanu,
who doted on her but died when Ke'elikolani was six. After Pauahi's
death, Kekuanaoa married Elizabeth Kina'u, and after the queen
regent's death they raised Ke'elikolani themselves—stability at last
in a childhood with too much sadness and loss.

Always large, she was considered attractive and her heritage,
having both Ka'ahumanu and Kina'u for mothers, made her a catch
no matter her looks. Her inheritance from the queen regent totaled
nearly a tenth of the entire kingdom; she was the richest woman in
the country. At fifteen she married the son of the great Kalanimoku,
William Pitt Leleiohoku, who fathered her first son, John William
Pitt Kina'u, before dying in the measles epidemic of 1848. This son
was one of the students at the Royal School, only two years old and
the last to be admitted. Kamehameha III had excluded Ruth from

the succession, but her son's stature—the Conqueror's only great-great-grandson, and descent from Kalanimoku and the kings of Maui on his father's side—overrode Christian legitimacy and merited his inclusion. In church processions he was often paired with Lydia Kamaka'eha, and by the time the Royal School folded he was considered one of the brightest lights of his young generation. His death of an unexplained accident in Kohala on the Big Island at the age of sixteen sent Ruth into an agony of mourning. The boy having died on September 9, 1859, the funeral was not until November 7, two months during which his lead coffin lay in his pagan mother's house, attended with unceasing chanting. In him Hawai'i might have lost a superb monarch. To the comfort of the Christian community, John had himself become a Christian, and his funeral at Kawaiaha'o Church drew a crowd of thousands.

Ruth's second husband, Isaac Young Davis, was the tall and handsome grandson of the British captive-gone-native. Their marriage was tempestuous to the point of physical battery. Ruth's face was disfigured when an infection in the end of her bulbous nose required its amputation—the result, gossip had it, of Young having broken her nose during one of their brawls. There was communal confidence, however, that she gave out better than she got; in her full flower the Leafbud of Heaven was well over six feet tall and weighed 440 pounds. From this vivid marriage came her second son, Keolaokalani Davis, born in the spring of 1863, whom she gave in *hanai* to her beloved first cousin Bernice Pauahi. Isaac Davis opposed the *hanai* vigorously, and the baby's death six months later helped seal the end of the marriage.

Ruth did not remarry. Of all her vast properties, she preferred living by the sea in Kona, in a spacious but not huge lava-rock mansion called the Hulihe'e Palace. Originally built by Governor John Adams Kuakini, he left it to his *hanai* son, who left it to his son Leleiohoku, who left it to his son, who left it to his mother. In this enchanting location, she eschewed the rock mansion for a traditional grass house, the *Hale Pili*, on the grounds, closer to the languorous sea breezes. And that love of the old life was what, in her maturity, presented the royal family with a dilemma. "Legitimacy" was a value judgment imposed by the Christian newcomers, but questioning her legitimacy may only have been a convenient and somewhat easy to dispose of her, because she presented the court with other problems. Some of it had to do with the court's image: At a time when all the Hawaiian royal ladies were trying their best to look Western, Princess Ruth had little choice but to embrace her startlingly Polynesian appearance. Her demeanor was often fierce, and one who knew her likened her voice to the rumble of distant thunder. More likely the need to marginalize her was rooted in her being vehemently anti-Western. She never converted to Christianity; she was eloquent in English but refused to speak it, forcing *haoles* who desired an audience to bring an interpreter. She therefore became something of a standard-bearer for anti-American sentiment among the natives, which was an embarrassment to Kamehameha III, who had given up his resistance to the *haoles*.

The king tried to make it up to her by naming her royal governor of Hawai'i Island in 1855, an office she held for nineteen years, which may explain at least in part why Kalakaua felt so threatened by her. He was a high chief of Kona, one district on the Big Island, the whole of which she had been royal governor for nearly twenty years, to the adoration of her people. At the change of dynasty, even an illegitimate Kamehameha might be able to make a claim to precedence over him—and perhaps, unreconstructed creature as she was held to be, she might like Liliha before her prepare to make a fight of it. But once secure on the throne Kalakaua displaced her as governor of Hawai'i Island, naming in her stead a crony from the legislature, Samuel Kipi.

Because of her bulk and her traditional ways, the white business community took to regarding Ruth as primitive and stupid. Over many years she had shown herself loving and loyal to her family,

and at social occasions such as the luau that Lydia Kamaka'eha gave
for the Duke of Edinburgh, she showed herself hearty and fun loving. But the Americans chose to characterize her by her looks, and
on this sentiment Ruth took her own measure of revenge.

After Kalakaua was able to present the sugar growers with a
reciprocity treaty, sugar growing itself underwent an interesting
change. Many of the plantations had undertaken to run the whole
process from start to finish, including refining their own sugar.
This put them in competition with a rather large sugar-refining establishment in California, and the industry leader there was a German immigrant-entrepreneur named Claus Spreckels. In this era of
laissez-faire capitalism, the early years of what Mark Twain came to
call the Gilded Age, when ruthless tycoons rose to fabulous wealth
on the ruin of their competitors, Spreckels became a master player.
What Cornelius Vanderbilt did with transportation and Andrew
Carnegie with steel, Spreckels did with sugar. After reciprocity
Spreckels took ship for Hawai'i. The growers in the islands would
find it more profitable, he said, not to finish refining their sugar
themselves. They could just ship it to him in its raw state, and his
mills in California would finish the job. His mills were soon the
destination for some seven thousand tons of Hawaiian raw sugar.
(Of course, he was also experimenting with sugar beets at home,
just in case.) He also befriended King Kalakaua, lending him forty
thousand dollars to pay down his debts.

But then, being a believer in vertical integration, he used part
of his fortune to acquire a whole or half interest in forty thousand
acres of Hawaiian government land, which he then wanted government permission to irrigate. When the ministers were slow with
their approval—perhaps they were beginning to realize just who
they were dealing with—the king had them awakened in the wee
hours of the morning to receive their resignations.[4] Perhaps no man
of commerce in the islands changed from best friend to bête noire
so quickly.

Ruth Ke'elikolani was among those who found him the essence

of everything they despised about *haole* businessmen. Spreckels knew that she owned more land than anyone else in the country. After pointed negotiations, he thought he had tricked her into a disastrous deal to sell him all her "right, title and interest" in the vast crown lands for only ten thousand dollars. She told him she thought it was half hers. Spreckels paid her willingly, only to learn later that the crown lands were the exclusive domain of the sovereign, and Keʻelikolani had no interest in them whatever: The crown lands had nothing to do with her personal holdings. Ruth outsmarted him and made an easy ten thousand dollars. (Spreckels, however, went to the government and received fee-simple title to a 24,000-acre *ahupuaʻa* on Maui in settlement for *his* interest, whatever that was, in the remainder of the crown lands).[5]

On November 5, 1880, Mauna Loa erupted with a powerful effluence of lava, which gave rise to an incident in which Princess Ruth's participation became legendary, though the legend has been called into question in more recent years. During the spring of 1881 the eruption continued, feeding a lava flow that made its way eastward, but heavy jungle impeded its progress toward the city of Hilo. By late summer the lava had burnt through most of the forest, and it became apparent that Hilo would be consumed. Prayer meetings were held; Liliʻuokalani sailed down from Honolulu, arriving on August 4. Urgent plans were made to try to save the city by diverting the lava either by erecting an earthen barricade or by dynamiting a diversion channel, but still the lava advanced.

Hawaiʻi's now sixty years of Christianization had left many pockets of people who, though many could read and write, never converted to any Christian denomination. (Visitors could still be unnerved by the islanders' frankness about sex: Dr. Nelson Bird, arriving in 1880 on the steamer *Australia* and finding the hotels full, rented a room in a commoner's house. Great was his consternation when his host "offered me any one of the women downstairs as a bed fellow, and wondered at my refusal. His wife smiled also at my innocence and offended . . . virtue."⁶) On the Big Island especially, people still feared Pele though there were no *kahunas* to continue her cult. The residents of Hilo went to their island's former governor, relying on her as the only royal who had never betrayed the traditional gods with a profession of Christianity, and implored her to make a sacrifice to Pele and stop the lava. Exactly what Ruth did is no longer known, for accounts of it, like a medieval miracle play, became exaggerated with retelling. Some have her progressing to the edge of the lava with chants and sacrificing *'ohelo* berries into the burning stream, which would make sense because those were known to be sacred to Pele. Other descriptions have her sacrificing a pig, or a bottle of brandy, and/or thirty red handkerchiefs, having raided Hilo merchants of all they had. One account had her laying down her 440-pound body for the night in the lava's path.

All that is known with certainty is that the lava halted on August 9. Ralph Kuykendall, Hawai'i's leading English-language historian, wrote in 1967 that the whole incident may have been apocryphal, for no contemporary newspaper accounts mention it. The Bishop Museum, however, preserves a couple of documents of the time that do. "Many thanks," wrote Hawai'i resident Ursula Emerson to her son, for his "account of the lava flow, or what had been the flow and had caused so much anxiety. . . . Keelikolani is not like the Kapiolani of olden time, who was so steadfast in her trust in Jehovah. . . . I fear she has not her piety." Kuykendall also wrote that Lili'uokalani made no mention of such an incident in her memoirs, but then, she hardly would have after having journeyed to Hilo for prayer meetings and consultations with her civil engineers, and been so thoroughly shown up.⁷

In spite of her ferocity, Ruth was known to be capable of great tenderness. When Miriam Likelike bore Victoria Ka'iulani to continue the Kalakaua dynasty, Ruth acted as her godmother and gave her ten acres of her Waikiki lands, which became the new heiress apparent's 'Ainahau estate in downtown Waikiki. Ruth watched over her upbringing, advocating that she receive the education that would best fit her for monarchical responsibility, despite her own exclusion. Kaʻiulani grew up addressing her as Mama Nui, her "Great Mother."

When Kalakaua was on his world tour, much talk in the country centered on the construction of the new ʻIolani Palace in Honolulu, which was being built to replace the old frame pavilions. Ruth, who preferred living on her Kona estate, decided to have a town house, Keoua Hale, built in Honolulu to reside there. Ruth used a different architect from the palace's, Charles J. Hardy of Chicago, then employed at a lumber mill in Honolulu, but the style—late Victorian Italianate with a Pacific accent—was so similar that the two dwellings could have come from the same drawing board. But where the palace repeated the mistake of the first ʻIolani Palace by being intended almost entirely for ceremonial purposes with a dearth of actual living space, Keoua Hale was designed for sumptuous, gracious living. As the house took shape, people saw a mighty stone edifice, its corners fully rusticated in the best Italian fashion, broad flights of steps surmounting a raised basement to a *piano nobile*, a second floor above that, a mansard roof with dormer windows above that, and a tower above that. Wings sprouted from the central bloc; there were bay windows, balconies, broad *lanais* on the first and second stories; and inside, plasterers sculpted the coat of arms of the kingdom in the ceiling of the grand drawing room.

Gossip flowed freely around Honolulu that Ruth had deliberately built Keoua Hale to outshine the just-completed ʻIolani Palace, pouring money into the gargantuan villa to spite Kalakaua,[8] and not coincidentally demonstrating that she was still vastly more wealthy than he—and that she did not owe the sugar planters for it. Nor could it have been a coincidence that Ruth inaugurated the grand home with a luau for a thousand people and an evening ball on February 9, 1882, perfectly timed to upstage the new palace and the eighth anniversary of the king's investiture.[9] The beautifully engraved invitations, not to make too fine a point, were surmounted by a generic-looking crown, and headed "Ka Mea Kiekie, Ka Alii Ruth Keelikolani: 'Her Royal Highness, the Chiefess Ruth Keelikolani.' "[10]

Not long after the vast mansion was finished, there was a small echo of the contest with Claus Spreckels when the sugar baron's son John insisted on showing off his new mansion to Queen Dowager Emma. As their carriage passed the Ali'iolani Hale, where the sugar barons were dining with Kalakaua, Emma lowered the veil from the brim of her hat, which Spreckels "firmly demanded that I open." Spreckels, whose father the sugar cabal regarded with increasing venom, wanted them to see what exalted company he was keeping. Emma was offended by the incident, kept her veil down, and later pronounced Ruth's Keoua Hale "much nicer from top to bottom" than the Spreckels mansion.[11]

Ruth paid for her grand gesture, though. After hosting in the vast house, her health began to decline. She returned to her favorite residence, the Hale Pili on the grounds of the Hulihe'e Palace in Kailua Kona, where she was most comfortable. She didn't know how sick she was. Not until some of her servants wrote to Bernice Bishop, entreating her to send a doctor, did the country learn of her condition. Bernice alerted Queen Dowager Emma, and together they hastened from Honolulu to her bedside, but upon arriving in Kailua Kona found the Hale Pili crowded with visitors, and Ruth propped up on her favored yellow cushions, laughing and holding court. She became quite provoked at the servants who had mailed Bernice the alarming letter, and she asked for the news from the capital. Kalakaua put into Kailua when he heard of her illness, and continued on to Hilo upon being assured that she was in no danger. That evening found her, according to Emma, "so cheerful and full of jokes" that her precipitous overnight decline took everyone by surprise.

She took a high fever, and both Bernice and Emma were with her when she died, "at 9 o'clock precisely on the morning of the 24th, Queen Victoria's birthday."[12] Ruth's body was taken to Honolulu, where she lay in state for three weeks in her magnificent Keoua Hale, with six men fanning her casket with *kahili*. It was an awkward time, for by custom the vigil was to be kept jointly by all nobles, and Bernice and Emma, the principal mourners, were seated with Lili'uokalani and Miriam Likelike. At the funeral Emma was given precedence, and the crown princess made no complaint, at least in public; Ruth was laid to rest in the Kamehameha crypt at Mauna 'Ala.

In her will Ruth provided land for a half dozen favored tenants living on her properties, but they were for life tenure only; at their deaths the lands would revert to her estate, the entirety of which she bequeathed to her much-loved cousin Bernice.[13] Ruth's concern was to keep the vast royal patrimony—some 353,000 acres, or nearly 10 percent of the entire country—intact. Bernice, too, honored this intent, and the Kamehameha lands became the nucleus of the trust that funds the Kamehameha Schools to this day.

To the Americans and American-Hawaiians intent on the country's cultural Westernization and economic grafting to the United States, Ruth Ke'elikolani had been a somewhat comical figure—crude, ungainly, primitive. But to the native people, both the *kanakas* who looked to her as Ku'u Haku, and her peers who understood her abilities and her intentions, she was a protectress of the island culture. She spent her life championing the language, the customs, and the heritage, and when she died her huge estate, which she had shrewdly managed and maintained intact, became the single greatest guarantee of their survival. That was a powerful legacy that has not been sufficiently appreciated.

16. Queen at Last

After the death of Princess Ruth, Bernice took up residence in the cavernous Keoua Hale, which her cousin had left her. Five years younger than Ruth, she also entered a decline. A voyage to San Francisco to consult a specialist resulted in a diagnosis of breast cancer, and she submitted to an operation to treat it. She returned to Hawai'i in the company of Likelike, took up residence first at her Waikiki retreat and then once more in Keoua Hale, but her mortality could not be stayed, and she died on October 16, 1884. Bernice's birth parents had been the *hanai* parents of Lili'uokalani, and despite the dynastic tension the two women had remained close. In her will Bernice left her numerous properties. Kalakaua benefited nothing from the Kamehameha lands, leaving him to finance his lifestyle and the government on his own, which meant increasing debt to the pro-American sugar industry. With increasing concern over his debts, he requested his sister to turn some of her lands over to him, and she caused something of a family rift when she refused.

No sooner had Bernice Pauahi passed from the scene than

Dowager Queen Emma began to fail noticeably. Only forty-nine, she had suffered a series of small strokes over the previous year, which may have affected her behavior,[1] and she died six months after Bernice, on April 24, 1885. After her death, as was the custom, she lay in state, at the capacious Rooke House, where her father had practiced medicine and entertained on the first floor as the family lived on the second, and which had been her principal residence her whole life. She was laid out in white silk trimmed with gold, a jeweled circlet on her brow. Four weeks was the usual time for a royal wake, but an incident occurred, almost stunning in its bad taste, that exhibited the reach if not the impudence of American arrogance. Early in the course of the vigil over Emma, her business manager, Alexander Cartwright, and several others spirited her remains away to Kawaiaha'o, the church of the American Congregationalists and the last place in the country that Emma would have wished to lie. Their justification was that Rooke House was not large enough to accommodate the throngs of mourners that they expected; that made sense, insofar that the Anglican cathedral for which Emma had raised money had barely begun construction, but the incident aroused the indignation of her "Emmaite" partisans and the sympathy even of others such as Lili'uokalani, who despite their differences regarded her with great respect.

Kalakaua had shown himself perhaps the most agnostic of all the monarchs, but that was less the cause of his discredit with the American and English element than his self-indulgent reign. He had proved himself a capable representative of the kingdom when abroad, but at home he was a profligate gambler and capacious drinker who should have been more careful about the friends he kept. He finally parted with Claus Spreckels, not over Spreckels's near-monopoly on the sugar industry, but because one night at cards when Kalakaua demanded to know where a missing king was, Spreckels carelessly remarked that *he* was the other king. It was an expensive divorce, but the king obtained it. After appointing Walter Murray Gibson to the house of nobles and then to a succession of cabinet posts, he had an able servant to deliver his legislative needs, but every time Gibson acted it seemed to cost the king *haole* support.

There may actually, though, have been a religious figure who was involved in Kalakaua's slow downfall—a mysterious man who appeared on the scene probably late in 1886, and enjoyed enormous influence over the king for the next year. That was Abraham Rosenberg, who claimed to be a rabbi and traveled with a Torah scroll and splendid silver *yad*, or pointer. As far as anyone could have known, during their long nighttime hours together Rosenberg was instructing the king in Jewish tradition and history, but he was almost universally known as the king's soothsayer.

One scholar has noted something salient about the effect that Jewish ritual would have had on Kalakaua. "Anyone who has heard such chanting must be struck by the remarkable similarity to Hawaiian chanting,"[2] an art form at which the king was highly proficient. And Rosenberg, whether he was actually a rabbi or merely a man versed in Jewish learning, could have augmented Bible stories with which Kalakaua was familiar with Talmudic commentary on their meaning, which would have made him seem (perhaps not inaccurately) more knowledgeable about them than the missionaries whom the king disdained. And Kalakaua could certainly have noticed the structural similarities between Hebrew and Hawaiian that struck Henry Opukaha'ia seventy years before. The political lobbies scoffed at Rosenberg, and the newspapers referred to him as "Holy Moses," but he held the king in thrall until his sudden decampment just weeks before the business element finally moved against the king.

It was singular how this upper echelon of the *ali'i*, no less than the commoners, kept one ear open to the call of the old ways. Praying someone to death, while long nominally debunked, was still feared and had been illegal for many years. Princess Ruth of course had never adopted Christianity, but even Queen Emma, who was the most devout of them, weakened to its charms at least once. Nearly two years after the queen dowager lost the bitter election to Kalakaua, one of Ruth's servants went to Emma with a recipe for hexing him and his whole clan to death. As Emma admitted in a letter to her cousin Peter Ka'eo, after a regimen of fasting and praying "that God would please place me on the Hawaiian Throne," a young lamb was sacrificed, and she drank a glass of brandy containing three drops of its gall and three drops of blood from its heart.[3] It is difficult to imagine a letter showing Emma in a worse light, but the fact that the ritual came from Ruth's *kahuna*, Kaiu, and was relayed by one of Ruth's servants, eloquently answers the question of how passively that formidable lady had been brooking Kalakaua's repeated insults.

Kalakaua was untroubled by spells cast in lamb's blood and brandy, but his expansive lifestyle, his rusticated palace with its electric lights and telephone and indoor plumbing, his entertaining and his gambling, left him in helpless need of money. The planters and factors could give it to him, but their terms became harder. Like an ant that had broken the edge of an ant lion's trap, Kalakaua sank into the cone of sugar. He had given them the reciprocity treaty he promised, and the sugar industry became gigantic. The 8,800 tons that Hawai'i exported in 1866 after the ramp-up to supply California during the Civil War seemed like a lot at the time. The industry's transformation after the United States ratified the reciprocity agreement in 1875, however, was stunning—the 9,400 tons that were exported in 1870 increased to 12,500 tons the year of the treaty, to 31,800 tons in 1880, on its way to nearly 130,000 tons in 1890. There were fifty-four major plantations in operation in 1879: twenty-four on Hawai'i, thirteen on Maui, seven each on Kaua'i and O'ahu, and three on Moloka'i. The larger among them covered as much as three thousand acres and employed a thousand or more workers. Irrigation now played a major role; rainfall on the islands was distributed so unevenly between windward and leeward sides that either artesian wells or channels diverting water from high in the forest on the wet sides to more arid regions were required to bring previously unsuitable lands into full cultivation. The shrewd Scotsman James Campbell, husband of Abigail Kuaihelani, took his profit from selling the Pioneer Mill and purchased land on the arid Ewa Plain on the dry side of Oʻahu, twenty miles west of Honolulu. By drilling artesian wells he quadrupled his money in sugarcane.[4] Even more dramatically, in the year after reciprocity the firm of Alexander & Baldwin—another one owned by missionary descendents—engineered a seventeen-mile irrigation ditch on Maui, from the wet, windward side of Haleakala to their acreage between Paʻia and Makawaʻo. Partner H. P. Baldwin proved himself indefatigable in getting it done. Despite having lost an arm in a mill accident, he shamed workers into finishing work in the dangerous Maliko Gorge by lowering himself on a rope with his one arm for daily inspections.[5] The ditch cost the extravagant sum of eighty thousand dollars, but delivered forty million gallons of water every day. That success led them to acquire more land and more mills until they became recognized as one of the so-called Big Five sugar combines.

Concentration of sugar production into fewer hands was the natural process of capitalism as larger companies acquired smaller ones, but the overall planted acreage continued to increase. Some others of what became the Big Five, such as Castle & Cooke, backed into sugar growing by having been the factor for plantations they eventually took over. Another one was H. Hackfeld & Co., founded by a German immigrant who marketed the sugar from the original Ladd & Co. plantation at Koloa. Another major player was Starkey, Janion & Co., British merchants who had run a store in Honolulu since 1846; one of their employees, Theo Davies, raised capital and assumed control of the company and its mercantiles, insurance business, and began buying plantations. The oldest of what became the Big Five had roots that extended all the way back to the sandalwood trade, which employed Henry Peirce, who eventually retired to become the American minister to the kingdom, as the company evolved into C. Brewer & Co., with Peirce's son as a partner—which made Henry Peirce something more than a disinterested bystander in the effort at reciprocity.

One important aspect of the plantation system at this time was mutual cooperation. With the American market apparently able to absorb all the sugar they could produce, there was no need to feel competitive against one another. So they shared irrigation networks where practicable, and agreed on slates of local officials who should be appointed, for instance district court judges, who could be counted on to decide contract-labor disputes in their favor. An even more serious effect of the spreading plantations was the eradication of local villages, with their remaining possibility of subsistence agriculture, forcing more *kanakas* to hang about the plantations for some kind of work.[6]

After 1879 Chinese immigration into Hawai'i under the controversial labor contracts increased to an average of some three thousand people a year. They presented one set of issues to the government, and other considerations to the planters. In China in 1881 Kalakaua had tried to limit immigration to those Chinese men who came with their wives. The native Hawaiian population was still in free fall, and it only exacerbated the problem when Chinese bachelors took Hawaiian wives and began having *hapa pake* (half Chinese) children. To the good side, somewhat more than half the coolies returned to China at the expiration of their contracts. The others presented a problem for the white element because, having hoarded their slender wages, they moved to the cities, went into business, and being shrewd and hardworking, undercut white-owned businesses. Sun De Zhang, for instance, more widely known as Sun Mei and the older brother by twelve years of Chinese republican leader Sun Yat-sen, came to Hawai'i in 1871 to work in his uncle's store, and by 1885 was the principal merchant on Maui, owned a six-thousand-acre ranch, and was known as the "King of Maui."[7] Sun Yat-sen himself lived in Hawai'i from 1879 to 1883 under his brother's sponsorship, but he was more interested in education than labor.[8] Chun Afong, for another case, one of the first Chinese to arrive back in 1849, opened a mercantile in Honolulu, folded his profits into real estate, and became that community's first millionaire. Perhaps most frightening to the *haole* community were men like Tong Yee, who made a fortune with his own Paukaa sugar plantation north of Hilo, married a chiefess on the Big Island—most Hawaiian women thought no worse of marrying a Chinese than an American, a notion the latter community had some trouble accepting—and had a daughter, Emma Aima, who became a leader in the fight against annexation.[9]

Overall the Chinese population in Hawai'i, which had stood at 2,038 in 1872, tripled to 6,045 in 1878, and tripled again to 18,254 in 1884—one-quarter of the population of the entire kingdom, before the government stepped in to regulate the flood. By 1886 Honolulu's "Chinatown" alone teemed with six to eight thousand residents, such a tightly packed warren of houses, shops, shacks, and lean-tos that a fire that year could not be extinguished before devastating most of it.[10] Plantation wages for them had increased to fourteen dollars per month, and still, despite Kalakaua's effort to limit the number of bachelors coming to the islands, sixteen Chinese immigrant men out of seventeen were unmarried.[11]

In 1881 both the Chinese government, newly alert to abuses in the coolie trade, and the Hawaiian government, fearful of being displaced from its own islands, each moved in its own way to restrict Chinese immigration, causing the planters to scout the globe for other ethnicities to bring to Hawai'i. As Kamehameha IV had envisioned, there was an attempt to recruit workers from elsewhere in Polynesia, with whom intermarriage would be less of an issue, but as laborers they proved to be not much more energetic than native Hawaiians. The Portuguese worked hard, settled with their families, and knew their place, but being white (albeit swarthy) they tended to want white wages, so the planters began to look elsewhere after bringing over several thousand.[12] In 1882 the United States passed the Chinese Exclusion Act; that did not directly affect Chinese contract labor in Hawai'i—except among those who foresaw a problem with annexation if the kingdom were overrun with people that the Americans would shun as undesirable. Still, it caused attention to turn to Japan, whose laborers also came mostly as single men but, unlike the Chinese, preferred to shop for wives in picture albums from home than seek out the diminishing number of native women.

In 1883 Kalakaua allowed himself to be drawn into a new scheme that added more tarnish to his reign, this one for Hawaiian coinage. It was not a bad idea; there were about half a million dollars in paper "silver certificates" circulating in the economy, but the law had been adjusted many times over the years, assigning values and depreciations to the many countries' coins that were accepted in the islands. People were wondering whether those certificates were actually redeemable for anything. It was Claus Spreckels, to whom the king was badly in debt, and who now held a mortgage as well on Walter Murray Gibson's Mormon paradise of the Palawai Valley, who came up with a solution: He would mint one million Hawaiian silver coins of various denominations, whose intrinsic worth could not be questioned. They would bear Kalakaua's profile on the obverse, the Hawaiian arms and motto on the reverse—a capital way to appeal to the king's ego. For this million dollars Speckels would be paid in government gold bonds bearing 6 percent. And that was after making $150,000 on the deal, because each face-value dollar of silver would cost him eighty-five cents for the metal and the minting. Some of the legislators, including Sanford Dole and William Castle, tried to block it but were unsuccessful. The coins were struck: half a million silver dollars, seven hundred thousand half-dollars, half a million quarters, and a quarter of a million ten-cent pieces. Spreckels then opened a bank in downtown Honolulu to compete with Bishop's,[13] and began laying plans for a Hawaiian National Bank that would be empowered to issue paper money. No one needed to be told who would be in charge of that. Hawaiian minister in Washington Henry A. P. Carter wrote a disgusted and confidential note to Dole: "Probably the next move will be to declare photographs of Mr. Spreckels legal tender for any amount."[14]

More capers over the next two years further eroded the king's standing with the business interests. A penultimate straw was the elevation of Gibson to the premiership at the end of June 1886, an office for him to hold while he also held the Interior Ministry.[15] For many downtown, the last straw was a bribery scandal that surrounded the king with too much smoke for anyone to believe there was no fire. In 1886 the legislature passed a bill to regulate the import of opium, which the religious quarter opposed, but the government saw little harm in allowing the now large Chinese community access to their traditional drug of choice. The newly appointed registrar of conveyances and friend of the king, Junius Kaae, importuned a wealthy Chinese named Aki, who wanted the opium-distributing license, into making a $75,000 gift to the king. However, the opium license went to a second Chinese in consideration of an even bigger gift to the king, and Kaae refused to give Aki his money back. Accepting one bribe would have been bad enough, but this was dishonor even among thieves. Aki went public, and both the British and American representatives reported that, while the government maintained that the king knew nothing of the dealing, public feeling against him on the part of those who wanted governmental reform—and that was most of the commercial element—was reaching the boiling point.

In November 1886 the nation celebrated Kalakaua's fiftieth birthday with bonfires, cannon salutes, and glittering balls and luaus. At a commemorative service on November 28 at the Kaumakapili Church (which had come to be known as the commoners' church, as the Christian *ali'i* increasingly claimed Kawaiaha'o as their own[16]), Prime Minister Gibson delivered a lengthy homage to the glories of the king's reign: "Is he not a Father beloved by his children? More than a Ruler revered by his subjects?. . . . He holds in his hands the sources of their welfare. And does he not shape all his action for the public good? For our King has inspired a great hope abroad, as well as at home, that his island realm was to advance, grow, and be glorified . . . that he, King Kalakaua, was the appointed man—the man of the Pacific, to lead onward to a higher destiny; to become a successful, beneficent and respected power." The powerful faction that abhorred Gibson and scoffed at the king would not restrain from vomiting much longer.

Kalakaua himself marked his birthday by establishing a secret organization, the Hale Naua Society, to promote "revival of the Ancient Science of Hawaii" to stand alongside the acquisitions of modern science from the West. The Western press bemoaned this validation of the "brutal and degraded past." Actually the Hale Naua was nothing so sinister. Genealogy was the armature of Hawaiian identity, and Kalakaua conceived the organization to preserve that tradition as well as further promote other elements of the native culture; Kapi'olani's sister Virginia Po'omaikelani was made president. But the Western community greeted the news with the darkest foreboding. It would "revive and vitalize the customs and usages of the barbarous and savage past," glowered the *Pacific Commercial Advertiser*. But given that Kalakaua had already inflamed the moral *haoles* with his open embrace of hula, and sponsored legislation that legalized the practice of native medicine, and given that the new society was imbued with some of the perceived hocus-pocus of Freemasonry and limited to people with native Hawaiian blood, suspicions were inevitably aroused.[17]

Reversion to heathen barbarity or preservation of indigenous culture was a matter of perspective. But adding the weight of the other events of 1886—the elevation of the despised Gibson to the premiership, the revelations of the latest bribery scandals—was finally enough to set the American and American-Hawaiian group into action. Early in 1887 they formed a secret society of their own, the Hawaiian League. The originator seems to have been Dr. S. G. Tucker, a homeopathic practitioner (perhaps not the best advertisement against native healers), who on Christmas Day, 1886, fatefully reined his buggy to a stop at the front gate of the young lawyer and missionary son Lorrin Andrews Thurston. "Thurston," he demanded. "How long are we going to stand this kind of thing?"

They discussed Kalakaua's shortcomings, and Tucker put forward the idea of forming a coalition of men who could compel the king to reform, or be deposed.

Thurston discussed the proposal with others, and they began meeting in January 1887, furtively. It is surprising that they were able to keep their business so secret, as the membership expanded to just over four hundred, many decisions undertaken by a central committee known as the Council of Thirteen, their names never written down although the composition changed. Thurston produced a constitution for the group, which quickly fractured into two camps, one favoring royal reform or else the creation of a republic, the other espousing annexation to the United States. The latter faction was narrowly voted down, which would explain the support for the group in the British community and among some *hapa haoles*.[18]

The Hawaiian League included other missionary scions, such as Sanford Dole and William Castle, who had previously been critical also of the sugar industry's labor excesses. Another member was N. B. Emerson, who understood Hawaiian well enough to have written "Smut" on that part of Kalakaua's coronation program describing hula in praise of the body. But Thurston, owing to the throbbing density of his discontent with the status quo, became the gravitational center of the Hawaiian League. He was only twenty-eight, a new member of the legislature, and grandson through union of the families of Asa Thurston and Lorrin Andrews, missionaries of the First and Third Companies, respectively. Like many of his contemporaries he was a product of the Punahou School, sent to the mainland to study law at Columbia before returning to Hawai'i in 1881, and currently publishing the *Pacific Commercial* ("revive . . . the barbarous and savage past") *Advertiser.*

Such an organization needs muscle, which they found in the volunteer militia company called the Honolulu Rifles. After the barracks mutiny of 1873, anything along the lines of a standing army for the kingdom had been allowed to lapse, and by 1886 it had recovered only to the point of having five volunteer rifle companies, in addition to the king's household guard. They drilled, marched in parades, and were otherwise decorative, and taken together they did comprise a kind of militia that could be called on in emergencies. Formation of the Honolulu Rifles early in 1884 was not thought suspicious. The appointment of Volney Ashford of Canada as its captain and drill instructor saw them become the class of the field, winning drilling competitions with the other volunteer companies.

Much of this ferment early in 1887 was obscured by an important approaching event, the Golden Jubilee of Queen Victoria, to culminate with a spectacular thanksgiving service at Westminster Abbey on June 21. Hawai'i readied a high-powered delegation to attend, with Queen Kapi'olani at its head, accompanied by Crown Princess Lili'uokalani and her husband, Governor Dominis; the king's chamberlain, Curtis Iaukea, to deliver a letter of congratulations from Kalakaua to Victoria, and others. On March 25 the Honolulu Rifles drilled before an audience of the finest—the king, privy council, several legislators, and members of the foreign diplomatic corps and their spouses. The king presented them with a Hawaiian flag, and traded extravagant blandishments with Ashford, now a lieutenant colonel, as the Rifles had expanded into three companies, two American and one Portuguese.

Packing her clothes into six gigantic *koa* wood trunks, Queen Kapi'olani sailed with her contingent on April 12 for Great Britain, via the United States, disembarking in San Francisco and crossing the country courtesy of the railroads. In Washington they were sumptuously feted by President Grover Cleveland, just at the midpoint of his first term, and by his wife of almost a year, Frances Folsom, twenty-seven years younger than he—a circumstance that Kapi'olani would have well understood.

Lili'uokalani moved easily in these circles but the queen, who had not been to the Royal School and spoke imperfect English, was more at sea. This became most apparent once they reached London. The evening before the jubilee celebration the British Foreign Office hosted a reception for visiting royalty; the two women went in different carriages, not knowing that owing to the complexities of protocol they would be routed to different gates. When Lili'uokalani entered the salon she discovered Kapi'olani standing unattended, with the room full of ranking dignitaries standing about in some apparent unease. She reached the queen, and once it was clear that the crown princess spoke English, a German grand duchess asked her, "Why does the queen not sit down, that the rest of us may be seated?" Kapi'olani had not been aware that at that moment, she was the ranking lady in the room. The Cookes' Boston Parlor training would have been useful to her.

For the grand service Kapi'olani selected a velvet court gown heavily trimmed with iridescent blue peacock feathers.[19] She and Lili'u were aware that by European standards their jewels were insignificant. Lili'u wore in her hair a butterfly of small diamonds; Queen Victoria's diamond collet necklace totaled 161 carats, and the other royals wore equivalent ensembles, whole parures of matching emeralds, sapphires, and rubies. Lili'u was taken aback at the sight of "little women who seemed almost bowed down" beneath the weight of them. "I have never seen such a grand display . . . in my life."[20] But the humble means of their country had no bearing on the reception they were given. In the procession to Westminster Abbey for the thanksgiving service, the coaches bore a majority of the crowned heads of Europe, but Victoria's Life Guards Household Cavalry escorted only two of them: the queen's own, and that of the Hawaiians. When thanked, Victoria remarked that it was the least she could do when they had come so far.

Others were less gracious. At the banquet King Albert of Saxony and the crown prince of Prussia (later Emperor Wilhelm II) objected to being seated next to the Hawaiian queen and crown princess because they assumed them to be Negroes. Not amused, Victoria detailed the Prince of Wales to escort Kapi'olani, and Prince Alfred the Duke of Edinburgh to attend Lili'uokalani, whom he knew from his visit to the islands. In her memoirs Lili'u omitted the entire incident—not the only artful dissimulation in her book— and maintained that she and the future Kaiser Willy were engaged in lively discourse for the duration.[21]

Back in the islands, politics reached a crisis. Gibson realized how vulnerable he was to the American business community, and responded by trying to promote Hawaiian nativism. He sent a tatty embassy to King Malietoa of Samoa on a converted tramp steamer manned by just-released juvenile delinquents, with a proposal to join Hawai'i in a federation. Malietoa agreed, but the larger result was that Germany, up to then a bystander in Pacific empire building, seized Samoa as a colony. Then various depositions of the opium bribery matter hit the newspapers. By the time the cabinet council met on May 23, the scope and aims of the Hawaiian League hit the open air, and the council passed resolutions to the attorney general and secretary of war to take steps to secure the country. The newspapers reacted with such ferocity that on May 26 the council authorized the attorney general to begin prosecuting them for defaming the king.

On the night of June 27, Kalakaua called American minister G. W. Merrill to the palace to ask his candid assessment of the situation, and his advice. Merrill told him plainly that the financial maladministration had created monolithic opposition, and that a change of cabinet was imperative to have a hope of salvaging the situation. The king had clung grimly to Gibson's obsequious services, even to the point of digging artillery emplacements around the palace and doubling the household guard, but now he collected the resignations of his cabinet at one o'clock in the morning.

The Hawaiian League went from meeting behind closed doors under cover of night to hosting a mass meeting in the Honolulu Rifles armory. Sanford Dole brought the meeting to order; Lorrin Thurston read five specific requirements to be made of the king, beginning with removal of the present cabinet. Charles Reed Bishop, widower of Princess Bernice, attended to read a letter from the king acquiescing in their demands and naming as new prime minister William L. Green, who was first on the League's list of four suggestions. He was English by birth, an adventurer who had settled in the islands after losing everything in the California gold rush, but his utility to the League was that he could deflect criticism that the bloodless coup was a purely American project.

The malcontents also wanted a new constitution, but like Kamehameha V before them, knew the obstacles to getting one. They wanted one immediately, and Lorrin Thurston set to drafting one. Volney Ashford, with a squadron of Honolulu Rifles behind him, arrested Walter Murray Gibson and locked him in a waterfront warehouse. He was preparing to hang him when Thurston stepped in and prevented it; within several days Gibson was allowed to sail for San Francisco, "for health reasons." Thurston, now the interior minister in the new cabinet, was able to edit the old 1864 constitution of Kamehameha V into a new document and have it ready for the cabinet to present for the king's signature on July 6. Upon reading it Kalakaua discovered that he had not been dethroned, but he had been defanged. Executive authority was no longer his alone but shared with the cabinet. He could still appoint ministers, but not dismiss them except upon a no-confidence vote of the legislature— votes in which the ministers themselves could no longer take part. Manipulation of the cabinet had been an important weapon in Kalakaua's ability to control the government. So, too, had been his power to appoint members of the house of nobles, and they were now to be elected. The king's veto power over legislation could now be overridden, and he was removed from any ability to amend the constitution in the future; that was solely the power of the legislature.[22]

It was to be sure bitter medicine. He would remain as a constitutional king, but the monarchy as a repository of meaningful power was finished. Kalakaua's new attorney general Clarence Ashford, brother of the colonel of the Honolulu Rifles, recalled that as the document was read to him, "His Majesty . . . listened in sullen, and somewhat appalling silence. And then came a general silence." At length Premier Green asked the king if he approved and would sign it. For some moments Kalakaua seemed to calculate furiously what chance he had of resistance, but with the rebel cabinet within and the Honolulu Rifles without, "his sullen and forbidding countenance . . . dissolved into a smile as sweet as seraphs wear," and he signed.[23]

The monarchy was maimed, but it survived—unlike Kalakaua's friend Walter Gibson, who died scarcely six months after his flight to the mainland. He had asked to be buried in the islands, a request that was granted on compassionate grounds. As he lay in state in the courthouse, several of those involved in the coup went to view the body—only to discover that embalming fluid had turned it "black as coal." Sanford Dole asked his brother George what he thought, and the latter remarked on the propriety that Gibson's complexion finally matched his soul.[24]

For the circumstances that surrounded it, the constitution of 1887 has become known as the "Bayonet Constitution," and as odious as it was, worse followed. Soon after his accession, Kalakaua had managed to secure the reciprocity treaty with the United States without having to cede Pearl Harbor. The Americans, however, never ceased lusting after the lochs below Pu'uloa, and during the decade of the treaty's life their avarice became harder to conceal. Kalakaua's man in Washington remained Henry A. P. Carter, son-in-law of Gerritt Judd, who had distinguished himself in winning European acceptance of the original treaty, and who had been on station in Washington now for four years. He had managed to win annual extensions of the treaty since its expiration in 1883, but had seen the American insistence over Pearl harden year by year.

As early as 1885 key American senators, such as John F. Miller of California and John Tyler Morgan of Alabama, broached a sudden but apparently idle interest in the place, and buttonholed Carter about the harbor's expanse and utility, and whether it was in private ownership. Carter was in the State Department on the kingdom's business "when I heard that a resolution was being prepared asking the President to take steps to secure Pearl River harbor." Alert instantly to the danger that the United States was going to hold the treaty hostage and demand Pearl Harbor as ransom, Carter scurried among Hawai'i's friends, warning them that the king and government would never agree to such a demand, and even if they did the legislature would not ratify it. "In a few days," wrote Carter, "I was told that the project was being pressed, and that there was danger" that senators who wanted to get American hands on Pearl Harbor would strike a deal with those who wanted to divest themselves of the Hawaiian treaty altogether "and make Pearl Harbor the price of non-abrogation."

Carter was able to keep the undeveloped harbor in Hawai'i's hands for another year, but by 1887 circumstances altered decisively in the Americans' favor. First, it had become increasingly obvious during the thirteen years of the treaty that Hawai'i, whose very survival now depended upon sugar, needed its continuation more than the Americans. Second, the British had come to accept their loss of place with the end of Kamehameha dynasty, and with typical good manners had not only dropped their objection to American primacy in the islands but often seemed to be promoting it—to which the United States responded with eager assurances of friendship and British access to the ports. Third, the Bayonet Constitution of July 1887 had crippled the king's position to maintain any demands about anything. Fourth—and what seemed to seal the deal—the Cleveland administration could credibly claim to be Hawai'i's friend, and when Cleveland's secretary of state, Thomas Bayard, assured Carter that lease of the inlet would not compromise the kingdom's independence, and that the United States would quit the place with the new treaty's expiration, Carter recommended that Pearl be signed over, rather than face the alternative of losing reciprocity altogether.[25] Carter also had Bayard's informal aside that the enormous cost of improving the harbor would probably dissuade the United States from actually doing anything with the property anyway.

Kalakaua was as entrenched as before and vowed to British commissioner Wodehouse that he would "never" sign it. The king, however, now browbeaten by a Reform cabinet and unable to muster enough allies in the legislature, had few options. The lease of Pearl Harbor was written up as a "supplementary convention" to the finally renewed reciprocity treaty, signed and published on November 29, 1887. The British Foreign Office later quietly removed Wodehouse from his posting in Honolulu, in an accommodation to amicable relations with the United States.[26]

News reports of dangerous unrest in Hawai'i had reached Europe all through the late spring and early summer of 1887, but the coup was only two days old and the new constitution four days from being signed, when the queen and crown princess left England on July 2. Henry Carter told them more when they reached New York, and the two women actually exulted in Gibson's fall, but discovered the depth of the situation when they reached Honolulu on July 26. The found the king deeply depressed and a pall cast over the palace; Lili'uokalani was dismayed at the wreck of his reign. "King signed a lease of Pearl Harbor to U. States for eight years to get R[eciprocity] Treaty," she wrote in her diary. "It should not have been done."[27]

Kalakaua played his powerless, bemedaled role for a further three years. During the summer of 1890 the Reform Party itself broke into factions and the government fell; it was a situation that the old Kalakaua might have been able to make something of, but the king had no fight left in him. He embarked on the USS *Charleston* for San Francisco hoping to recover his health. He declined, however, and was hospitalized; his servants ran down the street bearing his *kahili* from the hotel to the hospital to create a sacred space for him. Fascinated by technology to the end, he spoke his last words into an Edison wax cylinder: "Tell my people I tried." He expired on January 20, 1891.

First sight from Diamond Head of the returning *Charleston* sent a wave of celebration through the *kanakas* of Honolulu, but as she entered the harbor her crossed yards and black streamers told a different story. Queen Kapiʻolani had almost no time to absorb the news before the coffin was borne into the palace to lie in state in the throne room. She convulsed in grief; servants steadied her at the top of the long *koa* staircase lest she tumble down. The household was plunged into deep mourning, while Liliʻuokalani at fifty-two was proclaimed the first queen regnant of the Hawaiian Islands on January 29, 1891.

She was a large woman, but not by measure of the Hawaiian *aliʻi*; various of her forebears, Kaʻahumanu, Ruth Keʻelikolani, were far bigger. She had been left in peace at Washington Place since her mother-in-law's death two years before, although the two women had coexisted more peacefully for a time before that. Her husband Governor Dominis, elevated to "His Royal Highness, the Prince Consort," died the following August at fifty-nine. In the ʻIolani Palace throne room, the matrimonial chair next to hers would remain vacant, but in her marriage she had become quite accustomed to that.

Liliʻu's voluminous curly black hair, heavily streaked with gray, concealed many thoughts, even as her large frame concealed a conflicted heart. Her Christian upbringing had left her with a deeply persuaded faith, but her Polynesian heritage imbued her with a healthy skepticism of pomposity. She doubted whether Christ really demanded as many sacrifices of one's personal pleasure as the sour Calvinist missionaries did. Her polished English and high manners made her perfectly at home in the company of Queen Victoria, but she could be bawdy and she had a husky laugh. It was not often written about, for she was discreet, but she had lovers, handsome young Hawaiians. "Mrs. Dominis has a new love," Queen Emma once wrote to her cousin, "a native boy of Waikiki."[28] One would expect no less of a high chiefess who had been dumped by her American husband. She also, in strictest privacy, loved a good cigar.

A newspaperwoman from Chicago, Mary Krout, who in her

writings was frank, even brazen, in her opinion that the Anglo-Saxon race had a moral right to seize the Hawaiian government, obtained an audience with her, and found the queen's bearing so gracious that Krout almost forgot her convictions. She was also surprised that, although Lili'uokalani was often photographed, she did not really look like any of her pictures, and she would not have recognized her had Krout not been presented.

Kalakaua was buried on February 15 after a much shorter royal wake than was the custom in older days; he was laid to rest in a new crypt, prepared for his dynasty and separated from the Kamehamehas, at Mauna 'Ala. After the funeral the queen received the diplomatic corps to thank them for their condolences, including the American minister with whom she was destined to have a much trying acquaintance. John L. Stevens was seventy, a Maine man and Unitarian Universalist preacher, with white hair, sunken cheeks, and hollow eyes, as much of his chinless face as possible hidden under a scraggly white beard. He had some experience abroad, in South America as well as Scandinavia, and took the Hawai'i posting at the call of his former business partner, James G. Blaine, who had become secretary of state. Stevens was a boor who less and less privately advocated U.S. annexation of the kingdom. Where other countries' representatives had expressed their condolences and wishes for a happy reign, Stevens, with one leg swung over a chair arm, lectured her on the boundaries of her constitutional authority. Of course he couched his pedantry in phrases such as, he was happy to believe that she understood her limitations, but it was hard to think that he would have spoken to his own servants much differently. Lili'uokalani was deeply offended.

The reign had begun, however, and the queen had more than the requisite social presence to undertake her ceremonial duties. On June 22, 1891, she opened the Bernice Pauahi Bishop Museum of Hawaiian antiquities and natural history. Bernice had placed in trust the vast estate that she inherited from her Kamehameha cousin Ruth Ke'elikolani. Through this trust her husband established the museum as a memorial to her. Bishop fussed mightily over the details of construction; he actively curated and improved the collection, much of which was stored at Ruth's gigantic Keoua Hale, where Bishop was himself living while he directed the project. The museum also included the cultural treasures of the late Dowager Queen Emma.[29] Not limiting the museum's mission to cultural history, Bishop and the trustees reached out to Western scientists for the natural history of the Pacific—botany, ornithology, oceanography. The Bishop Museum began expanding no sooner than the doors were opened, with new halls dedicated in 1894, 1897, and thereafter, earning its reputation as the "Smithsonian of the Pacific." But lest anyone forget the source of so much knowledge, immediately to the left of the main entrance, in one of the most prominent spaces, lay the room reserved for displaying the tall feather *kahili* standards of Hawaiian royalty.

17. The Coup

Among the many letters of sympathy there was one from Robert Louis Stevenson, the author who had abandoned his native Scotland and begun roaming the Pacific in the summer of 1888, now resident on Samoa. "The occasion is a sad one," he condoled with the queen, "but I hope, and trust, that the event is for the ultimate benefit of Hawaii, where so much is to be hoped from, as much is sure to be effected by a firm, kind, serious and not lavish sovereign."[1] That was a remarkable sentiment for Stevenson to write, in view of the fact that Kalakaua had befriended and hosted him and his traveling suite generously enough.

Not many of those who offered Lili'uokalani advice, however diffident and sugarcoated it was, appreciated how keenly she in fact grasped her situation. She had a powerful mind of her own and knew how to express it, even in pointed criticism of her brother that she could deliver (privately) with such reckoning that it almost put the name he gave her—"Smarting of the Royal Ones"—in a new context. The business community became well acquainted with her strength of will during her stint as princess regent while Kalakaua was traveling the world. She had no hesitation in closing the ports to prevent the spread of smallpox, shutting off exports and blocking the influx of labor, unswayed by the heated editorials in the American press. That was when they first marked her as "bad for business"; they were wary of her, and it was perhaps no accident that when they moved against Kalakaua with the Bayonet Constitution, they did it when she was out of the country.

Now as queen, she did not wait for them to strike; she assembled her brother's *haole* cabinet and asked for their resignations. They demurred in something approaching disbelief, pointing out that under the new constitution, ministers could only be dismissed on a no-confidence vote of the legislature. Surely, she insisted, a new sovereign at the beginning of a reign was entitled to a cabinet that held her confidence. The chief justice of the supreme court was now Albert Francis Judd, and she took her case to him, with the additional argument that the present cabinet had performed in a way "hurtful to the standing of a good and wise government." The court agreed to consider the matter.

When word of this initial skirmish reached Charles Bishop in San Francisco, he realized that she might win this battle but set herself up to lose much more. Bishop's marriage to her *hanai* sister had been everything that her own marriage was not, and Bishop had the standing to offer private advice and encouragement to Lili'u that she likely would not have accepted from others. On March 5 he wrote her a long and loving—but at its heart didactic—letter:

> Your love for our dear Bernice would of itself win my regard. Were she living now her large heart would be full of sympathy for you in every trial, and of joy for every honor that you may gain. . . . Permit me now, dear friend, to congratulate you upon your grand opportunity for usefulness and honor—and to give some advice which you have not asked for, but which I trust will not seem to be bad. I regard the moral influence which you can execute upon the community, and especially upon your

own race, as of much more importance than anything you can do in the politics or business of the country. . . . In the politics and routine of the Government the Ministers have the responsibility, annoyances and blame—and usually very little credits. Let them have them, and do not worry yourself about them.

Bishop went on to register the opinion that the cabinet she found objectionable would likely resign whatever the supreme court decided, but he thought the justices would sustain them. If not, then they would surely resign, and she could begin her reign with a slate of her own choosing.[2] It was sage advice on constitutional government from an experienced man who cared about her very much. But as he perceived, she—like her brother and her distant relative Kamehameha V—was determined to rule. The Bayonet Constitution was an odious document whose legitimacy could be questioned as a historical exercise, but its ink was three years dry, and Kalakaua had closed out his reign obeying its terms. If she opened her reign by declaring war on that constitution, it would be a dark and dangerous business.

First, Kalakaua had won election as king by playing on the growing misogyny of the male legislators, and winning them over against the "petticoat rule" they would face under Emma Kaleleonalani. If anything, he succeeded too well in that, and in his seventeen years on the throne Hawai'i became that much more Westernized. Lili'uokalani was not Kamehameha V, the last great chief, and a constitutional abrogation that the people might have tolerated from him they would not accept from her, because she was a woman, because the times had come so far, and because a whole new political class—Lorrin Thurston, Sanford Dole, and the others—had come into being in the generation since Lot Kapuaiwa had quashed the previous constitution and issued his own.

Second, the issue of race had gained a different and uglier valence than it had had before. When Hiram Bingham brought the Congregationalist missionaries to Hawai'i in 1820, they and the eleven reinforcement companies that followed over the next two decades were confident that they were bringing the light of a Christian civilization to a benighted culture. That population happened to have dark skin. The missionaries would have felt the same had they evangelized newly discovered islands of Scandinavia. The early missionary letters and literature are remarkably free of overtly racist epithets, not least because they discovered the Hawaiians to be quick and perceptive, and intelligent enough to have emerged from a culture with no written language to the highest literacy rate in the world in less than a generation.

The missionaries' children, however, brought a different perspective. Sent to the mother country and welcomed back with their degrees from Harvard, Yale, and Columbia, many of them returned having absorbed the American racism of the late nineteenth century. William Richards could say of Timothy Ha'alilio, "He is not my servant, I am his," but that was not the starting point of the second and third generation *haoles*. In their minds it was but a small step from saying that the Kalakaua government was corrupt to saying that dark races are not capable of enlightened self-government. At the beginning of her reign the new queen, focused upon the recovery of meaningful royal power, had little notion of what a powerful obstacle she would face in simple racial prejudice. Social journalist Mary Krout was charmed by Lili'u's easy grace, but she still perceived the American side of the moment with perfect clarity: "When Queen Liliuokalani came to the throne more perverse than her brother; more determined to restore native rule in its most aggravated form, her subjects lost hope, and realised that there were but two alternatives—the relapse of the country into the state from which it had so painfully emerged, or the administration of the government by the Anglo-Saxon, aided by the natives of the better class."[3] By "subjects," of course, Mary Krout meant those of means and American descent.

Third, the new queen's support among the native and mixed-blood political class was not monolithic. At the time Lili'uokalani ascended the throne, the native population had continued on a downward drift of frightening inexorability. Even after the subsidence of the early postcontact epidemics, there had been a net loss of three to four thousand native inhabitants at each six-year census since early in the reign of Kamehameha V. And the census of 1890 was the first in which immigrants and island-born nonnatives (49,368) finally outnumbered the surviving native Hawaiians, including those of mixed race (40,662).[4] Many of the *maka'ainana* resented being disenfranchised by the property restrictions placed upon voting rights, and they turned for leadership to an unpredictable firebrand, Robert William Wilcox, who was the *hapa haole* son of a Maui chiefess and a Rhode Islander. Wilcox had been twenty-five when Kalakaua had plucked him out of the legislature, taken him on his grand tour, and deposited him at the Royal Military Academy at Turin for a Western military education. The reform government recalled him to save money, and back in Hawai'i he led an ill-advised putsch against the Bayonet Constitution that cost seven lives, and in which Kalakaua refused to get involved. At Lili'u's accession, Wilcox and his confederate John E. Bush sought government appointments from her, and when she refused they led as many of their party as they could command—but that was not everybody—against her, advocating a native republic not beholden to sugar, and to her anger they spread the rumor that she had taken her new half-Tahitian marshal of the kingdom, Charles B. Wilson, as a lover.[5]

Fourth, she came to the throne at perhaps the most threatening moment the sugar industry had yet known. The United States was bound to the reciprocity treaty, but now that they had finally squeezed Pearl Harbor out of Kalakaua, the rest of its provisions were a drag on free trade elsewhere. Under the leadership of Senator William McKinley of Ohio, the United States passed a bill that removed tariffs from all foreign sugar imports, but made up for it at home with a two-cents-per-pound bounty to grow domestic sugar. McKinley and his allies managed to wreck the treaty without technically breaking it, and the Hawaiian sugar growers were looking over a precipice not too different from what Kalanikupule saw at the Battle of Nu'uanu Pali.

Against this sea of troubles Lili'u took up arms, and she was a quick study in how to use what little remained of royal power. Before the Bayonet Constitution, her brother had usually managed to milk what he needed from the legislature by appointing and dismissing cabinets. That avenue was now closed; cabinets could not be dismissed without a no-confidence vote, and in fact the first government to fall in the 1892 legislature was her own preferred one, composed of members of her National Reform Party, brought down by a freakish alliance of the American-dominated Reform Party and the largely native Liberal Party. Soon, however, with the Reform Party unpopular and riddled with dissension, the queen discovered that by exercising a little trouble she could engineer no-confidence votes, bring a government down, and get a new cabinet just the same. To the fourth government of the session she appointed Reform Party members, which sufficiently angered members of the Liberal Party whose leaders had expected ministerial posts that they supported two revenue bills that she found crucial to keeping the government financed.

The members of the Reform Party, who had once risked their necks by conspiring to form the Hawaiian League, responded to the queen's machinations by forming a new, equally clandestine, organization whose very name made its purpose unmistakable: the Annexation Club. The 1892 legislature met contentiously for 172 days, the longest session in the history of the kingdom. The sugar industry, and therefore the economy, was close to ruin because the Americans' McKinley Act had gutted the reciprocity treaty, and much of the quarreling in the legislature was over how to raise revenue needed to sustain the government when its usual mainstay, sugar, was facing its bleakest hour.

Two notable proposals had been made in this regard: One was to begin a lottery, and the other was regulate and tax the import of opium. Both measures raised objections, mostly from the Americans in the legislature, on moral grounds. The queen was ambivalent on the subject of opium. She was grateful that the missionaries had brought the knowledge of Jesus to the islands. She spent most of her youth boarding in the Royal School, as she was reminded every day because the site of its building was now the barracks for her palace guard. Unlike Liholiho and Emma, she had remained loyal to that denomination and had her own pew in the Kawaiahaʻo Church, the first and still the largest church that they had founded. But the queen also knew them to be cold, dour people, and whether they actually preached it or whether it was because that was the way they lived their lives, they conveyed the message that the enjoyment of life was sinful. They took a dim view of both lotteries and opium. Nor did the Americans' hypocrisy escape her notice: They did not seem to mind working the Chinese to death, but they spun into a moral tizzy at the thought of opium.

Her feeling about the lottery was more ambivalent. "They are not native productions of my country," she wrote later, "but introduced into our 'heathen' land by so-called Christians, from a Christian nation, who have erected monuments, universities, and legislative halls by that method."[6] The queen's opinion of lotteries incorporated another point of view as well, which she confided freely enough to her diary but judiciously omitted from her memoirs. For some time she had been taking lessons in German from a tutor named Gertrude Wolf, who proceeded to insinuate herself into the queen's confidence as a medium and fortune-teller. Even as Kalakaua had never entirely abandoned his attraction to the occult, Liliʻu gave access and her attention to Fräulein Wolf. The company behind the lottery proposal had attempted a similar operation in Louisiana, and seeking an easier game in Hawaiʻi, probably had the acumen to use Fräulein Wolf to influence the queen.[7]

The preceding July 7, after a ball, the queen retired at 1:30 a.m. with Fräulein Wolf, who read her cards. "She told me," the queen wrote in her diary, "that at ten the next morning a gentleman will call on me with a bundle of papers where it would bring lots of money across the water. . . . She says I must have the House accept it, it would bring 1,000,000." Wolf ventured further—the strongest evidence that it was the lottery boosters who were behind her—and using initials only, instructed the queen what men should and should not be appointed to her next cabinet.

Wolf went home at 3:30 a.m. but returned to the queen at 9:00. "When she felt sure the man was in the house," the diary continued, "I sent her home. 10:25—sure enough—the man came up with the bundle of papers and spoke of lottery. How strange she should have told me."[8] A month later Fräulein Wolf indicated that if the lottery bill passed, the queen herself would profit by fifteen to twenty thousand dollars per annum, "pocket money."[9] This could only be called a bribe, but the queen was looking at least as hard at the public works projects to benefit the people that could be undertaken with such sums of money. Eventually the bills passed the legislature, and it was up to her to sign them or veto them. The kingdom needed revenue, and there was little chance at least in the near term of persuading the United States to repeal the McKinley Act. Taking pen in hand, she affixed her signature: Liliuokalani R.

During some of that 172-day session, at least her worst nemesis was out of her hair: Lorrin Thurston, firebrand of the Reform Party, had sailed to the United States to manage the continental end of his business affairs. Had she known what he was up to, she would have felt differently about his absence. During his "business" trip to the United States, Thurston visited Washington on behalf of the Annexation Club to ascertain the current sentiment there on the possible American acquisition of Hawai'i. He obtained a meeting with the chairman of the House Foreign Relations Committee, James H. Blount, a Democrat of Georgia, who thought Thurston was a seditious little troublemaker and gave him short shrift. Angling higher, Thurston turned toward the Republican administration, and met with Secretary of the Navy Benjamin Tracy, and with Secretary of State (and onetime presidential nominee) James G. Blaine, who had recruited Minister Stevens for the Hawai'i post. It would have seemed too conspiratorial for President Benjamin Harrison to him-self receive Thurston, but those two cabinet officers carried his case to the president and returned with an explicit statement of the U.S. position: "If conditions in Hawaii compel you to act as you have indi-cated, and you come to Washington with an annexation proposition, you will find an exceedingly sympathetic administration here."[10]

With the legislature's tasks nearly completed, the queen had a no-confidence vote called on Thursday, January 12, 1893; the cabi-net resigned, and she installed a new one that would be adequate to govern until the legislature was called again during the spring. The leaders of the legislature agreed that their session had finally come to its end, and the ceremony of prorogation, their dismissal, was set for noon on Saturday, January 14. The queen had her own reason for looking forward to that day, for just as Thurston had been scurrying about the United States making certain of American support for annexation, Lili'uokalani had been equally busy behind closed doors: She had written a new constitution.

This was not a closely held secret. She had previously given a draft of it to the man she now installed as her attorney general, Ar-thur P. Peterson, to comment on it and make suggestions; he returned it after a month with no recommended changes. One of her legisla-tive defeats during the session was that she tried and failed to per-suade the legislature to call a constitutional convention to debate, perfect, and enact the new fundamental law. So it was widely known that the queen had a new constitution ready to enact; the only ques-tion was whether she would limit herself to trying to put it into force through presently constitutional means, which would be difficult to impossible, or whether she would risk pulling down the monarchy around her in an attempt to restore the native franchise and her royal prerogatives by attempting to replicate Kamehameha V's bold step.

On Saturday morning before the ceremony, she conferred with the cabinet in the blue room of the palace. Once closeted with them, Lili'uokalani informed them that after she prorogued the legislature, she intended to abrogate the Bayonet Constitution and establish the new one. In it she would restore the vote to native Hawaiians, and—incorporating elements of the constitution of Kamehameha V—restore royal executive authority. Ministers would serve at her pleasure, she would appoint members of the house of nobles, and her sovereign acts would no longer depend upon the advice and consent of the cabinet. Her plan had only one breathtaking flaw: Under the provisions of the Bayonet Constitution then in force, she was barred from changing it except under the terms of its own admittedly all-but-insuperable amendment process.

Her four American ministers, in office for two days, were staggered. Most gravely shocked was Peterson. Born in the islands, the son of a business émigré from Plymouth, Massachusetts, he had attended law school at the University of Michigan and clerked for a Supreme Court justice. He was only thirty-three, but had previously served King Kalakaua as assistant attorney general and then attorney general toward the end of his reign. If any man in the government was positioned to know the angry mood of the American business community, it was he: His former law partner, W. A. Kinney, now practiced in the office of William O. Smith—whose partner was Lorrin Thurston. Before her sucker-punched ministers could recover, the queen further informed them of her intention to announce the new Constitution after she dismissed the legislature, first to an assemblage in the throne room, and again to the people from the palace balcony.

Bowing themselves away from this audience, Attorney General Peterson and the interior minister, John F. Colburn, beat a hasty retreat from the palace. Almost in panic at the queen's contemplated overthrow of the 1887 constitution, they hurried to a place where they could receive counsel on what to do. Whether it was an act of betraying the queen's plan (she later called it treason) or whether it was because they genuinely did not know where else to turn, they entered the law office of Lorrin Thurston.

Now returned with assurances of American sympathy toward annexation, Thurston knew exactly what to tell Peterson and

Colburn: They must oppose the queen, but for the moment they must endure her fury; they must not resign from the cabinet. If they resigned, Lili'uokalani would replace them with others who would do her bidding, and cabinet signatures on the new constitution would give it a greater appearance of legality. But once the legislature had been prorogued, she could not dismiss ministers until they convened again, and they would have her in the box in which their Bayonet Constitution was designed to keep her.

As the noon hour approached, Lili'uokalani and her entourage emerged in procession from the 'Iolani Palace and crossed the street to the Ali'iolani Hale, where the legislative chamber had been filling with members, dignitaries, and guests. Most noticeable about the assemblage was the absence of its representatives of American ancestry, the core of the Reform Party. As Lili'uokalani mounted the broad steps and passed through the rusticated Ionic portal of the Ali'iolani Hale, her view of the harbor was blocked by the neighboring music hall and she could not see the white, 3,300-ton U.S armored cruiser *Boston* slipping back through the narrows into Honolulu Harbor. She had been stationed there for some weeks and become a familiar sight, her two black eight-inch guns protruding from their blast shields, one on the bow and one on the stern, and the lesser five- and three-inch guns jutting like thorns down the length of her gun deck.

That vessel, one of the most powerful in the Pacific, had departed Honolulu only a few days before, for gunnery practice, and to convey U.S. minister Stevens on a visit to Hilo. Later it was alleged by natives and royalists that Stevens and Thurston, as aware as anyone that the queen was fiercely anxious to bring out the new constitution, had agreed that she was more likely to be tempted into an unconstitutional step if the *Boston* and her big guns were out of the harbor, and Stevens had the ship's captain, G. C. Wiltse, make speed back to Honolulu as soon as he heard the rumor racing like wildfire through the country that the queen was about to act.

Even as the warship dropped anchor, a launch hurried out

bearing an invitation to Captain Wiltse to attend the prorogation
ceremony, but he hesitated. Members of the Reform Party had previously conferred both with Stevens and separately with himself to
ascertain whether, if there was trouble and they appealed for marines to protect American lives and property, they could count on
the *Boston*. If it was true that the queen was planning to nullify the
1887 constitution and issue the new one, there was likely to be trouble. If it came to that, Wiltse would be needed aboard ship. He
therefore ordered Lt. Lucien Young into his dress uniform with all
haste, not just to attend the closing of the legislature, but to converse, eavesdrop, and learn what he could of the situation.

Lieutenant Young hurried ashore and was one of the last guests
to be seated. In the legislative chamber Young noticed immediately
that virtually all the lawmakers in attendance were from one or another of the native parties, and mostly sympathetic to returning the
islands to native rule. Young seated himself behind an *aliʻi* with
whom he had previously been acquainted, and greeted him. The
native chief seemed very pleased with things. "We have them at
last," he gloated. He could only have been referring to the absent
Americans' Reform Party. "Wait until we leave the hall and you will
see something. Come over to the palace when you go out."

Young guessed his meaning but determined to draw him out a
bit more. "Do you refer to the new constitution?"

The chief nodded and then gave his attention to the front of the
hall as the ceremony commenced. Young's recollection of the occasion was typical of what had come to be the American attitude toward Hawaiʻi, mocking the ceremony as buffoonery in blackface.
As the queen's entourage entered the front of the chamber from a
side door, Young wrote:

> First came the Chamberlain, supporting in front of him a large
> portfolio containing the Queen's message of prorogation. From
> it were streaming the ends of white and blue silk ribbons. Next
> came four dusky aides-de-camp in full uniform. . . . They were

stiff and pretentious, and exhibiting the air of fully realizing the importance of their exalted position. After them were the feather kahili bearers, supporting the emblems of savage royalty. These were followed by her Majesty the Queen, dressed in a light colored silk which tended to add somewhat to her dark complexion and negro-like features, and more plainly exhibiting in the facial outlines a look of savage determination. . . . Next came four homely ladies in waiting, dressed in the loud colors so much admired by all dark-colored races. Then the two royal princes, modest in demeanor, but dudish in appearance.

Only after these came the cabinet and the justices of the Hawaiian supreme court—the only American-Hawaiians in the queen's retinue—including Associate Justice Sanford Ballard Dole. Young marked him particularly, seeing a man "whose manly bearing and intellectual appearance gave a relief to what had preceded."

Dole was tall, now not quite fifty, still rail thin, his age denoted by his gray hair and long, square beard that affected a close impersonation of King Leopold II of the Belgians. His apple cheeks, however, and his unlined face and delicate features made him seem many years younger. Observers always felt that he conveyed great dignity. It was Lorrin Thurston and others who had prosecuted the revolution of 1887 and forced the king to sign the Bayonet Constitution, but it was Dole whose later approval made it seem solemn and acceptable.

The queen seated herself at the front desk, but not before she had tripped over her long train, which caused her to snap at her train bearers—the four "lackeys," Lieutenant Young called them, in knee breeches, blue velvet cutaway coats, and buckled slippers.[11] (The two "modest . . . but dudish" princes Young mentioned were David Kawananakoa and Jonah Kuhio Kalaniana'ole, twenty-four and nineteen, respectively, sons of Kapi'olani's sister Victoria Kinoiki, who had begun taking part in court life.) After the ceremony Lili'uokalani withdrew to an anteroom, and a receiving line formed for her to greet. When it came his turn, Lieutenant Young recorded that she received him coldly, but his presence was probably the first indication she had of the *Boston*'s return. She would naturally be sorry to see the ship back so quickly; any day that Minister Stevens was out of Honolulu was a good day.

Leaving the Ali'iolani Hale, the queen and her attendants crossed the square toward the 'Iolani Palace. Her palace guard was present, turned out in their dress uniforms for the greater ceremony to follow. On the palace grounds the Royal Hawaiian Band was playing light airs in the pavilion that her brother had built for his coronation. The queen was an expert pianist and composer, and always listened to the band and its German conductor with a more critical ear than did her people, who just enjoyed the music and always gathered when the band played.

After entering, on her left she saw that the marshal of the kingdom, her trusted friend Charles Wilson, stood at the entrance to the blue room. She paused and asked him if everything was ready, and he said that it was. All four of the arched doors on the right side of the hall passed into the throne room, which occupied the entire east side of the first floor. At the north end of the room, two thrones reposed upon the canopied dais, flanked by two tall *kahilis*. Before the thrones was a *kapu* stick to create a sacred space. Hawai'i was now a Christian country, but the principle of *kapu* had been an element of chiefs' courts for centuries, and it was retained in deference to tradition. The *kapu* stick was made of a seven-foot narwhal tusk that a whaling captain had presented to Kamehameha III, and since then it had been mounted on a gold sphere.

Lili'uokalani had come through the 1892 legislature with more wins than losses: she had successfully manipulated no-confidence votes, she had played the Liberal and Reform Parties against each other to obtain two means of income for the kingdom that might see it through until something could be done about the McKinley

Tariff Act. Hawai'i's leading historian has written that had she been content with that, the coup might have been averted.[12] But she could not let it go, and she would not continue to play the existing system for what good she could get from it. Once again in Hawaiian history, royal overreach led to mayhem.[13]

At the proper moment a procession of natives attired in morning dress entered the throne room. They were members of a patriotic movement, the Hui Kala'ia'ina. The first one carried an elegant folio that he presented to the queen, begging her to heed the many petitions of her people and proclaim this new constitution, and liberate them from the alienation they had suffered since 1887. It was impressive, but it was royal stagecraft; in fact the constitution they offered her was the one over which she herself had labored for months.

The queen decided to have the cabinet also sign the document, as was provided in the Bayonet Constitution anyway. She dispatched her chamberlain to fetch them, and she said that she would receive them in the Blue Room. As the crowd waited in the throne room, she crossed the grand hall and entered the palace's principal reception chamber, with its yellow-cream walls, royal blue draperies and upholstery, expansive cream-and-blue carpet, and—as throughout the palace—glowing wainscoting and trim of rare, exotic native woods. The room was dominated by the pompous 1848 portrait of Louis-Philippe. Watched over by the king of the French and other European monarchs who had sent their portraits as tokens of friendship, Liliuokalani waited—for three hours.

When the cabinet finally assembled, freshly coached by Thurston, they declined to sign the document, and urged on her the fatal irregularity of what she was about to do. Lili'uokalani was furious with them, alleging that she would not have proceeded with the constitution without their having encouraged her; accusing Peterson of playing her falsely in returning the draft after a month with no correction, from which she assumed that he found it acceptable. She raged, but they would not be moved. It was said that she even threatened to tell the restive crowd outside that it was her ministers who prevented her from issuing the new constitution. She hardly needed to remind them that during the riots in support of Queen Emma over Kalakaua, the mob had stormed the Ali'iolani Hale and cast an offending legislator from an upper-story window down to the natives who killed him. Steeling himself to the moment, Attorney General Peterson protested their loyalty but insisted that she stop and realize the danger. The step she was taking was unconstitutional, however defective she found that 1887 document to be. What she proposed to do would give the annexationists the only excuse they needed to arm themselves for revolution. With enormous difficulty Peterson and the others persuaded Lili'uokalani for her own safety's sake to postpone promulgating the new constitution.

It was almost unthinkable for an *ali'i* of her station to back down from such a confrontation, and it was four in the afternoon before Lili'uokalani returned to the throne room. "Princes, Nobles, and Representatives," she began, "I have listened to thousands of the voices of my people that have come to me, and I am prepared to grant their request. The present Constitution is full of defects, as the Chief Justice here will testify. . . . It is so faulty that I think a new one should be granted. I have prepared one in which the rights of all have been regarded—a Constitution suited to the wishes of the people. I was ready and expected to proclaim the new Constitution today as a suitable occasion for it . . . but with regret I have to say I have met with obstacles that prevent it. . . . You have my love and with sorrow I now dismiss you."

Now the humiliation would have to be repeated before the crowd that had gathered outside to welcome the restoration of their rights. Her people had despised the Bayonet Constitution that stole the vote from them, and they had petitioned her relentlessly to do what she had done. She knew they would rise up if she asked them to, but she did not want anyone's blood on her soul. More to the point, she knew that she would be blamed for any violence, and she knew that the United States would respond fiercely if any of their people, property, or investments were threatened. Although she was angry, the queen could not be responsible for any replay of the 1874 riots.

With bitterness but determination, the queen mounted the iridescent *koa* staircase and appeared on the palace balcony, motioning the crowd for quiet. She spoke in Hawaiian and in the style of the epic chants: "O, ye people who love the chiefs!" she hailed them. "Hereby I say unto you, I am now ready to proclaim the new constitution of my Kingdom, thinking that it would be successful. But look you! Obstacles have arisen. Therefore I say unto you, my loving people, go with good hope and do not be disturbed in your minds. Because within the next few days now coming, I will proclaim the new constitution."

The crowd grumbled and began to disperse, but the listening Americans—including Lorrin Thurston and others of the Annexation Club—buzzed among themselves. What had she said? Many of them spoke Hawaiian, but it was an ambiguous language: *Ua keia mau la.*[14] Had she actually meant the next few days now coming, in a short time, or had she merely meant sometime? They must not take the chance, and the members of the secret Annexation Club dispersed to gather again immediately at William O. Smith's law office.

Harking back to the French Revolution and the goodwill that it might buy them from the United States, they formed a Committee of Safety—mostly the same people as the Annexation Club—which decided breathlessly that the time had come to abolish the monarchy and establish a provisional government. They therefore set to work at what they did best—drafting documents.

The next day, Sunday, they shared their work with Peterson and Colburn, who were not prepared to go quite so far. After conferring with proroyalist leaders, they believed that the queen's pledge not to change the constitution would suffice to head off such a drastic step. By now word of a mass antigovernment meeting for Monday was abroad, with all the trouble that portended. Lili'uokalani sent urgently to U.S. minister Stevens to learn whether the government could count on American protection, of which Stevens declined to assure her. Some advised the queen to declare martial law and round up the conspirators before things went any further, but that could ignite the fighting she dreaded. Lili'u chose a milder course: simply calling a competing mass meeting for the next day, as though her supporters could merely shout down the annexationists.

On Monday afternoon, January 17, several hundred royalists gathered in Palace Square, having been adjured to be peaceful and give no excuse for an intervention. Wilcox and Bush, who were back in the queen's camp, addressed them, and read a statement that Lili'uokalani had issued, declaring that she would make no further attempt to change the constitution except by the means provided in the existing one.

That morning the Committee of Safety had sent their letter to Minister Stevens pleading for intervention to protect American lives and property:

> The Queen, with the aid of armed forces, and accompanied by threats of violence and bloodshed from those with whom she was acting, attempted to proclaim a new constitution; and while prevented for the time from accomplishing her object declared publicly that she would only defer her action. This [has] created general alarm and terror. We are unable to protect ourselves without aid and, therefore, pray for the protection of the United States forces.

The document's exaggerations are self-apparent; conspiracy to depose the queen could not be viewed as other than treason, and they needed to know where U.S. minister Stevens would stand. It was getting late in the day, but Thurston and two others hurried to his residence. Stevens was easy, declaring that it was the queen who had committed a revolutionary act and placed herself beyond his protection. He would send for the marines when they asked for them, and once they had secured the public buildings, he would recognize their provisional government. Another messenger boarded a launch out to the USS *Boston* to make certain of Captain Wiltse's position.

And Captain Wiltse was not just aware of the ferment in Honolulu, he was alive to the much, much larger question of America acquiring an empire, and the role forecast for the U.S. Navy in such a venture: For two generations Americans had vented their certainty in the perfection of their civilization with the pursuit of "Manifest Destiny." That was the idea that Providence had gifted all of North America to the growing nation to display the superiority of democracy and laissez-faire capitalism. First coined in 1839, the expression came into popular usage to justify the annexation of the Republic of Texas to the United States in 1845, advanced by Democrats for the glory of the nation, attacked by Whigs as a justification for naked conquest. But always Manifest Destiny had looked westward: across the Mississippi River, mastering the Great Plains and subduing the native Indians on them, over the Rockies, and backwashing from the Pacific Coast to fill in those corners leapfrogged in the westward hurry.

In 1893, however, the year of the Hawaiian crisis, the historian Federick Jackson Turner announced in a seminal paper to the American Historical Association that the frontier, which had formed the essence of the American character, was gone. Manifest Destiny was accomplished, and it had made the United States a continental nation but not a world power. Where now to direct the national energy?

In fact, the hour had already provided the man: Capt. Alfred Thayer Mahan, president of the Naval War College in Newport, Rhode Island, author of *The Influence of Sea Power upon History, 1660–1783*, which posited that no nation had ever sustained itself as a mighty world power without the service of an overpowering navy. It was one of the most influential books of its generation; scholars have noted that what *Uncle Tom's Cabin* did for abolitionism half a century before, Mahan did in 1890 for imperialism: He galvanized a large segment of the country behind a sense of purpose, that America must join Britain, France, Spain, Germany, and others as a colonial master. No one in the American navy, or foreign service, or in government at the national level was unaware of Mahan, his theories, or their implications for American expansion. And Hawaii's potential was clear: "In our infancy," wrote Mahan, "we bordered on the Atlantic only; our youth carried our boundary to the Gulf of Mexico; to-day maturity sees us upon the Pacific. Have we no right or no call to progress farther in any direction?"[15] And Hawaii, whose people had been spiritually and culturally captured seventy years before, and whose economy had been grafted to that of the United States twenty years before, was now in the crosshairs to become the first asset of an American empire.

Mahan considered himself a naval theoretician, not a historian, but in his historical writing he advanced the Hegelian "Great Man" theory and noted the times when strong men of conviction, in the right places and times, had wrought great changes in the story of civilization. In this tiny corner of the globe, such a well-placed man was Captain Wiltse of the USS *Boston*.

As the queen's mass meeting was under way on Palace Square, the Committee of Safety's meeting at the armory also commenced, and Lorrin Thurston tried his hand at oratory,[16] but as inflammatory rhetoric it was rather a dud, and the Committee of Safety sent word to Stevens that they were not ready yet, there were more plans to make for a new government. But it was too late. Triumphant that his moment had finally come, Stevens had already sent for the marines.

By five thirty in the afternoon the royalist meeting had dispersed, and the queen retired to the private second floor of the palace, when a disturbance became audible outside. American troops were landing on the wharf. From the front balcony the harbor was closer than it is today, for the landfills that extended the city out into the waterfront had not been created. Four launches from the *Boston* were unloading sailors and marine "bluejackets"; from the balcony the queen could plainly see two field guns, two ten-barreled Gatling machine guns, and the small caissons that carried their ammunition.

She watched the sailors and marines form into platoons and march into Palace Square. Seeing the queen on the balcony they gave her a "royal marching salute," of all things—"arms port, drooping of colors, and ruffles on the drums"[17]—before separating into two small squadrons and one large unit. One of the small groups continued on toward the American legation, the other turned up Nuʻuanu Street toward the residence of Minister Stevens. The remainder trooped into the opera house, next door to the Aliʻiolani Hale. As the queen's ministers continued to seek information from the unresponsive Stevens, the rest of the diplomatic corps advised her glumly not to resist. Thurston worked feverishly all night on a declaration of causes and justification for the coup; others set about trying to find a president for the new junta.[18]

Thurston at least recognized that he was not suitable, having been the prime mover in the affair, but there was always Dole, whose support would give much color of legitimacy to the enterprise. Dole weighed the situation carefully, resigned from the supreme court, and accepted. With the backing of the U.S. marines and the Honolulu Rifles, the junta took control of the public buildings, which they found virtually deserted, and proclaimed the new government. Also that afternoon, a deputation from the junta called at the palace, headed by a former finance minister, J. S. Walker. He told the queen that they had come on a painful mission: the matter of her abdication. With amazing composure she told Walker that she had no mind to do any such thing.

It was apparent that she would not get away without having to sign something, but abdication was a finality, or at least it could be argued as a finality even if it was compelled. Twice in the history of her kingdom, junior officers of foreign powers had seized the country, only to have those chagrined powers hand it back. With this history, and in view of their long-standing friendship with the United States, there might be a way out other than abdication, a middle way, a way to stall. The queen excused herself to confer with her secretary, and said when she returned that an appropriate document was being prepared.

Especially for having been composed in the exigency of the moment, it was a brilliant instrument. She ceded her authority, but only provisionally, noting that it was Stevens who had caused troops to be landed; she handed power not to the coup plotters but to the United States.[19] By alleging American collusion in surrendering power, she had in effect slammed the lid down on the cookie jar with the American hand still inside it. That was all she could do for now. She was aware that among her household guard and the volunteer rifle companies still loyal, her forces may have outnumbered the Honolulu Rifles and U.S. Marines by close to double. But she did not want bloodshed on her conscience, and sent word over to the police station giving Marshal Wilson permission to stand down, and with Wilson's assent, the annexationists disarmed 270 Royal Hawaiian troops. But the game was far from over, for the United States would have no choice but to respond.

18. The Inscrutable Mr. Blount

'Iolani Palace began a transition from royal residence to a make-shift capitol. In the coming days of the republic, the House of Representatives met in the throne room, the Senate in the blue room. When she retired to Washington Place, Lili'uokalani took with her many of the symbols and trappings of her reign. Other members of the family also rounded up royal keepsakes for safety. Archibald Cleghorn had been overseeing construction of a luxurious home in Waikiki, called 'Ainahau, as a residence for Ka'iulani when she returned from boarding school in England. A visitor to the almost-finished house found it "crowded with relics of Hawaiian royalty, evidently hastily gathered together—feather coronets, shell necklaces, pieces of furniture, and in a large box was one of the celebrated feather mantles like those worn by the nobles."[1]

At the new government headquarters Sanford Dole endorsed the queen's provisional cession of authority. He could have rejected it and insisted on an abdication, but it didn't occur to him that by accepting her wording, he was submitting the revolution to American approval and setting in motion another year's controversy.

Whatever Minister Stevens's posture of good faith about doing his duty and protecting American citizens and property, on February 1 he revealed his true bearing, and the object of his labors, in a letter to President Harrison's secretary of state, John W. Foster: "The Hawaiian pear is now fully ripe and this is the golden hour for the United States to pluck it."[2] Five representatives of the junta took ship for the United States, and the Harrison administration made good on its pledge to Thurston to be "exceedingly sympathetic." They negotiated, drafted, and finalized a treaty of annexation, which was signed on February 14, 1893—one month precisely after Lili'uokalani had brought the rafters down on her head. If haste could be unseemly, this seemed shameless.

Their timing was poor, however, for the Harrison administration had only days to live. Grover Cleveland, whom Harrison had unseated four years before, reclaimed the White House in the 1892 election, the only American president to serve two terms without them being consecutive. Cleveland chose for his secretary of state a Republican defector, Walter Q. Gresham, and one of his first acts was to withdraw the annexation treaty from Senate consideration. Harrison saw it coming. "I am sorry the Hawaiian question did not come six months sooner," he wrote, "or sixty days later, as it is embarrassing to begin without the time to finish."[3]

At the time the American administration changed, a new wrinkle appeared on the revolutionary front when it seemed that the junta's ends might be more quickly and easily met not by abolishing the monarchy but by accepting Lili'uokalani's abdication in favor of her niece, Victoria Ka'iulani, now seventeen and finishing her education in England. Her father Archibald Cleghorn had been present in the blue room as Lili'uokalani berated her cabinet for not signing her new constitution. He vented his temper in a nineteen-page letter to his daughter: "If she had followed my advice, she would have been firm on the throne, and Hawaiian Independence safe, but she has turned out a very stubborn woman and was not satisfied to Reign, but wanted to Rule. . . . If the Queen had abdicated . . . in your *favor*, the Throne I think could have been *saved*, but she did not think they would do as they did."[4] The princess's guardian Theo Davies who was one of Honolulu's richest sugar factors, pressed her to go to America and campaign to restore the crown.

The princess, escorted by the former finance minister E. C. Macfarlane, arrived in New York on March 1 and progressed to Washington; waif thin, doe-eyed, and the height of fashion (she traveled with eight bags and thirteen trunks[5]), she created a sensation. She delivered a series of wooden, melodramatic speeches and interviews, scripted by Davies, that reflected none of her natural flash and intelligence. "Today, I, a poor, weak girl," she had to say, "with not one of my people near me . . . have strength to stand up for the rights of my people." The new president and Mrs. Cleveland received her into the White House, while behind the scenes a flurry of letters circulated speculating on the advantages of accepting her as queen, rather than annexation. Joining the United States would not come without cost, as a new source of field labor would have to be found owing to the U.S. Chinese Exclusion Act. Ka'iulani was popular and could be controlled, at least during her minority, and it would deflect a growing wave of attacks on the coup in the American press that it was the project of adventurers out to get richer. Lilli'uokalani's lawyer in Washington, Paul Neumann, and his team were worried enough about the outcome that they investigated the American government's attitude toward the possibility of restoring the queen under an American protectorate.

It was a scenario not unfamiliar to Lili'uokalani, who late in her brother's reign had stood in the same relation to him. When politicians disgusted with Kalakaua sounded her out about his conditional abdication in her favor, she had not refused them outright, but said only that if they approached him about it, they should use only the most respectful language. As it was, Neumann and the others monitored the princess's appearances, wary of any hint that she was promoting her own benefit and not the queen's restoration.

"Kailuani's appearance on the scene will embarrass us very much," one wrote her, "more especially as she does not appear to care for anyone but herself, and wants the Throne at once."[6]

A good deal of discussion about Hawai'i in the United States did not concern itself with who should be queen or even with the morality of the coup; the examination was about geopolitical reality in the imperialist age and the future of America after the close of the frontier. And while the frontier may have gone, the sense of Manifest Destiny had not, and there was an earnest belief that the virtues of American democracy (as it was perceived) should continue their westward march across the Pacific.

One of the first people to react to news of the coup in Hawai'i was Capt. Alfred T. Mahan, the influential author and naval strategist, who noted the heavy importation of Chinese labor into the islands. "It is a question for the whole civilized world," he wrote the *New York Times*, "and not for the United States only, whether the Sandwich Islands, with their geographical and military importance . . . shall in the future be an outpost of European civilization, or of the comparative barbarism of China."[7] In his *Times* piece Mahan echoed the conclusion he reached in a second article, that "the annexation, even, of Hawaii, would be no mere sporadic effort . . . but a first fruit and a token that the [United States] in its evolution has aroused itself to the necessity of carrying its life—that has been the happiness of those under its influence—beyond the borders which heretofore have sufficed for its activities."[8]

As it developed, Cleveland withdrew the treaty, as Lili'uokalani had surrendered her powers not to the Dole junta but to the United States, and her lawyers had made a prima facie case that the entire affair could be laid to the collusion and bad faith of the American minister in Honolulu. Cleveland decided to send a special commissioner to Hawai'i to act as an honest broker of facts, to investigate and report on the actual conditions in the troubled country. At a glance, Cleveland's selection of the outgoing chairman of the House Foreign Affairs Committee, James H. Blount of Georgia, was so appropriate as to seem obvious. The choice, however, embraced a whole nest of interests and intrigues that bore materially on the question.

After nine terms in Congress, Blount had not stood for reelection in 1892, preferring to return to his plantation near Macon and, it was well believed, first seek an appointment abroad and then press his claims to the Georgia legislature for election to the U.S. Senate. He was a Confederate veteran, commonly addressed as "Colonel," and like most Southern politicians who had survived the horrors of Reconstruction, he was more interested in building the sectional and national economies from the poor up than he was in enriching Northern tycoons with empires either in the defeated South or abroad. Cleveland was aware of Blount's sympathies that might prejudice him against annexation, but a balance of other Southerners in his cabinet, representing the portfolios of Interior, Treasury, and Navy, pressed his case. The attorney general also favored him, respecting Blount's reputation as a dogged investigator.[9] Moreover, the new secretary of state, Walter Q. Gresham, blamed members of the outgoing administration for reverses in his own political aspirations. He had been a leading candidate for the Republican presidential nomination in 1888, but as a pro-West and proagrarian Republican, he fell from favor with the probusiness investor class that favored Harrison, as Harrison favored them. Thus despite Gresham's lead in the early ballots of the 1888 convention, the nomination eventually swung to Harrison. Gresham hated Benjamin Harrison's guts; he supported Cleveland in 1892, and as a reward became secretary of state. If the Republicans in Congress could be humiliated by torpedoing the Hawaiian annexation—well, the actual merits of the case could be looked at another day.[10]

Blount was in Macon, Georgia, when he read the telegram on Friday, March 10: "I ask you to come here immediately prepared for confidential trip of great importance to the Pacific Ocean." The following Sunday he was in Washington for briefings with Gresham in the morning; officially he was merely a fact finder, but unofficially he was to particularly investigate the conduct of Minister Stevens and American involvement in the coup. If he found it proper and advisable to do so, he was authorized to lower the American flag and raise the Hawaiian once more. On Monday, Blount was presented to the whole cabinet for a few seconds before being sent off with Cleveland's, "Now, Blount, you will let us hear from you."

Gresham cabled Stevens and Cleveland cabled Dole that Blount, his fact finder, was being dispatched. The full scope of his authority was not imparted. Other than the president and the cabinet, the only one who was given the whole story was Adm. John Skerrett, commanding U.S. naval forces in Honolulu. In Hawaii, members of the Dole government suspected that Cleveland was not their friend and knew some of the factors in play, but they fastened upon one bright ray of hope: Since he was a Confederate veteran and Georgia cotton planter, they could rely upon Blount's sympathy for the notion that the dark races were incapable of providing enlightened government. "As a Southerner," wrote Lorrin Thurston, "he is thoroughly familiar with the difficulties attendant upon government with an ignorant majority in the electorate, and will thoroughly appreciate the situation upon this point."[11]

Blount departed for San Francisco the day after he was trotted before the cabinet, finding upon his arrival there the insubstantial U.S. Coast Guard cutter *Richard Rush* waiting to take him aboard. A 140-foot schooner, displacing less than two hundred tons, rigged for sailing in case her single-screw steam engine failed, she was a minimal vessel in which to cross the vast Pacific, but she headed gamely through the Golden Gate. And at 9:30 a.m. on March 29 the telephone station on Diamond Head rang down to the city to notify the government and the American legation of the *Rush*'s imminent arrival at Honolulu. As the *Rush* coasted through the harbor the first ship she passed was a sobering one: the Japanese armored cruiser *Naniwa*, dispatched to Hawaii at first news of the coup with sufficient marines to protect Japanese citizens. British-built to Japanese specifications and armed to the teeth, the 300-foot, 3,700-ton

Naniwa was the most powerful cruiser on earth at the time she entered service; the Emperor Meiji himself had reviewed his rapidly modernizing fleet from her deck. If violence were to suddenly erupt, *Naniwa* would be more than a match for the newer USS *Boston*, and she could give a full account of herself. Dispelling any hostile intent, however, one of *Naniwa*'s guns saluted the *Rush* smartly as she passed, which *Rush* answered with her single six-pounder. One reporter in Honolulu remarked of the comical disparity in the ships' respective capabilities that the American cutter's answering salute was "like the yap of a terrier echoing the deep bellow of a boar hound."[12]

This correspondent on the dock was one of a large throng who produced more flags and bunting, she wrote, than she imagined could be in all of Honolulu. Both factions, annexationists nearly all white, waving American flags, and monarchists nearly all native, waving Hawaiian flags, were present to cheer on their cause. While the junta knew whom to expect, the crowd believed that the American commission to hear the case for annexation would consist of General Schofield, Admiral Brown, and an authority on international law, Justice Thomas M. Cooley of Michigan. Thus the consternation was general when the commission proved to be the single former congressman from Georgia, "a commonplace, rather sullen-looking man of sixty, clad in ill-fitting clothes of blue homespun and a Panama hat," accompanied by his wife and secretary.

From the moment the *Rush* dropped anchor, Blount was courted by all factions, and the games began. Minister Stevens, unaware that his own recent conduct was to be an object of Blount's special attention, motored out on a launch to greet him, accompanied by a committee of the Annexation Club (a new one, reconstituted and no longer secret), which had rented for Blount an elegant mansion, fully furnished, including servants and carriage. Blount declined with thanks. The ex-queen sent her personal carriage to convey him to his hotel; determined to maintain his neutrality, he declined with thanks. Once it was clear that Blount would not become a partisan for their side, the proannexation press turned on him. His refusal of Dole's favors became "insulting," his very appearance "loathsome." Admiral Skerrett paid his compliments, and offered use of the navy's coded cipher for his communications back and forth to Washington. Considering the navy's implication in the events of January 17, he declined with thanks. He did not trust Skerrett not to share his messages with Stevens.

Calling on President Dole, Blount handed him a letter from President Cleveland, advising that Blount spoke for the United States and that his authority over the American mission and military was paramount. The contents of the letter were made public, after which the ex-congressman became known as "Paramount Blount." From the inability of virtually everyone to draw out his thoughts, he also became known as "Minister Reticent."

From his cottage at the Hawaiian Hotel, Blount began taking testimony from virtually all comers. By the third day he had heard enough to order Dole to lower the American flag and restore the Hawaiian. That evening, before the order was carried out, Minister Stevens called on Blount, introducing and endorsing the worth of a Mr. Walter G. Smith, who Blount learned was a member of the Annexation Club and editor of the *Honolulu Star*, an American mouthpiece. Smith imparted his certain knowledge that Lili'uokalani had colluded with the Japanese commissioner, and agreed that the removal of the American flag and marines was the signal to land troops from the *Naniwa*, and restore the monarchy in a counterinsurgency. Blount wrote, "I was not impressed much with these statements," and his inquiries quickly exploded the story; indeed the Japanese commissioner was so mortified that the presence of an imperial warship would lend color to such a tale that he asked his government to withdraw the powerful cruiser, which it did.[13]

In the days after the Hawaiian flag was restored, it became apparent that the fate of Hawai'i and its "revolution" was being decided by the parade of witnesses trailing into Paramount Blount's cottage at the Hawaiian Hotel. Mary Krout noticed that a huge yellow mastiff had taken up residence there, semiadopted by some Portuguese bellboys. As it happened, one day a black mongrel of equal size appeared and tried to muscle in on the arrangement, and the two hounds fell upon each other in a terrifying brawl in the hotel's main corridor. "That," remarked one of the foreign reporters from the safety of the staircase, "is the first real fight I have seen since the Revolution began."[14]

Blount made an almost impossibly quick study of Hawaiian history, but he succeeded to the point that, when A. F. Judd of the Hawaiian supreme court was giving him a précis of events leading up to the forced constitution of 1887, Blount interrupted him more than once with trenchant questions that induced a more even-handed narrative of events.[15] Judd found Blount's method of operating peculiar: "Mr. Blount has not observed the usual course in Diplomatic [illegible] at all. He did not tell Mr. Stevens of his intention to remove the Protectorate. . . . But the Prov Govt's authority is not questioned & maintains itself well & keeps order so that quietness reigns. The 'Annexation Club' now numbers about 2500 and grows daily. Mr. Blount sees everybody and is getting information from all quarters. The royalists are working [and] have at him too."[16] Most of the maka'ainana had been disenfranchised by the Bayonet Constitution of 1887. They could no longer vote, but Thurston and Dole could not keep them and their side of the issue away from Blount. Even with no more notice than they'd had, the commoners were able to give Blount petitions with more than seven thousand names on them protesting against annexation. To counter this landslide, Thurston suggested to Dole that he should collect a number of proannexation common natives and parade them before the special commissioner to bolster their case. Dole's response was that the only way to accomplish this would be to first convince some natives that annexation was the best and only improvement they could expect over the provisional government, and then "pay their expenses." It was probably too late for such a scheme to succeed, anyway, because Blount had already gotten an earful from the Hawaiian Patriotic League and other royalist groups.

In his assessment of the events of January 14–17, Blount was critical of Stevens's overhasty recognition of the provisional government, and noted that the sailors and marines of the *Boston* had been positioned in the city not for the protection of American property but to support the ongoing coup. Stevens was recalled, but not before his daughter accidentally drowned. Least sorry to see Stevens depart was the queen, who referred to his bereavement as a judgment from God. With Stevens gone, Secretary of State Gresham awarded his credentials to Blount, making him both special commissioner with paramount powers, and minister as well. Blount quickly realized that representing the interest of the United States might well conflict with his interest in getting to the bottom of the Hawaiian situation, and he resigned Stevens's job as soon as it was given him. One Panama hat was quite enough for him to wear in Honolulu.

When the Blount Report was made public in July, its shock waves rattled all the interested parties. To the extent that Thurston and Dole relied on Blount's Southern heritage to color his view of the racial component of the situation, the Georgia planter blasted their hopes without mercy. After stating what credit the native Hawaiians reflected upon themselves with their high literacy rate, Blount went on to characterize the natives as "over-generous, hospitable, almost free from revenge, very courteous—especially to females. Their talent for oratory and the higher branches of mathematics is unusually marked. . . . The small amount of thieving and absence of beggary are more marked than among the best races in the world. What they are capable of under fair conditions is an unsolved problem."[17] In his report, Blount did not venture to advise President Cleveland on a course of action. His conclusions, however, were unmistakable: "The undoubted sentiment of the people is for the Queen, against the provisional government and against annexation. A majority of the whites, especially Americans, is for annexation."

As a Southerner who had survived congressional Reconstruction, Blount was uniquely qualified to spy out chicaneries by which the forms of "democracy" could be touted while ensuring that a genuinely democratic outcome was impossible. And what carpetbaggers had done to Southern Democrats, the latter had been doing to blacks since the end of the occupation. Blount summarized and then lambasted the American-Hawaiians' shenanigans that guaranteed elections would reach a predetermined result—placing a wealth restriction on the franchise for Hawaiians that gave the Americans three-quarters of the votes for the house of nobles, for instance, while making it possible for illiterate foreigners such as the Portuguese (and they were almost uniformly illiterate, and only eight had become naturalized Hawaiians) to be taken to polls by plantation managers and vote as they were told. "The annexationists," Blount concluded, "expect the United States to govern the islands by so abridging the right of suffrage as to place them in control of the whites."

Replacing Stevens as U.S. minister to Hawai'i was Albert Willis, fifty, a former five-term congressman from Kentucky, with large blue eyes under a prominent balding dome. His first task was to approach Lili'uokalani with an inquiry. President Cleveland was frank in his assessment that Minister Stevens had had no justification for offering American support for the coup, but his encouragement once offered made the United States responsible to a degree for the rebels' safety. Thus Willis asked whether she would grant amnesty to the Americans who staged the coup, in exchange for Cleveland's help, perhaps even intervention, in regaining her government. In a thoughtless moment the former queen, a Christian woman who could have saved her throne if she had taken some lives when she had the chance, finally bridled. The "Americans" who seized the government were born in the islands, subjects of the crown, and "American" only by ethnicity, or had become naturalized. She would not grant such an amnesty. She may have said, or at least Willis came away believing that he heard her say, they should be beheaded. Whatever the exact exchange was, the story gained currency in the press that Lili'uokalani had vowed to take their heads as in the old days.

Much of the story about the queen swearing to take rebel heads if she were restored smacks of being someone else's invention. The Conqueror a century before was known to offer the heads of his enemies as sacrifices to his war god, but they were harvested from corpses after battle. In the premissionary days, the usual mode of dispatch was strangulation, sometimes clubbing, or a woman who broke *kapu* might be thrown off a cliff. And for as long as almost anyone could remember, the approved mode of criminal capital punishment in Hawai'i had been American-style hanging. But to circulate the mental image of Hawai'i's dark-skinned queen lopping off the heads of white American businessmen contains just the telltale mixture of cultural ignorance and racial baiting to have become exaggerated, even if it did not originate, among her enemies. The tale raced as far away as Massachusetts, where the 1894 Republican Party platform, written by their longtime senator George Frisbie Hoar, included the plank, "No barbarous Queen beheading men in Hawaii."[18]

Benefiting from such stories, if not propagating them, was Lorrin Thurston, scurrying from meeting to meeting in Washington to promote the provisional government's cause. It became increasingly apparent that he considered Sanford Dole a weak sister in revolutionary fervor, and bombarded him with telegrams and letters to cave in to no inducements to restoration, in fact advising that they deport the queen to some other Pacific island.[19]

On December 18 the former queen thought better of her intransigence and indicated that an amnesty might be possible, but she was too late. On that same day Cleveland had sent a detailed recapitulation of relations with Hawai'i dating back to his withdrawal of Harrison's annexation treaty in the opening days of his administration, along with all the relevant documents accumulated since that time. "If national honesty is to be disregarded," the president began, "and a desire for territorial extension . . . ought to regulate our conduct, I have entirely misapprehended the mission and character of our government." He would not, he advised the Congress (and instructed Willis to inform the Hawaiian junta), resubmit the Hawaiian annexation treaty, for the reason that without the malfeasance of American minister to Hawai'i John Stevens there would have been no coup: "I believe that a candid and thorough examination of the facts will force the conviction that the provisional government owes its existence to an armed invasion by the United States. Fair-minded people . . . will hardly claim that the Hawaiian Government was overthrown by the people of the islands or that the provisional government had ever existed with their consent. I do not understand that any member of this government claims that the people would uphold it . . . if they were allowed to vote on the question."

Stevens had bombarded Harrison's State Department with his vociferous advocacy of annexation both before and after the coup, and Cleveland now quoted the damning documents at length. He declared in his final summation that "but for the lawless occupation of Honolulu under false pretexts by the United States forces, and but for Minister Stevens' recognition of the provisional government when the United States forces were its sole support . . . the Queen and her government would never have yielded to the provisional government." What Cleveland's broadside disregarded, however, was the fact that Stevens, with or without formal instruction, had been effecting the Harrison administration's wishes. Britain's minister to the United States, Sir Julian Pauncefote, perceived as much and expressed some sympathy for Stevens: "It is unfortunate for him that a change of Administration should have taken place just after he had succeeded in carrying out the annexation Policy."[20] Pauncefote was correct, as Harrison's secretary of state Foster cabled Stevens on January 28 to approve of his recognizing the junta and advising his continued cooperation with Captain Wiltse to protect American interests.[21]

But Cleveland's conditions to the queen, "that the past should be buried, and that the restored government should reassume its authority as if its continuity had not been interrupted . . . have not proved acceptable to the Queen, and though she has been informed that they will be insisted upon, and that, unless acceded to, the efforts of the President to aid in the restoration of her Government will cease, I have not thus far learned that she is willing." Cleveland had no way of knowing that Lili'uokalani had capitulated on that very day; as it was he submitted the whole knotty issue "to the extended powers and wide discretion of the Congress," with his assurance that he would cooperate in "any legislative plan which is consistent with American honor, integrity, and morality."[22]

Lili'uokalani had surrendered her powers not to the junta but to the United States, on the gamble that that country would show the same honorable shame that Britain and France had done when misguided minions of theirs had seized the government in years past. And it almost worked, but once again a royal blunder—her distaste for and delay in accepting the deal that Willis offered—cost Hawaii its continued existence as an independent nation.

On December 23, 1893, the junta formally rejected Cleveland's request to stand down and return sovereign power to the queen. The revolution and provisional government, they declared, were faits accomplis; Hawai'i was an independent country, and the United States had no right to order its citizens about. "Our only issue with your people," declared the Dole regime, "has been that, because we revered its institutions of civil liberty, we have desired to have them extended to our distracted country, and . . . we have stood ready to add our country, a new star, to its glory, and to consummate a union. . . . If this is an offense, we plead guilty to it." The junta's conscience was untroubled by the irony that they had provoked American intervention by pleading that their American lives and property were in danger, but now proclaimed for themselves this new national Hawaiian identity in order to tell the United States to get lost.

❧

With the hope of annexation gone for the present, the task of preparing for an extended national existence now presented itself, and they discovered that sustaining a government involved a plethora of small tasks. Typical of their extemporizing was the postal department, where royal issues that were still in use, all the way back to Victoria Kamamalu, had to be recalled and overprinted with a typeset "Provisional GOV'T. 1893" until a new set of stamps could be prepared. Of greater moment was the need for a new constitution, and it would have to be an artful one, for a genuinely democratic document would have resulted in a return to native power after a single election. For advice President Dole turned to John W. Burgess of Columbia University, widely acknowledged as the "father of political science" in the United States.[23] Dole wrote Burgess on March 24, 1894, and again on March 31; there were two points particularly that he wished Dr. Burgess to address. First, "There are many natives and Portuguese who had the vote hitherto, who are comparatively ignorant of the principles of government, and whose vote from its numerical strength as well as from the ignorance will be a menace to good government." Dole proposed to blunt this menace by imposing stiff property requirements on all candidates for the legislature, and also for voters in casting ballots for the upper house, which could block ignorant natives in the lower house from enacting undesirable laws. Second, Dole wanted Burgess's endorsement that a Hawaiian constitution embrace a strong central executive. Dole had read Burgess's books on political science, and complimented him on his espousal of a virile executive with "a veto power, a military power, and an ordinance power active enough and strong enough to defend his constitutional prerogatives." The irony seemed lost on him that a new constitution with just such sweeping executive powers was exactly why they had pulled the throne out from under Lili'uokalani.

Paramount Blount may have disappointed the junta in exposing the naked racism of the coup, but in Burgess Dole found a kindred spirit. Burgess, during graduate study at the University of Göttingen, had been converted to the German notion that the right to democratic self-determination was not universal and natural but determined by innate intelligence, which was determined by race, and the Teutonic Aryan was superior. As he wrote the following year, "No other peoples or population have ever given the slightest evidence of the ability to create democratic states."[24] Let alone the dark races, even other European races such as Huns, Slavs, and Celts were rightly directed by Teutonic nationalities until they could be educated into those values.

The constitutional convention had been called for May 5, and Dole urged Burgess to hasten his reply. He answered on April 13, approving of most of Dole's ideas, which would "place the government in the hands of the Teutons, and preserve it there, at least for the present." He did not favor Dole's first idea to have the lower house elect the upper, and the upper house elect the president, as potentially ceding too much power to the wrong element. He strongly seconded Dole's predilection for a strong executive, and as a final redoubt against the lower class, warned that the judiciary should be chosen from among the Teutonic element.[25]

On the same points Dole turned to Lorrin Thurston, who urged Dole to have a look at the recent (1891) constitutional convention in Mississippi for pointers on "how to keep the upper hand over a large, undesirable element in the population."[26] This was an urgent consideration, as made plain by the 1890 census, which showed that there were 9,554 native and part-native registered voters (of whom 8,777 were pure natives) as opposed to only 637 of American extraction.[27]

To these cautions the junta ultimately added two further layers of protection in arranging the election of delegates to the constitutional convention: Only Hawaiian-born or naturalized citizens could vote, which cut out the Chinese and Japanese. And then, most native participation was precluded with a further stroke: No one could cast a vote who did not first pledge allegiance to the provisional government. Then and only then did the regime risk public ballot-ing for delegates who would craft the constitution. Before he left office, Benjamin Harrison had suggested that the junta hold a pleb-iscite so that the coup would have some "semblance of having been the universal will of the people," but even he would have been em-barrassed at the charade of voting on the constitution.

19. Countercoup and Annexation

The constitutional convention finally convened on May 30, 1894, with thirty-seven delegates. Only five of the eighteen who were elected were native Hawaiians, but the junta still held an absolute majority with nineteen votes—the executive council, the advisory council, and the president. Dole's attorney general, the original Annexation Club member William O. Smith, defined their task clearly enough: "In general terms the problem to be solved is, how to combine an oligarchy with a representative form of government."[1]

Thurston and Dole provided the draft document, and the essential features that they planned from the beginning—literacy and property restrictions, an oath not to support a restoration of the monarchy—survived into the finished Constitution of the Republic of Hawai'i, adopted on July 3 and effective, emblematic of their hopes, the following day. The dethroned queen protested, but the United States had already abandoned her, and the British—who were realists—quickly recognized the new government, as did the other major powers.

Shut out of the political process, the queen's supporters began laying plans for a countercoup. They stockpiled guns, ammunition, and a few crude bombs, intending to rise up on January 7, 1895. The junta had long been alert to disloyalty, and on the night of January 6, tips sent police and helpful citizens to Waikiki to look for an arms cache. The rumor proved correct; a gunfight erupted, killing an important annexationist named Charles L. Carter. The junta fielded its riflemen and volunteers as the would-be freedom fighters scattered into the hills above Honolulu. Some held out for nearly two weeks, but they eventually surrendered or were flushed out. At their head, and it was something of a surprise, was Robert Wilcox, the Italian-trained *hapa haole* who had changed sides so many times no one was quite sure where he would materialize next, and also Volney Ashford, formerly colonel of the Honolulu Rifles.

Lili'uokalani was arrested on January 16. The republic's government had moved into the 'Iolani Palace, with the house of representatives meeting in the former throne room. The ex-queen was escorted in under guard and confined upstairs in the southeast bedroom, overlooking Palace Square and the Ali'iolani Hale, which was now the Judiciary Building. As confinements go it was not harsh—at least this was the bedroom with the private bath, and she occupied herself with music and quilting. Sadly for her cause, a search of Washington Place revealed an arms cache buried in a flower bed—thirty or more rifles with a thousand rounds of ammunition, coconut-shell bombs, swords, and sidearms. She was tried as Lili'uokalani Dominis, convicted, and sentenced to pay a fine of five thousand dollars and serve five years at hard labor. Probably she was guilty, but the irregularities of her trial—under U.S. law it would have been illegal to try a civilian in a military court when there was no fight ongoing; sudden reduction of the charge from treason, which could not stick, to misprision of treason; the lack of time given her to prepare a defense—placed the whole proceeding under a cloud.[2]

Hers was the most prominent trial; one prince of the House of

Kalakaua, Jonah Kuhio Kalanianaole, received a one-year jail term and had his photo taken in prison stripes; 191 others were tried; Wilcox and four others were sentenced to death. Lili'uokalani finally abdicated in the hope that it would save the lives of the condemned. She was told rather insolently that former queens could not abdicate, but there was little stomach in the country for the harsh sentences, and all went free by the following January, except for the ex-queen. After eight months' confinement in the palace, she was placed under house arrest at Washington Place for five months more, and confined to the island for another eight.

After the countercoup was suppressed, the Dole government (not risking an election, the constitution appointed him president for the first six-year term) gained expertise in the seeding of confidential informants in hostile organizations and environs, ready to root out further disloyalty wherever it was uncovered. Sometimes their gumshoes made asses of themselves. One government monitor whose job it was to translate native-language newspapers for the junta was taken aback by the headline, "The Glad Tidings: Methodist Missionary Steamer Wrecked." Thinking that he had caught someone in a wicked thought, he read on, and had to report (to his apparent disappointment) that the native reporter was not exulting in the death of missionaries—the name of the vessel was the *Glad Tidings*, "which removes our first impression."[3]

Lorrin Thurston was sent to Washington as the Hawaiian minister, perhaps not the best appointment, as the American secretary of state was still Walter Gresham, who was left with a bad taste of the whole revolution. Thurston made himself obnoxious enough that Gresham requested his recall, but then the annexationists received some good news, that the United States had elected a Republican president, William McKinley, the man who as a senator from Ohio had had much to do with tariff relations between Hawai'i and the United States. The possibility of annexation seemed alive again, as the fate of Hawai'i continued to thump like a shuttlecock back and forth with each change in the occupancy of the White

House—Democratic in 1884, Republican in 1888, Democratic in 1892, and Republican again in 1896.

Thurston and Commissioners William Kinney and Francis Hatch took ship for America, and in June 1897 worked out a new deal for annexation as a territory. McKinley signed it and transmitted it to the Senate for ratification, with the beatific endorsement that the failure of annexation in 1893 not only demonstrated the virtuous disinterest of the United States, but that annexation now would be not a change but a consummation. Of ninety senators in that body, McKinley needed the votes of sixty—two-thirds—to approve the treaty. From the beginning he knew that he could safely rely on fifty-eight. Finding two more who could be persuaded to add these magnificent islands to the American family should not be difficult—especially in view of the fact that the Senate had discarded James Blount's hotly critical report and replaced it with a shameless whitewash of the coup authored by the new chairman of the Senate's Foreign Relations Committee, John Tyler Morgan of Alabama, who was the perfect combination of racist and imperialist to meet the new republic's needs. The Morgan Report held the provisional government blameless in the coup and laid all the fault on the queen, without ever sailing to Hawai'i or interviewing a single witness who was not partial to the revolution.

To save the lives of her supporters Lili'uokalani had sworn allegiance to the junta, but after her release it would have been disastrous publicity to prevent her from political advocacy and opposition any more than they could any other Hawaiian. Once she was freed from house arrest, it being painfully obvious that there was no opposing the march toward annexation within Hawai'i, Lili'uokalani went to the place where she might still derail the move. Mortgaging Washington Place and some other properties to raise money, she relocated to Washington, D.C., and stayed there for six months.[4] Her presence alone was meant as a reproach to the annexationists—as indeed it proved to be: Unable to get a private audience with McKinley, the ex-queen, shortly before leaving for New York, crashed McKinley's weekly reception for the general public in the

White House. After sending her card—"Liliuokalani of Hawaii"—upstairs, an usher showed her and her suite to a group of chairs in a corner of the East Room farthest from the waiting file of well-wishers and patronage seekers. The president appeared and greeted his way through the hundred or so waiting to bend his ear to their particular needs. Liliʻuokalani rose as he approached, and she wrote that they chatted amiably for several minutes. Only Mrs. McKinley's illness, said the president, prevented him from inviting her up for a more private visit. In her mind one head of state paid an informal social call on another; McKinley was the one who needed to explain why he had agreed to steal her country.

Back in Hawaiʻi word of the new treaty, along with news that the proannexation senator John Tyler Morgan, who had buried the Blount Report, would arrive in September, set into motion two native organizations from former times. In the wake of the 1887 Bayonet Constitution, native activists had formed the *Hui Kalaʻiaʻina* to preserve some base for their political action. And after the 1893 coup, angry Hawaiians had coalesced into a political group, the *Hui Aloha Aina* (or Patriotic League) that had two divisions, the Queen's Women and the Queen's Men. The Hawaiian *makaʻainana*, the commoners, had been mostly disenfranchised by the Bayonet Constitution of 1887, and they mattered even less after the takeover, but they had been too indoctrinated over too many decades in the propaganda of American democracy to believe that there was absolutely nothing they could do now. A mass meeting was announced for Palace Square on September 6, 1897.

Despite threats published in the annexationist papers that they could be arrested for treason, the square was jammed with natives. James Keauiluna Kaulia, the lawyer and president of the Queen's Men who had given Blount an earful when he was taking depositions, stoked the crowd:

We, the nation, will never consent to the annexation of our lands, until the very last patriot lives. . . . If the nation remains steadfast in its protest of annexation, the Senate can continue to strive until the rock walls of Iolani Palace crumble, and never will Hawaii be annexed to America! . . . Let us take up the honorable field of struggle . . . Do not be afraid, be steadfast in aloha for your land and be united in thought. Protest forever the annexation of Hawaii until the very last *aloha aina* [patriot]![5]

Kaulia was followed on the podium by the leader of the older *Hui Kala'ia'ina,* David Kalauokalani, who made certain that the crowd understood exactly what annexation as a territory meant. Public lands and crown lands, and all infrastructure and improvements, would be handed over to the United States. The American Congress would rule the islands, but the protections of U.S. law would not necessarily come with it.

The instruments of their protest would be two petitions, one remonstrating against American annexation of the islands, the other seeking restoration of the queen, to be signed by as many native Hawaiians as they could muster. Petitions were drafted and printed, and only five days after the rally on Palace Square, James Kaulia was on Maui, collecting signatures for the Queen's Men. Organizing the petition drive for the Queen's Women was its formidable president, Abigail Kuaihelani Campbell. Now thirty-nine, she had been nineteen in 1877 when she married Scotch-Irish sugar baron James Campbell, a man thirty-two years her senior. That year he sold his interest in the Pioneer Mill for half a million dollars, a fortune he doubled and redoubled by buying and irrigating the Ewa Plain on Oahu. What was good for sugar was good for her family, but they were aligned with the British interests; Campbell had been a friend of King Kalakaua, who had appointed him to the house of nobles during and after the Bayonet Constitution, and he was close to Archibald Cleghorn, father of the heiress presumptive. Abigail, moreover, was descended from the Kalanikini line of Maui royalty, with a solid reputation for noblesse oblige and charity toward native people.[6]

Petitions in hand, Campbell and her aide, Mrs. Emma Aima

Nawahi, sailed for Hilo on the interisland ship *Kinau*. Nawahi, secretary of the Hilo chapter, was the recent widow of Joseph Nawahi;
the former legislator and publisher of the *Ke Aloha Aina* had died
in San Francisco the preceding November of the tuberculosis he
may have contracted while imprisoned by the junta. Unbowed,
Aima Nawahi continued publishing their antiannexation newspaper
and would do so until 1910. Hilo was her hometown, where she was
popular as the daughter of a chiefess and the Chinese businessman
Tong Yee, founder of the Paukaa Sugar Plantation.[7] It was an accurate expression of native temper, albeit organized by the local chapter of the *Hui Aloha Aina,* that the ship was met by a traditional
twin-hulled canoe, with chairs of honor on its deck draped with
leis, to bring Campbell and Nawahi into Hilo harbor.

Not known at the time, but made clear by recent research in
Hawaiian-language letters, was that the petition drive did not materialize purely from these organizations. In fact it was the queen who
suggested the idea, put forward some of the wording, and corre-
sponded actively with Kaulia, Kalauokalani, and with Aima
Nawahi, who shared her letters with Kuaihelani Campbell.[8]

The American journalist Miriam Michelson of the *San Francisco Morning Call* interviewed Campbell, cleverly (as she thought)
leading Campbell into asserting that no Hawaiians supported annexation. "I met a woman at Hana," Michelson rejoined pluckily,
"on the island of Maui. She was."

Campbell was unfazed. "Was she in the government's employ?"
Michelson admitted that she was a teacher.

"Ah, I thought so. You see, the government will employ no one
who does not swear allegiance. Even the schoolteachers." (And not
just teachers. All but sixteen players in the Royal Hawaiian Band
were fired when they refused the oath.[9])

While Campbell and Nawahi gathered signatures in Hilo, Laura
Mahelona worked the Kona Coast on the west side of the Big
Island, her boat stopping at every village from Kona south to Kau to
leave blank petitions, after which she reversed course back up the

coast to gather them again, along with 4,216 names on the documents.

Back in Honolulu, Miriam Michelson got James Kaulia, president of the Queen's Men, to pause for an interview on the hotel veranda. He verified Abigail Campbell's assertion that government workers had given empty pledges of allegiance in order to secure their jobs. "Take the police now," he said, "who have sworn allegiance, of course. Some of them have signed our petition against annexation." Seven thousand natives had signed the petition since the preceding Thursday.[10]

Such a number spoke more eloquently than any interview. The men's and women's sections of the *Hui Aloha Aina* had to work fast. The annexation treaty was set to be debated at the winter session of Congress; they had to select and fund a delegation, travel to Washington, divine a lobbying strategy—and October was nearly upon them. Known as the *Ku'e* petitions, when they were finally rounded up they bore some twenty-one thousand signatures—more than half of the surviving native population of the islands and the equivalent, in the United States at that time, of a petition bearing thirty-five *million* names.

Before sailing, when the *Hui Aloha Aina* for men and women and the *Hui Kala'ia'ina* learned that their former monarch had moved on to New York without pressing their case to McKinley, they sent her a perplexed letter requesting that she return to the American capital. With a delegation soon to take ship bearing the petitions of their last hope, Lili'uokalani had to recognize that crashing the president's public reception for a handshake was hardly sufficient, and she headed back to Washington. The groups decided to send four of their leaders as *elele lahui*, messengers, to make their case in Washington: Kaulia, Kalauokalani, the Maui attorney John Richardson, with William Auld as their secretary.[11]

While they expected the core of their support to be among the Democrats, the Hawaiian delegation was invited to the opening of the Senate session on December 6 by an important Republican, Richard F. Pettigrew. A onetime frontier surveyor and the first U.S.

senator from South Dakota, he was also, happily for them, an amateur archaeologist with a fascination for indigenous cultures, and a
committed anti-imperialist. Like a select few other senators, he was
inclined to break with his Republican colleagues over matters of
conscience such as this—a sinful habit for which the South Dakota
legislature booted him from the Senate two years later.

In a meeting with the queen at her hotel, Ebbitt House, on December 7, the delegation decided to streamline its presentation. The
petition of the *Hui Kalaʻiaʻina* called for the restoration of the monarchy, which might not be received well in such an antiroyalist
country as the United States, and further it might be (erroneously)
construed as being at cross-purposes with the petition of the *Hui
Aloha Aina*, which merely protested annexation. The petition calling for the queen's return was dropped in favor of this one.[12]

The next day, December 8, the delegation braved ice on the
streets to call at the home of Senator George Frisbie Hoar, Republican of Massachusetts. It was a bold move, for he had supported
annexation three years earlier. He was an early convert to the strategic naval theories of Alfred T. Mahan—that Hawaii in American
hands was preferable to Hawaii in the hands of a potential enemy.
They were surprised to be ushered into the presence of such an *el-
emakule*, an "old man." Hoar was just shy of seventy-two, and after
twenty years in the Senate this grandson of Roger Sherman (a signer
of the U.S. Declaration of Independence and the Constitution) had
risen to become a lion of conscience in that body. He had been also
a consistent supporter of extending the voting franchise to minori-
ties whether women, freedmen, or American Indians. The Hawaiians thought it significant that Hoar shook hands with them; they
had seen enough of mainland *haole* politics to know that persons of
darker skin pigmentation lived a different reality from the whites.
As it happened, their visit came just at a time when Hoar's thoughts
about American empire were changing. It was becoming increasingly clear to him that it was fundamentally inconsistent for the
United States, the world's beacon of democracy, to engage in colonial

exploitation in the manner of the European powers. Far better, it seemed to him, for America to spread its civilization and ideals without snatching others' countries and cultures.

Hoar listened intently as John Richardson explained the whole gambit of revolution and annexation from the beginning—the collusion of the American minister Stevens with the Missionary Boys, the involvement of the *Boston* and the marines, and they saw tears well up in Hoar's eyes. Hoar was quite familiar with the Blount Report, and the subsequent whitewash of the Morgan Report. Now, it seemed to him, Blount had been right. The Hawaiian delegation should, said the old senator, entrust their petition to him, and be in the Senate gallery on the following day. From the floor of the chamber on December 9 Hoar intoned the text of the petitions into the record, which protested "against the annexation of the said Hawaiian Islands to the said United States of America in any form or shape." A representative leaf of the 556 pages of signatures bore thirty-eight names, the petitioners ranging in age from fourteen to eighty-six, the variety of penmanship attesting to their literacy, pride, and expectations.[13]

Hoar had the documents accepted for consideration with the proposed "treaty." And Hoar was a Republican, the party of the expansionist president. To have made an ally of him was a huge step in the right direction.

The next day Richardson, Kaulia, Kalauokalani, and Auld had a far less sympathetic audience with McKinley's secretary of state, John Sherman (no relation to Roger), to present him a memorial in protest of annexation. Then came rounds of lobbying; some senators they found courtly but unpersuaded. The Hawaiian delegation learned to polish ready answers when confronted by the alleged policy justifications—apart from imperial landlust—why Hawaii should be annexed. Might not Japan seize Hawai'i if the United States refused annexation? The Japanese had been powerful enough to take the islands for half a century; why would they wait until now to challenge President Tyler's doctrine, which was still in force, that a foreign conquest of Hawaii would not be allowed to stand? Might not the British or French gain too much influence there? On the contrary, it was the British and French who had vouchsafed Hawaiian independence in the wake of seizures of the islands by their own jingo-driven naval officers, whereas it was an American cruiser and marines who had bolstered the coup that toppled the constitutional government. For the United States to question the motives of England and France in this circumstance could only be regarded as a bad joke. Besides, the United States had vetted its own growing ties to Hawai'i with both France and Britain for decades without them registering any objection.

Thurston and the annexationists did all they could to discredit the *Ku'e* petitions. In Washington on March 4, 1898, Thurston submitted a carefully typewritten rebuttal with handwritten underscoring and insertions. Thurston claimed that as many as 10 percent of the signatures were either forgeries or had fraudulently entered the ages of children who were really as young as two. Moreover, he alleged, many natives had signed the petition for the simple reason that, in that setting and circumstance, it would have been rude not to. In Hawai'i, furthermore, "it is common knowledge . . . that there is little feeling of responsibility attached to signing a petition. Among the native Hawaiians especially the feeling is that it is rather an honor to see ones [*sic*] name attached to a petition."[14] Even if Thurston's allegations could have been borne out, however, the remaining signatures still comprised virtually half of all the natives on the islands. That was a monolithic expression of sentiment that no quibbling over handwriting could overcome.

Still, Thurston recapitulated his arguments in an eighty-three-page tract titled *A Hand-Book on the Annexation of Hawaii*. He demonstrated Hawai'i's existing importance to American trade, enumerating its 1896 imports from the mainland in meticulous detail, from 4.1 million board feet of redwood lumber to fourteen thousand tons of fertilizer, from 937 sewing machines to nearly half a million yards of denim cloth. His main amplification, however, was to include the texts of U.S. diplomatic papers relating to Hawai'i dating back to the 1840s. The document was an effective polemic but deceitful in its selection of facts and context. Thurston's citation of Kamehameha III's offered cession of the islands in 1851 made no mention that it was done in the wake of French and British seizures of the country. He dealt curtly with the charge that the coup was accomplished with American collusion. "This accusation is ancient history. If it were true, which is not admitted, it would have no more effect today upon the status of the Hawaiian Republic than does the fact that French troops assisted Washington to overthrow the British monarchy."[15] (The French government, of course, actually *knew* that its army and navy were aiding Washington.)

Thurston also included testimonials of notable Americans on the subject. Surprisingly—at least it was surprising if he had the goal of masking U.S. conspiracy in the overthrow—Thurston actually included a testimonial from Capt. G. C. Wiltse of the USS *Boston*. Or rather, it was an excerpt from Wiltse's statement in a Senate report, made to appear as a testimonial that "there is a large and growing sentiment, particularly among the planters, in favor of annexation . . . everything seems to point to an eventual request." Perhaps weightier were extracts from Mahan's imperialist tracts on Hawai'i's "strategical position," and more from Gen. John Schofield. The latter took issue with the point of view that the islands would be a political drag on the rest of the country, pointing out that the Chinese and Japanese would be excluded from participation. He also noted that citizens of Hawai'i would become citizens of the United States (omitting that "citizens" as defined two months after the coup also excluded the native islanders). But failing to extend America's protection to Hawai'i's citizens "would be a crime."[16] The endpapers of Thurston's little handbook displayed a map of the Pacific showing Hawai'i as the hub of its commerce—which was accurate enough—and then, to emphasize how much of the globe was at stake, they creatively overlaid that map on one of the Atlantic; if Hawai'i were in the center of the Atlantic, it would command a wedge of the planet from San Francisco on the west to Madagascar on the east.

Additionally, now that most *kanakas* were disenfranchised back home and the only issue before the Congress was whether or not to annex the islands, the racial undercurrent erupted to the surface as it had seldom done before. Thurston's close confederate, the fifty-four-year-old Reverend Sereno Bishop, sent a private note to the formerly "Paramount" Blount. Bishop was no relation of Bernice Pauahi's husband, Charles Bishop, but he was the son of Artemas and Elizabeth Bishop of the Second Company of missionaries. His parents had sent him to the mother country for an education, and he came back to the islands in 1851 with a degree from Auburn Theological Seminary; after a stint as seaman's chaplain in Lahaina, he edited *The Friend* (monthly newsletter of the Seamen's Friend Society) for many years. His letter to Blount was a prime exhibit of how the views of the missionary offspring had sunk to the most stupefying racism. In denying the native Hawaiians' right to self-determination, he held that "such a weak and wasted people prove by their failure to save themselves from progressive extinction . . . the consequent lack of claim to continued sovereignty. . . . Is it not an absurdity for the aborigines, who under the most favorable conditions, have dwindled to having less than one third . . . of the whole number of males on the Islands, and who are mentally and physically incapable of supporting, directing or defending a government, nevertheless to claim sovereign rights?"

When it came to actual debate in the Senate, the Hawaiians found most of their allies among the Democrats, such as David Turpie of Indiana, chairman of the Democratic Conference, who held the singular distinction of having taken his Senate seat away from Benjamin Harrison. When the Hawai'i issue reached the floor, it was Turpie who spearheaded the drive to submit the question to a plebiscite of the whole Hawaiian people. Thurston had anticipated this, and his *Hand-Book* argued hotly against any constitutional necessity of submitting annexation to a popular vote.[17] Nevertheless, knowing that such a referendum would go down in an avalanche of defeat if the native Hawaiians were allowed to vote, Senate Republicans were forced to kill the measure, thus admitting that democracy had no part in the junta's continuing control of the islands.

With time and argument, and 556 pages of petitions signed by Hawai'i's highly literate native population—more literate by a large percentage than Americans on the mainland—support for the annexation treaty fell in the Senate from fifty-eight votes to forty-six, far fewer than the sixty needed for passage. In a jubilant frame of mind the four *elele lahui* departed Washington on February 27, three months and a week after they left Hawaii. Had they understood American politics better, they would have waited to celebrate.

Two weeks earlier the U.S. battleship *Maine* had blown up in Havana harbor, killing 276 American sailors. Coming after months of heightening tensions between the United States and Spain over a revolutionary insurgency in Cuba, many Americans and certainly the more sensationalist element of the American press were certain that the *Maine* had been sunk as the result of sabotage.[18] On April 25 Congress issued, not an outright declaration of war against Spain, but an authorization for McKinley to utilize the naval and land forces of the United States in forcing American will on Spain. Officially it was to vindicate American honor and free a suffering Cuba; the subtext was that the Spanish empire had been in decline for two centuries and its remnants could be had for the taking.

War with Spain made it likely that the United States would attack the then Spanish Philippine Islands in the western Pacific, which necessitated a secure coaling station in midocean. It was true that the United States had squeezed Pearl Harbor out of King Kalakaua by holding the reciprocity treaty over his head in 1887, but they had never developed the harbor. Clearly annexation offered the easiest solution. With a two-thirds majority vote lacking in the Senate, the expansionists seized on a stratagem last employed when the United States annexed the Republic of Texas in 1845. The U.S. Constitution is not specific on how territory may be annexed; in 1845, when the treaty majority was lacking, Texas was annexed by joint resolution, which required only a simple majority of both houses.

Hawaiian annexation resolutions were reported out of the Senate and House on March 16 and May 17, respectively, ready for a final round of grand debate. Sugar was part of it. By the 1890s the sugar industry had changed Hawai'i in fundamental ways—not just the economy but the ecology of the land, the makeup of the population, and the solidification of a social class system far different from, but as entrenched as, the *kapu* system a century before. But at the end sugar was not the reason for the overthrow of the monarchy. Most of the sugar planters actually opposed annexation, for the reason that bringing in the American exclusion law would put an end to importing more Chinese labor. Growing sugarcane on American soil would not, in their minds, adequately compensate them for the declining number of coolies.[19]

War with Spain was now under way, and not to accept the strategic islands being offered seemed simply unpatriotic. Opponents of annexation were reduced to turning the Dole government's antidemocratic racism back on them. If Hawai'i became a state, railed James Beauchamp Clark of Missouri, "How can we endure our shame when a Chinese Senator from Hawaii, with his pigtail hanging down his back . . . shall rise from his curule chair and in pigeon [*sic*] English proceed to chop logic with George Frisbie Hoar or Henry Cabot Lodge?"[20] It was a losing effort and they knew it. The House approved the annexation resolution by 209 to 91 on June 15, the Senate by 42 to 21 three weeks later.

Among the senators giving his assent was Massachusetts' George Frisbie Hoar, but he did not come to the decision easily. After introducing the *Ku'e* petitions that sank the original treaty in the Senate, he had continued to follow the Hawaiian saga, and had come to an appreciation of the former queen. On various occasions on the floor of the Senate, he regretted that he had bought the tale of Lili'uokalani vowing to take the heads of the junta if she were restored to power. "I ought not to have accepted the story without investigation," he wrote. "I learned afterward, from undoubted authority, that the Queen is an excellent Christian woman; that she has done her best to reconcile her subjects of her own race to the new order of things . . . and that she expended her scanty income in educating and caring for the children of the persons who were about her court who had lost their own resources by the revolution."[21]

Hoar was troubled that the Hawaiian question had come to be dominated by jingoes interested not in the welfare of the native people but in the establishment of an American empire. While he accepted Mahan's assertion that Hawai'i was vital to the protection of the U.S. West Coast, the notion of empire for its own sake was thick in the air, and he sensed something deeply hypocritical about the intended annexation. By his own admission he was unable to commit himself to it. At one point McKinley summoned him to the White House, ostensibly to ask his advice on how to win the vote of Vermont's Justin Smith Morrill, an eighty-eight-year-old legend whom McKinley was loath to pressure. Hoar came to the real point quickly, however: "I ought to say, Mr. President, in all candor, that I feel very doubtful whether I can support it myself."

Since being swayed by the *Ku'e* petitions, Hoar had settled it in his own mind that the native Hawaiians, still by population a huge majority, had had five years to overthrow the cabal of sugar planters; if that government was so odious to them, they could have risen up. (Actually, they *had* risen up: In the countercoup of January 7, 1895, a number of them had been killed and nearly two hundred convicted and sent to prison.) Then too, although it saddened him and he felt sympathy for them, "The native Hawaiians were a perishing race. They had gone down from 300,000 to 30,000 within one hundred years," and the remnant desired only "a quiet, undisturbed life, fishing, bathing, supplied with tropical fruits, and [to] be let alone." (The shock of seeing the *Ku'e* petitions and their cry for real democracy had certainly worn off by the time he composed his memoirs.) Hoar's actual sticking point on annexation was what he perceived to be the real reason that it was being pressed, as a forward military base to take part in the dismembering of China. "I told President McKinley . . . I did not like the spirit with which it was being advocated. I instanced several distinguished gentlemen indeed . . . who were urging that we must have Hawaii in order to help us get our share of China." China, which had been Alfred Mahan's original bugbear and perceived threat in 1893, had since been humiliated in a catastrophic war with Japan. European powers were now in hot competition to divide the prostrate Chinese coast into spheres of influence, and American expansionists were half-crazed with jealousy that the United States was apparently seeking no spoils.

McKinley, to Hoar's satisfaction, expressed a repugnance equal to his own for the notion of establishing an empire in the Orient. But there was still another factor to consider that weighed against such idealism. "Well, I don't know what I shall do," said McKinley. "We cannot let those Islands go to Japan. Japan has her eye on them. Her people are crowding in there. I am satisfied they do not go there voluntarily, as ordinary immigrants, but that Japan is pressing them in there, in order to get possession before anybody can interfere." The president cited the instance of supposed "immigrants" marching off their ship in lockstep, like soldiers, after which Hawai'i [the Dole government] cut off further arrivals, and the Japanese responded by sending a warship, which McKinley had warned them to withdraw. But according to the president, "Japan is doubtless awaiting her opportunity."[22]

No credible evidence has ever surfaced that Japan had injected occupying troops into Hawai'i under the guise of immigrant labor. It was true, however, that relations between the Hawaiian Republic and Japan had become very tense over the labor issue. In 1894 the U.S. Congress passed the Wilson Act, which discontinued the domestic two-cent sugar bounty and restored Hawai'i's advantages under the reciprocity agreement. The Hawaiian sugar industry entered another boom, but the country was now angling toward annexation, and they had to be mindful of the U.S. Chinese Exclusion

Act, which meant finding a new source of labor. Naturally enough the plantations looked to Japan, and there came such a flood of Japanese laborers that by 1896, they comprised almost a quarter of the country's population. In alarm the Hawaiian government tried to stem the tide, at one point refusing to allow some twelve hundred Japanese to land. The two countries traded sharp notes, Japan lodged a claim for damages against Hawai'i, sent the powerful cruiser *Naniwa* back to Honolulu to remind the upstart country who they were dealing with, and protested to the United States when the annexation question came back to life that Hawai'i as an American territory would complicate satisfaction of their claims.[23]

What neither McKinley nor Hoar was aware of was that Japan was on the cusp of something much more drastic than monitoring the situation for an opening. The Japanese minister in Washington, Toru Hoshi, secretly cabled Foreign Minister (soon to be prime minister) Shigenobu Okuma, "strictly confidential . . . I desire to submit to your consideration . . . that taking advantage of the present strained relations between Japan and Hawaii a strong naval armament should be at once dispatched for the purpose of occupying the islands by force."

Hoshi was both irascible and a master of dissimulation; he had already made statements to the American press that the Hawaiian government had trumped up the recent immigration troubles as a publicity stunt to promote annexation to the United States, and that Japan had no interest in acquiring the islands. Okuma took the same stance in Japan. However, American naval analysts—not least among them Assistant Secretary of the Navy Theodore Roosevelt—were not interested in Hoshi's truthfulness or lack of it. They knew that two powerful, modern battleships, the *Fuji* and the *Yashima*, were being built for the Japanese under contract by British yards. *Fuji* was almost ready to sail, and Roosevelt put out a call to American diplomats worldwide to monitor and report her movements. If the Japanese seized Hawai'i, their fleet would have a forward coaling station that would leave California vulnerable to attack,[24] and

Captain Mahan's worst nightmare would be realized. With a seven-thousand-mile cruising range on eleven hundred tons of coal, the new Japanese battleships could steam from Hawai'i, reach the U.S. West Coast with nearly three thousand miles of operational steaming time to wreak destruction and still have fuel to return. *Fuji* and *Yashima* were only the first two of an envisioned class of six battleships, although they were the only two completed before being superseded by a still larger and deadlier design. They simply could not be allowed to operate from Hawai'i. Okuma, not ready to precipitate war with America, brushed aside Hoshi's prodding, but Roosevelt and the naval high command were already drawing up contingency plans on how to meet the Japanese threat. The crux, repeatedly, was Hawai'i.

Hoar voted for annexation but he did so in light, he said, of the Teller Amendment, which attempted to put a brake on the imperialist tilt of the coming conflict with Spain by affirming the self-determination of people in territories acquired in the course of the war. It did not save Hoar from bitter recrimination, from Democrats and antiempire Republicans, who accused him of speaking one way and voting the other.[25]

The ignobility of the Hawaiian coup is a matter of history. It is also necessary, however, to look at the islands' subsequent annexation in light of those imperialist times. Even Kalakaua had perceived that Hawaii was too weak to exist indefinitely as an independent nation, with no army or navy and no resources or population to defend itself. He believed that the islands must pass to either Japan or to the United States. His experience with the duplicitous, bullying sugar boys, weighed against the royal courtesies extended to him by Emperor Mutsuhito, led him to prefer the latter, indeed to offer his niece, Princess Ka'iulani, in a marriage alliance to the imperial house. Japan's performance as an imperial power over the next half century, however, gives sufficient hint of what horrors Hawai'i was spared at not becoming a Japanese protectorate.

As the legal drama played out in the United States, back in Hawai'i the government and pro-American element extended themselves in welcoming American soldiers and sailors en route to the Philippines. While waiting for word about annexation, four extra coal-storage yards were allocated to American use; the Dole government offered a hundred volunteers to fight in Cuba; Princess Ka'iulani offered the grounds of her 'Ainahau estate for the recreation of American soldiers and sailors; pending annexation, the government offered its alliance. The Hawaiian government agreed to an American suggestion to pay the Japanese $75,000 to satisfy their claims and go away. The anxious wait ended on July 13 when the long, slender White Star liner *Coptic* entered Honolulu Harbor. Even before coming to rest she ran up signal flags: ANNEXATION. The Americans were delirious.

Lili'uokalani returned from the mainland on August 2, and ten days later shuttered herself, family, and retainers into Washington Place during the ceremony at the palace that rendered her country an American territory. Before a huge throng, the U.S. minister to Hawai'i, Harold Sewall, read aloud the Joint Resolution of Hawaiian annexation. Sanford Dole then rose for a short address, concluding, "I now, in the interest of the Hawaiian body politic and with full confidence in the honor, justice and friendship of the American people, yield up to you as representative of the Government of the United States, the sovereignty and public property of the Hawaiian Islands." Minister Sewall accepted the transfer and the two bands, the (formerly Royal) Hawaiian and the one from the USS *Philadelphia*, together played "Hawai'i Pono'i" as the national flag was lowered. Tears flowed freely.

In its stead a thirty-six-foot Stars and Stripes was hoisted up the central flagpole of the 'Iolani Palace, to the accompaniment of "The Star Spangled Banner." At this, several members of the Hawaiian band abandoned their instruments and quit the scene, unable to continue.[26]

20. Angry Lu'aus

With annexation in 1898 the capture of paradise was accomplished. Hawai'i entered the United States with a healthy balance sheet; in each of the last two years of the junta, the value of exports approximately doubled the value of imports. Sugar production, after the McKinley disability was removed, increased to 220,000 tons.

Princess Ka'iulani, the heiress presumptive, died on March 6, 1899, at the age of only twenty-three. She had been horseback riding near Kawaihae with friends, scorned to wear a raincoat, and was drenched in a storm. The cold she caught deepened into pneumonia; she was returned to her Waikiki estate where she lingered for several weeks, the pneumonia no doubt exacerbated by a lack of will to live. Among the mourners who filed into 'Ainahau to view her laid out in white silk was Dowager Queen Kapi'olani,[1] who at sixty-four had only three months to live herself. When Ka'iulani died the presumptive heir to the Hawaiian crown became Prince David Kawananakoa, Kapi'olani's nephew, who had been betrothed to Ka'iulani, who nicknamed him "Koa" for the strong, beautiful native wood.

Nearly three years after Kaʻiulani's death, on January 6, 1902, Kawananakoa married Abigail Campbell, daughter of the redoubtable Kuaihelani Campbell of the *Kuʻe* Petitions. Their wedding had been in a California hotel, but they received more proper recognition after they returned home, and Abigail was requested to preside over a Mardi Gras ball. The brothers had been favorites of the ex-queen, and Liliʻuokalani herself, bearing a hefty casket, was waiting as Abigail arrived for the occasion. "I may no longer be queen," she announced as the crowd gathered, "but I have jewels fit for a queen." As Abigail stood breathless Liliʻu fitted her with a diamond-studded girdle and pearl rope, and then to gasps she lifted the Hawaiian crown from the casket and settled it on her dark tresses.[2] As the hopes of the House of Kalakaua passed to the House of Kawananakoa, Abigail produced three children in the next three years to carry forward their claims, a son bracketed by two daughters. When not starting a dynasty Kawananakoa was active in starting the Hawaiian Democratic Party, and in 1900 became the first royal prince to take part in a presidential nominating convention. The son, Edward David Kalakaua, shouldered the mantle at the age of four when David died in 1908.[3]

Hawaiʻi's position as a U.S. territory gave it a voice, albeit a nonvoting voice, in the Congress. While it was Prince David who established their family as the dynasty-in-waiting, it was his brother Prince Jonah Kuhio Kalaniʻanaole who represented the islands on the mainland. However, the first elected Hawaiian representative to Congress was in fact the ubiquitous gadfly, Robert Wilcox. When he entered Congress in 1900, instead of submitting the usual résumé, he handed in a short autobiography describing himself as fearless and indefatigable, a champion of the poor. The U.S. Congress was a body in which windy self-promotion was usually considered a virtue, but it was not welcome from a newcomer who had to use the "colored" facilities, and his term was not a success.

Prince Kuhio, who unseated Wilcox in the 1902 election, was leading an interesting life. During the year he served in prison, his fiancée, Elizabeth Kahanu Kaʻauwai (younger cousin of Kapiʻolani and niece of Queen Emma's chaplain Hoapili), sang to him daily and brought him food to keep his spirits up. Upon his release they married and traveled abroad, usually received as royalty, but he also volunteered and fought in the Second Boer War in South Africa. While touring Europe, in one happy aftermath of the Germans' behavior to his aunt at Queen Victoria's jubilee, a German duke made an unkind observation about their skin color; Kuhio, drawing upon his superior rank and boxing skill, punched him out.

Back in Hawai'i, seeing that the Democrats were historically not very successful in matters pertaining to Hawai'i, and not finding the collection of home-rule sort-of radicals under Wilcox very useful, Kuhio joined the Republican Party. It was a keenly astute move; they were delighted to have the legitimacy of a royal prince in their midst, and they accommodated him in a number of projects. He organized the territorial counties and made certain to staff the civil service positions with natives—a convenient marriage of the ancient watchfulness of the ali'i over his people with modern political patronage. Kuhio died in his tenth term, on January 7, 1922, all too aware that much work remained to restore the stature of the Hawaiian natives. "Stick together," he enjoined a friend from his deathbed, "and try to agree to the best of your ability to meet the most important problem: the rehabilitation of our race."[4]

Kuhio died with some hope that he had helped achieve that, although his bill to establish Hawaiian statehood, which was the first, went nowhere. He had better expectations of the Hawaiian Homes Commission Act of 1920, an attempt to undo the evils of the Great *Mahele* of 1848. In the preceding few years leases on about a quarter of a million acres had expired, and for native rehabilitation Hawaiians of 50 percent blood or more were allowed to apply for homesteads. Wise to the flaws of the *Mahele*, they would lease the land and not be able to turn around and sell it. To overcome opposition, productive cane fields were excluded from homesteading, and for environmental protection (rather a first for the islands), forest reserves were excluded as well. Kuhio did not live to see the act misfire on about the same scale as the *Mahele*, this time because *kanakas* were given leases to inferior and often remote and unproductive lands. To the Anglo governor of the territory, however, the act removed the pressure for the government to step in and further "help" anybody. To his way of thinking, the *kanakas* had had land made available to them, and if they could not improve their lives by it, that was their own fault.[5]

With the stability of American sovereignty, Lorrin Andrews Thurston began a long slow mellowing from walleyed firebrand to a leading private citizen who steadily advanced the interests of the territory. During the years of the provisional government he had remarried (his first wife having died in childbirth) and with annexation, aged forty, he stood down from active politics and bought the *Pacific Commercial Advertiser*, an admirable platform from which to pursue his projects. Some of them came to nought. After World War I he backed legislation to restrict the activities of Japanese-language schools, but the U.S. Supreme Court struck it down. He was ahead of his time in trying to ban billboards, but he was prescient in the promotion of tourism as a contributor to the islands' economy. Thurston understood the economic boon that shiploads of sightseers, especially from the mother country, would bring to Hawai'i. He was an amateur vulcanologist, and as a boy on Maui he had often led tourists up the ten-thousand-foot ascent of Haleakala. Now he was instrumental in creating Hawaii Volcanoes National Park.

Also important to developing tourism in the territory was a visit in 1907 by America's most celebrated writer, the novelist and social critic Jack London. The recent author of *The Call of the Wild* (1903), *The Sea-Wolf* (1904), and *White Fang* (1906) felt that he had exhausted the literary possibilities from his gold-seeking trek to the Yukon, and had come in search of a whole new universe of story ideas. He sailed to Hawaii in his own thirty-five-foot yacht, the *Snark*, with his wife and a small crew, having (rather dangerously, but typically for him) taught himself navigation while en route.

Thurston, vigorously seconded by Lucius Pinkham, secretary of the Board of Health, importuned London to visit Moloka'i and the much-maligned leper colony there, and write a piece showing that it was not the hopeless hellhole it was commonly believed to be. Indeed, as London himself had neared Honolulu and the *Snark* entered the Kaiwi Channel, they passed Moloka'i and London pointed it out to his crewman Martin Johnson as the most cursed spot on earth. Now London accepted Thurston's challenge. He and his wife, Charmian, crossed the channel to Kalaupapa and stayed two days, celebrating the Fourth of July with its residents, practicing on their shooting range with them, and interviewing the doctors and nurses. They were impressed with the colony's superintendent, Jack McVeigh, who in five years' residency had stemmed the slide into drunken despair. London gratified Thurston with a brave, frank article under the title "The Lepers of Molokai" in a leading magazine, the *Woman's Home Companion*, depicting the colony in a more positive light. It was, according to Thurston, "a value to Hawaii that cannot be estimated in gold and silver."

Also in London's crew on the *Snark*, however, was another young man named Bert Stolz. Once in Honolulu he revealed to London that his purpose in working for his passage to Hawai'i was to visit the grave of his father, Deputy Sheriff Louis Stolz, shot down by a native named Ko'olau, who had been diagnosed with leprosy, evaded capture, and hidden in the mountains of Kaua'i for more than two years, until his death.[6] In response London wrote the short story "Koolau the Leper," which depicted in London's famously clinical style the horrors of the disease and the terror of natives desperate to avoid capture. Thurston was furious with him, referring to him as a "sneak of the first water, a thoroughly untrustworthy man and an ungrateful and untruthful bounder," turns of phrase that Lili'uokalani might well have used of Thurston.

Of greater importance to Hawai'i's fledgling tourism industry, Jack London also discovered surfing. It had been a royal sport for generations, the massive size and weight of those early surfboards providing sufficient testimony to the strength of those who indulged.

Mark Twain was aware of its existence during his visit in 1866, and wrote of its pursuit as lunatic. During the missionary period it had declined, along with chants, hula, and other aspects of the native culture. As headline-making celebrities, London and his wife were lodged in a beach house at Waikiki near the Swimming Club, with whose members he became familiar. Electrified at his first sight of surfing, he determined to teach himself but made a failure of it for over an hour. His efforts were spied by Alexander Hume Ford, a South Carolina journalist who had been traveling to Australia, stopped in Hawai'i to see if he could learn to surf, and had never left. He gave London the necessary tips and launched him onto a likely wave, which London rode, breathless, all the way to the beach. "From that moment," he wrote, "I was lost." Again for the *Woman's Home Companion*, he wrote "A Royal Sport: Surfing in Waikiki," describing the sight of a native surfer:

> And suddenly, out there where a big smoker lifts skyward . . . appears the dark head of a man. Swiftly he rises through the rushing white. His black shoulders, his chest, his loins, his limbs—his feet planted in the churning foam, the salt rising to his knees, and all the rest of him in the free air and flashing sunlight, and he is flying through the air, flying forward. . . . He is a Mercury, a brown Mercury. His heels are winged, and in them is the swiftness of the sea.[7]

Once he learned how, London surfed for hours, whooping, unable to come in from the blistering tropical sun. He was bedridden for the next four days with what the doctor called the worst sunburn he had ever seen, but his article and the force of his celebrity behind it firmly established surfing as part of Hawai'i's identity.

A. H. Ford, for his part, shortly sought funding from Queen Emma's estate to establish the Hawaiian Outrigger Canoe Club, which was founded on May 1, 1908, with surfing as an integral part, neighboring the Moana Hotel. Their facility boasted dressing rooms and a traditional grass hut for storing surfboards. The club thrived, and began staging competitions with the already ongoing *hui nalu*, a native surfing group that regularized its existence in 1911. One of its founders, Duke Paoa Kahinu Kahanamoku, was only just beginning a long career of spreading the gospel of surfing. He carried it to Australia in 1915 and caused a sensation there, while another surfer whom London wrote about in his article, the Irish-Hawaiian George Freeth, gave a demonstration in California at the invitation of Henry Huntington to promote one of his railroads. On his return visit to Hawaiʻi in 1915, London was stunned to see that the Outrigger Canoe Club had grown to more than twelve hundred members. Hawaiian tourism was on its way.

While in Hawaiʻi in 1907 London also became friends with Prince David Kawananakoa. The two went fishing by torchlight, one of many experiences that London had in Hawaiʻi that caused him to rethink his previous advocacy of "racialism," which was supplanted by an appreciation of the native culture. Kawananakoa at thirty-eight was in the last year of his life before the family hopes would fall on his small son—but Liliʻuokalani was still very much alive, although bitter[8] and usually reclusive within Washington Place. She did respond to invitations to state occasions and events that she thought important for the unity of her people, although the rebuke of her presence could dampen a festive atmosphere. A famous photograph captures her seated, her hair now quite white, with Sanford Dole and territorial governor Lucius Pinkham, brought together for a concert to promote the Allied cause in World War I. Standing behind them is Henry Berger, for forty years conductor of the (Royal) Hawaiian Band. They all look miserable. The legislature had voted her a pension of four thousand dollars per year and the income from a large sugar plantation that had belonged to her brother—but she did not regard that as much compared to the losses for which she repeatedly sued, without success.

On their return visit to Hawaiʻi in 1915, Jack and Charmian London were presented to her at a New Year's Day party. Charmian was struck by the former queen's "narrow black eyes [which] gave the impression of being implacably savage in their cold hatred of everything American. . . . I offered her a dubious paw, which she touched gingerly, as if she would much prefer to slap it."⁹ Lili'uokalani was seventy-nine when she passed away on November 11, 1917, and was accorded a state funeral and interment in the Kalakaua vault at Mauna 'Ala. Little remarked in the American press was the death of another elderly lady in Hawai'i on December 20, 1928, which marked the end of an era. Elizabeth La'anui Pratt was ninety-four, great-grandniece of the Conqueror and last surviving graduate of the Royal School. Late in her life she wrote a paean to her great-great-grandfather titled *Keoua, Father of Kings*, a precursor of literary interest in Hawaiian royal history and genealogy.

Considering that Hawaiian annexation was far less about sugar than it was about denying a coaling station to a frightening new generation of Japanese battleships, the United States was quite slow to actually develop Pearl Harbor. Blowing up the coral bar to the lochs and scooping out a channel two hundred feet wide and thirty feet deep began in 1900, followed by massive dredging to deepen the harbor. An actual naval base was not authorized until 1908, when some port facilities and a drydock were begun. This first attempt at a drydock was nearly completed when it spectacularly collapsed, and World War I had come and gone before it was fixed and finished. United States neutrality in the early years of that conflict reinforced Hawai'i's critical location, as German vessels called freely to resupply. German ships then in port were impounded with America's sudden entry into that conflict in 1917.

The international naval disarmament treaty of 1925 drew attention away from Pearl Harbor, but loss of confidence in that agreement preceded massive development starting in 1931 into a fully serviced fleet anchorage. By the end of that decade, with Europe again embroiled in war, Pearl Harbor fulfilled Captain Mahan's vision of it as America's forward defense bastion—not that it did them much good on December 7, 1941.

❧

In one tragic way, the thirties also reminded the native Hawaiians that they had become strangers in their own land, as a sensational murder provided an object lesson in mainland-style justice for dark-skinned people. On the night of September 12, 1931, navy wife Thalia Massie, who did not like to drink or dance, accompanied her submariner husband Thomas and several of his friends to the Ala Wai Inn, a restaurant and dancing venue in Waikiki.[10] Late in the evening one of his friends said something fresh to Thalia; she slapped him and left, intending to make her way home alone. She was beaten and alleged that she was raped by a carload of locals: two Japanese, one Chinese-Hawaiian, and two Hawaiians. It was not the joyriders' only incident that evening, and after being apprehended for the other trouble they quickly fell under suspicion for the Massie assault.

Adm. Yates Stirling, a Southerner commanding Pearl Harbor, was frank in his assessment that some rope and a strong tree would see justice done. At trial, however, want of evidence resulted in hanging the jury instead. Of five whites and seven nonwhites on the panel, there were five votes to convict, seven to acquit. The American community was outraged. Thalie Massie's mother, Grace Fortescue, rushed out from the mainland to comfort her daughter. After the trial, in company with her son-in-law and others, they seized, beat, and shot dead Joe Kahahawai, who was visibly the darkest of the rape defendants. Grace Fortescue, Thomas Massie, and others were apprehended with Kahahawai's body wrapped in a sheet, intending to dump him off Koko Head. They were tried for murder, defended by Clarence Darrow, convicted of manslaughter and sentenced to ten years. Admiral Stirling, however, brought pressure to bear on the territorial governor, Lawrence Judd, who commuted their sentences to one hour to be served in his office. Race relations in Hawai'i probably reached their lowest ebb ever as the *kanakas* realized what American justice would mean for them. Of equal significance, the scandal set the campaign for statehood back by decades—not because of any perceived deficiency in the justice system, but because it caused members of Congress to question whether it was any benefit to the country to admit a state populated by violent, dark-skinned people.

At about the time the Massie trial ended, an effort to promote mainland tourism to Hawaii went into high gear with entry into service of the sleek, white, 26,000-ton ocean liner SS *Lurline* of the Matson Line.[11] She, other ships, and eventually airliners disgorged paying passengers who were garlanded with leis, hosted at luaus, entertained with hula (which was sanitized, no longer scandalous, but an exotic tourist attraction)—and who never had a clue what their hosts might be thinking.

Race relations came to the fore in a different way during World War II, because about one-quarter of the population of the islands was of full or partial Japanese ancestry. On the West Coast, Japanese-Americans were rounded up and concentrated into internment camps; in Hawai'i that was simply not workable. They were questioned, and watched, and lived under martial law, but ironically those of Japanese ancestry in the only part of the nation to suffer a major attack had a far easier lot than those thousands of miles in the rear. Ultimately, most Japanese-Americans who volunteered for the war were formed into the 442nd Regimental Combat Team and were sent to Europe, where there would be no question of friendly fire; they saw their fiercest action in the Italian campaign. After the war one tally revealed that of all Hawaiian service members killed in battle, four in five were of Japanese ancestry—an imperishable monument to valor and patriotism.

In fact, during the next run made for statehood in 1946, the congressional report allowed that according to both army and navy intelligence, "not a single act of sabotage was committed by any resident of Hawaii before, during, or after the attack on Pearl Harbor." The report went on to acknowledge "the important patriotic service rendered, under the most critical conditions . . . by all citi-

zens of Hawaii, regardless of racial origin." The U.S. Supreme
Court reached a similar conclusion the same year, when it finally
ruled (rather after the fact) that wartime martial law in the territory
had been unconstitutional, and was based on "the mistaken prem-
ise that Hawaiian inhabitants are less entitled to constitutional protection than others."

When statehood finally came in 1959, it was attended by some
lovely ironies. The last-appointed territorial governor, Republican
and Anglo William F. Quinn, was elected first governor of the state,
to be sworn in by Justice Masaji Marumoto. The former speaker of
the territorial House of Representatives, Hiram Fong, who had
been an energetic leader in the campaign for statehood, was elected
one of the state's first two (and the nation's first Asian-American
and first Chinese-American) senators to go to Washington—where
his seat was directly across the aisle from Strom Thurmond's.
James Kealoha, the state's first lieutenant governor, was Chinese-
Hawaiian; to the House of Representatives in Washington they
sent Daniel Inouye, a Japanese-American war hero who lost an
arm in Italy and won the Congressional Medal of Honor. Thus
Hawai'i entered finally the American union with its full ethnic
rainbow in display.

After a decade of statehood, interest in Hawaiian language and
culture led in the islands to what became known as the Second
Hawaiian Renaissance, the first having been the resuscitation of native culture by Kamehameha V and Kalakaua. One inspiration for
it was the writing, publishing, and cultural advocacy of an articu-
late and reflective *hapa haole*, John Dominis Holt. A trustee of the
Bishop Museum and chief of Topgallant Publishing, Holt was 45
when his essay *On Being Hawaiian* appeared in 1964. His was an
appropriate voice, as his heritage contained a thorough mixture of
ancestries, and he was born at a time when his own parents were
less than eager to relate his Hawaiian genealogy. Equally at home in
New York or Europe, Holt supported the revival of Hawaiian arts,
and was himself the author of a novel and several short stories, a

treatise on traditional featherwork, and a history of the monarchy that was as insightful as it was all too brief.

Because of his recognition that pre-*haole* Hawai'i was in fact no paradise, that some practices from the old days had been rightly discarded, and his stance that all of Hawai'i's past and its influences contain elements that can be salvaged to fashion a healthy modern culture, Holt came to be disparaged by the more radicalized element of the cultural renaissance.[12] By the time of his death in 1993 he had won a place at the table, but the fact was that his literary interpretation of the Hawaiian mixed-blood experience, which is to say the experience of a majority of the islands' people, fought uphill to gain the recognition of academia and the new cultural elite.

The cultural renaissance, as it grew, was all too often "highly fragmented and contains little sense either of unity among Hawaiians or of cross-cultural harmony within the wider society."[13] The way of *aloha* all too often goes wanting in the resentments expressed about the past—and the history itself often seems poorly understood by the angriest of partisans. In a time-transport back to those days, a native Hawaiian would stand 999 chances in 1,000 that he or she would be a fisherman and taro digger, even more impoverished than now, and, subject to chiefly whim or sacrifice, tied to a tree and strangled. That does not excuse the overthrow, which was indefensible. But political appeals to Hawai'i's history could use a reality check. There were no good old days.

To the independence movement after the turn of the twenty-first century, the boot heel of oppression is increasingly seen in virtually every aspect of the American presence, no matter how much respect was intended. One scholarly article published in 2005 savaged construction of the Waikiki War Memorial and Natatorium, dedicated in 1927, and criticized it on the ground that only eight Hawaiians had died in combat during World War I; for the monument to commemorate the lives of the further ninety-three Hawaiians who died of illness or accident while in American or British service was allegedly designed to exaggerate Hawai'i's participation, and is therefore a monument to American domination. One suspects, however, that if the monument had honored only the eight battle dead, and ignored the other ninety-three, the criticism would have been even more shrill. The same article also lamented that the memorial occupies the site of the Papa'ena'ena *heiau* (the Pacific War Memorial), and thus mourned the loss of an important native religious site—never mind that the *heiaus* were destroyed on the order of Queen Ka'ahumanu and the chief priest, Hewahewa, before any missionaries arrived, let alone that its loss had nothing to do with Americans or World War I. One might further note that after the Battle of Nu'uanu Pali in 1795, Kamehameha sacrificed the conquered *ali'i* of Oahu at this *heiau*, an aspect of native religious practice that does little to validate today's wash of nostalgia. The article even sees the monument's heroic Western architecture as an insult to its Pacific location, despite its being within the vernacular of worldwide memorial design at the time. A monument to Hawai'i's war dead constructed of traditional thatched grass could have been equally criticized for paying them little regard.[14] Modern times cannot put a foot right when it comes to the old days.

In 1993, the centenary of the overthrow, President Bill Clinton did the only proper thing to mark the occasion: On behalf of the rest of the United States, he apologized. Another event of cultural significance to the islands that occurred in 1993 was the repatriation of the remains of Henry Opukaha'ia, the youthful refugee from the Kamehameha conquest whose zeal for the new God set the missionaries in motion and changed Hawaiian history forever. An effort was coordinated by collateral descendents, who raised money and support, and shipped a glowing casket of koa wood to Connecticut. In July a team led by the state archaeologist painstakingly excavated the grave at Cornwall; their hopes sank as they found only discolored soil in the outline of the original coffin, which had been dissolved by the acetic soil. To their great surprise, however, Opukaha'ia's nearly intact skeleton slowly emerged from the earth. Washed and articulated in a bed of foam rubber in the koa coffin, he returned home and was reburied on August 15 in the cemetery of the Kahikolu Church, close by Kealakekua Bay from where he had escaped the butchery of the conquest two centuries before.[15] Originally constructed in 1852–55, the Kahikolu Church was one of only two stone churches built on the Big Island in the missionary era. Felled by the earthquake of August 21, 1951, it lay in ruins for many years before being restored and reopened for services in 1999.

A much more important restoration has been the stunning resurrection of the 'Iolani Palace, seat of the Kalakaua monarchy. Immediately after the coup the building was appropriated to house the junta's government, for a time during which the queen was locked in her bedroom directly overhead. Much of the original woodwork had been lost to insects and rot incident to the climate, and was meticulously re-created. Similar to the experience of the French palace of Versailles, a call was put out to return furniture and precious objects that had been dispersed. While the project is not complete, the people's response has been eloquent testimony of their endorsement of the project.

In 1994 another site of cultural importance was recovered when the U.S. Navy relinquished control of the sacred island of Kaho'olawe. Once settled and agricultural—albeit thinly because it lies in the rain shadow of Haleakala and is semidesert—it had been uninhabited since being commandeered as a bombing and naval gunnery range during World War II, a use that continued through the Korean and Vietnamese Wars. In one test, to see whether a retired cruiser could withstand a nearby blast, five hundred tons of TNT were set off, ruining the island's only well. Shattered by the decades-long rain of high explosives, the forty-four-square-mile island was designated an environmental and cultural reserve, and is being restored by young natives reconnecting to their Polynesian traditions.

Hawai'i in the twenty-first century, despite having contributed a president to the United States, is still in ferment. Protests, such as those that periodically occupy the 'Iolani Palace grounds, continue to the present day, carried out by what is collectively known as the "Independence Movement." It is angry and vigorous but disunited, with perhaps half a dozen principal groups, some headed by one or another royal descendent, each claiming the throne for herself. Some things, it seems, never change.

But Hawai'i's social ills—poverty that is demonstrably an after-effect still of the *Mahele* more than a century and a half ago; youth crime and disaffection that come of having one's cultural heritage ripped apart and never mended; the restoration of native identity and the just desire for the return of some amount of autonomy, which for decades was never accorded a status equal to that even of American Indians; the natural environment that was nearly obliterated in the worship of sugar; and more, need to be not just addressed but com-prehensively, meaningfully—and probably expensively—addressed.

But they are not addressed by nostalgia for the chiefly days. People who espouse reincarnation always fancy themselves to have been Henry VIII or Marie Antoinette. No one channels his past as some humble, downtrodden medieval plowman. In old Hawai'i 999 people in 1,000 were *kanakas*, digging taro, netting fish, trying to hide their one pig from the chief's steward, being throttled on an altar if their shadow crossed an *ali'i*. Modern cultural sensitivity obscures an important fact: Hawai'i never was a paradise.

In its own way the Western-dominated nineteenth century was as merciless as precontact warfare. The Age of Imperialism had no room for small but strategically vital countries. Kamehameha III sensed that when he prepared to cede his kingdom to the United States in preference to the French or British. Kalakaua realized it when he tried to marry off Princess Ka'iulani to a Japanese imperial prince. The Second World War gave sufficient examples of how the Japanese governed their client states for the Hawaiians still to be counting their blessings that he failed.

What is needed, by the government and on the mainland, is a clear grasp of the history and what Westernization has done to the islands and people. Precontact Hawaiians had no iron, but that did not make them a Stone Age culture. They had by most measures a highly evolved society, albeit retaining some brutal remnants of a more primitive time whose eradication need not be mourned. But there was also a large extent to which contact meant exploitation— economic more than cultural—and that is what needs to be put right. Over generations as an American territory and then state, Hawaiians have often struggled to maintain the spirit of *aloha*—the "face of breath," from the ancient greeting of inclining close in greeting, and sharing the air. That is the most famous part of their culture, and mainlanders have come to expect that of them.

But Hawaiians have another important concept: *Ho 'oponopono*— reconciling, the making right of a bad situation. In the ancient days there were ceremonies to achieve it, to cleanse the minds of anger or selfishness, and to come together earnestly and in good faith to rectify and satisfy. Hawai'i deserves to have it made right.

Notes

Preface

1　Docents at Queen Emma's summer "palace" in the Nuʻuanu Valley, and at Princess Ruth Keʻelikolani's Huliheʻe "palace" in Kailua-Kona, regularly contest this characterization, with some reason, although these two residences were residential retreats and did not function as a nexus of royal power in the same sense as did the ʻIolani Palace.

2　Menton, "A Christian and 'Civilized' Education," 222–29.

3　Nogelmeier, *Mai Paʻa I Ka Leo*, 110.

4　Bird, *Six Months in the Sandwich Islands*, 316.

5　http://hawaii-inns.com/history/index.htm.

6　Nogelmeier, *Mai Paʻa I Ka Leo*, 144–52.

7　The *ʻokina* question has beset plenty of other editors. See for example Eloise Christian's preface to the 1951 annotated edition of Malo, *Hawaiian Antiquities*, xx. Similar considerations led me to the opposite conclusion, and I have omitted using the macron, the bar over a vowel that lengthens its sound. The thick tongue of the mainland outweighed the additional accuracy of pronunciation.

8　See the writings of the early missionary William Ellis, published in 1825: "In the year 1819, Tamehameha, king of the Sandwich Islands, died, and his son Rihoriho succeeded to his dominions." *Journal of a Tour around Hawaii*, iii.

Antecedent: Captain Cook

9　By far the premier scholar of Captain Cook has been John Cawte Beaglehole, author of the biography *The Life of Captain James Cook* in 1974, and editor of Cook's journals from his three voyages. His works cemented Cook's august reputation, to which John Ledyard, the American corporal of marines aboard the *Resolution*, took such exception.

10　Westervelt, *Hawaiian Historical Legends*, 102–3.

11　Ibid., 104–5. In this account it was the mother of Kaumualiʻi, later king of Kauaʻi, Kamakahelei, who advocated giving their daughters for the gods' pleasure, she first among them.

12　Writing in the mid-nineteenth century, the native historian and commentator Davida Malo dismissed the notion that the difference in size between the lordly *aliʻi* and the lorded-over *makaʻainana* stemmed from any different ethnicity, but acknowledged that the difference was unexplained. *Hawaiian Antiquities*, 52, 60. Much has since been learned about the aboriginal Hawaiian migration, but the issue is still unresolved.

13 Cook, *The Journals*, quoted in Smith, "John Ledyard Revisited," 59.

14 Ledyard's importance to the historiography of Captain Cook is well expounded in Smith, " 'We Shall Soon See the Consequences of Such Conduct': John Ledyard Revisited."

15 Ledyard, *Journal of Captain Cook's Last Voyage*, 102.

16 See Braden, "On the Probability of Pre-1778 Japanese Drifts to Hawaii," 86, and works there cited.

17 Dye, "Population Trends in Hawai'i before 1778," 15.

18 Key elements of the religious system originated in Tahiti (or in old Hawaiian, "Kahiki"), where such *ki'i* images were known as *tiki*.

19 Wichman, *Kaua'i: Ancient Place-Names and Their Stories*, 94–95. Other accounts have the eyeball eating at the beginning of the season. See www.donch .com/lulh/heiau1.htm. Other various circumstances in which the eyeballs of sacrificial victims were consumed, sometimes floating in a cup of *'awa*, are outlined in Beckwith, *Hawaiian Mythology*, 49–50. The practice of eating the eyeballs of sacrifices seems to have been imported from Tahiti when that group conquered Hawai'i, although some sources maintain that in Tahiti, the sacrificed eyeball was raised to the chief's lips but not actually ingested. Still, at the time the French imposed their protectorate over Tahiti, the reigning Queen Pomare IV's given name was *'Aimata*, or "Eye Eater."

20 That precontact Hawaiians actually took Cook for Lono was expounded by the anthropologist Marshall Sahlins, and quickly challenged by the Sri Lankan scholar Gananath Obeyesekere, who denied "the right of any non-Polynesian to speak with authority" on the subject. Smith, "John Ledyard Revisited," 45. While that particular dispute degenerated into an epic pissing match of political correctness over who has the "right" to study non-Western cultures—itself a stunningly antiintellectual notion—the timing of Cook's visit, his circumnavigation of Hawai'i Island during *makahiki*, his landing in Kealakekua Bay of all places, Ledyard's memory of his acclamation as "Orono," the reception accorded him, and the forbearance demonstrated by the natives at his partial dismantling of the Hikiau *heiau* seem to justify a conclusion that he was regarded, at first, as more than a mortal visitor. Although they may not rise to the level of historical testimony, the sources used by the folklorist W. D. Westervelt included a rather lengthy excerpt of the prayers offered to Cook as Lono; indeed, in Westervelt's account, the natives of Kaua'i had debated and concluded him to be Lono the year before, but apparently made less fuss over him since Hawai'i Island was the locus of his cult. Westervelt, *Hawaiian Historical Legends*, 104, 108–9. See also Obeyesekere, *The Apotheosis of Captain Cook: European Mythmaking in the Pacific* (Princeton: Princeton University Press/Honolulu: Bishop Museum Press, 1992); versus Sahlins, *How "Natives" Think: About Captain Cook, For Example* (Chicago: University of Chicago Press, 1995).

1. The Loneliness of a God

1 The appearance of the south shore today is remarkably different; Hurricane Iniki scoured away the sand, and it is now a pebble beach of lava and coral, the chunks worn smooth by the waves but as startlingly black and white as a chessboard, studded with boat-crunching spikes of newer lava.

2 Ledyard, *Journal of Captain Cook's Last Voyage*, 103.

3 See, for instance, Grant and Ogawa, "Living Proof," 140–41, and works there cited.
4 Beaglehole, *Voyage of the Resolution and Discovery, 1776–1780*, Part 2, 1234. Samwell's own memoir, *The Death of Captain Cook and Other Writings*, lives in reprint, edited by Martin Fitzpatrick et al., Cardiff: University of Wales Press, 2007.
5 Ledyard, *Journal of Captain Cook's Last Voyage*, 104.
6 Derivative of the kava plant (*Piper mythesticum*), still familiar today as "kava-kava." Habitual use also leads to skin scabs, which Kalaniopuʻu also evinced.
7 Thrum, *Hawaiian Annual*, 42, is among those who cite a traditional paternity of Kahekili, but Keoua is more commonly accepted as the Conqueror's father, and the usual genealogies stem from him. But rather like the Romanovs after Catherine II, it is a genealogy of common consent with the possibility of biological accuracy.
8 Fornander, *Polynesian Race*, 2: 24.
9 Silverman, "Young Paiea," 105, doubted this, pointing out that Keoua was one of Alapaʻi's closest confederates, but this assumes first, that Keoua was indeed his father, and second, the birth year of 1758, which is disputed. Silverman is a good source for many of the malleable aspects of the Conqueror's biography—that he may have been named Paiʻea later, after showing himself inflexible in battle, etc. The best a reader can do is accept an account of his life as true in its impressionistic whole but subject to dispute in its particulars. See for instance Kamakau, *Ruling Chiefs*, 66–120. It is Kamakau who asserts that Alapaʻi died in 1754, so if he had any cognizance of Kamehameha at all, the latter must have been born about 1750 at the latest for the traditional rendition of his early years to be true, which would still make him less than seventy at the time of his death.
10 The degree to which infanticide was practiced among the commoners, and the controversy over accepting early accounts, is dealt with in chapter 4, infra.
11 Sahlins and Barrère, "William Richards on Hawaiian Culture," 23. The missionary Richards's estimate was a guess only, but it seems well-enough borne out by contemporary descriptions of what the *kanakas* lost each year "via taxes, arbitrary confiscations, and voluntary offerings." La Croix and Roumasset, "Evolution of Private Property," 832.
12 Westervelt, *Hawaiian Historical Legends*, 108.
13 Smith, "John Ledyard Revisited," 49, quoting Ledyard, *Last Voyage of Captain Cook*, 98.
14 Westervelt, *Hawaiian Historical Legends*, 110. Use of the term *aikane* was later broadened to include nonsexual male companions, but the nature of the relationship in chiefly circles at this time is well established. Malo, *Hawaiian Antiquities*, 67. See a more detailed discussion of *aikane* in chap. 5, nn. 16–21.
15 There is an alternative theory of Captain Cook's death: that it was an assassination carried out on the order of Kamehameha. See Valdemar R. Wake, "Who Killed Captain Cook?" *Australian Quarterly* 75, no. 3 (May–June 2003).
16 Mookini, "Keopuolani," 7.
17 Silverman, "Young Paiea," 104.
18 Kamakau, *Ka Moʻolelo Hawaiʻi*, 73, cited in Kuykendall, *Hawaiian Kingdom*, 1: 25.
19 Simon Metcalf to S. I. Thomas et al., 22 March 1790, http://apps.ksbe.edu/kaiwakiloumoku/makalii/historical-photos/manuscript/metcalfletter.

20 For a biography see Miller, "Ka'iana, the Once Famous 'Prince of Kaua'i,'"
   1–21.
21 Silverman, "Young Paiea," 103.
22 Kuykendall and Day, *Hawaii: A History*, 25.

2. "Disobey, and Die"

1 She was the daughter of Kamehameha's popular brother Keli'imaika'i, long
  remembered in Kohala as "the good chief." "Royal Lineages of Hawai," Bishop
  Museum, Honolulu.
2 Daws, *Shoal of Time*, 38.
3 Equally likely, as the Kona chiefs who had supported Kamehameha's first war
  against Kiwala'o died, their sons took their places, and they displaced Ka'iana
  in the king's regard. Miller, "Ka'iana," 14.
4 The number and paternity of Keopuolani's children differs among the native
  chroniclers, one of whom identifies Kamehameha as the father of all her children. See Langlas and Lyon, "Davida Malo's Unpublished Account of Keopuolani," 40–41. One of her alternate names was Makuahanaukama, meaning
  "Mother of Many Children." Richards, *Memoir of Keopuolani*, 9.
5 www.hawaiilink.net/~ems/Pila/AAOK_files/v26.Waimea.Temples.html.
  Modern Western society, one might note, is not the only one where each side
  thinks that the deity is rooting for them.
6 Del Piano, "Kalanimoku," 3. Oddly, it took until 2009 for the known facts of
  Kalanimoku's life to be pulled together into this first biographical article.
  Ka'ahumanu would have been in a good position to advance him at court, but
  there is a second story that, like Kamehameha being the cousin of Kiwala'o,
  he was taken captive after the Battle of Moku'ohai, noticed, spared, and favored by the king.
7 Schmitt, "Brief Statistical History of Hawaii," 48.
8 See www.donch.com/lulh/heiau1.htm.
9 The falls are located on Nu'uanu Stream, just east now of the Mauna 'Ala royal
  cemetery. It was a favorite bathing spot of Queen Lili'uokalani, who bequeathed
  it to the country, and it is now part of the Lili'uokalani Botanical Garden.
10 Kuykendall, *Hawaiian Kingdom*, 1: 49–51; Papa 'I'i, *Fragments*, 81–83.
11 The stole remains on display in the Bishop Museum in Honolulu.
12 Malo, *Hawaiian Antiquities*, 194–96, outlines the complex etiquette of master
  and servant class. See also La Croix and Roumasset, "The Evolution of Private Property," 832.
13 During the voyage of the *Thaddeus*, Lucy Thurston asked the captain whether
  he thought the natives would kill the missionary company, and he replied no,
  unless by poison. Thurston, *Life and Times*, 24.
14 That Kaumuali'i was using Schäffer to reestablish his independence from Kamehameha at least as much as Schäffer was using him was a point of view
  expounded in Mills, "A New View of Kaua'i," 91–102.
15 Johnson, "Wily Savage," 17–18.
16 Birkett, "Hawai'i in 1819," 76, 89.
17 See Okihiro, *Island World*, 147.
18 Bryant & Sturgis to Captain James Hale, August 31, 1818, quoted in Kuykendall, *Hawaiian Kingdom*, 1: 88.
19 Kuykendall and Day, *Hawaii: A History*, 37.

3. The Suicide of *Kapu*

1   Sources differ as to the year of the *Kanawai Mamalahoe*. Kuykendall, *Hawaiian Kingdom*, 1: 34, offering 1783, is probably one of the best informed.

2   Dwight, *Memoirs of Henry Obookiah*, 4–5.

3   Ibid., 10–12.

4   Hopu, *Memoirs*, 42–43. There seems to have been a third Hawaiian on board, whom Hopu identifies as a son of Kamehameha whom the king sent abroad to see what the world was like. *Memoirs*, 44. Dwight, *Memoirs of Henry Obookiah*, 13, mentions the presence of a third Hawaiian but does not identify him, but both agree that after the *Triumph* returned from North America with furs, the third one remained behind on Oʻahu, Hopu writing that it was because the king changed his mind. This interesting vignette seems not to have been picked up by later chroniclers.

5   Dwight, *Memoirs of Henry Obookiah*, 13.

6   Ibid., 18–19. It was Dwight who edited and pieced together the memoir of Opukahaʻia, with his own observations interjected among those of his principal.

7   Ibid., 22.

8   All these developments are described in greater detail in Lyons, "Obookiah Memoir," 4–6.

9   Dwight, *Memoirs of Henry Obookiah*, 41.

10 Ibid., 41–46.

11 Ibid., 51.

12 Ibid., 60.

13 Bell, "Owhyhee's Prodigal," 27. For a more recent and complete biographical treatment see Warne, "Story Behind the Headstone," *HJH* 43 (2009).

14 Bell, "Owhyhee's Prodigal," 26.

15 Quoted in Kikukawa, *Ka Mea KoʻAla*, 64.

16 "Extract from a Sermon, Preached at the Funeral of Obookiah, Feb. 18, 1818, by Lyman Beecher, D.D.," in Dwight, *Memoirs of Henry Obookiah*, 120.

17 Clement, "From Cook to the 1840 Constitution," 53–54.

18 A *muʻumuʻu* that belonged to Kaʻahumanu is preserved in the guest room where she often stayed at the Mission Houses Museum in Honolulu. While unsized, it reveals her to have been a very large woman indeed.

19 See Wichman, *Kauaʻi: Ancient Place-Names and Their Stories*, 94.

20 Bingham, *Sandwich Islands*, 73.

21 Alexander, "Overthrow of the Ancient Tabu System," 41.

22 Holt, *Monarchy in Hawaii*, 7.

23 There is a variety of political and sociological aspects attending the end of *kapu* that do not bear directly on the story of Hawaiʻi's Americanization. For more detail, see Seaton, "Hawaiian *Kapu* Abolition of 1819," 193–206.

24 Papa ʻIʻi, *Fragments*, 99.

25 Mookini, "Keopuolani," 3.

26 Seaton, "Hawaiian 'kapu' Abolition of 1819," 201.

27 Mookini, "Keopuolani," 4.

28 Ibid., 17.

29 Very likely Kamehameha would have chosen a daughter by his favorite, Kaʻahumanu, but the two were childless together, and her sister, Kalakua Kaheiheimalie, was the next-closest relative.

30 Bingham, *Sandwich Islands*, 164.

31 Charles S. Stewart (1823 memoir), quoted in Ariyoshi, *National Geographic Traveler*, 52.

32 Thurston, *Life and Times*, 20.

33 Holman, *Journal of Lucia Ruggles Holman*, 15–17.

4. Abhorring a Vacuum

1 Zwieck, "Sending the Children Home," 40, 65n4.

2 "I witnessed a sight to-day that I never did before," wrote a newcomer to the islands some years later. "It was the killing Cooking of a dog." Dogs were killed in the same way as most sacrifices, by strangling them with cords, then they were scalded and baked in an *imu*. "We ate some and found it very good, if I had not known what it was I should have called it Pig. But knowing it was a dog I did not Eat but a little, I think not enough to make me bark." Quoted in Martin, "Maui during the Whaling Boom," 61. It took years of incremental American disapproval, and eventually a *haole*-backed tax on dog ownership that priced them out of the *kanakas'* hands, for dogs to fall from favor in the Hawaiian diet.

3 Bingham, *Sandwich Islands*, 126.

4 Geschwender et al., "Portuguese and Haoles," 516.

5 Bingham, *Sandwich Islands*, 131.

6 Ibid., 207–8.

7 Thrum, *Hawaiian Almanac for 1923*, 44–45.

8 Judd, *Honolulu Sketches*, 79. This was in January 1841. What an ironic end that would have made for one who had heard so much preaching about fire and brimstone.

9 Alexander, "The 'Hale o Keawe' at Honaunau, Hawaii," 159–61.

10 Morris, "Kapiolani," 41.

11 Judd, *Honolulu Sketches*, 76–77.

12 Byron, *Voyage of H.M.S. Blonde*, 111.

13 MacAllen, "Richard Charlton: A Reassessment," 56.

14 Byron, *Voyage of H.M.S. Blonde*, 117.

15 Goodrich to American Board, Nov. 11, 1825, in Bingham, *Sandwich Islands*, 272.

16 The Congregationalist missionaries left a shelf heavy with memoirs, which taken together provide an induplicable look at mid-nineteenth-century Hawai'i. See for instance Bingham, *Sandwich Islands*, Ellis, *Narrative of a Tour through Hawaii*, Stewart, *Journal of a Residence in the Sandwich Islands*, and Laura Judd, *Honolulu, Sketches of Life in the Hawaiian Islands*.

17 Bingham, *Sandwich Islands*, 78. Textual commentary on Ka'ahumanu's usage of the missionaries to enhance her own position is not very common, but see Karpiel, "Mystic Ties of Brotherhood," 364.

18 Kuykendall, *Hawaiian Kingdom*, 1: 74–75.

19 Stauder, "George, Prince of Hawaii," 42. Alexander, "Funeral Rites of Prince Keali'iahonui," 26, quoted Reverend Stewart's muttering that the queen regent's marriage bonds were, in this instance, "not altogether silken." No fool, she.

20 Stewart, *Journal of a Residence*, 313–14.

21 Judd, *Honolulu Sketches*, 5, 9. These passages have become often quoted. See for instance Grimshaw, "Cult of True Womanhood," 72; H. A. P. Carter, *Kaahumanu*, 26.

22 Holman, *Journal*, 19–20, 31.
23 Stewart, *Journal of a Residence in the Sandwich Islands*, 133. Kalaniopu'u also had been of lesser bulk than the average *ali'i*. Malo, *Hawaiian Antiquities*, 52, maintained that "the chiefs and the common people . . . were the same; they were all of one race; alike in features and physique." However, he based this on their mythological common descent from Wakea and Papa, a sort of native Adam and Eve, which might not hold up to genetic scrutiny. The editor's note to that passage at p. 62 echoes the notion of *ali'i* descending from different ethnic stock as "flattery and bosh," and attributes their looming bulk to better "feeding and grooming." Still, one looks back to the first Marquesan settlers' conquest by Tahitian warriors, and the centuries of *kapu* against marrying into the lower class, and wonders whether *ali'i* and *kanaka* descended from different ethnicity—politically incorrect speculation against which this author has been gently warned.
24 Daws, *Shoal of Time*, 66.
25 Schmitt, "Population Policy in Hawai'i," 91, 106.
26 Ellis, *Tour*, 298.
27 Stewart, *Journal of a Residence*, 251.
28 Quoted in Dye, "A Memorial of What the People Were," 53.
29 Ariyoshi, *Traveler Hawaii*, 110; Dorrance, *O'ahu's Hidden History*, 131. O'ahu's Waimea Valley is not to be confused with the mighty canyon on Kaua'i. Waimea ("reddish water") is a common place-name in Hawai'i; there is a third Waimea in the highlands of the Big Island.
30 Lili'uokalani, *Hawaii's Story*, 3.
31 Stewart, *Journal of a Residence*, 152.

5. The New Morality

1 Hackler, "The Voice of Commerce," 42.
2 For a biography see Gast, *Contentious Consul: A Biography of John Coffin Jones*.
3 Dye, "Memorial of What the People Were," 60. A more detailed treatment of ministry to sailors in Hawai'i is Martin and Jackson, "The Honolulu Sailor's Home," 105–21.
4 Keali'iahonui remarried, lived a creditable life, and became one of the first members of the house of nobles after creation of the constitution. Alexander, "Funeral Rites of Prince Keali'iahonui," 26–28.
5 The incident did not damage the career of Kuakini. Known to Westerners as "John Adams" Kuakini, he served as royal governor of Hawai'i Island from 1820 until his death in 1844.
6 For a summary of Boki's baleful history see Daws, *Shoal of Time*, 82–86.
7 "No Ka Moe Kolohe," Sept. 21, 1829, broadside, Hawai'i Judiciary History Center.
8 Their mother, Keopuolani, already wielded the prostration *kapu*, and was herself the daughter of a half-sibling marriage and granddaughter on her mother's [?] side of a full-sibling marriage. Distillation of royal *mana* into a fifth generation would have been virtually unprecedented.
9 Judd, *Honolulu Sketches*, 41–42.
10 The marriage was also opposed on the same grounds by Kalama's own *hanai* mother, Kekauluohi, herself later *kuhina nui*. Kalama adopted Albert, but his

illegitimacy removed this last grandson of the Conquerer from the line of succession.

11 Stewart, *Journal of a Residence in the Sandwich Islands*, 154.

12 Ibid., 156.

13 Martin, "Maui during the Whaling Boom," 59. For a complete discourse on this pest, see Haas et al., "The Flea in Early Hawaii," 59–74.

14 Daws, *Shoal of Time*, 61–65, introduces the missionaries in a vein that is particularly sarcastic.

15 Quoted in Dye, "Memorial of What People Were," 54.

16 Grimshaw, "Cult of True Womanhood," 83.

17 First-generation scholar Davida Malo's annotator explained it delicately: *"Aikane*, now used to mean an honest and laudable friendship between two males, originally meant the vice of that burnt-up city." *Hawaiian Antiquities*, 67n5.

18 See for instance Robert J. Morris, "Translators, Traitors, and Traducers: Perjuring Hawaiian Same-Sex Texts through Deliberate Mistranslation," *Journal of Homosexuality* 51, no. 3 (2006): 225–47.

19 Ledyard, *Journal of Captain Cook's Last Voyage*, 132. Ledyard did remark that this custom was limited to the chiefly class; it was not observed among the *maka'ainana*. See also various quotes throughout Bettinger, "Historically Speaking: A Quick Look at Homosexuality and Gender-Roles in Pre-Contact Hawai'i."

20 Malo, *Hawaiian Antiquities*, 65.

21 Bingham, *Sandwich Islands*, 128; Del Piano, "Kalanimoku," 5.

22 Malo, *Hawaiian Antiquities*, 56. See also Robert J. Morris, *"Aikane*: Accounts of Hawaiian Same-Sex Relationships in the Journals of Captain Cook's Third Voyage (1776–80), *Journal of Homosexuality* 19, no. 3 (1990); Curt Sanburn, "Men of the First Consequence: The *Aikane* Tradition: Homosexuality in Old Hawaii," *Honolulu Weekly*, May 12, 1993.

23 Boyd Bond, interview, Kohala, October 17, 2010.

24 Daws, *Shoal of Time*, 78.

25 Bartholomew, *Maui Remembers*, 11.

26 Quoted in Busch, "Whalemen, Missionaries, and the Practice of Christianity," 97.

27 Daws, *Shoal of Time*, 80–81.

28 Quoted in Martin, "Maui during the Whaling Boom," 63.

29 *Missionary Herald* 39, no. 1 (January 1833): 20–21.

30 Dye, "Memorial of What People Were," 59.

31 Gutmanis, "The Law . . . Shall Punish All Men Who Commit Crime," 143–45.

32 Davida Malo to Kina'u, August 18, 1837, quoted in Kuykendall, *Hawaiian Kingdom*, 1: 153.

6. Becoming Little Americans

1 Kamakau, *Ruling Chiefs of Hawaii*, 298 (1992 ed.)

2 Kuykendall, *Hawaiian Kingdom*, 1: 104. This theme has come to be reiterated often in the scholarly literature. See for example Menton, "A Christian and 'Civilized' Education," 214–15. For Hawai'i, though, the latter's assertion that the purpose of the Chiefs' Children's School was to put the "civilized" (her quotes) *ali'i* "in a position to perpetuate the work of the Sandwich

Islands Mission" carries disapproval beyond accuracy. Once the king and chiefs were converted, it became their show, with the goal of raising up a Christian nobility to guide the kingdom. True, they might still support, even warmly support, the mission, but the missionaries' own misgivings about providing a special education for noble children undercut at least some of the modern cynicism.

3 One recent scholar questions how much of the work was really Mahune's, and how much by William Richards. See Osorio, *Dismembering Lahui*.

4 See Morse, "Lahainaluna Money Forgeries," 95–101.

5 Kuykendall, *Hawaiian Kingdom*, 1: 111–12.

6 Modern writers have focused on the depopulation as the result of foreign-introduced diseases, which was accurate among the *maka'ainana*. Rare among academics who consider the possibility that the infertility among the *ali'i* might have been a result of five centuries of incest are Langlas and Lyon, "Davida Malo's Unpublished Account of Keopuolani," 41.

7 Ruth and Bernice were both granddaughters of Pauli Ka'oleioku, the Conqueror's son by a minor wife. Ruth was Ka'oleioku's granddaughter by his first wife, Keouawahine, and Bernice by his second wife, Luahine. "Royal Lineages of Hawaii," Bishop Museum.

8 Gerrit Judd to R. Anderson, draft of October 8, 1835, quoted in Kuykendall, *Hawaiian Kingdom*, 1: 112.

9 Stewart, *Journal of a Residence*, 138.

10 Papa 'I'i, *Fragments*, 166–67.

11 Ibid., 168.

12 Juliette Cooke to Martha Montague, May 5, 1840, quoted in Menton, "A Christian and 'Civilized' Education, 226.

13 Brown to My Dear Wife & Children, 14 November 1843, Brown Papers, Honolulu Historical Society. Brown's estimate of twenty children included the Cookes' own, who by then attended alongside the nobility.

14 Judd, *Royal Palaces and Forts of Hawaii*, 66–67.

15 Papa 'I'i, *Fragments of Hawaiian History*, 167–68. There was probably another level of humor here, in knowing that Victoria Kamamalu, if she did not inherit the throne, would herself one day serve as *kuhina nui*.

16 Lunalilo School Notebook, Honolulu Historical Society.

17 Ibid.

18 Quoted in Taylor et al., *From Land and Sea*, 31.

19 Ibid.

20 Abigail and Jane were descended from Kame'eiamoku on their father's side, and from King Kahekili II of Maui on their mother's side, whether by blood or *hanai* is uncertain.

21 No more than other women of her station, Abigail Maheha did not suffer in silence for long. She petitioned for divorce in 1855 on the grounds that her forced husband could not and could never support her in the manner fitting to her. Menton, "A Christian and 'Civilized' Education, 235.

22 Brown to My Dear Wife & Children, 14 November 1843, Brown Papers, Honolulu Historical Society.

23 Bishop, *Memoirs of Hon. Bernice Pauahi Bishop*, 28–29. Lieutenant Wilkes's equating of light-skinned people with good behavior and motive, and dark-skinned with the problematical was a recurrent motif of American ob-

servation. See Lt. Lucien Young's account of Liliʻuokalani's prorogation of the legislature in ch. 17, infra.

24 Cooke to Rufus Anderson, November 7, 1847, quoted in Menton, "A Christian and 'Civilized' Education," 233.

25 The missionaries, in one scholar's estimation, had no appreciation that the native society they encountered "was characterized by a highly developed social system, a complicated land-use organization, and a sophisticated division of labor . . . a society in which religion, government, social structure and cultural practices were inextricably intertwined." Menton, "A Christian and 'Civilized' Education," 216–17. Possible inequities of that native society, such as infanticide, human sacrifice, and rule by terror are not considered suitable subjects for outside judgment.

26 Quoted in Zwiep, "Sending the Children Home," 47.

27 All quoted in ibid.

28 Grimshaw, "The Cult of True Womanhood," 71. See also Kashay, "Missionaries, Gender, and Language," 41–58.

29 The land had been taken by Kamehameha I at the conquest of Oʻahu; he gave it to his loyal chief, Kameʻeiamoku (the one who had been whipped by Simon Metcalfe); he gave it to his son, Hoapili (last husband of Keopuolani), who gave it to Liliha, who was his daughter. It is probable that Kaʻahumanu was the one who shook it loose from Liliha to give to Bingham. For a history of its early years, see Alexander, Dodge, and Castle, *Punahou, 1841–1941*.

30 Kuykendall, *Hawaiian Kingdom*, 1: 366.

7. A Sweet Taste

1 Nagata, "Early Plant Introductions," 35–36.

2 Papa ʻIʻi, *Fragments*, 94; see generally Cushing, "Begnnings of Sugar Production," 17–20.

3 Taylor et al., *From Land and Sea*, 72, identify Wilkinson as an Australian.

4 Kuykendall, *Hawaiian Kingdom*, 1: 172–73.

5 www.laddfamily.com/Files/Koloa%20Plantation/Hawaii.htm.

6 Burlin, *Imperial Maine and Hawaiʻi*, 29.

7 Kuykendall and Day, *Hawaii: A History*, 93.

8 Bingham, *Sandwich Islands*, 493–96.

9 Quoted in Kuykendall, *Hawaiian Kingdom*, 1: 177–78.

10 Frost, "The Spinning Wheel and Loom," 116–17.

11 Duensing, "Hawaiʻi's Forgotten Crop," 161.

12 Joesting, *Uncommon History*, 103–7. While in Hawaiʻi, Douglas described ninety plant species that were new to science. The escaped Australian convict with whom Douglas spent the preceding night was also suspected in his death, but nothing could be proved. The incident is recounted in more detail in Greenwell, "Kaluakauka Revisited," 147–69.

8. Captains and Cannons

1 Wilkes, *Narrative of the Expedition*, 4: 504–6.

2 Pilon, Maxime, and Daniele Weiler, *The French in Singapore: An Illustrated History* (Singapore: Didier Millet, 2012), 34–36.

3 This is at some variance with Daws, *Shoal of Time*, 94–95, but Bachelot and

Short returned to Hawai'i the next year in the belief that they would be allowed in on the same terms.

4 Castle, *An Account of the Visit of the L'Artemise*, 2–3.
5 *Sandwich Islands Mirror*, January 15, 1840.
6 Taylor et al., *From Land and Sea*, 54.
7 For a thoughtful perspective on his personal and theological molding, see Miller, "The Making of a Missionary," 36–45.
8 Canning to Barrow, October 4, 1842, quoted in Kuykendall, *Hawaiian Kingdom*, 1: 186.
9 MacAllen, "A Reassessment," 54–55.
10 *British Foreign and State Papers*, 1023; an extensive selection of the exchange can be found in Jarves, *Hawaiian Islands*, 176–78. Indicative of the respect in which Charlton held Kamehameha III was a letter complaining of the theft of some stock which he began, "Dear King." Jarves, 171.
11 Quoted in Kuykendall, *Hawaiian Kingdom*, 1: 214.
12 Judd, *Honolulu*, 93–94.
13 Ibid., 94.
14 Kuykendall, *Hawaiian Kingdom*, 1: 215–16.
15 Judd, *Honolulu*, 94.
16 Quoted in Kuykendall, *Hawaiian Kingdom*, 1: 218–19.
17 Judd, *Honolulu*, 95–96.
18 *British State and Foreign Office Papers*, 1030.
19 Lord George Paulet's career survived his Hawai'i missteps. He fought with gallantry in the Crimean War and was made naval aide de camp to Queen Victoria in 1854, retiring a full admiral in 1866.
20 *Ka Nonanona*, quoted in Solomine, "Hawaiian Restoration Day, July 31, 1843," 18.
21 From *Ka Nonanona*, August 8, translated by Solomine, in ibid., 22–24.
22 Ibid., 34.
23 Quoted in Taylor et al., *From Land and Sea*, 42.
24 Judd, *Honolulu*, 90–91.
25 Brown to My Dear Wife, 1 January 1844, Brown Papers, Honolulu Historical Society.

9. A Nation among Nations

1 These figures and many more are found in Jarves, *Hawaiian Islands*, 238–40, and were used extensively in Greer, "Honolulu in 1847," 59–95.
2 Clement, "From Cook to the 1840 Constitution," 55. "Hawai'i nei" can be taken to mean "our Hawai'i," or more literally, "the Hawai'i right here," but carrying a connotation of such deep affection that it is sometimes rendered, "beloved Hawai'i."
3 Silverman, "Imposition of a Western Judicial System," 48.
4 Daws, *Shoal of Time*, 108; Kuykendall, *Hawaiian Kingdom*, 1: 236–37. Ricord's adaptability and discretion were attested to by the fact that he had also previously served as private secretary to Houston's predecessor and bitter enemy, David G. Burnet, Tyler et al., eds., 6 vols., *New Handbook of Texas* (Austin: Texas State Historical Association, 1996), 5: 577; Haley, *Sam Houston* (Norman: University of Oklahoma Press, 2002) 182–84.
5 Daws, *Shoal of Time*, 108.

6   Fox, *Macnamara's Irish Colony and the United States Taking of California*, 83–86.
7   Kanahele, *Pauahi*, 41.
8   Quoted in Kuykendall and Day, *Hawaii: A History*, 64–65.
9   This is the principal interpretation of him in Daws, *Shoal of Time*, 128–29.
10 Judd, *Honolulu*, 131.
11 Greer, "Honolulu in 1847," 83–84; Tyler et al., *New Handbook of Texas*, 5: 577.
12 Quoted in Charlot, "An 1849 Hawaiian Broadside," 97.
13 Dunn, "Letters from Hawaii," 75.
14 Charlot, "An 1849 Hawaiian Broadside," 97.
15 Dunn, "Letters from Hawai'i," 75.
16 Bates, *Sandwich Island Notes*, 47.
17 Original documents quoted in Kuykendall, *Hawaiian Kingdom*, 1: 398–402.

10. The Great *Mahele*

1   In later years, the papers that Wyllie squirreled away were recovered "from the attic and basement of the old royal palace, from under counters in the tax office, the vaults of the treasury and from various isolated public buildings." Taylor, "Intrigues, Conspiracies and Accomplishments," 18.
2   It is sad, even maddening, that his papers did not survive him by long. His eventual successor as foreign minister, the former French consul Charles de Varigny, was Wyllie's principal executor, and likely destroyed the state papers because they contained incriminating references to himself. Charles Judd, son of Gerrit, took up residence at Rosebank and cast further boxes of papers out to the elements "as rubbish." Raeside, "Journals and Letter Books of R. C. Wyllie," 90.
3   The Hudson's Bay steamer *Beaver* had called at the islands eleven years before, but its paddle wheels were not fitted until later. Schmitt, "Some Transportation and Communication Firsts," 100.
4   Schmitt, "Some Firsts in Island Leisure," 102.
5   Kuykendall, *Hawaiian Kingdom*, 1: 373–74.
6   W. L. Lee to Catherine Scott, October 1, 1848, quoted in Dunn, "Letters from Hawai'i," 69.
7   Steiner, "Numerals: Hawaiian Kingdom Stamps," 58.
8   Ibid., 59.
9   William Richards to Lt. Charles Wilkes, March 15, 1841, quoted in Kuykendall, *Hawaiian Kingdom*, 1: 270. Wilkes was the commanding officer of an American exploring expedition.
10 Quoted in Kuykendall, *Hawaiian Kingdom*, 1: 274.
11 Greer, "Notes on Early Land Titles," 34.
12 Kuykendall, *Hawaiian Kingdom*, 1: 270–71.
13 Greer, "Notes on Early Land Titles," 48–50.
14 Baldwin to Edward B. Robinson, December 15, 1848, quoted in Schmitt and Nordyke, "Death in Hawai'i," 6.
15 Kamakau, *Ruling Chiefs of Hawai'i*, 236–37. Schmitt and Nordyke, "Death in Hawai'i," 8–10, track the decline in both population and birth rate through census figures.
16 Daws, *Shoal of Time*, 127.

17 Dunn, "Letters from Hawai'i," 87.
18 See Anderson, *The Hawaiian Islands.*
19 David Greene to Sandwich Islands Mission, November 11, 1844; Anderson to Sandwich Islands Mission, April 10, 1846, quoted in Kuykendall, *Hawaiian Kingdom,* 1: 337.
20 Quoted in Taylor et al., *From Land and Sea,* 45.
21 Ibid.
22 Ibid., 75.

11. The Anglican Attraction

1 Diary of Prince Alexander Liholiho, Honolulu Historical Society, msp. 243 ff. The quote appears at 107 of the published rendition.
2 Judd to Anderson, May 1, 1861, quoted in Daws, "Decline of Puritanism," 32.
3 Kanahele, *Emma,* 78–79.
4 Silverman, "To Marry Again," 68, 71.
5 Bishop Museum. The source at Pu'ukohola Heiau National Historic Park gives the date as "about 1840." Local sources place her birth in Kohala, others maintain that she was born in Honolulu, as inscribed on her casket; a source at the Queen Emma Foundation indicates that her birthplace is actually uncertain. Greg Cunningham to author, August 30, 2011.
6 Emma's father was High Chief George Na'ea, her mother High Chiefess Fanny Kekelaokalani Young, daughter of John Young. Fanny's sister, High Chiefess Grace Kama'iku'i Young, was married to Dr. Rooke, and they had no children of their own.
7 For a short biography see White, *National Cyclopædia of American Biography,* 9: 32.
8 Kuykendall, *Hawaiian Kingdom,* 2: 48–52.
9 Taylor, "Intrigues, Conspiracies and Accomplishments," 21.
10 www.pdavis.nl/ShowBiog.php?id=1113.
11 Kuykendall, *Hawaiian Kingdom,* 2: 86.
12 Wyllie to Kamehameha IV, September 27, 1859, quoted in Kanahele, *Emma,* 114.
13 Wyllie to Hopkins, December 5, 1859 (two letters), quoted in Kuykendall, *Hawaiian Kingdom,* 2: 87.
14 Jennings, *Chronology,* 59.
15 The founding of the Queen's Hospital is chronicled in detail in Greer, "Queen's Hospital," 110–45.
16 In corresponding with her father, Emma asked him to correct her letter, but not let anyone else see it. Kanahele, *Emma,* 75–76.
17 Some steps to set apart the dignity of the king were certainly in order, as foreign ship captains particularly treated the monarch with no more moment than they had in the era of discovery. Taylor, "Intrigues, Conspiracies and Accomplishments," 23.
18 Kuykendall, *Hawaiian Kingdom,* 2: 93, as well as in Semes, "Hawai'i's Holy War," 119, which contains the most detailed account of the spiritual guerrilla war that the Congregationalist community prosecuted against Staley during his tenure.
19 Kuykendall, *Hawaiian Kingdom,* 2: 95, quotes Synge's report for the death date of the twenty-seventh. Kanahele, *Emma,* 139, cites August 23.
20 Kanahele, *Emma,* 140.

12. Useful Marriages

1   Cole, "Native Hawaiians Served on Both Sides during the Civil War," *Honolulu Advertiser,* May 31, 2010, http://the.honoluluadvertiser.com/article/2010/May/31/ln/hawaii5310346.html.

2   "Palawai Mormon Experiment: Early History of Mormon Settlers on Lanai," www.lanaichc.org/lanai-mormons/Palawai_Mormon_Experiment.html. See also "Selected Accounts of the Mormon Settlement."

3   Quoted in Daws, *Shoal of Time,* 222–23. For the closest thing to a biography of this character see Gould, "Filibuster of Walter Murray Gibson," 7–32.

4   Kanahele, *Emma,* 175–77.

5   See Tayman, *The Colony,* for an outstanding history of Kalaupapa.

6   Quoted in Taylor et al., *From Land and Sea,* 35.

7   Kanahele, *Emma,* 79.

8   Daws, *Shoal of Time,* 156.

9   See Kovacevic, "Descent of John Owen Dominis," 3–24.

10 Kanahele, *Emma,* 330. See also archives.starbulletin.com/2007/10/28/travel/tsntsumi.html.

11 Ibid. Kunuiakea was for a time betrothed to Miriam Likelike (Lili'uokalani, *Hawaii's Story,* 33), although he constantly embarrassed the family as a wastrel and spendthrift. Kanahele, *Emma,* 257–58.

12 Their correspondence is largely reproduced and annotated in Hackler, "Dear Friend," 101–30.

13 Kanahele, *Emma,* 199–200.

14 Ibid., 221.

15 Twain, *Letters from Hawaii,* 125.

16 See Zmijewski, "Man in Both Corners," 55–73, and A. Grove Day, introduction to Twain, *Letters from Hawaii,* v–xvii.

17 Kuykendall, *Hawaiian Kingdom,* 2: 169–70; Schmitt, "Some Transportation and Communication Firsts," 100.

18 Twain, *Letters from Hawaii,* 126–27.

19 Both R. C. Wyllie and David Kalakaua had supported the bill to allow sale of alcohol to natives, and were shocked by Lot's veto. Alexander, "Brief Sketch," 11.

20 Day, introduction to Twain, *Letters from Hawaii,* viii.

21 Quoted in Austin Shelley Fishker, ed., *A Historical Guide to Mark Twain* (Oxford University Press, 2002), 231–32. Like much effective art, Twain's letters sometimes inspire readers to discover their own predispositions. Defenders of the native culture find his depiction disrespectful; others find him shilling for further sugar investment. James E. Caron, "Mark Twain Reports," 39. This he may have done, but I found his sympathy for the natives genuine and his observations accurate, albeit expressed in the humorous vernacular people expected of him.

22 Lili'uokalani, *Hawaii's Story,* 32–34.

23 Kamehameha V to Emma, June 9, 1871, quoted in Kuykendall, *Hawaiian Kingdom,* 2: 96.

24 Kanahele, *Emma,* 258.

25 The French being skilled in matters of the heart, it was Varigny in whom the king confided, and who approached Emma on his behalf. Kuykendall, *Hawaiian Kingdom,* 2: 240.

13. Mountains of Sugar

1 Taylor et al., *From Land and Sea*, 76.
2 Varigny, *Fourteen Years*, 205, quoted in La Croix and Grandy, "The Political Instability of Reciprocal Trade," 177.
3 Tate, *Reciprocity or Annexation*, 54, 74–75.
4 Rowland, "Contract Labor Question," 251–53.
5 Taylor et al., *From Land and Sea*, 77.
6 S. N. Castle to *Pacific Commercial Advertiser*, April 24, 1869, quoted in Kuykendall, *Hawaiian Kingdom*, 2: 188.
7 Kanahele, *Emma*, 264–66.
8 The Conqueror's father, Keoua (assuming the genuineness of that paternity over Kahekili), had a secondary wife, Kamakaeheikuli, and they were the great-grandparents of Lunalilo. His maternal grandmother was Kalakua, the sister of Ka'ahumanu, who bore Kina'u and Kamamalu to the Conqueror before marrying Lunalilo's grandfather. "Royal Lineages of Hawaii," Bishop Museum.
9 Latter-day Emmaites reject this interpretation, and peg the kings' disapproval to Lunalilo's refusal to sign a prenuptial agreement. Della Kua'ana, Interview, October 20, 2010. Ms. Kua'ana, a member of the Daughters of Hawai'i, is a docent at Hanaiakamalama, Emma's summer "palace."
10 Holt, *Hawaiian Monarchy*, 20; Lili'uokalani, *Hawaii's Story*, 14–15, has Lunalilo proposing to her while he was still engaged to Kamamalu, and committing other ungentlemanly indiscretions until she decided on her own to reject him.
11 Castle to Edward & May, December 17, 1872, reproduced in Taylor et al., *From Land and Sea*, 111.
12 This of course again assumes Keoua's paternity of Kamehameha. "Royal Lineages of Hawai'i," Bishop Museum. The Conqueror's grandfather Kekaulike was Kapi'olani's great-great grandfather by a secondary wife. She was also the granddaughter of Kaumuali'i of Kaua'i and brought that royal line to the marriage as well.
13 Twain, *Letters from Hawaii*, 133.
14 Entry for June 9, 1849, Lunalilo School Workbook, Honolulu Historical Society.
15 Secretary of War to Schofield, June 24, 1872 [confidential], quoted in Kuykendall, *Hawaiian Kingdom*, 2: 248.
16 *Hawaiian Gazette*, February 26, 1873.
17 Daws, *Shoal of Time*, 193–95; Kuykendall, *Hawaiian Kingdom*, 2: 259–61.
18 Kanahele, *Emma*, 274.
19 Nordhoff, *California, Oregon and the Sandwich Islands*, quoted in Thurston, *Life and Times of Lucy G. Thurston*, "Introduction to the Second Edition," d.
20 Thurston, *Life and Times*, iv.

14. Taffy Triumphant

1 Green, "Trollope in Hawaii," 301–2. Trollope was returning home after having spent several months in Australia helping in the dissolution of his son's failed agricultural enterprise.
2 "Royal Lineages of Hawai'i," Bishop Museum.
3 Lunalilo was the great-grandson of the Conqueror's father Keoua (assuming that paternity) by his secondary wife Kamakaeheikuli. Kame'eiamoku was her

second husband, and that pair were Kalakaua's great-grandparents. Thus Lunalilo and Kalakaua were second cousins through the same great-grandmother, but there was no actual blood tie between Kalakaua and the Kamehamehas descending from Keoua. Kameʻeiamoku, however, was Keoua's cousin, so Kalakaua could claim a royal tincture from further up the line, hence his and his sisters' eligibility to the succession. http://en.wikipedia.org/wiki/Royal_ School_(Hawaii), accessed November 15, 2010; "Royal Lineages of Hawaiʻi," Bishop Museum.

4 Kuykendall *Hawaiian Kingdom*, 3: 6.
5 Ibid.
6 Emma to Peter Kaʻeo, September 26, 1873, quoted in Kanahele, *Emma*, 276.
7 Liliʻuokalani, *Hawaii's Story*, 39–45. She also wrote that she found Emma's avoidance of Kapiʻolani incomprehensible, even though she must have known very well that Emma blamed Kapiʻolani for the death of her son. Liliʻuokalani's partisanship for her brother is understandable, but here is one of many indications that her memoir is to be used with caution.
8 Karpiel, "Ties of Brotherhood," 382.
9 Quoted in Kanahele, *Emma*. 289.
10 See Williams, "Prince of Entertainers," 153 ff.
11 Bird, *Six Months in the Sandwich Islands*, 317.
12 Daws, *Shoal of Time*, 199.
13 Chauvin, "Astronomy in the Sandwich Islands," 199–201.
14 Summarized in much more detail in Daws, *Shoal of Time*, 202–5.
15 Kalakaua to Harris, March 15, 1881; Kalakaua to Green, March 10, 1881, Foreign Office Papers, HSA. The king also got a lesson on the mortality of monarchs who lose favor with their subjects, as he reported without comment the assassination of the Emperor of Russia.
16 Marumoto, "Vignette of Early Hawaii-Japan Relations," 52.
17 Kuykendall, *Hawaiian Kingdom.*, 3: 230.
18 Ibid., 3: 238–39.
19 Kalakaua to Green, April 6, 1881, Foreign Office Papers, HSA.
20 Kalakaua to Green, April 21, 1881; Kalakaua to Dominis, May 12, 1881, Foreign Office Papers, HSA.
21 Kalakaua to Liliʻuokalani, June 21, 1881, Foreign Office Papers, HSA.
22 Menton, "A Christian and 'Civilized' Education," 241.
23 Daws, *Shoal of Time*, 219–20.
24 Twain, *Letters from Hawaii*, 70–71.
25 Honolulu: *Pacific Commercial Advertiser*, 1881.
26 Green, "Trollope in Hawaii," 208.

15. A Voice Like Distant Thunder

1 Nogelmeier, "Ruta Keanolani Kamuʻolaulani Keʻelikolani Kanahoahoa: A View from Her Time," 5.
2 Twain, *Letters from the Sandwich Islands*, 69–70.
3 Ibid., 129–30.
4 Daws, *Shoal of Time*, 226–27.
5 Kuykendall, *Hawaiian Kingdom*, 3: 60–61.
6 Bell, "Journal of Dr. Nelson J. Bird," 119.
7 Kuykendall, *Hawaiian Kingdom* 3: 236–37; Ursula Sophia Newell Emerson to

Nathaniel Emerson, August 31, 1881, Bishop Museum Archives, online at www.hawaiialive.org/realms.php?sub=Wao+Lani&treasure=356&offset=0.

8 Kanahele, *Emma,* 346.

9 See *Pacific Commercial Advertiser,* February 15, 1882.

10 Luau Invitation, Bishop Museum, online at www.hawaiialive.org/realms.php ?sub=Wao+Lani&treasure=356&offset=0.

11 Emma to Lucy Peabody, March 25, 1882, quoted in Kanahele, *Emma,* 346.

12 Emma to Ihilani Jones, May 29, 1883, quoted in ibid., 356.

13 Will of Ruth Ke'elikolani, Kamehameha Schools Archives, online at http:// kapalama.ksbe.edu/archives/historical/wills/ruth.php.

16. Queen at Last

1 Lili'uokalani, *Hawaii's Story,* 108.

2 Adler, "Rosenberg," 56.

3 Emma to Peter Ka'eo, December 17, 1875, quoted in Kanahele, *Emma,* 306–7. Lili'uokalani too in her turn would allow herself to be influenced by the mysterious Fräulein Wolf. Kuykendall, *Hawaiian Kingdom,* 3: 544.

4 James Campbell, Vertical File, Honolulu Historical Society.

5 Kuykendall and Day, *Hawaii: A History,* 153.

6 MacLennan, "Hawai'i Turns to Sugar," 102.

7 www.sunyatsenhawaii.org/en/research/a-humanities-guide/101-sun-yat-sen -and-hawaii.

8 See Soong, "Sun Yat-sen's Christian Schooling," 151 ff.

9 Nellist, *Women of Hawaii,* 206.

10 Greer, "Sweet and Clean," 33–51.

11 Nordyke and Lee, "Chinese in Hawai'i," 200–203.

12 Rowland, "Contract Labor Question," 254.

13 Daws, *Shoal of Time,* 230–31; Kuykendall, *Hawaiian Kingdom,* 3: 86–91.

14 Quoted in Kuykendall, *Hawaiian Kingdom,* 3: 91.

15 Gibson, Walter Murray, Office Record, HSA.

16 Fuchs, *Hawaii Pono,* 78.

17 Silva, *Aloha Betrayed,* 104–7.

18 Kuykendall, *Hawaiian Kingdom,* 3: 348–49.

19 The accompanying pillbox hat and one of the queen's massive koa trunks are on display at the Hulihe'e Palace.

20 Lili'uokalani, *Hawaii's Story,* 148.

21 Ibid., 156–57; Giles St. Aubyn in *Edward VII Prince & King* (New York: Atheneum, 1979), 249, allows that the future kaiser survived the meal, but was so "furious" at being seated with what he took to be Africans that he quit the gathering early "in a huff." Loomis, *For Whom Are the Stars?,* 33, notes how purposeful Lili'uokalani's selective memory could be, citing the example of her claim of having no option but to sign the controversial lottery bill before the coup that deposed her.

22 The rapidly tumbling kaleidoscope of events is recounted in Kuykendall, *Hawaiian Kingdom,* 3: 356–67; Daws, *Shoal of Time,* 243–49.

23 Ashford, 25–29, quoted in Kuykendall, *Hawaiian Kingdom,* 3: 367.

24 Daws, *Shoal of Time,* 250.

25 Bayard's protestation of America's innocent intentions was a masterpiece of diplomatic molasses: "No ambiguity or obscurity in that amendment is

observable, and I can discern therein no subtraction from Hawaiian sovereignty over the harbor to which it relates, nor any language importing a longer duration for the interpolated Article II than is provided for in Article I of the supplementary convention. . . . I can see no cause for any misapprehension by your Government as to the manifest effect and meaning of the amendment in question. I therefore trust that it will be treated as it is tendered, in simple good faith, and accepted without doubt or hesitation." Kuykendall, *Hawaiian Kingdom*, 3: 396–97.

26   What occasioned Wodehouse's actual removal was his voicing his doubts over a later supplement to the Pearl Harbor agreement, which would have allowed the United States to land troops under certain circumstances. Tate, "Hawaii: A Symbol of Anglo-American Rapprochement," 563.

27   Quoted in Morgan, *Pacific Gibraltar*, 26.

28   Emma to Peter Ka'eo, September 2, 1873, quoted in Kanahele, *Emma*, 277.

29   The codicil of Emma's will that contained her intention to donate the items to the museum that Bernice envisioned had not been legally witnessed, but the trustees of the Queen's Hospital, her primary beneficiary, willingly agreed to the transfer. Kent, *Charles Reed Bishop*, 290–91.

17. The Coup

1   Quoted in Siler, *Lost Kingdom*, 179.

2   Bishop to Lili'uokalani, March 5, 1891, reproduced in Kent, *Charles Reed Bishop*, 346.

3   Krout, *Hawaii and a Revolution*, ix.

4   Population of remaining native Hawaiians (including mixed-race) were 58,765 in 1866, 51,531 in 1872, 47,508 in 1878, 44,232 in 1884, 40,662 in 1890. Kuykendall and Day, *Hawaii: A History*, 298. Kalakaua's efforts to restore native culture had had its effects, one of which was that people felt more free to eschew *haole* doctors and return to native practitioners. The queen's friend and Bernice Pauahi's widower, Charles Reed Bishop, wrote her soon after her accession, "The decrease of the Hawaiians which the recent census shows is still going on, in the adults, at least—is caused mainly by two things: intemperance, and the influence of Kahunas. Is there no hope of winning the people to wiser and better habits? The children are better cared for and are doing better than in times past, but the adults and old people are behaving badly." Kent, *Charles Reed Bishop*, 346.

5   For a biography of this mercurial figure, see Andrade, *Unconquerable Rebel*.

6   Lili'uokalani, *Hawaii's Story*, 240. Russ, *Hawaiian Revolution*, 62–65, depicts the queen as more active in securing the bills' passage. This is the most detailed and documented account of the revolution.

7   This is suggested in Siler, *Lost Kingdom*, 193–94.

8   Loomis, *For Whom Are the Stars?*, 34–36. From none of the sources is there an indication that Lili'uokalani had any suspicion that Fräulein Wolf was playing her.

9   Kuykendall, *Hawaiian Kingdom*, 3: 544.

10   Thurston, *Memoirs of the Hawaiian Revolution*, 23–32. Among them, Stevens, Blaine, and Tracy were taking the point in effecting a policy that would be too risky for Harrison to be seen advocating, given the lack of broad public sup-

port for establishing an American empire. See Baker, "Benjamin Harrison and Hawaiian Annexation," 302–3.

11 Young, *The Boston at Hawaii*, 161–63.

12 Kuykendall and Day, *Hawaii: A History*, 176.

13 "Of the occurrences of January 14 and the three following days, in which were involved the queen, the cabinet ministers, the diplomatic representatives of foreign governments, Captain Wiltse of the U.S.S. *Boston*, and various members of the civilian population, there are available, in print, accounts by nearly all. . . . None of these is complete, and there are between and among them a large number of discrepancies, some irreconcilable differences, and a good many actual contradictions." Kuykendall, *Hawaiian Kingdom*, 3: 583. Kuykendall's treatment therein, pp. 582–605, is the clearest.

14 Daws, *Shoal of Time*, 272.

15 Mahan, "Hawaii and Our Future Sea Power," in *The Interest of America in Sea Power*, 35.

16 Quoted in Daws, *Shoal of Time*, 273–74.

17 Young, *Boston at Hawaii*, 187.

18 Jennings, ed., *Chronology*, 79–83.

19 Liliʻuokalani, *Hawaii's Story*, 387–88.

18. The Inscrutable Mr. Blount

1 Krout, *Hawaii and a Revolution*, 106.

2 *Papers Relating to the Foreign Relations of the United States*, appendix 2 (Washington: USGPO, 1895), 400, quoted in Heffernan, "From Independent Nation to Client State," 209.

3 Harrison to C. C. Hines, February 3, 1893, quoted in Kuykendall, *Hawaiian Kingdom*, 3: 615.

4 Cleghorn to Kaʻiulani, January 28, 1893, quoted in Siler, *Lost Kingdom*, 226.

5 Webb and Webb, *Kaʻiulani*, 111.

6 T. E. Evans to Liliʻuokalani, February 25, 1893, quoted in Siler, *Lost Kingdom*, 231.

7 *New York Times*, January 31, 1893. 978-0-312-60065-5.

8 Mahan, "Hawaii and Our Future Sea Power," in *The Interest of America in Sea Power*, 49.

9 McWilliams, "James H. Blount," 29–30.

10 See generally Calhoun, "Morality and Spite," 292 ff, and McWilliams, "James H. Blount," 29–30. One close scholar found no dissonance between his temper and his policy. Stevens, *American Expansion*, 245–46. This Gresham should not be confused with the Texas Congressman, Walter Gresham, of the same era. See Tyler et al., eds., *New Handbook of Texas* (Austin: Texas State Historical Society, 1996), 3: 333.

11 Fuchs, *Hawaii Pono*, 32.

12 Krout, *Hawaii and a Revolution*, 144.

13 *Blount Report* (not paginated). www.hawaiiankingdom.org/blounts-report.shtml.

14 Krout, *Hawaii and a Revolution*, 169.

15 In his summary of Hawaiʻi history, Blount also heavily criticized the Great *Mahele* for having disempowered the common people. *Blount Report*.

16 Judd to Dear James and Sophie, April 8, 1893, Mission Houses Museum, Children's Collection.

17 *Blount Report.* Other passages of Blount's report did fall into a predictably patronizing assessment of the native Hawaiians ("In person they have large physique, good features, amid the complexion of the brown races. They have been greatly advanced by civilization, but have done little towards its advancement") but his respect and sympathy for them are by far the more salient feature of his report.

18 Hoar, *Autobiography of Seventy Years*, II, 264.

19 Russ, *Hawaiian Revolution*, 249.

20 Quoted in Kuykendall, *Hawaiian Kingdom*, 3: 629.

21 Devine, "Foster and Annexation," 35.

22 *Report of the Committee on Foreign Relations, United States Senate, with accompanying testimony, and Executive documents transmitted to Congress from January 1, 1883 to March 10, 1894*, 1253 ff.

23 See http://c250.columbia.edu/c250_celebrates/remarkable_columbians/john _burgess.html. Burgess (1844–1931) was the author of the highly influential *Political Science and Comparative Constitutional Law* (1890) which Dole would have seen, and several other books written after the time of the Hawaiian coup.

24 Burgess, "The Ideal of the American Commonwealth," *Political Science Quarterly* 10 (1895): 407. Burgess was the founder of the journal.

25 Castle, "Advice for Hawaii: The Dole-Burgess Letters," 28.

26 Russ, "The Role of Sugar in Hawaiian Annexation," 349, citing Thurston to Dole, 10 March 1894, United States, Ministers and Envoys to Washington, Hawaii State Archives.

27 Ibid., 341.

19. Countercoup and Annexation

1 Quoted in Daws, *Shoal of Time*, 280.

2 Hawai'i Judiciary History Center, "Trial of a Queen," 7–8.

3 "Résumé of Editorials and Newspaper Articles," May 31, 1895. Insurrection of 1895, Hawaiian Newspapers Translations, Hawaii State Archives.

4 Lili'uokalani, *Hawaii's Story by Hawaii's Queen*, 364–65.

5 Silva, "The 1897 Petitions Protesting Annexation," Digital Collections, University of Hawaii Manoa, http://libweb.hawaii.edu/digicoll/annexation/pet -intro.html.

6 Vertical files, James Campbell, Alice Campbell, Hawaii Historical Society; www.campbellfamilyfoundation.org/james_abigail.cfm; http://en.wikipedia .org/wiki/Abigail_Campbell.

7 Joseph Nawahi was well acculturated to American values, having been raised by Hilo missionaries David Lyman and his wife. Nellist, *Women of Hawaii*, 205.

8 Silva, *Aloha Betrayed*, 192.

9 Kuykendall, *Hawaiian Kingdom*, 3: 607.

10 *San Francisco Morning Call*, September 30, 1897.

11 Silva, *Aloha Betrayed*, 157–58.

12 While the junta did not prevent Lili'uokalani from traveling to the United States, they engaged in considerable discussion whether the effort at annexation would be furthered by retiring the ex-queen on a generous pension, and how much it might cost to buy her out. At least one member of the *hui aloha aina* lent some credibility to the notion that she might have been not alto-

gether unwilling. "Queen Liliuokalani want only money. . . . She did not help our delegation. We do not want her. We want our young princes." Loomis, *For Whom Are the Stars?*, 221.

13 The *Ku'e* petitions are preserved online at http://libweb.hawaii.edu/annexation /petition.html. See also Senate Journal of December 9, 1897.

14 Thurston, "Report of Lorrin A. Thurston," 10.

15 Thurston, *Hand-Book on the Annexation of Hawaii*, 50, 42.

16 Ibid., 71–72.

17 Ibid., 37–38.

18 The explosion may have been the result of spontaneous combustion in a coal bunker, touching off a powder magazine, as concluded by a 1976 study by Adm. Hyman Rickover. A 1999 expedition to the wreck site by the National Geographic Society discovered inward distension of hull plates, evidence that the initial explosion had indeed been external—a mine—and not internal.

19 The various aspects in which sugar advantage did not play a part are fleshed out in Osborne, *Empire Can Wait*, 17–27.

20 Champ Clark went on to become Speaker of the House during World War I. Quoted in Daws, *Shoal of Time*, 290.

21 Hoar, *Autobiography of Seventy Years*, 2: 265.

22 Ibid., 2: 307–9.

23 Summarized in Kuykendall and Day, *Hawaii: A History*, 186–87.

24 Morgan, *Pacific Gibraltar*, 211–13. Roosevelt had lectured at the Naval War College during Mahan's tenure; they were warm friends, and TR was intimately familiar with the strategic import of Hawaii. It is clear that he was also thinking in larger, even imperial, terms, as he embraced the fates of both Hawai'i and Samoa with the envisioned canal across Panama in American defense. Anderson, "Pacific Destiny," 52.

25 Hoar, *Autobiography of Seventy Years*, 2: 311.

26 Loomis, "Summer of 1898," 97.

20. Angry Luaus

1 Webb and Webb, *Ka'iulani*, 199–200.

2 Newspaper clipping, Vertical File, Alice Kamakila Campbell, Hawaii Historical Society. Kuaihelani the matriarch of the clan could be equally proud of her other daughters' outcomes. Muriel married William Charles, High Chief Ke'eaumoku V of Maui, and Alice Kamakila Campbell became a linchpin of dissent in the Americanization of the islands.

3 Prince Edward died without children in 1953, making successivees presumptive of his sisters, Princess Abigail Kapi'olani (1903–61) and Princess Lydia Lili'uokalani (1905–69). http://en.wikipedia.org/wiki/David_Kawānanakoa.

4 Omandam, "Kuhio's Advice Still Relevant Today," *Honolulu Star-Bulletin*, September 20, 1999, archived at http://archives.starbulletin.com/1999/09/20 /news/story4.html. Kuhio's complicated and frustrating tenure in Congress is summarized in Fuchs, *Hawaii Pono*, 167–72.

5 Daws, *Shoal of Time*, 298–99.

6 See Frazier, "True Story of Ko'olau the Leper," 1–41.

7 Quoted in Haley, *Wolf*, 247–48.

8 Webb and Webb, *Ka'iulani*, 208.

9 Charmian London, *Jack London and Hawaii* (London: Mills & Boon, 1918), 51.

10 The whole episode is explored in much more detail in Daws, *Shoal of Time*, 319–27.
11 Joesting, *Uncommon History*, 323.
12 Hershinow, "John Dominis Holt: Hawaiian–American Traditionalist," 70–71.
13 Ibid., 61.
14 Ireland, "Remembering and Forgetting at the Waikiki War Memorial Park," 53 ff.
15 Park, "A Hawaiian in Connecticut," in *Biological Anthropology*, 7–10.

Bibliography

Manuscripts and Published Documents

Blount, James H. *Report of Special Commissioner James H. Blount to U.S. Secretary of State Walter Q. Gresham Concerning the Hawaiian Kingdom Investigation.* www.hawaiiankingdom.org/blounts-report.shtml.

British and Foreign State Papers, 1842–43. London: James Ridgway and Sons, 1858, vol. 31.

Hawaiian Historical Society, Honolulu. George Brown Papers.

———. Broadside Collection.

———. Henry Opukahaia, A Short Elementary Vocabulary of the Owhyhe Language.

———. Journal of Prince Alexander Liholiho.

———. Lunalilo School Notebook.

———. Vertical Files.

Hawaii Judiciary History Center, Honolulu. Broadside Collection.

Hawaii State Archives, Honolulu. Charges & Specifications Preferred Against Liliuokalani Dominis.

———. Foreign Office Papers.

———. Series 506, Insurrection of 1895.

Lanai Cultural Heritage Center. "A History of the Mormon Mission at Palawai." Manuscript in progress. www.lanaichc.org/lanai-mormons/lanai-mormons-and-the-palawai-experiment-nov-2009.pdf.

Hawaiian Mission Houses Historical Site and Archives, Honolulu. Castle & Cooke Records.

———. Church Records.

———. Mission Children's Collection.

———. Solomine, Lisa. "Hawaiian Restoration Day July 31, 1843: Hawaii in the 1800's, the Restoration Ceremony and the King's Speech." Hawaiian Mission Houses Historical Site and Archives, 2012.

University of Hawaii Manoa Library, Hawaiian & Pacific Collections. Lihue Plantation Papers.

Letters, Memoirs, and Reportage

American Board of Commissioners for Foreign Missions. *A Narrative of Five Youths from the Sandwich Islands, Now Receiving an Education in This Country.* New York: J. Seymour, 1816.

Anderson, Rufus. *The Hawaiian Islands: Their Progress and Condition under Missionary Labors.* 2nd ed. Boston: Gould and Lincoln, 1864.

Bates, George Washington. *Sandwich Island Notes*. New York: Harper & Bros., 1854.

Beaglehole, John Cawte. *The Journals of Captain James Cook on His Voyages of Discovery*. Vol. 3, parts 1 and 2. Cambridge, UK: Cambridge University Press, 1974.

Bingham, Hiram. *A Residence of Twenty-one Years in the Sandwich Islands*, etc. 3rd rev. ed. Canandaigua, NY: H. D. Goodwin, 1855.

Bird, Dr. Nelson J. Edited by Susan N. Bell. "Hawaii in 1880: The Journal of Dt. Nelson J. Bird." *Hawaiian Journal of History* (hereafter cited *as HJH*) 18 (1984).

Bishop, Sereno Edwards. *Reminiscences of Old Hawaii, with a Brief Biography by Lorrin A. Thurston*. Honolulu: Hawaii Gazette Co., Ltd., 1916.

Bloxam, Andrew. *Diary of Andrew Bloxam, Naturalist of the "Blonde," on Her Trip from England to the Hawaiian Islands, 1824–25*. Honolulu: Bernice P. Bishop Museum, Special Publication No. 10 (1925).

Botta, Paul-Emile. "Paul-Emile Botta, Visitor to Hawaii in 1828." Edited and translated by Edgar C. Knowlton, Jr. *HJH* 18 (1984).

Castle, William N. *An Account of the Transactions Connected with the Visit of the L'Artemise*. Honolulu: Privately printed, 1839.

Cooke, Amos Starr. *The Hawaiian Chiefs' Children's School*. Tokyo: Charles E. Tuttle, 1970.

Corley, J. Susan. "The British Press Greets the King of the Sandwich Islands: Kamehameha II in London, 1824." *HJH* 42 (2008).

De Varigny, Charles. *Fourteen Years in the Sandwich Islands: 1855–1868*. Translated by Alfons L. Korn. Honolulu: University Press of Hawaii, 1981.

Dunn, Barbara E. "William Little Lee and Catherine Lee, Letters from Hawaiʻi, 1848–1855." *HJH* 38 (2004).

Dwight, Edwin Wells. *Memoirs of Henry Obookiah*. Philadelphia: American Sunday School Union, 1830.

Gast, Ross H., and Agnes C. Conrad, eds. *Don Francisco De Paula Marin: The Letters and Journal of Francisco De Paula Marin*. Honolulu: University of Hawaii Press, 2002.

Hackler, Rhoda E. A. "My Dear Friend": Letters of Queen Victoria and Queen Emma." *HJH* 22 (1988).

Haole, A. See Bates, George Washington.

Hoar, George F. *Autobiography of Seventy Years*. New York: Charles Scribner's Sons, 1903.

Holman, Lucia Ruggles. *Journal of Lucia Ruggles Holman*. Honolulu: Bernice P. Bishop Museum, Special Publication No. 17 (1931).

ʻIʻi, John Papa. *Fragments of Hawaiian History, As Recorded by John Papa Iʻi*. Translated by Mary Kawena Pukui. Edited by Dorothy B. Barrère. Honolulu: Bishop Museum Press, 1959.

Jennings, Helen, ed. *Chronology and Documentary Handbook of the State of Hawaii*. Dobbs Ferry, NY: Oceana Publications, 1978.

Johnson, Donald D. "The 'Wily Savage,' A Tale of Kamehameha's Time." *HJH* 13 (1979).

Kekuaokalani. *The Letters of Peter Young Kaeo to Queen Emma, 1873–1876*. Edited by Alfons L. Korn and Mary Pukui. Berkeley: University of California Press, 1963.

Kono, Hideto, and Kazuko Sinoto, "Observations of the First Japanese to Land in Hawai'i." *HJH* 34 (2000).

Krout, Mary H. *Hawaii and a Revolution: The Personal Experiences of a Newspaper Correspondent in the Sandwich Islands during the Crisis of 1893 and Subsequently.* London: John Murray, 1898.

————. *Memoirs of the Hon. Bernice Pauahi Bishop.* New York: Knickerbocker Press, 1908.

Ledyard, John. *A Journal of Captain Cook's Last Voyage to the Pacific Ocean,* etc. Hartford: Nathaniel Patten, 1783.

Lili'uokalani, H. M. Queen. *Hawaii's Story by Hawaii's Queen.* Boston: Lee and Shepard, 1893.

Malo, Davida. *Hawaiian Antiquities.* Honolulu: Bishop Museum, 1951.

Martin, Kenneth R. "Maui during the Whaling Boom: The Travels of Captain Gilbert Pendleton, Jr." *HJH* 13 (1979).

Richards, Williams. *Memoir of Keopuolani, Late Queen of the Sandwich Islands.* Boston: Crocker & Brewster, 1825.

Stewart, Charles. *Journal of a Residence in the Sandwich Islands by C. S. Stewart, the Years 1823, 1824, and 1825.* 3rd ed.; facsimile. Honolulu: University of Hawaii Press for Friends of the Library of Hawaii, 1970.

Thurston, Mrs. Lucy G. *Life and Times of Mrs. Lucy G. Thurston, Wife of Rev. Asa Thurston, Pioneer Missionary to the Sandwich Islands.* 2nd ed. Ann Arbor, MI: S. C. Andrews, 1882.

Trollope, Anthony. Edited by Bradford Allen Booth. *The Tireless Traveler: Twenty Letters to the Liverpool Mercury.* Berkeley/Los Angeles: University of California Press, 1941.

Twain, Mark. *Mark Twain's Letters from Hawaii.* Edited by A. Grove Day. New York: Appleton-Century, 1966.

Wilkes, Charles, U.S.N. *Narrative of the United States Exploring Expedition, During the Years 1838, 1839, 1840, 1841, 1842.* Philadelphia: C. Sherman, 1844.

Zmijewski, David. "The Man in Both Corners: Mark Twain, The Shadowboxing Imperialist." *HJH* 40 (2006).

Biographies

BOOKS

Andrade, Ernest. *Unconquerable Rebel: Robert W. Wilcox and Hawaiian Politics, 1880–1903.* Niwot: University of Colorado Press, 1996.

Beaglehole, John Cawte. *The Life of Captain James Cook.* Stanford, CA: Stanford University Press, 1974.

Gast, Ross H. *Contentious Consul: A Biography of John Coffin Jones.* Los Angeles: Dawson's Book Shop, 1976.

Haley, James L. *Wolf: The Lives of Jack London.* New York: Basic Books, 2010.

Kanahele, George Hu'eu Sanford. *Emma: Hawai'i's Remarkable Queen.* Honolulu: Queen Emma Foundation, 1999.

————. *Pauahi: The Kamehameha Legacy.* Honolulu: Kamehameha Schools, 1986.

Mellen, Kathleen Dickenson. *The Magnificent Matriarch.* New York: Hastings House, 1952.

Kent, Harold Winfield. *Charles Reed Bishop: Man of Hawaii.* Palo Alto, CA: Pacific Books, 1965.

Pratt, Elizabeth La'anui. *Keoua: Father of Kings.* Honolulu: Privately printed, 1920.

Siler, Julia Flynn. *Lost Kingdom: Hawaii's Last Queen, the Sugar Kings, and America's First Imperial Adventure.* New York: Atlantic Monthly Press, 2012.

Sinclair, Marjorie. *Nahi'ena'ena, Sacred Daughter of Hawaii.* Honolulu: University Press of Hawaii, 1976.

Taylor, Frank J., Earl M. Welty, and David W. Eyre. *From Land and Sea: The Story of Castle & Cooke of Hawaii.* San Francisco: Chronicle Books, 1976.

Webb, Nancy, and Jean Francis Webb. *Kaiulani: Crown Princess of Hawaii.* New York: Viking Press, 1962.

White, James Terry. *Cyclopædia of American Biography.* New York: James T. White Co., 1971.

ARTICLES

Alexander, W. D. "A Brief Sketch of the Life of Kamehameha V." In *First Annual Report of the Hawaiian Historical Society.* Honolulu: Hawaiian Gazette Co., 1893.

Del Piano, Barbara. "Kalanimoku: Iron Cable of the Hawaiian Kingdom." *HJH* 33 (2009).

Frazier, Frances N. " 'The Battle of Kalalau': As Reported in the Newspaper *Kuokoa.*" *HJH* 23 (1989).

———. "The True Story of Kaluaiko'olau, or Ko'olau the Leper." *HJH* 21 (1987).

Gould, James Warren. "The Filibuster of Walter Murray Gibson." In *Sixty-eighth Annual Report, for the Year 1959.* Honolulu: Hawaiian Historical Society, 1960.

Hackler, Rhoda E. A. "The Voice of Commerce." *HJH* 3 (1969).

Kamins, Robert M., and Jacob Adler. "The Political Debut of Walter Murray Gibson," *HJH* 18 (1984).

Langlas, Charles, and Jeffrey Lyon. "Davida Malo's Unpublished Account of Keopuolani." *HJH* 42 (2008).

MacAllan, Richard. "Richard Charlton: A Reassessment." *HJH* 30 (1996).

Miller, Char. "The Making of a Missionary: Hiram Bingham's Odyssey." *HJH* 13 (1979).

Miller, David G. "Ka'iana, the Once Famous Prince of Kauai'i." *HJH* 22 (1988).

Mookini, Esther T. "Keopuolani, Sacred Wife, Queen Mother, 1778–1823." *HJH* 32 (1998).

Silverman, Jane. "Young Paiea." *HJH* 6 (1972).

Stauder, Catherine. "George, Prince of Hawaii." *HJH* 6 (1972).

Taylor, Albert Pierce. "Intrigues, Conspiracies and Accomplishments in the Era of Kamehameha IV and V, and Robert Crichton Wyllie." *Papers of the Hawaiian Historical Society* 16 (1929).

Warne, Douglas. "The Story Behind the Headstone: The Life of William Kanui." *HJH* 43 (2009).

Williams, Riánna. "John Adams Cummins: Prince of Entertainers." *HJH* 30 (1996).

MYTHOLOGY AND FOLKLORE

Alameida, Roy Kakulu. *Na Mo'olelo Hawai'i o ka Wa Kahiko: Stories of Old Hawaii.* Honolulu: Bess Press, 1997.

Beckwith, Martha. *Hawaiian Mythology.* Honolulu: University of Hawaii Press, 1970 [repr.] Also archived on line at www.sacred-texts/pac/hm/.

Thrum, Thomas G. *Hawaiian Folk Tales.* Chicago: A. C. McClung & Co., 1907.

————. *More Hawaiian Folk Tales*. Chicago: A. C. McClung & Co., 1923.

Westervelt, W. D. *Hawaiian Historical Legends*. New York: Fleming H. Revell Co., 1923.

————. *Hawaiian Legends of Ghosts and Ghost-Gods*. Boston: George E. Ellis Co., 1916.

————. *Hawaiian Legends of Old Honolulu*. Honolulu: George E. Ellis Co., 1915.

————. *Hawaiian Legends of Volcanoes*. Honolulu: George E. Ellis Co., 1916.

————. *Maui: The Demi-God*. Honolulu: Hawaiian Gazette Co., 1910.

Wichman, Frederick B. *Kaua'i: Ancient Place-Names and Their Stories*. Honolulu: University of Hawaii Press, 1998.

Secondary Sources

BOOKS

Alexander, Mary C., Charlotte P. Dodge, and William R. Castle. *Punahou, 1841–1941*. Berkeley: University of California Press, 1941.

Anthony, J. Garner. *Hawaii under Army Rule*. Stanford, CA: Stanford University Press, 1955.

Barber, Joseph, Jr. *Hawaii: Restless Rampart*. New York: Bobbs-Merrill, 1941.

Bartholomew, Gail. *Maui Remembers: A Local History*. Honolulu: Mutual Publishing, 1994.

Burlin, Paul T. *Imperial Maine and Hawai'i: Interpretive Essays on the History of Nineteenth-Century American Expansion*. Lanham, MD: Lexington Books, 2008.

Cozad, Stormy. *Images of America: Kauai*. Charleston, SC: Arcadia Publishing, 2008.

Daws, Gavan. *Shoal of Time: A History of the Hawaiian Islands*. Honolulu: University of Hawaii Press, 1974 (reprint).

Dodge, Charlotte P. *Punahou: The War Years, 1941–1945*. Honolulu: Punahou School, 1984.

Dougherty, Michael. *To Steal a Kingdom: Probing Hawaiian History*. Waimanalo, HI: Island Style Press, 1992.

Ellis, William. *A Narrative of a Tour through Hawaii, or Owhyhee, with Remarks on the History, Traditions, Manners, Customs and Language of the Inhabitants of the Sandwich Islands*. Honolulu: Hawaiian Gazette Co., Ltd., 1917.

Fornander, Abraham. *The Polynesian Race, Its Origins and Migrations*. London: Trübner & Company, 1880.

Fuchs, Lawrence H. *Hawaii Pono: A Social History*. New York: Harcourt, Brace & World, Inc., 1961.

Hawaii Judiciary History Center. *Trial of a Queen: 1895 Military Tribunal*. Rev. ed. Honolulu: Hawaii Judiciary History Center, 1996.

Holt, John Dominis. *Monarchy in Hawaii*. Honolulu: Star-Bulletin Printing Co. 1964.

Judd, Walter F. *Palaces and Forts of the Hawaiian Kingdom*. Palo Alto, CA: Pacific Books, 1975.

Kamakau, Samuel Manaiakalani. *The People of Old*. Honolulu: Bishop Museum Press, 1961.

————. *Ruling Chiefs of Hawaii*. Honolulu: Kamehameha Schools, 1992 (reprint).

Kauanui, J. Kehaulani. *Hawaiian Blood: Colonialism and the Politics of Sovereignty and Indigeneity*. Durham, NC/London: Duke University Press, 2008.

Korn, Alfons L. *The Victorian Visitors*. Honolulu: University of Hawaii Press, 1958.

Kuykendall, Ralph S. *The Earliest Japanese Labor Immigration to Hawaii*. Honolulu: University of Hawaii, 1935.

———. *The Hawaiian Kingdom*. 3 vols. Honolulu: University of Hawaii Press,
1938–67.

———. *A History of Hawaii*. New York: Macmillan Co., 1926.

——— and A. Grove Day. *Hawaii: A History from Polynesian Kingdom to American Commonwealth*. New York: Prentice-Hall, Inc., 1948.

Jarves, James Jackson. *History of the Hawaiian Islands: Embracing Their Antiquities, Mythology, Legends, Discovery by Europeans*. 3rd ed. Honolulu: Charles
Edwin Hitchcock, 1847.

Johannessen, Edward. *The Hawaiian Labor Movement: A Brief History*. Boston:
Bruce Humphries, 1956.

Lind, Andrew. *An Island Community: Ecological Succession in Hawaii*. Chicago:
University of Chicago Press, 1938.

———. *Hawaii's People*. Honolulu: University of Hawaii Press, 1974.

Loomis, Albertine. *For Whom Are the Stars? An Informal History of the Overthrow
of the Hawaiian Monarchy in 1893 and the Ill-Fated Counterrevolution It Evoked*.
Honolulu: University Press of Hawaii/Friends of the Library of Hawaii, 1976.

Mahan, Alfred Thayer. *The Interest of America in Sea Power, Present and Future*.
London: Sampson Low, Marston and Company, 1897.

Morgan, Theodore. *Hawaii: A Century of Economic Change, 1778–1876*. Cambridge,
MA: Harvard University Press, 1948.

Mrantz, Maxine. *Women of Old Hawaii*. Kihei, Maui: Aloha Publishing, 1975.

Nellist, George F. *Women of Hawaii*. Honolulu: Paradise of the Pacific, Ltd., 1938.

Okihiro, Gary Y. *Island World: A History of Hawai'i and the United States*. Berkeley: University of California Press, 2008.

Osborne, Thomas J. *"Empire Can Wait": American Opposition to Hawaiian Annexation, 1893–1898*. Kent, OH: Kent State University Press, 1981.

Osorio, Jon Kamakawiwo'ole. *Dismembering Lahui: A History of the Hawaiian Nation to 1887*. Honolulu: University of Hawaii Press, 2002.

Park, Michael Allen. *Biological Anthropology*. McGraw-Hill, 2009.

Potter, Norris W. *The Punahou Story*. Palo Alto, CA: Pacific Books, 1969.

Rhodes, Linda W., and Diane Lee Green. *A Cultural History of Three Traditional
Hawaiian Sites on the West Coast of Hawai'i Island*. U.S. National Park Service, 1993.

Russ, William Adam, Jr. *The Hawaiian Revolution (1893–94)*. Selinsgrove, PA:
Susquehanna University Press, 1959.

Silva, Noenoe K. *Aloha Betrayed: Native Hawaiian Resistance to American Colonialism*. Durham, NC/London: Duke University Press, 2004.

Smith, Jared G. *Plantation Sketches*. Honolulu: Advertiser Press, 1924.

Stanton, Joseph, ed. *A Hawai'i Anthology: A Collection of Works by Recipients of
the Hawai'i Award for Literature, 1974–1996*. Honolulu: State Foundation on
Culture and the Arts, 1997.

Stevens, Sylvester K. *American Expansion in Hawaii, 1842–1898*. Harrisburg: Archives of Publishing Co. of Pennsylvania, 1945.

Takaki, Ronald. *Pau Hana: Plantation Life and Labor in Hawaii, 1835–1920*. Honolulu: University of Hawaii Press, 1983.

Tate, Merze. *Hawai'i: Reciprocity or Annexation*. East Lansing: Michigan State
University Press, 1968.

Thrum, Thomas G., comp. *Hawaiian Almanac and Annual for 1923.* Honolulu: Thomas G. Thrum, 1922.

ARTICLES

Adler, Jacob. "Elias Abraham Rosenberg, King Kalakaua's Soothsayer." *HJH* 4 (1970).

Alexander, W. D. "Funeral Rites of Prince Keali'iahonua." *Fourteenth Annual Report of the Hawaiian Historical Society, for the Year 1906.* Honolulu: Hawaiian Historical Society, 1907.

———. "The 'Hale o Keawe' at Honaunau, Hawaii." *Journal of the Polynesian Society* 3 (1894). Johnson Reprint Corp., 1965.

———. "Overthrow of the Ancient Tabu System in the Hawaiian Islands," *Report of the Hawaiian Historical Society, for the Year 1916* (1917).

Anderson, Stuart. "Pacific Destiny and American Policy in Samoa, 1872–1899." *HJH* 12 (1899).

Baker, George W. "Benjamin Harrison and Hawaiian Annexation: A Reinterpretation." *Pacific Historical* Review (hereafter cited *as* PHR) 33, no. 3 (August 1964).

Bell, Susan N. "Owhyee's Prodigal." *HJH* 10 (1976).

Bettinger, Keith. "Historically Speaking: A Quick Look at Homosexuality and Gender Roles in Pre-Contact Hawaii." *Honolulu Weekly,* June 20, 2007.

Birkett, Mary Ellen. "The French Perspective on the Laplace Affair." *HJH* 32 (1998).

———. "Hawai'i in 1819: An Account by Camille de Roquefeuil." *HJH* 34 (2000).

Braden, Wythe E. "On the Probability of Pre-1778 Japanese Drifts to Hawaii." *HJH* 10 (1976).

Bradley, Harold Whitman. "Hawaii and the American Penetration of the Northeastern Pacific, 1800–1845." *PHR* 12, no. 3 (September 1943).

Busch, Briton C. "Whalemen, Missionaries, and the Practice of Christianity in the Nineteenth-Century Pacific." *HJH* 27 (1993).

Calhoun, Charles W. "Morality and Spite: Walter Q. Gresham and U.S. Relations with Hawaii." *Pacific Historical Quarterly* 52 (1983).

Caron, James E. "Mark Twain Reports on Commerce with the Hawaiian Kingdom." *HJH* 44 (2010).

Chapin, Helen Geracimos. "Newspapers of Hawai'i, 1834 to 1903: From 'He Liona' to the Pacific Cable." *HJH* 18 (1984).

Chapman, Abraham. "Hawaii Seeks Statehood." *Far Eastern Survey* 15, no. 14 (July 17, 1946).

Char, Wai-Jane. "Chinese Adventurers and Sugar Master in Hawaii: 1802–1852." *HJH* 8 (1974).

Charlot, Jean. "An 1849 Hawaiian Broadside." *HJH* 4 (1970).

Chauvin, Michael E. "Astronomy in the Sandwich Islands: The 1874 Transit of Venus." *HJH* 27 (1993).

Clement, Russell. "From Cook to the 1840 Constitution: The Name Change from Sandwich Islands to Hawaiian Islands." *HJH* 14 (1980).

Corley, J. Susan. "Kamehameha II's Ill-Starred Journey to England Aboard *L'Aigle,* 1823–1824." *HJH* 44 (2010).

Cushing, Robert L. "The Beginnings of Sugar Production in Hawai'i." *HJH* 19 (1985).

Deringil, Selim. "An Ottoman View of Missionary Activity in Hawai'i." *HJH* 27 (1993).

Devine, Michael J. "John W. Foster and the Struggle for the Annexation of Hawaii." *PHR* 46, no. 1 (February 1977).

Duensing, Dawn E. "Hawai'i's Forgotten Crop: Corn on Maui, 1851–1951." *HJH* 42 (2008).

Dye, Bob. " 'A Memorial of What the People Were': The Sandwich Islands Institute and *Hawaiian Spectator*." *HJH* 31 (1997).

Dye, Tom. "Population Trends in Hawai'i before 1778." *HJH* 28 (1994).

Frost, Rossie Moodie. "King Cotton, the Spinning Wheel and Loom in the Sandwich Islands." *HJH* 5 (1971).

Geschwender, James A., Rita Carroll-Seguin, and Howard Brill. "The Portuguese and Haoles of Hawaii: Implications for the Origins of Ethnicity." *American Sociological Review* 53, no. 4 (August 1988).

Grant, Glen, and Dennis M. Ogawa. "Living Proof: Is Hawaii the Answer?" *Annals of the American Academy of Political and Social Science* 530. Interminority Affairs in the U.S.: Pluralism at the Crossroads (November 1993).

Green, Carleton. "Trollope in Hawaii." *Trollopian* 3, no. 4 (March 1949).

Greenwell, Jean. "Kaluakauka Revisited: The Death of David Douglas in Hawai'i." *HJH* 22 (1988).

Greer, Richard A. "The Founding of the Queen's Hospital." *HJH* 3 (1969).

———. "Honolulu in 1847." *HJH* 4 (1970).

———. "Notes on Early Land Titles and Tenure in Hawai'i." *HJH* 30 (1996).

———. "Sweet and Clean: The Chinatown Fire of 1886." *HJH* 10 (1976).

Grimshaw, Patricia. "New England Missionary Wives, Hawaiian Women, and 'the Cult of True Womanhood.' " *HJH* 19 (1985).

Gutmanis, June. "The Law . . . Shall Punish All Men Who Commit Crime . . ." *HJH* 8 (1974).

Haas, Glenn E., P. Quentin Tomich, and Nixon Wilson. "The Flea in Early Hawaii." *HJH* 5 (1971).

Hammett, Hugh B. "The Cleveland Administration and Anglo-American Naval Friction in Hawaii, 1893–1894." *Military Affairs* 40, no. 1 (February 1976).

Hart, Albert Bushnell. "Pacific and Asiatic Doctrines Akin to the Monroe Doctrine." *American Journal of International Law* 9, no. 4 (October 1915).

Herman, R. D. K. "The Aloha State: Place Names and the Anti-Conquest of Hawai'i." *Annals of the Association of American Geographers* 89, no. 1 (March 1999).

Hershinaw, Sheldon. "John Dominis Holt: Hawaiian-American Traditionalist." *Multi-Ethnic Literature of the United States* 7, no. 2, Between Margin and Mainstream (Summer 1980).

Howay, Judge F. W. "Captain Simon Metcalfe and the Brig 'Eleanora.' " In *17th Annual Report of the Hawaiian Historical Society* (Honolulu: Paradise of the Pacific Press, 1910).

Ireland, Brian. "Remembering and Forgetting at the Waikiki War Memorial Park and Natatorium." *HJH* 39 (2005).

Jones, Stephen B. "Geography and Politics in the Hawaiian Islands." *Geographical Review* 28, no. 2 (April 1938).

"K." "Honolulu Letter." *Science* 8, no. 181 (July 23, 1886).

Karpiel, Frank J., Jr. "Mystic Ties of Brotherhood: Freemasonry, Ritual and Hawaiian Royalty in the Nineteenth Century." *PHR* 69, no. 3 (August 2000).

Kashay, Jennifer Fish. " 'O That My Mouth Might Be Opened': Missionaries, Gender, and Language in Early 19th-Century Hawai'i." *HJH* 36 (2002).

Kosaki, Richard H. "Constitutions and Constitutional Conventions in Hawaii." *HJH* 12 (1978).

Kuykendall, Ralph S. "Introduction of the Episcopal Church into the Hawaiian Islands." *PHR* 15, no. 2 (June 1946).

La Croix, Sumner J., and Christopher Grandy. "The Political Instability of Reciprocal Trade and the Overthrow of the Hawaiian Kingdom." *Journal of Economic History* 57, no. 1 (March 1997).

La Croix, Sumner J., and James Roumasset. "The Evolution of Private Property in Nineteenth-Century Hawaii." *Journal of Economic History* 50, no. 4 (December 1990).

Loomis, Albertine. "Summer of 1898." *HJH* 13 (1979).

MacLennan, Carol A. "Foundations of Sugar's Power: Early Maui Plantations, 1840–1860." *HJH* 29 (1995).

———. "Hawai'i Turns to Sugar: The Rise of Plantation Centers, 1860–1880." *HJH* 31 (1997).

Martin, B. Jean, and Frances Jackson. "The Honolulu Sailor's Home." *HJH* 20 (1986).

Marumoto, Masaji. "Vignette of Early Hawaii-Japan Relations: Highlights of King Kalakaua's Sojourn in Japan on His Trip around the World as Recorded in His Personal Diary." *HJH* 10 (1976).

Maurer, Evan. "Kamehameha I and the NEH." *Art Journal* 40, nos. 1–2. Modernism, Revisionism, Pluralism and Post-Modernism (Autumn–Winter 1980).

———. "The Royal Isles." *Bulletin of the Art Institute of Chicago* 74, no. 3 (July–September 1983).

McWilliams, Tennant S. "James H. Blount, the South, and Hawaiian Annexation." *PHR* 57, no. 1 (February 1988).

Meller, Norman. "Missionaries to Hawaii: Shapers of the Islands' Government." *Western Political Quarterly* 11, no. 4 (December 1958).

Menton, Linda K. "A Christian and 'Civilized' Education: The Hawaiian Chiefs' Children's School, 1839–50." *History of Education Quarterly* 32, no. 2 (Summer 1992).

Mills, Peter R. "A New View of Kaua'i as 'The Separate Kingdom' after 1810." *HJH* 30 (1996).

Morse, Peter. "The Lahainaluna Money Forgeries." *HJH* 2 (1968).

Nagata, Kenneth M. "Early Plant Introductions in Hawai'i." *HJH* 19 (1985).

Nordyke, Eleanor C., and Richard K. C. Lee. "The Chinese in Hawai'i: A Historical and Demographic Perspective." *HJH* 23 (1989).

Pearce, George F. "Assessing Public Opinion: Editorial Comment and the Annexation of Hawaii: A Case Study." *PHR* 43, no. 3 (August 1974).

Pratt, Julius W. "The Hawaiian Revolution: A Re-Interpretation." *PHR* 1, no. 3 (September 1932).

Quinn, William F. "Politics of Statehood." *HJH* 18 (1984).

Raeside, James D. "Journals and Letter Books of R. C. Wyllie: A Minor Historical Mystery." *HJH* 18 (1984).

Rolle, Andrew F. "California Filibustering and the Hawaiian Kingdom." *PHR* 19, no. 3 (August 1950).

Rowland, Donald. "The Establishment of the Republic of Hawaii, 1893–1894." *PHR* 4, no. 3 (September 1935).

———. "The United States and the Contract Labor Question in Hawaii, 1862–1900." *PHR* 2, no. 3 (September 1933).

Russ, William A., Jr. "Hawaiian Labor and Immigration Problems before Annexa-
tion." *Journal of Modern History* 15, no. 3 (September 1943).
———. "The Role of Sugar in Hawaiian Annexation." *PHR* 12, no. 4 (December
1943).
Sahlins, Marshall, and Dorothy Barrère. "William Richards on Hawaiian Culture
and Political Conditions of the Islands in 1841." *HJH* 7 (1973).
Schmitt, Robert C. "Population Policy in Hawai'i." *HJH* 8 (1974).
——— and Eleanor C. Nordyke. "Death in Hawai'i: The Epidemics of 1848–49."
HJH 35 (2001).
Seaton, S. Lee. "The Hawaiian 'Kapu' Abolition of 1819." *American Ethnologist* 1,
no. 1 (February 1974).
Semes, Robert Louis. "Hawai'i's Holy War: English Bishop Staley, American Con-
gregationalists, and the Hawaiian Monarchs, 1860–1870. *HJH* 34 (2000).
Silva, Noenoe K. *"He Kanawai E Ho'opau I Na Hula Kuolo Hawai'i: The Political
Economy of Banning the* Hula." *HJH* 34 (2000).
Silverman, Jane L. "To Marry Again." *HJH* 17 (1983).
Smith, Roger C. "We Shall Soon See the Consequences of Such Conduct: John
Ledyard Revisited." *HJH* 41 (2007).
Soong, Irma Tam. "Sun Yat-sen's Christian Schooling." *HJH* 31 (1997).
Souza, Blase Camacho, "Trabajo y Tristeza—Work and Sorrow: The Puerto Ricans
of Hawaii, 1900–1902." *HJH* 18 (1984).
Spitz, Allan. "Democratic Transplantation: The Case of Land Policy in Hawaii."
Land Economics 42, no. 4 (November 1966).
Taeaber, Irene B. "Hawaii." *Population Index* 28, no. 2 (April 1962).
Tate, Merze. "Great Britain and the Sovereignty of Hawaii." *PHR* 31, no. 4 (No-
vember 1962).
———. "Hawaii: A Symbol of Anglo-American Rapprochement." *Political Science
Quarterly* 79, no. 4 (December 1964).
———. "Twisting the Lion's Tail over Hawaii." *PHR* 36, no. 1 (February 1967).
Weigle, Richard D. "Sugar and the Hawaiian Revolution." *PHR* 16, no. 1 (Febru-
ary 1947).
Whitehead, John. "Hawaii: The First and Last Far West?" *Western Historical Quar-
terly* 23, no. 2 (May 1992).
Zwiep, Mary. "Sending the Children Home: A Dilemma for Early Missionaries."
HJH 24 (1990).

Acknowledgments

As colleagues of mine learned that I had opened work on a book about the Americanization of Hawai'i, I was warned that I would be rapping on a hornet's nest. "You know, they really don't like Americans poking into their history over there." "Don't be surprised if they don't give you much cooperation."

I did not find this to be the case whatsoever. What I found was that in Hawai'i the spirit of *aloha* remains an important touchstone of cultural identity. I was welcomed and encouraged, occasionally squinted at askance and adjured but in the best-intended way. Suspicion that I might not be the first choice to write such a book as this was generously masked with wonderfully helpful pointing of direction and willingness to allow me continuing engagement. It is a pleasure to acknowledge these debts:

At the Hawai'i State Library and Archives: Luella Kurkjian.

At the University of Hawai'i at Manoa Library and Archives, Hawaiian and Polynesian Collection: Lynette Furuhaka.

At the Hawaiian Historical Society: Barbara E. Dunn and Ipo Santos-Bear.

At the Mission Houses Museum: Mike Smola and Carol White.

At the Hawaiian Judiciary Center: Keahe Davis and Toni Han Palermo.

With the Daughters of Hawai'i: Della Kua'ana at Queen Emma's Summer Palace and B. K. Calder at the Hulihe'e Palace.

At Kilauea National Park: Helene Buntman.

At Pu'ukohola National Historic Site: Joon So.

More than by anyone else, I was bowled over by the knowledge and passion of independent scholar Boyd Bond of Kohala, descended from the Judds and the Bonds, blue-eyed but as native as can be. Producing a grand unifying theory of Hawaiian history and culture that has universal approbation may prove as elusive as producing one of the universe itself, but if I met anyone with the voice and the temperament to do it, he can.

In the writing of history, one does not meet many genuine game changers. However, the effort to resuscitate Hawaiian language sources has been given an electric shock by M. Puakea Nogelmeier at the University of Hawai'i at Manoa, and his kind reception and encouragement are deeply appreciated.

In commercial publishing, the term "meritorious" is the kiss of death. Most of my best book ideas will never see light of day, because while they are acknowledged as quality projects that would be edifying to the public, they are not perceived as profitable. For *Captive Paradise*, huge thanks are due to my literary agent, Jim Hornfischer, who strongly advocated moving this project ahead of others that were pending; to my editor, Charles Spicer at St. Martin's, for perceiving that once Hawai'i's story was presented to the mainland audience, they would actually buy books.

And above all: not until this effort have I had to work so fast as to engage a research assistant—a term that he modestly awarded to himself—but this book would not have happened without Jody Edward Ginn, in real life a Ph.D. candidate at the University of North Texas and producer with Texas History Films. His omnipresence as my right-hand man (which, being left-handed, I found particularly useful) was indispensable. Because of the unforgiving nature of clock and calendar, I had to trust him to evaluate whole collections of documents, and his eye for spotting the glint of gold in the folder of gravel saved me months of work.

For many other kindnesses and paving my way, thanks are due to Paul and Rachel Sheffield, Greg Hermida and Laura MacLay, Quinn Argall, Laurence Jackson, Evan Yeakel, Craig Eiland, Jim Kunetka, and especially Brent and Gina Bliven.

Index